NEW ORLEANS

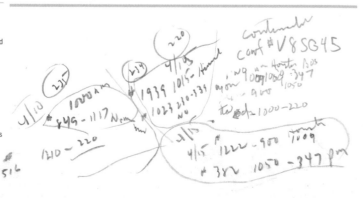

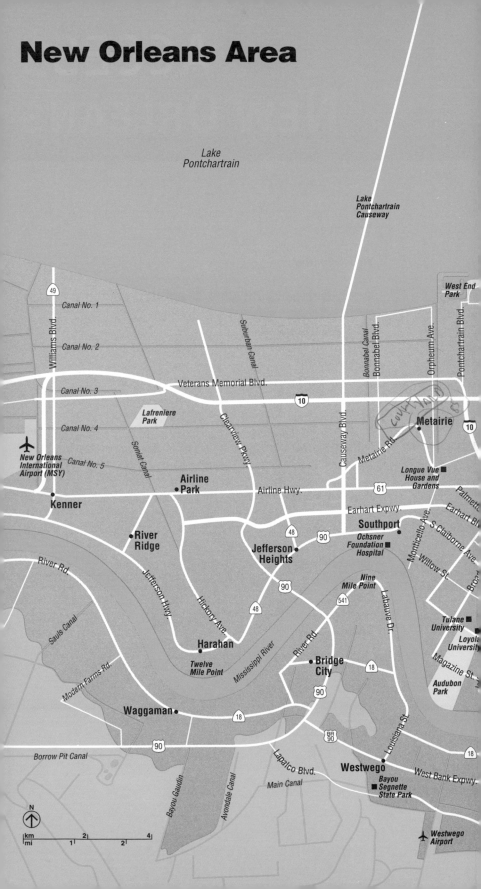

Carved from a swamp and comfortably settled a good ten feet below the water level of the Mississippi, New Orleans is a gorgeous mistake, a flawed paradise of wild culture, ambrosial food, and unpunished sin. On this inland archipelago, where even a funeral is an occasion for a parade, you'll find an excess of everything but parking spaces and moral indignation.

People in "The City that Care Forgot" learned long ago to take life one day at a time, though perhaps not in the manner of the 12-step programs. The blithe cynicism and institutionalized laziness can mystify visitors accustomed to Yankee ideals and the Protestant work ethic. You can spot the newcomers on **Bourbon Street**, reeling and howling, relaxing as hard as they can. Natives take their pleasures more calmly, without a lot of fuss. Overindulgence is their birthright, along with Catholic absolution and a French-Spanish heritage that lets backsliders shrug it off and try again *mañana*. Civilized pagans, genteel paupers, and amiable misanthropes who visit the city will fit right in. You'll also find ample evidence that God watches over fools and drunks—and looks the other way on Mardi Gras. Rules are made to be loosely interpreted, and everything your mother told you is wrong. Take candy from strangers. Don't sit up straight. Enough is *not* enough.

New Orleans has been called everything from the Paris of the Americas to the northernmost banana republic. To early French settlers, it was *le flottant* (the floating land), and Napoléon Bonaparte called it *Ile d'Orléans*. Dominated by water, the city is bordered on one side by the nation's grandest river and on the other by 610 square miles of **Lake Pontchartrain**. On average, residents live five feet below sea level and resign themselves to an annual rainfall greater than Seattle's. Historic neighborhoods that sprang up on isolated ridges of high ground remain connected by a system of bridges and ferries, and city streets follow the crazy bends of the Mississippi instead of a logical grid pattern.

Over the past 300 years, New Orleans has been battered by hurricanes, floods, and generations of *laissez le bon temps rouler* (let the good times roll) government. Between 1682 and 1803, the Louisiana Territory was transferred from France to Spain, then back to France, before being sold (20 days later) to the United States. It was one of history's most spectacular land flips, but the Louisiana Purchase could not buy blind allegiance from the insular Creoles, a distinctly Mediterranean society that took root long before *les Américains* hit town in 1803.

To this day, the multicultural Creole spirit continues to resist Americanization, a fact most readily apparent in the complex flavors of the city's cuisine. The New Orleans pot has been stirred by French, Spanish, African, and Caribbean settlers, and spiced by the Irish, Italian, German, and Asian immigrants who followed. Here fast food still means a sack of boiled crawfish or a crusty muffuletta, stacked with Italian meats and cheeses and dripping with chopped olive salad. Sophisticated Creole fare is sautéed in butter, simmered in rich bisques, or étoufféed into dark and garlicky stews. Jambalaya is a revved-up version of paella, and piquant redfish court bouillon is smothered in a Spanish-style mélange of tomatoes, peppers, and onions. From Africa come yams, okra, and filé gumbo, spiced with ground sassafras leaves. Even ham and cheese sandwiches are served on fresh French bread, unless you're crazy enough to specify "sliced."

Rollicking ethnic festivals fill New Orleans's calendar as well, led by Mardi Gras, which crowns a month-long season of parades and masked balls. Then for two full-tilt weeks in April and May, the annual Jazz and Heritage Festival crams the New Orleans Fair Grounds and clubs throughout town with a roundup of jazz, blues, R&B, rock, and gospel music. Meanwhile, smaller fests are scheduled nearly every weekend throughout Louisiana, and die-hard party animals can bark around the clock on frenetic Bourbon Street in the French Quarter.

The other narrow streets of the French Quarter are dense with steep-roofed Creole cottages and majestic town houses laced with ironwork. But this 90-square-block living museum is above all a busy neighborhood where more than 7,000 permanent residents sleep, eat, work, and carouse. Many claim they seldom cross over into the real world, finding just about everything they need to sustain life—or shorten it—within walking distance. The Quarter's downtown boundaries are Faubourg Marigny (a 19th-century "suburb" with a 21st-century bohemian bent) and Treme (former site of the scandalous red-light district of Storyville, now home turf for a tight community of world-famous jazz musicians). Along the uptown border, the relatively recent Riverfront development has created a festive zone of steamboat docks, promenades, shopping centers, and tourist attractions (including the popular Aquarium of the Americas), extending through the French Quarter and Central Business District (CBD) to the modern arts colony of the Warehouse District. From here the St. Charles Avenue Streetcar rumbles past the architectural gems of the Garden District and the Uptown/University area to Audubon Park's first-class zoo. Roads less traveled lead to the historic racetrack and neighborhood bars of Mid City, the nautical calm of the Lakefront, and the funky eccentricity of the Ninth Ward and St. Bernard Parish.

Or if all that sounds like it would take just too much energy, snag a sidewalk table at Café du Monde and watch the world pass by. After all, *demain* is another day.

Jackson Square

KEELY EDWARDS

5

How To Read This Guide

ACCESS NEW ORLEANS is arranged by neighborhood so you can see at a glance where you are and what is around you. The numbers next to the entries in the following chapters correspond to the numbers on the maps. The text is color-coded according to the kind of place described:

Restaurants/Clubs: Red

Hotels: Purple | Shops: Orange

🏵 **Outdoors: Green** | Sights/Culture: Blue

♿ Wheelchair accessible

WHEELCHAIR ACCESSIBILITY

An establishment (except a restaurant) is considered wheelchair accessible when a person in a wheelchair can easily enter a building (i.e., no steps, a ramp, a wide-enough door) without assistance. Restaurants are deemed wheelchair accessible *only* if the above applies, and if the rest rooms are on the same floor as the dining area and their entrances and stalls are wide enough to accommodate a wheelchair.

RATING THE RESTAURANTS AND HOTELS

The restaurant star ratings take into account the quality, service, atmosphere, and uniqueness of the restaurant. An expensive restaurant doesn't necessarily ensure an enjoyable evening; however, a small, relatively unknown spot could have good food, professional service, and a lively atmosphere. Therefore, on a purely subjective basis, stars are used to judge the overall dining value (see the star ratings at right). Keep in mind that chefs and owners often change, which can drastically affect the quality of a restaurant. The ratings in this guidebook are based on information available at press time.

The price ratings, as categorized at right, apply to restaurants and hotels. These figures describe general price-range relationships among other restaurants and hotels in the area. The restaurant price ratings are based on the average cost of a dinner entrée for one person, excluding tax and tip. Hotel price ratings reflect the base price of a standard room for two people for one night during the peak season.

RESTAURANTS

★	Good
★★	Very Good
★★★	Excellent
★★★★	An Extraordinary Experience
$	The Price Is Right (less than $10)
$$	Reasonable ($10-$15)
$$$	Expensive ($15-$20)
$$$$	Big Bucks ($20 and up)

HOTELS

$	The Price Is Right (less than $75)
$$	Reasonable ($75-$150)
$$$	Expensive ($150-$225)
$$$$	Big Bucks ($225 and up)

MAP KEY

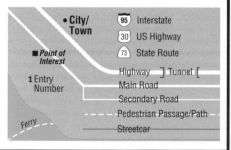

• City/Town
■ *Point of Interest*
1 Entry Number
Ferry

95 Interstate
30 US Highway
73 State Route
Highway] Tunnel [
Main Road
Secondary Road
- - - - Pedestrian Passage/Path
Streetcar

AREA CODE 415 UNLESS OTHERWISE NOTED.

Getting to New Orleans

Airports

New Orleans International Airport (MSY)

New Orleans International Airport is perched a heady four feet above sea level in suburban **Kenner**, about 11 miles west of downtown New Orleans. Elevators are located in the east and west ends of the terminal building and in the parking garage, and telephone display devices (TDDs) are on each of the four concourses. A post office and full-service **Whitney National Bank** (with ATM) are located across from the **American Airlines** ticket counter; additional ATMs are located in the baggage claim area in the west end of the terminal. In the west lobby, an **American Express** machine gives cash advances or traveler's checks, and

the **Mutual of Omaha Business Service Center** offers travel insurance, currency exchange, photocopies, and emergency cash, and they will wire money. Information desks in the west lobby and baggage claim area are staffed by multilingual workers. The **Traveler's Aid Booth** in the baggage claim area provides tourist information as well as help for those in distress. The airport complex is fully accessible to the handicapped traveler.

AIRPORT SERVICES

Airport Shuttle	465.9780
Business Service Center	465.9647
Customs	441.9179
Ground Transportation	464.2701
Immigration	467.1713

Information and Paging	464.0831
Lost and Found	464.2671
Parking	464.0204
Security and Emergencies	464.2700
Traveler's Aid Booth	464.3522

AIRLINES

Aeromexico	800/237.6639
AirTran	800/825.8538
American	800/433.7300
ComAir	800/354.9822
Continental	800/525.0280
Delta	800/221.1212
LACSA	800/225.2272
MetroJet	888/638.7653
Northwest	800/225.2525
Southwest	800/435.9792
TACA	800/535.8780
TWA	800/221.2000
United	800/241.6522
US Airways	800/428.4322
US Airways Express	800/428.4322

Getting to and from New Orleans International Airport

By Bus

Airport/Downtown Express (737.7433, 737.9611) operates from 5:30AM to 11:30PM. Buses depart from the west side of the terminal's upper level every 10 minutes during peak hours (6AM to 9AM and 3PM to 6PM), and every 23 minutes at other times. During the day (5:30AM to 5:40PM), buses deliver passengers to **Tulane Avenue** (between Elks Pl and Saratoga St) in the CBD. After 5:40PM, all buses terminate at the intersection of Tulane and **Carrollton** Avenues in Mid City. Schedules may fluctuate slightly on weekends and holidays. The fare is $1.50.

To get to the airport from town, follow the above instructions in reverse: Catch the airport bus on Tulane Avenue (between Elks Pl and Saratoga St) from 6:09AM to 6:30PM. After 6:30PM, you'll have to take a **Regional Transit Authority (RTA)** bus (*Tulane* line) to the corner of Carrollton and Tulane Avenues. When you get off the bus, go to the **Burger King**, where the airport bus picks up from 7PM to midnight on the hour.

Airport Shuttles (522.3500) depart every 10 minutes and run between the airport and various drop-off points around town. Ticket desks and pickup are on the lower level of the terminal near the baggage claim area; the one-way fare is $10. Each passenger is limited to three normal-sized pieces of luggage (boxed freight items don't count).

The Coastliner (800/647.3957) provides van service between the airport and Mississippi's **Gulf Coast** beaches (and points in between) daily from 8AM to 11:30PM. Ticket booths are on the lower level next to **Delta** baggage claim; call for schedules and prices.

By Car

To get into the city, follow the signs from the airport's parking garage or rental-car lots to the airport access road, then stay in the left lane and follow signs for New Orleans. The access road will converge with **Interstate 10 (I-10)**, which goes through town.

To get to the airport, follow the well-marked exits off I-10 or **Highway 61**, better known as **Airline Highway**. Overhead signs at airport entry roads direct you to short- or long-term parking areas. Overnight and weekly rates are lower at **Park and Fly** (1017 Airline Hwy, 464.0183) and **US Park** (1025 Airline Hwy, 469.9942); both are open 24 hours and provide free shuttle service. Rental-car agencies operate on the ground floor of the terminal.

Rental Cars

The following rental-car companies have counters at the airport:

Alamo	469.0532, 800/327.9633
Avis	464.9511, 800/331.1212
Budget	467.2277, 800/527.0700
Hertz	468.3695, 800/654.3131
National	466.4335, 800/227.7368
Payless	441.5700, 800/729.5377
Thrifty	463.0800, 800/367.2277

By Taxi

Cabs can be hailed outside the baggage claim on the terminal's lower level. Fare to the Central Business District runs around $21. For three or more passengers, the cost is $8 per person.

Bus Station (Long-Distance)

Greyhound buses arrive at and depart from **Union Terminal** (Loyola Ave, between S Rampart and Girod Sts, 524.7571). The ticket office is open daily from 5:30AM to 11PM. There's a taxi stand just outside the front entrance of the terminal.

Cruise Ships

Commodore's *Enchanted Isle* sails year-round from New Orleans on seven-night cruises to Playa del Carmen, Cozumel, Grand Cayman, and Montego Bay; the *Enchanted Capri* offers weekend "cruises to nowhere" and five-day cruises to Playa del Carmen and Cozumel; call 800/832.1122. **Carnival's** *Celebration* also departs New Orleans year-round for seven-night cruises to the western Caribbean; call 800/327.9501. **Holland America Line's** *Nieuw Amsterdam* cruises the western Caribbean from New Orleans seasonally (October through April); contact your travel agent. These three lines dock at the **Julia Street Wharf**. From the nearby **Robin Street Wharf**, the **Delta Queen Steamboat Company** offers river cruises (3 to 14 nights) aboard authentic steam paddle wheelers; call 586.0631 or 800/543.1949.

Train Station (Long-Distance)

Amtrak trains run between **Union Terminal** (Loyola Ave, between S Rampart and Girod Sts) and New York City, Chicago, Los Angeles, and Miami; call 800/872.7245

Getting Around New Orleans

Bicycles

Potholes and reckless drivers can be hazardous, but the city's flat terrain is ideal for cycling, and it's one of the best ways to breeze right past the traffic jams and parking problems of Carnival and other special events. **French Quarter Bicycles** (522 Dumaine St, between Decatur and Chartres Sts, 529.3136) rents mountain bikes by the hour, day, or week; helmets and locks are included in the price. **Bicycle Michael's** (622 Frenchmen St, between Chartres and Royal Sts, 945.9505) rents mountain bikes, tandems, and three-speeds by the hour, day, or week; locks included, helmets extra.

Buses and Streetcars

Public transportation in New Orleans is administered by the **Regional Transit Authority (RTA).** Bus routes, both local and express, are extensive and service is frequent; most routes run daily around the clock. The fare is $1.25 and transfers are a dime; express buses charge $1.50. Drivers cannot make change, so have exact fare ready and purchase transfers when boarding. Ask the driver to call out your stop if you're unfamiliar with the route. The buses on the heavily trafficked **Canal Line** follow that street all the way from the Mississippi River, through Mid City, to Lake Pontchartrain; service is available daily, 24 hours. The **Esplanade Line** travels the oak-shaded avenue of the same name from the river to **City Park** and the **New Orleans Fair Grounds** daily from 4:45AM to 12: 45AM. On the beaten tourist track, the **Vieux Carre Shuttle** crisscrosses the French Quarter Monday through Friday from 5AM to 7PM, Saturday and Sunday from 8AM to 6PM. Just watch for the quaint trolley buses that look like escapees from a theme park.

The streetcars also are quaint, but they aren't even the slightest bit cutesy. The **St. Charles Avenue Streetcar** is the world's oldest continuously operating street railway and is listed on the National Register of Historic Places. It clangs past the downtown shopping area, the Garden District, uptown to **Tulane** and **Loyola Universities, Audubon Park, Riverbend,** and **Carrollton.** The **Magazine Line** services the famous shopping street of the same name from the CBD to **Audubon Zoo.** Both of these lines charge a $1.25 fare and operate daily around the clock. The **Riverfront Streetcar,** more of a Disneyesque apparition, follows the Mississippi from the lower French Quarter to the Warehouse District. It runs Monday through Friday from 6AM to 11PM, and Saturday and Sunday from 8AM to midnight; the fare is $1.25. A good option for travelers is the **VisiTour Pass,** which is available for either one day ($4) or three consecutive days ($8) of unlimited travel on all forms of public transportation. Passes are sold at information counters in many hotels and shops; call the 24-hour **RTA RideLine** (248.3900) for the name of the nearest distributor.

for information. The ticket office is open daily from 5:50AM to 8:30PM. Taxis are available at the front entrance of the terminal.

It's always a good idea to double-check the public transportation hours listed above with the **RideLine,** as schedules may change. The **RideLine** operators also offer routing advice—tell them where you are, where you want to go, and when you plan to leave and they'll provide the location of the nearest stop, the approximate time of the next trip, and details on necessary connections. See the overview map of **RTA** routes on the inside back cover of this book.

Driving

Negotiating traffic in New Orleans is a trip in itself. Nowhere is the warning to drive defensively more crucial than in a town where beer is sold in gas stations and the highway median is called the "neutral ground." Natives are not shy about blowing their horns, and liberal interpretations of traffic laws can be quite a shock for the uninitiated. If you insist on driving, keep the following tips in mind. Speed limits are strictly enforced in school zones, along **Lakeshore Drive,** and on the airport approach roads. Don't even try to cross any of the Mississippi River bridges during rush hours. Traffic lights blink after dark in the less fashionable neighborhoods, which is a signal to slow down and check for other cars before continuing briskly on your way. Take the hint. And, finally, a word about potholes: everydamnwhere.

Ferries

You can cross the Mississippi River to **Algiers** daily except Christmas. The boats leave the **Canal Street** dock every half-hour beginning at 6AM, with the last round trip leaving from Canal Street at 11:30PM and returning at 11:45PM. (The boat docks for the night at 12:15AM in Algiers, where you really don't want to be stuck after dark, as muggings are all too common in the isolated riverfront neighborhood. Just to be sure, always ask about the return crossing when boarding after 9PM.) Pedestrians ride free; cars pay $1 only for the return trip from Algiers.

Parking

Be sure to obey all parking signs in the French Quarter to the letter, as violators will certainly be towed. Never park within three feet of a driveway.

In the CBD, expect to pay 25 cents at a meter for every 15 minutes of parking time (up to two hours). Be sure to read all of the nearby signs, as it is illegal to park at meters in designated "rush-hour zones" from 7AM to 9AM and 4PM to 6PM. During special events, additional restrictions may be posted and bags will be placed over meters in high-traffic areas. Never park at a bagged meter, as your car will certainly be towed. Extremely complicated signs identify street-cleaning routes, which are patrolled by tow trucks on alternate sides at alternate times. To confirm your worst fears, contact the **Claiborne Auto Pound** (400 N Claiborne Ave, at Conti

St, 565.7450). Be prepared to identify your vehicle by license number, make, color, and (former) parking location.

Canal Place Parking Garage (Canal and N Peters Sts, 522.9200) is ideally located at the Riverfront on the border between the CBD and the French Quarter. All-day and nighttime rates are reasonable, and area attractions validate tickets for short-term discounts. All-day rates are downright cheap at the parking garage in the **Louisiana Superdome** (587.3663), where you can park Monday through Friday from 8AM to 6PM and hop a city bus to Canal Street.

TAXIS

They're easy to find in the French Quarter and outside most hotels, but they can be scarce on rainy days. Cruising cabs are rare, so to get to and from most destinations you have to call for pickup. Use **United Cabs** (522.9771), **Yellow-Checker Cabs** (525.3311), or **White Fleet Cabs** (948.6605). Rates are reasonable, but be aware that a flat fare of $3 per passenger (or the regular meter rate, if greater) is in effect during special events, such as Mardi Gras, Jazz Fest, arena concerts, **Sugar Bowl**, and **Saints** home games. Drivers have been known to overcharge, but the **Taxicab Bureau** (565.6272) advises visitors to refuse payment and summon a police officer if there is a discrepancy. The bureau oversees all licensed taxis, limousines, horse carts, and tour buses that operate within the city of New Orleans.

FYI

ACCOMMODATIONS

No matter when you plan to visit, make hotel reservations well ahead of time. The exceptions to that rule are the summer months, when bookings are at their lowest and bargain rates abound. For special events like Mardi Gras and Jazz Fest, think about booking as far as a year in advance, and be prepared to pay through the nose. Even the crummiest places fill up early, and without a reservation you'll be sleeping on the airport floor. Non-hotel types can choose alternative accommodations from modest family houses to posh historic inns. For information and reservations, contact **Bed and Breakfast Inc. Reservation Service** (1021 Moss St, PO Box 52257, New Orleans, LA 70119, 504/488.4640, 800/729.4640; fax 504/488.4639; bedbreak@gnofn.org); **New Orleans Bed and Breakfast and Accommodations** (671 Rosa Ave, Suite 208, Metairie, LA 70005, 504/838.0071; fax 504/838.0140; info@neworleansbandb.com); or **Bed & Breakfast Access** (PO Box 1665, Metairie, LA 70004, 504/834.7726, 888/766.6707; fax 504/834.2677; bnbaxces@bellsouth.net).

CLIMATE

Natives say New Orleans has two seasons—summer and February—but even February can be kind of muggy. The usual forecast is sun, followed by rain, followed by steam. Bring cool, loose-fitting clothes to allow for the climate (and the cuisine). In winter months it's wise to overpack, because temperatures can change drastically

TOURS

To join the crowd for bus tours of city, swamps, or plantations, contact **Gray Line** (569-1401; fax 587.0742; www.graylineneworleans.com) or **New Orleans Tours** (592.0560; fax 527.0093; www.visitnola.com). Riverboat excursions and dinner cruises are offered by **New Orleans Steamboat Company** (586.8777; fax 587-0742; www.steamboatnatchez.com) and **New Orleans Paddlewheelers** (524.0814; fax 524.6265; www.visitnola.com). Rangers from the French Quarter Unit of **Jean Lafitte National Historical Park** (589.2636) lead free walking tours of the French Quarter and Garden District every day; reservations are required. **Friends of the Cabildo** (523.3939) leads two-hour walking tours of the French Quarter; the tour fee includes admission to two of the **Louisiana State Museum** buildings. **Save Our Cemeteries** (525.3377) is a nonprofit group that sponsors walking tours of historic cemeteries to help fund their ongoing maintenance and preservation projects. For details on more specialized tours, see page 53.

WALKING

Walking is unquestionably the best way to see the French Quarter, Faubourg Marigny, Warehouse District, and the CBD. The picturesque old streets and sidewalks can be treacherous so watch your step. And be sure to wear sensible shoes for dodging mimes and for dancing in the streets.

from day to day. And, although the temperature rarely falls to freezing, the wind off the river combined with high humidity can make it feel colder. Then there's hurricane season, which runs from 1 June to 30 November, with most storm activity between 15 August and 30 September. In general, the best months to be outdoors are October and May. August and September are great for mad dogs and Englishmen, but the rest of us may be a little uncomfortable.

MONTHS	AVERAGE TEMPERATURE (F°)
December-January	53
March-May	69
June-August	82
September-November	70

DRINKING

The legal drinking age is 21. Some bars stay open around the clock, but most shut down for a few hours about 5AM. Wine and liquor are widely available and can be purchased in convenience shops, supermarkets, drugstores, and even drive-thru daiquiri stands. It's legal to drink on the streets, but not from glass containers; virtually all bars sell drinks in plastic "go cups."

GAMBLING

In 1992, the Louisiana Legislature voted to allow a single land-based casino to operate in New Orleans near the French Quarter. Construction was begun on a permanent facility on the site of the former **Rivergate**

(Canal St, between Pl de France and S Peters St); however, the building remains unfinished and work has been stalled indefinitely due to political and legal squabbling. Meanwhile, the 1991 legalization of gambling boats has introduced two paddle wheelers to Lake Pontchartrain: **Bally's Casino, Lakeshore Resort** (see page 127) at **South Shore Harbor** in New Orleans and the **Treasure Chest Casino** (see page 156) in the western suburb of Kenner. Both boats operate around the clock, either dockside or cruising the lake, as weather dictates.

HOURS

Opening and closing times for shops, attractions, etc. are listed only by day(s) if normal hours apply (opening between 8 and 11AM and closing between 4 and 7PM Monday through Saturday, and opening at noon and closing between 5 and 6PM on Sunday). Coffeehouses (of which there are many in New Orleans) generally stay open until at least 10PM. In unusual cases, specific hours are given (e.g., 6AM-2PM, daily 24 hours).

MONEY

Foreign currency may be exchanged at **American Express** (201 St. Charles Ave, at Common St, 586.8201); **First National Bank of Commerce** (210 Baronne St, between Gravier and Common Sts, 561.1371); or the **Whitney National Bank** (228 St. Charles Ave, between Gravier and Common Sts, 586.7272). Banks are generally open Monday through Friday from 9AM to 3PM. There are plenty of ATMs throughout the city, and traveler's checks are accepted virtually everywhere.

PERSONAL SAFETY

It's a strange fact of life in New Orleans that a block of meticulously maintained mansions may be followed by a row of bombed-out slums, so it is important to pay close attention to your surroundings if you go exploring. The famous aboveground cemeteries (aka "cities of the dead") are very dangerous for lone tourists, so visit only with a guided group; the sole exception is **Lake Lawn Metairie Cemetery** in Mid City. **Armstrong Park** draws good crowds for its afternoon concerts, but pass on by when it's deserted, even in daylight. **Audubon** and **City Parks** are reasonably safe during the day, but after dark avoid all parks and side alleys. Take a cab in the Garden District and Uptown after dark unless your destination is directly on the streetcar line. The loud drunks and strip shows may be offensive, but Bourbon Street is well patrolled and probably the safest place to walk in the French Quarter after dark. **Royal** and **Decatur Streets** are more pleasant than Bourbon and usually pretty crowded, but by all means keep to the beaten paths. If you're venturing farther afield, it's a good idea to take a cab.

POSTAL SERVICE

The main post office is at 701 Loyola Avenue (at Girod St) in the CBD; the French Quarter branch is at 1022 Iberville St (between Burgundy and N Rampart Sts). Call 589.1111 for general information.

PUBLICATIONS

Check the Friday edition of the city daily, the *Times-Picayune*, for *Lagniappe*, a pull-out section of entertainment reviews and listings. The weekly tabloid *Gambit*, another good source for area listings, is available free at restaurants and retail outlets (or for a nominal charge at newsstands and coin boxes). *Offbeat* covers the local music industry and club scene. *New Orleans Magazine* and *Louisiana Life* are regional slicks. Gay and lesbian publications include *Ambush Magazine* and *Impact Gulf South Gay News*. The *New Orleans Tribune*, which serves the black community, the Spanish-language *Aqui New Orleans*, and *The Jewish Civic Press* are all published monthly.

RADIO STATIONS

AM:

690	WTIX	Oldies
870	WWL	News/Talk
990	WGSO	CNN
1350	WSMB	News/Talk
1450	WBYU	Adult Pop

FM:

89.9	WWNO	National Public Radio/Cultural
90.5	KTLN	National Public Radio/Cultural
90.7	WWOZ	Community/Jazz/Blues
91.5	WTUL	Progressive
92.3	WCKW	Rock
94.3	WTIX	Oldies
97.1	WEZB	Contemporary
98.5	WYLD	Urban
99.5	WRNO	Classic Rock
101.1	WNOE	Country
105.3	WLTS	Contemporary
106.7	KKND	Alternative

RESTAURANTS

Reservations are essential for both lunch and dinner at old-line Creole establishments like **Commander's Palace, Antoine's**, and **Brennan's**, and at fashionable bistros such as **Bayona, Emeril's**, and **Nola**. Although dress codes have slipped considerably in recent years, coats and ties still separate the men from the tourists at more formal establishments. Casual types may be more comfortable at the beloved local institutions known collectively as "neighborhood restaurants" (**West End Cafe** or **Liuzza's**, for example), where excellent seafood, Italian, and French Creole dishes are rich and plentiful.

Restaurants are mobbed during Mardi Gras and Jazz Fest, when the quality of food and service can suffer. Business slows across the board in summer, so eateries all over town cook up tempting promotions to fill tables. Throughout December, Reveillon dinners at French

> Louisiana's first commercial sugar crop was produced in 1794–95 on the plantation of Etienne de Bore, which was in the area now known as Audubon Park.

Quarter restaurants are prix-fixe holiday feasts (522.5730 for details).

SHOPPING

First stop is the French Quarter, for everything from world-class art to outré undies. **Magazine Street** offers six colorful miles of shops proffering antiques, collectibles, and assorted junk. The galleries of the Warehouse District are filled with works by regional and international artists, both emerging and established. The city's best malls are all in the CBD: there's the highrise **Canal Place**, anchoring Canal Street at the river; the waterfront **Riverwalk Marketplace**, which made headlines for being rammed by a freighter in late 1996; and the glitzy **New Orleans Centre**, near the **Superdome**.

SMOKING

City ordinances prohibit smoking in public buildings and theaters and on public transportation. Restaurants that seat more than 50 people must designate separate sections for smokers and nonsmokers, but it's okay to light up in bars and at indoor sporting events.

STREET PLAN

Hang on to your maps; it's going to be a bumpy ride. To get to the **West Bank**, head due *east* on the **Crescent City Connection Bridge**. To get to **Slidell** on the *north* shore of Lake Pontchartrain, take Interstate 10 *east*. Main drag **North Claiborne Avenue** goes *northeast* for a few blocks, then turns due *east* and finally continues to the *southeast* for most of its length. **South Claiborne Avenue**, on the other hand, heads mostly *northwest*. Just put a Dixie cup over your dashboard compass and do what the natives do—go with the flow. The main source of the confusion is Old Man River. Streets that follow the twists the Mississippi make conventional directions useless, so get accustomed to the four points that define the city for locals: "toward the river" versus "toward the lake," and "Uptown" (above Canal Street) versus "Downtown" (below Canal Street). Street signs only add to the confusion. Even in New Orleans, most people call it the French Quarter, but someone put *Vieux Carré* on the freeway exit signs. If you don't want to sound like a tourist, **Burgundy Street** is pronounced Bur-*gun*-dy, **Calliope** is *Kal*-ee-ope, **Carondelet** is Ka-*ron*-da-let, **Chartres** is *Char*-ters, **Conti** is *Con*-tie, **Fontainebleau** is *foun*-ten-blow, **Milan** is *My*-lan, and everyone's favorite, **Tchoupitoulas**, is easier than it looks. Just say Chop-a-*too*-lus. By the way, if you travel more than two blocks without spotting a street sign, you have probably wandered into a neighborhood where metal salvage is a cottage industry. Turn back before they get yours.

Phone Book

EMERGENCIES

Ambulance/Fire/Police	911
AAA Emergency Road Service	837.1080
Child Find	800/426.5678
Mercy/Baptist Hospital	483.5777
New Orleans Bar Association	525.7453
New Orleans Dental Association	834.6449

Throughout Louisiana, parishes are the equivalent of counties. **Orleans Parish** defines the city limits. The closest suburban neighborhoods are in surrounding **Jefferson, St. Bernard**, and **St. Tammany Parishes**.

TAXES

Sales tax in Orleans Parish is 9 percent, with an additional 3-percent hotel tax, bringing room rates to a hefty 12 percent. An amusement tax (which includes sales tax) adds up to 14 percent; it applies to concert and theater tickets and to the cover charge in bars that feature live entertainment. Foreign visitors with a valid passport and a round-trip international airline ticket that is good for less than 90 days (Canadians can present a birth certificate or driver's license instead) can take advantage of a **Louisiana Tax-Free Shopping** perk. Merchants who display the Louisiana Tax Free logo will give sales tax refund vouchers to qualified customers, who can then cash them in at the airport or by mail. Call 568.5323 for details.

TICKETS

Ticketmaster (522.5555; www.ticketmaster.com) is the one source for sports, theater, dance, and music events. If you prefer to pay cash, ask about their outlets located throughout the city and suburbs.

TIME ZONE

New Orleans is located in the central time zone, one hour behind New York City.

TIPPING

A 15-percent tip is standard for cab drivers and restaurant servers. Kick it up to 20 percent for good service, especially in swank establishments where servers may have to share tips with other personnel. Many restaurants tack on a 15-percent gratuity for parties of six or more; the staff will be happy to keep mum and pocket double tips from unaware diners. Hotel and station porters expect one dollar per bag. If a concierge offers useful advice or performs any other special favors, hand over at least $5.

VISITORS' INFORMATION CENTERS

The **New Orleans Metropolitan Convention and Visitors Bureau** (566.5011; 800/672.6124; fax 566.5046; www.neworleanscvb.com) manages three information desks at **New Orleans International Airport**; all are open daily. In the French Quarter, make your first stop the **New Orleans Welcome Center** (529 St. Ann St, between Decatur and Chartres Sts, 568.5661; fax 568.5664). The center is open every day except Mardi Gras and Christmas and provides maps, brochures, and good advice.

Orleans Parish Medical Society	523.2474
Poison Control	800/256.9822
Red Cross Language Bank (foreign language assistance)	586.8191
Touro Infirmary	897-8663
Traveler's Aid Society	525.8726
Tulane Medical Center	588.5711

VISITORS' INFORMATION

Amtrak 800/872.7245

Better Business Bureau..................................581.6222

Chamber of Commerce 527.6900

New Orleans Metropolitan
Convention and Visitors Bureau 566.5011
....800/672.6124

New Orleans Multicultural Tourism Network....523.5652

Greyhound Bus Lines 524.7571

Louisiana State Office of Tourism 568.5661

Marine Recreational Forecast 465.9215

RTA RideLine...248.3900

Ticketmaster 522.5555

Time (fee charged) 976.1111

US Passport Office 589.6728

Weather 828.4000

MORE BON TEMPS IN NEW ORLEANS

Everybody knows about **Mardi Gras** (see "Motley Krewes: The Unbridled Excess of Mardi Gras," page 33, and "The Skinny on Fat Tuesday: A Survival Guide," page 29) and the **New Orleans Jazz and Heritage Festival** (see "All That Jazz Fest," page 92), but Southern Louisiana's calendar of events is booked solid year-round. Here's just a brief sample of the other *bon temps* (good times) that keep rolling all year long. They are either in New Orleans or an easy day trip from the city.

January

Sugar Bowl Classic Originated in 1935, this most famous of the football bowl games fills the **Superdome** on or about **New Year's Day** (depending on television scheduling). For more information, call 525.8573.

Carnival Everyone hits the streets for weeks of parades and masquerades, a citywide bacchanal that always kicks off on **Twelfth Night**, or the **Feast of the Epiphany** (6 January), and ends the day before **Ash Wednesday**, known as **Mardi Gras** (Fat Tuesday). For more information, call 566.5019, 800/672.6124.

Battle of New Orleans Musketeers hit town from around the globe to reenact the famous climactic battle of the War of 1812 at **Chalmette Battlefield**, a colorful event scheduled on the weekend closest to 8 January. (Actually, the battle took place after the war was officially over, but New Orleans still takes pride in the city's defeat of the British.) For more information, call 589.4428.

February

New Orleans Boat and Sportfishing Show The largest in the region, a display of boating and fishing supplies and exhibits occupies the **Superdome** the last weekend in February. For more information, call 582.3000.

March

St. Patrick's Day and the Feast Day of St. Joseph At around the same time each March, two of the strongest ethnic groups that have shaped the character of New Orleans, the Irish and the Italians, celebrate the feast days of St. Patrick and St. Joseph, their respective patron saints. At these neighboring festivals (St. Patrick's Day on 17 March and Feast Day of St. Joseph on 19 March), different social clubs sponsor parades throughout the week; there are plenty of food displays (particularly food-laden altars, a tradition connected with St. Joseph); and other colorful festivities

are held. For more information on St. Patrick's Day festivities, call 525.5169; for information on Feast Day of St. Joseph, call 522.7294.

Tennessee Williams Literary Festival Around the third weekend in March, a three-day series of plays, readings, and lectures is held at various locations, mostly in the French Quarter. For more information, call 581.1144.

April

French Quarter Festival This small, cozy neighborhood festival is always overshadowed by the larger, splashier **Jazz Fest**, which begins right afterward; however, it is certainly worthy of attention in its own right. The event, usually held the second weekend in April, showcases hundreds of local musicians and the wares of some 40 restaurants at various locations throughout the French Quarter. Among the freewheeling traditions is the annual waiter's race (they weave through the streets bearing trays) and "The World's Largest Jazz Brunch," an incredible array of food booths and live jazz performances in **Jackson Square** and **Woldenberg Riverfront Park**. For more information, call 522.5730.

May

Louisiana Crawfish Festival The state's favorite crustacean is highlighted during a weekend festival held in **Breaux Bridge**, the heart of Cajun country and the self-proclaimed "Crawfish Capital of the World." Food vendors, street performers, and arts and crafts booths are featured. For more information, call 318/322.3655.

Greek Festival A hugely popular blowout featuring folk dancing, crafts, and terrific homemade foods, it is held at the **Hellenic Cultural Center** at the **Greek Orthodox Cathedral of the Holy Trinity** (1200 Robert E. Lee Blvd, between St. Bernard Ave and Wisner Blvd, 282.0259) on the third or fourth weekend of the month.

June

Great French Market Tomato Festival Cooking demonstrations, tastings, and music are presented in the historic open-air **French Market** on the first weekend of June. For more information, call 522.2621.

Reggae Riddums Festival On the second weekend of the month, reggae, calypso, and soca musicians from around the world converge on **City Park**. In addition, authentic African arts and crafts, food, and beverages are available. For more information, call 367.1313, 800/367.1317.

Carnival Latino The largest celebration of Hispanic heritage and culture in the Gulf South (i.e., the Southern states that front the **Gulf of Mexico**) takes over the **Riverfront** on the last weekend of the month. For more information, call 566.5019, 800/672.6124.

New Orleans Wine & Food Experience In this annual event held over a long weekend in late June or early July, top international wineries and local restaurants present seminars, special dinners, and daylong "grand tastings." For more information, call 529.WINE.

July

Go 4th on the River This event celebrates **Independence Day** with fireworks over the **Mississippi** and music, food, and discounts at **Riverfront** attractions. For more information, call 587.1791.

August

White Linen Night On the first Saturday of the hottest month of the year, the smart set chill out at art galleries throughout the **Warehouse/Arts District** in this moonlit block party. Canopies are set up all along **Julia Street** for stylish food and drink vendors, informal performances by members of the **New Orleans Opera** and the **Louisiana Philharmonic Orchestra**, ice carvings (splendid but short-lived), and other artistic activities. For more information, call 523.1216.

The Blessing of the Fleet In a beautiful and vibrant ceremony to commemorate the opening of the white shrimp season (on the third Monday in August), several isolated fishing communities in lower **St. Bernard Parish** hold a colorful parade of decorated working boats on the two preceding Sundays. For more information, call 576.3719.

September

Madisonville Wooden Boat Festival Held in this **North Shore** community across **Lake Pontchartrain** on the third weekend in September, the festivities include boat-building demonstrations and workshops, contests, a marine auction, and a trade show along the **Tchefuncte River**. For more information, call 845.9200.

Alligator Festival Man bites gator (fried, sausage, served with sauce piquante, etc.) at this event held in **Boutte** on the last weekend of the month. There is also a fun community fair featuring craft booths, athletic events, Cajun and country bands, and children's rides. For more information, write to: Alligator Fest, PO Box 1066, Luling, LA 70070-1066.

October

Swamp Festival Held on the first and second weekends of the month at **Audubon Zoo**, here is a vibrant roundup of authentic Cajun country music, crafts, and hands-on introductions to bayou critters, among other events. For more information, call 581.4629.

Art for Arts' Sake The annual fundraiser for the **Contemporary Arts Center**, this gala festivity also marks the opening of the season for Warehouse/Arts District galleries. With music, food, and outré theatrics, it's held every year on the first Saturday of the month. For more information, call 523.1216.

Gumbo Festival The savory signature dish of Louisiana is saluted in three days of cookoffs, tastings, various entertainment, and crafts at **Angel Square** in **Bridge City**, which is across the river from New Orleans. For more information, call 436.4712.

Washington Parish Free Fair The largest free county fair in the US, it offers a full slate of house tours, rodeos, cooking contests, and other Old South festivities. The fair takes place in **Franklinton**, about 70 miles north of the city, the third week of the month. For more information, call 839.2314.

Ghostly Gallivant In a fundraiser sponsored by the **Friends of the Cabildo**, tours of historic French Quarter houses and courtyards are led by costumed spirit guides who spin tales of historic hauntings. Appropriately, it's held the weekend before Halloween. For more information, call 568.6968.

November

All Saints Day On 1 November, New Orleans residents visit cemeteries all over town to clean family tombs and decorate them with fresh flowers. It's the best time for visitors to tour New Orleans's usually secluded and potentially dangerous "cities of the dead." For more information, call 525.3377.

Destrehan Plantation Fall Festival On the second weekend in October, tours of a historic manor house (on River Road in Destrehan, about 20 miles west of New Orleans) are offered, as well as crafts exhibits, food, and entertainment. For more information, call 764.9315.

Bayou Classic This football game is the traditional end-of-the-season grudge match between **Southern and Grambling Universities**; it's held at the **Superdome** on the last weekend of the month. For more information, call 587.3800.

December

Christmas, New Orleans Style! The city schedules a number of special events throughout the month to celebrate the holiday season. (For more information, see "Santa Flies South" on page 126.)

New Orleans's average annual rainfall is 57.4 inches. The quantity of rain over its 57,000 acres amounts to more than 11 billion cubic feet of water weighing nearly 360 million tons.

At 2,350 miles, the Mississippi is the longest river in the US and the third-longest in the world, after the Nile and the Amazon. Its name is an Algonquin word meaning "Father of Waters."

The most devastating storm in New Orleans in recent years was Hurricane Betsy, on 9 September 1965. It caused 61 deaths and millions of dollars in property damage. Even today it's common for residents of the hardest-hit neighborhood, suburban St. Bernard Parish, to categorize other events as "before Betsy" or "after Betsy."

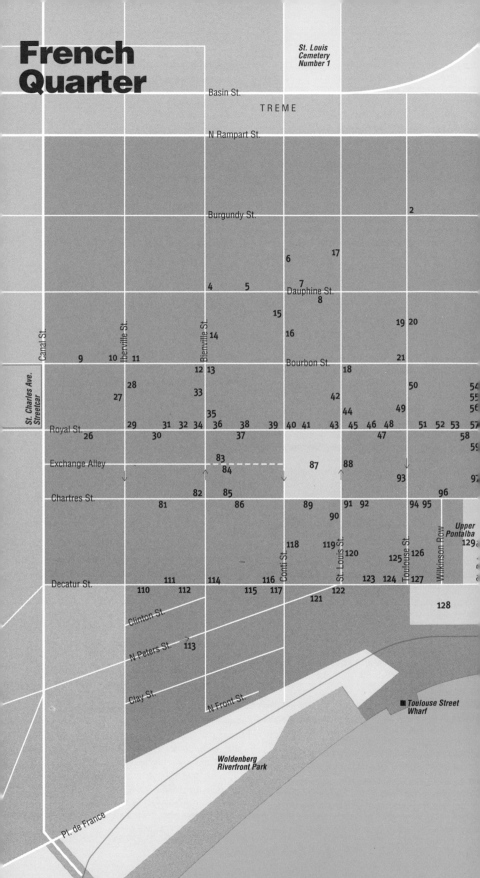

French Quarter

St. Louis Cemetery Number 1

Basin St.

TREME

N Rampart St.

Burgundy St.

2

17

6

7

4   5   Dauphine St.

8

15

19 20

Canal St.

Iberville St.

Bienville St.

14   16

9   10   11   Bourbon St.   21

12 13   18

28   33   50   54
27   42   55
35   44   49   56
29   31 32 34 36   38   39 40 41 43 45 46 48 51 52 53 57

Royal St.   47   58
26   30   37   59

St. Charles Ave. Streetcar

Exchange Alley   83   87 88
                          84   93   97

Chartres St.   82 85   96

81   86   89 91 92 94 95

Upper Pontalba
129

90

118   119 St. Louis St.
                  120   Toulouse St.   Wilkinson Row
Conti St.   125 126

Decatur St.   111   114   116   123 124 127

110 112   115 117 121 122   128

Clinton St.

N Peters St.   113

Clay St.

N Front St.

Toulouse Street Wharf

Woldenberg Riverfront Park

Pl. de France

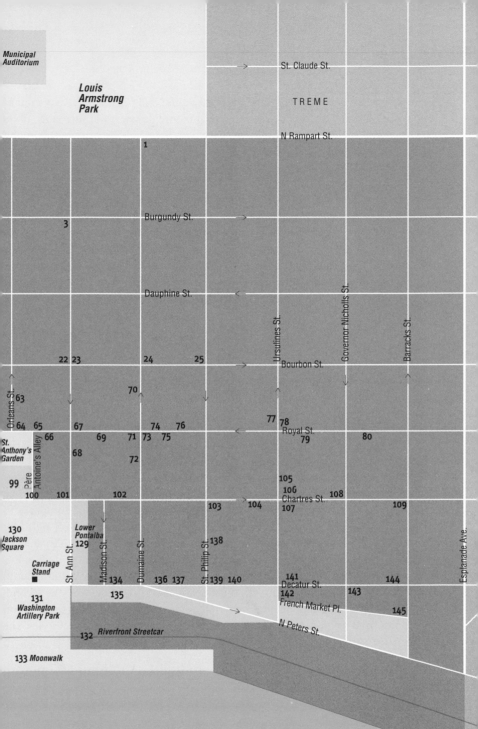

Municipal
Auditorium

**Louis
Armstrong
Park**

St. Claude St.

TREME

N Rampart St.

1

Burgundy St.

3

Dauphine St.

Ursulines St.

Governor Nicholls St.

Barracks St.

22 23   24   25

Bourbon St.

Orleans St.
63   70

64 65   74 76   77 78
    66 67 69 71 73 75   Royal St.
        68   79
            72   80

St.
Anthony's
Garden

Père Antoine's Alley

99   105
100 101   102   106   108
                        103   104 Chartres St.
                                    107   109

130
Jackson
Square

Lower
Pontalba
129

Madison St.
Dumaine St.
St. Philip St.   138

St. Ann St.

Carriage
Stand

134   136 137 139 140   141
135   Decatur St.
                                142   143
                                    French Market Pl.   145
                                                144

131
Washington
Artillery Park

132 **Riverfront Streetcar**

N Peters St.

133 **Moonwalk**

Esplanade Ave.

*Mississippi
River*

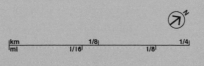

km
mi   1/8
        1/16   1/8   1/4

Mornings are the best time here. The streets are quiet and filled with yeasty aromas from the bakers, who fire their wood ovens before dawn, rewarding early risers with hot croissants and baguettes. Residents pace their balconies in bathrobes, drinking coffee and watering plants. And shopkeepers open their shutters and mutter as they hose down the sidewalks, washing away another night of frantic sinning. Today the square mile known as the French Quarter (bordered by the **Mississippi River, Rampart and Canal Streets,** and **Esplanade Avenue**) is New Orleans's prime tourist attraction.

As Quarter residents walk upriver to offices beyond Canal Street, they pass a different breed of worker streaming down to **Jackson Square** to ply the tourist trade. A buggy driver shouts at his mule, fast-trotting to line up for the first catch of the day. A curbside master hangs out his shingle—a chess game for hire. Caricaturists and other quick-draw penslingers set up camp under vibrant beach umbrellas. Street entertainers clatter into place with their fire batons, tuba quartets, tarot cards, unicycles, and wineglass xylophones.

The earliest visitors hurry to claim their reservations for breakfast at **Brennan's** by 8AM. Before noon, swarms of tourists crowd the world-class antiques shops and art galleries that line **Royal Street.** Already having exceeded their fat and calorie allowances for the day, many of these once upstanding citizens are tipsy, unaccustomed to vodka-spiked orange juice and Champagne with their ham and eggs.

When the same area was settled in 1718 under Jean-Baptiste Le Moyne, Sieur de Bienville, it comprised the entire city—or, more precisely, the small French colony of *La Nouvelle Orléans*. A shifty Scot named John Law had ordered Bienville to establish the Louisiana outpost in the name of Philippe, *Duc d'Orléans*, regent to the child-king Louis XV. A big-time hustler in the French court, Law had finagled a 25-year charter to exploit the vast territory that had earlier been claimed—and named—for Louis XIV. Then he publicized the wonders to be found in the New World and lured scores of Europeans to the exciting new colony. Fresh off the boats, the émigrés were excited all right: by hurricanes, yellow-fever epidemics, floods, and the alarming sight of the crude palmetto huts that housed the first settlers.

Little remains from those days. Two disastrous fires swept through the young colony: The first, in 1788, destroyed virtually all of the original French structures; the second, in 1794, wiped out a large part of the recovering community. Most of the Quarter you see today dates from the mid-19th century and reflects Spanish architectural styles. The only undisputed survivor of Bienville's town, the **Old Ursuline Convent,** is a superb example of pure French-Colonial design.

You can easily imagine the narrow streets and flagstone alleyways teeming with Creole gentry, buccaneers, voodoo queens, and all of the other wild characters who populated the booming port colony. Thanks to the pioneering **Vieux Carré Commission,** a model for similar preservationist groups nationwide, old New Orleans is jealously guarded and painstakingly conserved. Small two- and three-story structures of worn brick or pastel-painted masonry are decked with cast-iron balconies or liberal dollops of gingerbread. Dormers and chimneys poke through high-pitched slate rooftops and baskets of flowers dangle from the eaves. French doors, flanked by tall shutters, overlook ancient courtyards lavish with subtropical plants and softly gurgling fountains.

After dark, antique street lamps and storefront gaslights flicker on; brassy background music seeps down the alleyways as **Bourbon Street** bars swing wide open; and night-blooming jasmine competes with the seductive scents from block after block of extraordinary restaurants. Serene strollers, fat and happy, window-shop after a voluptuous old-line binge at **Antoine's** or **Galatoire's**, or a stylish feast at the newer **Bayona, Mr. B's Bistro, or NOLA.** Jackson Square is shadowy and filled with echoes, washed with soft light from the illuminated cathedral. Solitary musicians play romantic songs for lovers on the **Moonwalk**, and foghorns answer from the ships along the river. Nearby, a starstruck entrepreneur props his telescope next to **Café du Monde** and chalks the evening's target—maybe Saturn or Jupiter—on the sidewalk.

As the rest of the French Quarter calms down, Bourbon Street grows more frenetic. Whiskey-voiced barkers outside the strip joints promise oil wrestlers, "French orgies," and worse. Whooping college students, last guests at the party in the town that never sleeps, reel from one dive to the next until sunrise. Then there's still time for the repentant to make 6:30AM Mass at **St. Louis Cathedral**, as the cycle begins all over again.

1 PERISTYLE

★★★★$$$ Reservations can be scarce in this highly popular restaurant, especially for Friday lunch when every table is usually claimed by regular local customers. Chef/owner Anne Kearney, one of the leaders in the culinary charge back to the basics, presents a chic retake of comfort food—a deftly polished collection of Southwestern French classics that changes with the season. Offerings could include seared foie gras with housemade cranberry conserve, grilled loin of lamb with ratatouille, thick veal chops with roasted fennel, rustic apple tarts, or fruit sorbets spiked with fresh herbs. The 19th-century building and the no-nonsense dining room fitted with dark woods, terrazzo floors, bentwood chairs, white linens, and flickering candles are well suited to the cuisine. Note Alonzo Lansford's huge oil paintings of architectural structures in **City Park,** including the restaurant's namesake Peristyle. The paintings were created in the 1930s for the old **Gentilich** family restaurant that formerly occupied these premises. ♦ Contemporary French ♦ Tu-Th, Sa dinner; F lunch and dinner. Reservations recommended. 1041 Dumaine St (at N Rampart St). 593.9535

2 MAISON DUPUY HOTEL

$$ This hotel's seven balconied 19th-century buildings surround a gorgeous palm-shaded courtyard with a heated pool and sun deck. The 200 guest rooms and suites are decorated in sunny French Provincial style. Other amenities include cable TV, marble bathrooms, a small health club and an excellent restaurant. ♦ 1001 Toulouse St (at Burgundy St). 586.8000, 800/535.9177; fax 525.5334; www.maisondupuy.com &

Within the Maison Dupuy Hotel:

DOMINIQUE'S

★★★$$$ A native of the little island of Mauritius off the eastern coast of Africa, Chef Dominique Macquet established his local reputation at chic The Bistro at Hotel Maison de Ville before opening his namesake here in 1977. His fusion cuisine continues to attract national attention—particularly such exotica as brochette of sweetbreads skewered on sugarcane, foie gras Napoleon with fig confit, duck prosciutto with marinated melons and chestnut vinaigrette, and flash-broiled lobster with Mauritian-spiced couscous and a lavender-scented sauce. An in-house pastry chef produces additional temptations, from dessert soufflés to an extra-creamy cappuccino tiramisù. Dark woods and deep green wallpaper are brightened by twinkling votives, fine china and crystal, and fresh orchids. Upholstered armchairs are especially roomy and comfortable and tables are well spaced. ♦ International ♦ M-Sa lunch and dinner; Su brunch and dinner. Reservations recommended. 522.8800 &

3 THE RAWHIDE

Their annual costume contest on an outdoor stage is one of the highlights of Mardi Gras. This leather/Levi bar draws an older crowd of mostly gay men. ♦ Daily 24 hours. 740 Burgundy St (at St. Ann St). 525.8106

4 CHATEAU LE MOYNE

$$ Four 19th-century town houses, designed by **James Gallier Sr.,** are incorporated into an unusually attractive Holiday Inn property with 171 rooms and suites, lacy galleries, four courtyards, and a large swimming pool. Some of the suites have exposed bricks and cypress

beams. **Cafe Bienville** restaurant serves breakfast daily. ✦ 301 Dauphine St (at Bienville St). 581.1303, 800/HOLIDAY; fax 523.5709 ♿

5 GRENOBLE HOUSE

$$$ An inconspicuous etched-glass door is the entrance for 17 spacious suites (one is 1,500 square feet) in a carefully restored 1834 complex. All of the units are self-contained with fully equipped kitchens (handy since there is no restaurant). The decor is attractive and traditional, with exposed brick walls and high ceilings adding charm to the modern conveniences. The suites share a large brick courtyard with Jacuzzi and pool. A continental breakfast buffet is included in the room rate. ✦ 323 Dauphine St (between Bienville and Conti Sts). 522.1331, 800/722.1834; fax 524.4968

MUSÉE CONTI
HISTORICAL MUSEUM

6 MUSÉE CONTI HISTORICAL WAX MUSEUM

A fun half-hour stroll along the cool, dark passageways takes you past 300 years of local history staged in brilliant tableaux. The figures were made in Paris, the eyes are optical glass from Germany, and the human hair, imported from Italy, was painstakingly inserted strand by strand with a special needle. Wax, like human skin, is slightly translucent and the coloring was added beneath the final layer for a startling resemblance to living flesh. This quaint and meticulously detailed museum offers a fine introduction to Andrew Jackson, pirate Jean Lafitte, voodoo queen Marie Laveau, Mardi Gras Indian Chief Montana, Louis Armstrong, Pete Fountain—even former Governor Edwin Edwards. The requisite chamber of horrors presents Frankenstein, Dracula, the Wolf Man, and other mild shocks. ✦ Admission. Daily. 917 Conti St (between Dauphine and Burgundy Sts). 525.2605, 800/233.5405; fax 566.7636 ♿

7 DAUPHINE ORLEANS

$$$ It's not the grandest property in town, but this pleasant motor hotel has 111 rooms, secured on-site parking (a rare amenity in the French Quarter), a palm-filled courtyard with swimming pool, a small exercise center, and free downtown van service (but no restaurant). The **Audubon Room** meeting facility is located in a cottage where the famous naturalist once painted, and the lounge, **May Bailey's Place,** was formerly a bordello (ask for a copy of the original city license). Request one of the 14 **Dauphine Patio** rooms, with original 19th-

century brick and cypress detailing. All guests are treated to complimentary breakfast in a bright yellow dining nook, with a gratis morning newspaper. ✦ 415 Dauphine St (between Conti and St. Louis Sts). 586.1800, 800/521.7111; fax 586.9630; dohfq@aol.com ♿

8 BAYONA

★★★★$$$ Susan Spicer's lusty New World cuisine has an ideal setting in an early 19th-century cottage, where the walls are decked with photographs of historic Italian gardens and a trompe l'oeil Mediterranean mural. In fair weather, ask for a table in the lush courtyard, landscaped with banana trees, flowering shrubs, a fish pond, and a fountain. The menu changes seasonally, but Spicer's signature cream of garlic soup is a constant. Other great choices are grilled duck breast with pepper jelly, sweetbreads with lemon-caper butter, and rabbit with rosemary and sundried tomatoes. Pronounced Buy-ah-na, the restaurant's name comes from **Camino de Bayona**, which is what Dauphine Street was called during the Spanish regime. ✦ International ✦ M-F lunch and dinner; Sa dinner. Reservations recommended. 430 Dauphine St (between Conti and St. Louis Sts). 525.4455

9 RED FISH GRILL

★★$$ Giant "oyster shell" mirrors over the bar set the theme for Ralph Brennan's casual New Orleans seafood eatery. A school of metal fish "swims" in neon overhead. The real creatures are served grilled, jerked, broiled, marinated, pecan-crusted, and fried, as well as in bisques, jambalayas, po-boys, omelettes, and gumbo. The menu changes daily. ✦ Seafood ✦ M-Sa lunch and dinner, Su brunch and dinner. 115 Bourbon St (between Canal and Iberville Sts). Phone 598-1200, fax 598-1211 www.redfishgrill.com

9 STORYVILLE DISTRICT

In collaboration with Jazz Fest producer Quint Davis, music impresario George Wein, and project architect **Arthur Davis,** restaurateur Ralph Brennan opened this 10,000-square-foot music complex adjoining his **Red Fish Grill** in 1999. A variety of music, ranging from full jazz bands to solo performances, is presented here in multiple venues under one roof. There's no cover charge, and patrons are free to wander from room to room, sampling traditional New Orleans sounds. Flashy black-and-white decor, backed by an oyster and cocktail bar, adds Roaring 20s glamour to the **Corner Room**. The **Blues Alley** is a back-street fantasy of lacy iron balconies and exposed 1909 masonry. The **Jazz Parlor,** a plush extravaganza with red velvet curtains and haunting photographs of Jazz Age "working girls," recalls the dark and sultry brothels where Jelly Roll Morton and Louis Armstrong once played. All three rooms also feature limited menus of first-rate seafood, sandwiches, and Creole/Cajun fare, from duck-and-andouille gumbo to Lady in Red Velvet cake. ✦ Daily 11:30AM-2AM; live music noon-3PM and 5PM-2AM; Su jazz brunch 10AM-2PM. 125 Bourbon St (between Canal and Iberville Sts). 410.1000; fax 410.1200

10 CHATEAU SONESTA HOTEL NEW ORLEANS

$$$ Housed in the former **D.H. Holmes Department Store,** a fixture on mainline Canal Street for generations, this spacious and quietly elegant newcomer is in a prime location for exploring the French Quarter, CBD, and Warehouse/Arts District. The 251 guest rooms are individually decorated in traditional style and feature 12-foot ceilings and towering windows; some also have balconies overlooking Bourbon or Dauphine Streets, while others face the courtyard or pool. There's also a restaurant. ✦ 800 Iberville St (at Bourbon St). 586.0800, 800/SONESTA; fax 586.1987; www.chateausonesta.com &

11 GALATOIRE'S

★★★★$$$ Every Sunday afternoon they come down from their Garden District or Audubon Place mansions, or just stroll over from their French Quarter town houses—past the topless/bottomless bars and female impersonator clubs. The gentlemen are outfitted in perfectly tailored suits, ladies in broad-brimmed hats and couturier dresses. They're on the way to this historic Parisian-style bistro with mirrored walls, crisp white linens, and whirring ceiling fans. It's one of the best places in town to get a close-up look at a real live uppercrust New Orleanian. (**Antoine's** and **Commander's Palace** are a couple of other good bets.) They order their lamb chops béarnaise or buttery broiled pompano crowned with lump crabmeat, wave excitedly across the room to old friends they haven't seen since last Sunday, and table-

hop to catch up on the latest gossip. If you can dine at only one of the grand Creole landmarks, many locals think this should be the one. Reservations are not accepted, so be prepared to stand in a line that sometimes stretches down the sidewalk. But meals are served continuously all day, and you can avoid the crowds by arriving at off-hours. ✦ French/Creole ✦ Tu-Su lunch and dinner. Jacket and tie required for dinner and all day Sunday. 209 Bourbon St (between Iberville and Bienville Sts). 525.2021

12 THE ABSINTHE HOUSE

Here is yet another of the many sites where Andrew Jackson and Jean Lafitte reputedly met to map out strategy for the 1815 Battle of New Orleans. (Apparently the general and buccaneer conspired about as often as George Washington slept. Some historians claim the two never actually met at all.) The 1805 building is now a funky old bar, with worn-out football helmets drooping from the ceiling and peeling walls papered with business cards from all over the world—not to be confused with the nearby **Old Absinthe House Bar** (400 Bourbon St, at Conti St, 525.8108), which rattles with live music. ✦ Daily from 9:30AM. 240 Bourbon St (at Bienville St). 523.3181

13 ROYAL SONESTA HOTEL

$$$ The massive Spanish-style brick complex, rich with green canopies and cast-iron galleries, has a large courtyard shaded by orange trees and a grand pink marble lobby that shimmers with fountains and crystal chandeliers. The 500 rooms and suites are furnished with antique reproductions and high-tech phones, and many have French doors that open onto balconies (ask to face the courtyard, rather than Bourbon Street, if you're here to sleep). Other amenities include several restaurants and bars; a heated outdoor pool; health club; and business center with computer rentals, secretarial services, and fax and photocopy machines. The key-access **Tower Level** offers extra perks. ✦ 300 Bourbon St (at Bienville St). 586.0300, 800/SONESTA; fax 586.0335; www.royalsonesta.com &

Within the Royal Sonesta Hotel:

BEGUE'S

★★★$$$$ The French Provincial setting is lightened by baskets of flowers and a wall of windows overlooking the courtyard. Farm-raised quail is pan fried and served with wild rice pilaf and wild mushrooms. Seared baby salmon is presented on a bed of braised fennel with horseradish mashed potatoes. Vegetable strudel and a fig-and-ginger

Restaurants/Clubs: Red | Hotels: Purple | Shops: Orange | Outdoors/Parks: Green | Sights/Culture: Blue

compote accompany the honey-glazed duck breast. Ask about the seasonal table d'hôte menu, which offers four luxe courses at a good price. ♦ Creole/Continental ♦ Daily breakfast, lunch, and dinner. Reservations recommended for dinner, and for all meals Friday through Sunday. 586.0300 &

MYSTICK DEN

Home base for celebrated jazz pianist Ronnie Kole, the plush and clubby lounge is a fine place to sink back and hear one of the local lions roar. Kole performs the third Thursday of every month and the regular house band is the Richie Moten Trio. ♦ Daily from noon; music starts at 9PM. 586.0300

14 ARNAUD'S

★★$$$ Count Arnaud Cazenave (dubbed with the faux title for his courtly ways) opened his famous Creole restaurant in 1918 and was succeeded by his daughter, the late Germaine Wells, for 30 years following his death in 1948. Current owner Archie Casbarian gave the labyrinthine complex of dining rooms a much-needed facelift when he took over in 1978. Today the meticulously restored mosaic tile floors, leaded glass windows, potted palms, high ceilings, and slowly revolving ceiling fans evoke old New Orleans. Try signature appetizer oysters Bienville or spicy shrimp remoulade. A mellow trio of musicians wanders around the room during the sit-down jazz brunch on Sundays. ♦ Creole ♦ M-F lunch and dinner; Sa dinner; Su brunch and dinner. Reservations recommended; jacket recommended. 813 Bienville St (between Bourbon and Dauphine Sts). 523.0611; fax 581.7908 &

Within Arnaud's:

GERMAINE WELLS MARDI GRAS MUSEUM

A tribute to a true original—Germaine Wells, the daughter of the restaurant's founder—this museum opened in 1952 as the **Carnival Memory Room**. The display of the family's elaborate costumes and memorabilia became increasingly ragtag with the passing years, until 1983, when current proprietor Archie Casbarian relocated the collection to a luxurious display area on the second floor. From 1937 to 1968, Ms. Wells reigned as queen at 22 Carnival balls, more than anyone else in New Orleans history. The public is welcome to stop in during restaurant hours to view her regalia, including the

spectacular spangled number she wore as Queen of Naiades in 1954. Don't miss the display of Easter bonnets from her annual buggy parade through the French Quarter. (Bourbon Street entertainer Chris Owens has carried on the tradition, but the ladies now parade in convertibles.) ♦ Free. M-F, Su 11:30AM-2:30PM, 6-10PM; Sa 6-10PM. 523.0611

15 PRINCE CONTI HOTEL

$$ The European pension-style hotel offers 50 guest rooms (many furnished with antiques), secured parking, and complimentary café au lait and croissants in the breakfast room. **The Bombay Club** is a clubby gathering spot for locals. ♦ 830 Conti St (between Bourbon and Dauphine Sts). 529.4172, 800/366.2743; fax 581.3802; www.frenchquarter.com

16 BROUSSARD'S

★★★$$$ Chef/owner Gunter Preuss and his wife Evelyn made their reputation at the late, lamented **Versailles** restaurant in the Garden District. Since they took over this beautiful old Creole restaurant in 1995, it has been attracting a loyal local following. Indecisive types can start with shrimp in two remoulades or an oyster trio that teams those tasty mollusks prepared in the Bienville, Rockefeller, and house Broussard styles. Louisiana bouillabaisse is stocked with shrimp, crabmeat, and oysters; *panéed* veal medallions are topped with herbed lump crabmeat; and a wild game grill changes daily. The courtyard is gorgeous, and don't miss the old hand-painted tiles along the entry walls that depict women (nude except for aprons) roasting pigs, making wine, and other culinary naughtiness. ♦ Creole ♦ Daily dinner. Reservations recommended. 819 Conti St (between Bourbon and Dauphine Sts). 581.3866; fax 581.3873

Hermann-Grima Historic House

17 HERMANN-GRIMA HISTORIC HOUSE

This National Historic Landmark is generally considered to be the earliest and best example of American architecture in the French Quarter. Built in 1831 by **William Brand** for wealthy merchant Samuel Hermann, the two-story brick mansion was purchased in 1844 by Judge Felix Grima, whose family lived here for five generations. The house has been meticulously restored to depict the gracious lifestyle of a prosperous Creole family in the years 1830-60. Elegant furnishings include family portraits, fine American Empire and Rococo Revival pieces, wool carpets woven on antique English looms, and silk damask draperies reproduced by Scalamandré. Guided tours take in the house, stable, flower-filled courtyards, and working 1831 French kitchen. Cooking demonstrations use the open hearth, baking oven, and *potager* (Mediterranean stew hole) on Thursdays October through May. ◆ Admission; children under 8 free. M-Sa; last tour at 3:30PM. 820 St. Louis St (between Bourbon and Dauphine Sts). 525.5661 ⅋

18 CHRIS OWENS CLUB

As the story goes, the Texas native was discovered by Walter Winchell when she was dancing at El Morocco in New York. The exact date of that event is not recorded, but let's just say the lady has been around long enough to become a legend (she is remarkably well preserved). Clad in shimmering sequins and plumes, Owens belts out high-energy versions of top 40, country/western, and jazz tunes. Trumpeter Al Hirt follows her act on Thursdays and Saturdays. The band continues between shows for dancing. ◆ Cover. Daily from noon; Chris Owens performs W and F at 10PM, Th and Sa at 9:30PM; Al Hirt performs Th and Sa at 10:30PM. 500 Bourbon St (at St. Louis St). 523.6400

19 OLIVIER HOUSE

$$ Architect **J. N. B. DePouilly** designed this rambling town house in 1836 for Marianne Bienvenue Olivier, widow of a wealthy planter, to accommodate a family that included 50 grandchildren. Jim and Kathryn Danner renovated the property as a guest house in the 1970s, and the atmosphere remains casual and friendly, with Danner grandkids often playing around the parlor and swimming pool. The tropical courtyard is lush and authentically crumbly, deliberately unmanicured. Europeans love the Old World easiness here. Each of the 42 rooms and suites is different: Some are furnished with antique canopy beds and carved armoires, while others are modern

lofts, many with kitchenettes and microwaves. Quality varies (as does price) and some rooms are noisy, especially those at street level, which open off the lobby or overlook the sidewalk. For privacy and luxury, ask about the honeymoon cottage with private courtyard. ◆ 828 Toulouse St (between Bourbon and Dauphine Sts). 525.8456; fax 529.2006

20 HOTEL STE. MARIE

$$ A half block from Bourbon Street, these 94 traditionally furnished rooms, some with balconies, share a small courtyard and swimming pool. An extensive renovation was completed in late 1996. There's also a small cafe that serves breakfast and dinner daily. ◆ 827 Toulouse St (between Bourbon and Dauphine Sts). 561.8951, 800/366.2743; fax 581.3802; hotels@frenchquarter.com ⅋

21 THE INN ON BOURBON

$$$ The 186-room Best Western motel sits at the corner of Toulouse and Bourbon Streets, where the music blaring out of surrounding clubs creates one of the noisiest intersections in town—if not the world—and the lobby's rowdy piano bar contributes to the din. But if you like to be at the center of the storm, this is it, especially during Carnival when the balconies are jammed with drunken guests tossing trinkets to the mob on the streets below. (Some rooms are reserved up to three years in advance for Mardi Gras.) The motel is on the former site of the **French Opera House,** which (prior to its 1919 destruction by fire) was the scene of many grand productions and glamorous fetes. The on-site restaurant serves breakfast only. ◆ 541 Bourbon St (at Toulouse St). 524.7611, 800/535.7891; fax 568.9427; www.innonbourbon.com ⅋

22 FRITZEL'S EUROPEAN JAZZ PUB

Traditional jazz by house band Jack Maheu and Friends—and frequent visits by traveling jazz groups from Germany—draws a fun crowd to this rustic European pub with crumbling brick walls and a small "beer garden" patio. The club is an after-work stopover for many local musicians, and impromptu late-night jams are common. ◆ M-Th from 11AM; F-Su from 10AM. 733 Bourbon St (between Orleans and St. Ann Sts). 561.0432; fax 523.8747

23 THE BOURBON PUB

A slightly mixed crowd, primarily gay men, shouts above the din from banks of monitors blaring music videos. Upstairs, the **Parade Disco** has a dazzling light show, huge dance floor, and commanding views from a balcony that's always mobbed at Carnival time. ♦ Cover charge for disco. Daily 24 hours. 801 Bourbon St (at St. Ann St). 529.2107

24 CAFÉ LAFITTE IN EXILE

The mahogany walls and gas-flame brick fireplace add plenty of old New Orleans atmosphere to the club, a gay men's bar since 1952. A pool table and video poker are upstairs. ♦ Daily 24 hours. 901 Bourbon St (at Dumaine St). 522.8397

25 LAFITTE'S BLACKSMITH SHOP

No one is willing to let go of the myth that the picturesque cottage that houses this popular bar was once a front for the smuggling operation of brothers Jean and Pierre Lafitte. Ownership records date back to the early 1770s, with no evidence that it was ever a blacksmith shop for pirates or anyone else. It is, however, one of the few remaining examples of the *brique-entre-poteaux* (French for "brick-between-posts") houses built by the early Creoles. A neighborhood hangout for decades, it has devoted fans who love the ancient walls and crude wooden furnishings. Tennessee Williams was a regular. ♦ Daily from noon. 941 Bourbon St (at St. Philip St). 523.0066

26 HOLIDAY INN

$$$ The Royal Street link in the chain has 276 rooms and suites, covered parking, an indoor pool, exercise area, lounge, and **TGI Friday's**. Upper rooms on the river side have good views of the Mississippi. ♦ 124 Royal St (between Canal and Iberville Sts). 529.7211, 800/HOLIDAY; fax 447-2830. &

27 ACME OYSTER HOUSE

★★$ Generations of New Orleanians have bellied up to one of the city's greatest—and most crowded—oyster bars. Be prepared to wait for a table, where you can order excellent fried seafood, gumbo, or po-boys. ♦ Seafood ♦ Daily lunch and dinner. 724 Iberville St (between Royal and Bourbon Sts). 522.5973. Also at: 7306 Lakeshore Dr (just north of Lake Ave). 282.9200

Rex, Carnival's king of kings, who presides over the main festivities on Mardi Gras, first reigned in 1872 as the monarch of a parade and masked ball held in honor of the visiting Grand Duke Alexis of Russia.

28 FELIX'S RESTAURANT AND OYSTER BAR

★$ Three of the city's most enduring debates are Democrat vs. Republican, Catholic vs. Protestant, and **Acme** vs. **Felix's**—and in the last case, the contenders square off across the street from one another. Though some old-timers may be put off by its touristy atmosphere, **Felix's** is larger and the menu is longer. Here, in addition to raw and fried, you can order oysters en brochette, Rockefeller, Bienville, broiled, and stewed. ♦ Seafood ♦ Daily lunch and dinner. 729 Iberville St (between Royal and Bourbon Sts). 522.4440; www.felixs.com

29 MR. B'S BISTRO

★★★$$ Owned by the Brennan family branch that oversees **Commander's Palace, Palace Cafe,** and **Bacco,** this is a clubby and very fashionable bistro with marble-topped tables, etched-glass windows, brass trim, lace cafe curtains, and an open hickory grill. Pasta jambalaya (with spinach fettuccine in place of rice) provides a novel touch to the spicy Cajun classic tossed with Gulf shrimp, andouille sausage, duck, and chicken. The bread pudding is bathed in Irish whiskey, and Mr. B's chocolate cake is layered with ultra-rich mousse and topped with chocolate ganache. ♦ International ♦ M-Sa lunch and dinner; Su brunch and dinner. Reservations recommended. 201 Royal St (at Iberville St). 523.2078; fax 521.8304 &

30 THE MONTELEONE

$$$ In 1886, Antonio Monteleone—a shoemaker who came to New Orleans from Contessa, Italy, and prospered at his French Quarter boot factory—bought the 14-room **Commercial Hotel** and gave it his name. After a multimillion-dollar renovation under the direction of Antonio's grandson, William, this place has recaptured its reputation as a grand hotel. The 16-story building is graced by a Baroque granite facade, ceiling frescoes, and ornate chandeliers. Liveried doormen add another touch of class. Decor differs in each of the 600 rooms and suites, but all have rich fabrics and elegant furnishings; some feature four-poster beds with mirrored canopies. Restaurants are the **Hunt Room Grill** for dinner only, **Le Café** for breakfast and lunch, and the **Aft Deck Oyster Bar** for lunch and dinner. Other special facilities are the

revolving **Carousel Bar,** a health club, rooftop pool, and business center. ◆ 214 Royal St (between Iberville and Bienville Sts). 523.3341, 800/535.9595; fax 528.1019; www.hotelmonteleone.com &

Within the Monteleone:

CAROUSEL BAR

The ornate revolving bar, just off the lobby, is a landmark meeting place for local business and professional people. ◆ Daily from 11AM. 523.3341 &

31 ALEX PATOUT'S LOUISIANA KITCHEN

★★$$ Patout is a native of New Iberia in Cajun country, and he brings to New Orleans three generations of family recipes. The gumbos are smoky and flavorful; other decent bets are *cochon de lait* (roasted pork sliced in a dark and peppery gravy with sweet potato praline casserole and spiced apple chutney), smothered duck (served on a bed of oyster dressing), and étouffée stocked with shrimp and crab. The menu changes with the seasons. ◆ Cajun ◆ Daily dinner. Reservations recommended. 221 Royal St (between Iberville and Bienville Sts). 525.7788

31 FRENCH ANTIQUE SHOP, INC.

Gleaming French bronze and Baccarat crystal are standouts in one of the South's largest inventories of fine chandeliers. Other specialties are bronze statuary, Oriental vases, antique French furniture, and hand-carved 19th-century French marble mantels. ◆ M-Sa. 225 Royal St (between Iberville and Bienville Sts). 524.9861; fax 524.9985

32 HANSON GALLERY NEW ORLEANS

Works by pop master Peter Max and sports artist Leroy Neiman are prominently featured, along with Frederick Hart's lucite and bronze sculptures, and the surreal paintings of Raymond Douillet. Regional and local talent includes realist painter Adrian Deckbar and photographer Barbara Kline. The emphasis is on contemporary painting, sculpture, and photography. ◆ Daily. 229 Royal St (between Iberville and Bienville Sts). 524.8211; fax 524.8420 &

33 THE SAINT LOUIS

$$$ Although built in the 1960s, the cream stucco facade with broad fanlights and colonnaded entry blends well with its 19th-century neighbors. Wide Spanish arches surround a brick courtyard studded with tables, a white stone fountain, and baskets of flowers. The 79 rooms and suites, furnished in peaches-and-cream French provincial style, have bidets and phones in the bathrooms. Amenities include 24-hour concierge and room service from the swank **Louis XVI** restaurant. ◆ 730 Bienville St (between Royal and Bourbon Sts). 581.7300, 800/535.9706; fax 524-8925; www.stlouishotel.com &

Within The St. Louis:

LOUIS XVI

★★★★$$$$ With brass wall sconces and hues of gold and burgundy that evoke the Art Deco chic of Paris in the 1920s, the restaurant has won national awards for its European-style service. Waiters maneuver *gueridons* (little carts) to each table to put finishing touches on rack of lamb, beef Wellington, and tournedos draped in rich Madeira-and-mushroom sauce, or crêpes suzette flamed with great ceremony. Chef Agnes Bellet, a native of France, has added her own signature, topping fresh fish with sautéed banana, red bell pepper, and meunière butter sauce. In July and August, patrons are treated to lighter (and less expensive) table d'hôte specials, in addition to the regular menu. ◆ Continental ◆ Daily breakfast and dinner. Reservations recommended; jackets required. 581.7000, 800/535.9706 &

34 DIXON & DIXON OF ROYAL

A regal collection of French, English, and Dutch antique furnishings, European oil paintings, Persian rugs, and antique and estate jewelry fills the 20,000 square feet of gallery space. You may find an Edwardian brooch, dating from 1905 and encrusted with diamonds and opals, or a pair

---

of gilded Napoleon III armchairs with a matching mahogany cabinet. Prices are not exactly in the garage sale range. ♦ Daily. 237 Royal St (between Iberville and Bienville Sts). 524.0282, 800/848.5148; fax 524.7378 &

34 ROTHSCHILD'S ANTIQUES

Fine custom-made jewelry, estate jewelry, 18th- and 19th-century French and English furnishings, and elegant chandeliers are among the treasures on display. ♦ M-Sa. 241 Royal St (at Bienville St). 523.5816 & Also at: 321 Royal St (between Bienville and Conti Sts). 523.2281

35 VINCENT MANN GALLERY

Lesser-known 19th- and 20th-century French masters showcased at this gallery include painter and author Françoise Gilot (the mother of Paloma Picasso) and Luc Didier (one of the finest living French Impressionists). The only American artist among the featured Impressionists and Post-Impressionists is Charles Allard, celebrated for his brightly colored, formal beach scenes. ♦ M-Sa. 713 Bienville St (between Royal and Bourbon Sts). 523.2342 &

36 ROYAL ANTIQUES, LTD.

Nanette Keil Shapiro's enormous store houses an outstanding collection of 18th- and 19th-century French and English furniture, chandeliers, decorative accessories, and antique jewelry. ♦ M-Sa. 309 Royal St (between Bienville and Conti Sts). 524.7033; fax 523.4834 &

37 A GALLERY FOR FINE PHOTOGRAPHY

Continuous exhibitions of works by Ansel Adams, Diane Arbus, Helmut Newton, Annie Leibovitz, and more than 150 other classical and contemporary photographers fill two floors. Casual or serious collectors also will find a good selection of rare photo books. ♦ Daily. 322 Royal St (between Bienville and Conti Sts).www.agallery.com; 568.1313

38 KEIL'S ANTIQUES

In 1899, Hermina and Jacob Keil came to New Orleans and founded what was then called **The Royal Company**. Today the Keil family still operates this establishment, which specializes in French and English antique furnishings, marble mantels, opulent chandeliers, and decorative objets d'art. Other family members established the neighboring **Royal**

Antiques and **Moss Antiques**. ♦ M-Sa. 325 Royal St (between Bienville and Conti Sts). 522.4552; fax 522.8754 &

39 WALDHORN & ADLER COMPANY, INC.

Spanish Colonial architect **Barthelemy Lefon** designed this balconied building for the **Bank of the United States** around 1800, when Royal Street was the financial center of the city. Occupying over 15,000 square feet of space, its three floors are filled with antique French and English furniture and estate and modern diamond engagement rings. The company was acquired in 1997 by **Adler's** (see page 52), which added a stock of Rolex, Pavek, and Cartier watches. ♦ M-Sa. 343 Royal St (at Conti St). 581.6379; fax 581.6381 &

40 MANHEIM GALLERIES

The old board of directors' room of the former **Louisiana State Bank** building, designed in 1820 by **Benjamin Latrobe** now houses one of the world's largest collections of archaic and antique hand-carved jade art pieces. An extensive selection of antique European and Oriental furnishings and accessories includes porcelains, paintings, vases, and urns. The gallery also offers exquisite handmade reproductions of antique furniture. ♦ M-Sa. 403 and 409 Royal St (between Conti and St. Louis Sts). 568.1901, 800/265.4986; fax 568.9430

40 RAYMOND H. WEILL CO., RARE STAMPS

Hambros Bank Ltd. of London bought out the entire stock in 1989 for $14 million—the largest single sale in the history of stamp collecting. The internationally recognized Weill (who has been at this location since 1933) subsequently rebuilt the collection and continues to offer the philatelic world a substantial inventory. ♦ M-F until 3PM. 407 Royal St (between Conti and St. Louis Sts). 581.7373; fax 581.7385

41 MOSS ANTIQUES

Another Keil-Moss enterprise (along with **Keil's Antiques,** see at left), this shop features antique and estate jewelry, as well as French and English furnishings, chandeliers, paintings, and other decorative artworks.♦ M-Sa. 411 Royal St (between Conti and St. Louis Sts). 522.3981, 522.8754; fax 522-3508&

41 BRENNAN'S

★★★★$$$$ Festive milk punch or Bloody Marys begin the famous "Breakfast at Brennan's"—served from 8AM to 2:30PM daily—but the prices are the biggest eye-opener of all. Worth every pretty penny, though, are the eggs Benedict or eggs Sardou (on a bed of creamed spinach and artichoke bottoms, topped with hollandaise), piquant turtle soup, and signature bananas Foster (sautéed in butter, brown sugar, cinnamon, and banana liqueur, then flamed tableside with white rum and heaped over vanilla ice cream). For dinner, try oysters Rockefeller, trout Kottwitz (with diced artichokes and mushrooms in a lemon butter sauce), or veal Alana Michelle (smothered in lump crabmeat and béarnaise). The wine selection is one of the city's greatest. The seven dining rooms are richly furnished with comfortable tapestry chairs and crystal chandeliers. Ask to be seated on either the glassed-in terrace or the balcony, which overlooks the tropical courtyard. Built in 1795 for Spanish merchant José Faurie, the mansion was home to world chess champion Paul Morphy in the late 1850s. ◆ French/Creole ◆ Daily breakfast, lunch, and dinner. Reservations required; jacket and tie preferred for dinner. 417 Royal St (between Conti and St. Louis Sts). 525.9711

42 LUCKY CHENG'S

★★$$ Talk about a great gimmick: The "dragon queen" waitresses at this film noir version of a Chinese restaurant are actually men in drag. The elegant lounge has more than a touch of decadence, with gold-fringed green velvet chairs, embroidered silk pillows, and deep burgundy walls. A thoroughly modern menu travels the Orient, from sesame-crusted salmon to crawfish rock 'n' roll (a tempura sushi roll filled with crawfish cream sauce). New Orleans native Hayne Sutton also created the sister operation in New York City. ◆ Asian/Creole ◆ M-Th dinner; F-Su lunch and dinner. 720 St. Louis St (between Royal and Bourbon Sts). 529.2045; fax 524.3486 &

43 DYANSEN GALLERY

This branch of the Dyansen family of art galleries (also located in New York and San Francisco) showcases one of the country's largest collections of sculpture, graphics, and original gouaches by Erté, as well as works by Leroy Neiman, Angelo Basso, and Chinese graphic artist/sculptor Jiang. Be sure to see the etchings, bronzes, and drawings by contemporary satirist Nechita. ◆ M-Th, Su; F-Sa until 9PM. 433 Royal St (between Conti and St. Louis Sts). 523.2902, 800/211.6984; fax 523.3125; www.dyansengallery.com &

43 JAMES H. COHEN & SONS

A wooden Indian guards the entrance to this cavernous storehouse of rare coins and currency (including ancient Roman coins. Confederate paper money and authentic pieces of eight), antique watches, jewelry, carved ivory miniatures, and Frederic Remington's bronco-bustin' cowboys. The fourth generation of the Cohen family specializes in historic weaponry, and their stock includes 18th-century British flintlocks, sabers, bayonets, Civil War muskets, cannonballs, muzzle loaders, and pistols. ◆ Daily. 437 Royal St (between Conti and St. Louis Sts). 522.3305, 800/535.1853; fax 523.7603 &

ANTOINE'S

44 ANTOINE'S

★★★★$$$ If they seat you in the front room, you're in Siberia, despite the pretty Austrian drapes. You'll know you've arrived when you're led to the **Rex Room,** surrounded by glass cases filled with Carnival regalia, and given your own private waiter. The maze of 15 dining rooms is rich with dark woods, gleaming chandeliers, and antique furnishings. Since Antoine Alciatore established the city's oldest and most famous restaurant in 1840, the formally clad staff has served the Duke and Duchess of Windsor, Count Albrecht Von Bismarck, Cecil B. DeMille, Mick Jagger—ask for a free booklet listing hundreds of illustrious guests. Don't miss the celebrated *pommes de terre soufflés* (twice-fried potato puffs filled with air), oysters Rockefeller (the much-imitated dish was created here), and pompano *en papillote* (topped with lump crabmeat and shrimp, cooked in sealed white parchment). As soon as you settle in, order dessert; the signature football-shaped baked Alaska, which serves two, requires this advance notice. Before leaving, stroll to the back and peek into the 25,000-bottle wine cellar. ◆ French/Creole ◆ M-Sa lunch and dinner. Reservations recommended for dinner; jacket required. 713 St. Louis St (between Royal and Bourbon Sts). 581.4422; fax 581.3003 &

Restaurants/Clubs: Red | Hotels: Purple | Shops: Orange | Outdoors/Parks: Green | Sights/Culture: Blue

Royal Street Shopping

IBERVILLE STREET

Hurwitz-Mintz *furniture*

menswear Gentlemen's Quarter

womenswear Ladies' Quarter Ltd.

French Antique Shop
Hanson Gallery
Birjand Oriental Rugs

First National Bank of Commerce
24-hour ATM

Dixon & Dixon *antiques*
Rothschild's *antiques*

BIENVILLE STREET

Touchstone Gallery
Maison Royale Art Gallery
animation art Bryant Galleries
DuMonde Gallery
A Gallery for Fine Photography

ROYAL STREET

Currents *fine jewelry*
Royal Antiques

Jack Sutton *antiques*
Rumors Too *masks/jewelry*

Keil's *antiques*

J. Herman & Son Ltd. Galleries *antiques*
Waldhorn & Adler Company Inc. *antiques*

CONTI STREET

Manheim Galleries *antiques*
Raymond H. Weill *rare stamps*
Moss Antiques

Vintage 429 *autographs/movie memorabilia*

Dyansen Gallery *art gallery*
James H. Cohen & Sons
rare coins/antique weaponry

ST. LOUIS STREET

brass decorative arts The Brass Lion

Barrister's Gallery
tribal jewelry/Southern folk art
Le Petit Soldier Shop
miniatures/military artifacts
Elliot Art Gallery

Jack Sutton *jewelry/objets d'art*
Gerald D. Katz *antiques*
Martin Laborde Gallery
Rumors *masks/jewelry*
Kurt E. Schon *gallery*

The Ré Gallery *vintage posters*
Dansk *factory outlet*

TOULOUSE STREET

hand-painted clothing/gifts Lazybug
souvenirs Crab Bag
masks/dolls/gifts
jewelry/collectibles Lord Jim
fine jewelry Royalties
jewelry/antiques Peacock Galleries
antiques M. S. Rau

Great Expectations *jewelry*

Galleria Veronese *gallery/jewelry*
Old Town Praline Shop *pralines/gifts*

Fischer-Gambino
womenswear/collectibles
Richard Russell *gallery*

ST. PETER STREET

womenswear Fleur de Paris

Royal St. A&P *regional foods/souvenirs*
Accents *gifts/collectibles*
Chinese-American Co.
Oriental art/collectibles

ORLEANS STREET

posters/prints Bergen Galleries
Bottom of the Cup Tearoom
occult/tarot cards/readings

Indonesian crafts Importícos
Guthrie Rinard Gallery

Rodrigue Gallery

L. M. S. *antiques/Russian art*

ST. ANN STREET

Royal Street Shopping, continued

ST. ANN STREET

cotton clothing **California Drawstrings**
Casell Gallery
vintage linens/quilts **The Front Porch**
Hové Parfumeur

home accessories **The Gothic Shop**

sterling jewelry **La Mina**

Vieux Carré Hair Store
theatrical makeup/wigs
Joan Good *antiques*
Crafty Louisianians *Louisiana crafts*
Hello, Dolly *doll shop*
Cotton Market *cotton clothing*
Three Dog Bakery

Mystic Curio *collectibles*

DUMAINE STREET

Gallerie Louisiane
antiques **Barakat**
jewelry **Sabai**
antiques **Patout/Dozier**
clothing **Royal Ltd.**
French Quarter Postal Emporium
postal services/copy machines

ROYAL STREET

Grace Note *art-to-wear/exotic curios*

Guess Bridges Gallery *antiques*
Sigle's Antiques & Metalcraft *metalworks*
Maggio Gallery

ST. PHILIP STREET

Native American crafts **Vision Quest**

URSULINES STREET

Royal Pharmacy

GOV. NICHOLLS STREET

women's occult books/herbs **More Magic**

BARRACKS STREET

45 MARTIN LABORDE GALLERY

MARTIN LABORDE GALLERY

Collectors take note: Artist Martin LaBorde, a longtime local favorite with a solid following of international patrons, signed an exclusive contract in 1996 with impresario Richard Steiner. It was Steiner who helped promote Cajun artist George Rodrigue and his trademark blue dog to superstar status via similar galleries in New Orleans (see **Rodrigue Gallery of New Orleans** on page 31), Carmel, Munich, and Tokyo. LaBorde's current works are also sparked by a recurring icon, a little magician named Bodo, who lives in a spiritual landscape dominated by deep-hued skies, with a crescent moon observing the scene below. Unbound by gravity, Bodo "floats" among pyramid-shaped mountains, often accompanied by one of his familiars—a dog, cat, elephant, sea turtle, or the occasional human. The visual poetry is enhanced by titles like "Just as My Big Toe Left the Ground, Sparky Decided to Stay" and "She Dreams the Dreams of the Blue Moon." Among other awards, LaBorde received the 1972 Pushkin Medal of Honor from the Hermitage Museum in St. Petersburg. His work has also been exhibited in Chicago, Mexico City, Munich, and Tokyo. ♦ Daily. 509 Royal St (between St. Louis and Toulouse Sts). 587.7111 &

45 RUMORS

The work of more than a hundred artisans is represented in the spectacular handcrafted masks and jewelry in this shop, including more than 10,000 pairs of earrings that range from humorous bangles to late-night chic. The collectible masks (fashioned in bold-colored leathers, they make startling wall decorations) are priced from $25 to $3,000. There are also medieval-style papier-mâché masks with long pointy snouts, which are imported from Florence, Italy. ♦ Daily. 513 Royal St (between St. Louis and Toulouse Sts). 525.0292; fax 568.1816. Also at: 319 Royal St (between Bienville and Conti Sts). 523.0011

46 KURT E. SCHON, LTD.

A sweeping staircase, dazzling chandeliers, and 18-foot ceilings create the perfect setting for America's largest inventory of 19th-century European paintings. More than 600 works can be seen here, including those of British and French Impressionists and Post-Impressionists, and members of the Royal Academy and the French Salon. Around 150 paintings are housed in the Royal Street browsing gallery,

---

most priced from $20,000 to $100,000. Serious collectors can view approximately 450 more at the St. Louis Street branch (by appointment only), where the collection ranges from late 18th-century Neo-Classics, through the Romantic period of Delacroix, to the Pre-Impressionist Barbizon painters. ♦ M-Sa. 523 Royal St (between St. Louis and Toulouse Sts). 524.5462; fax 524.6233 ﾕ Also at: 510 St. Louis St (between Decatur and Chartres Sts). 524.5462; fax 524.6233

47 LE PETIT SOLDIER SHOP

Look closely at the miniature warriors (average height, two inches) and you may recognize a few faces: Napoleon, Churchill, Patton, Eisenhower, Hitler, Mussolini, Lincoln, Grant, Lee. Six local artists work full time to stock the window displays and inside cases with hundreds of tiny figures dating from ancient Greece through modern times. Owner Dave Dugas loves to talk military history, and his auxiliary stock includes authentic medals and decorations, as well as British Royal Family commemoratives from weddings, coronations, and jubilees. ♦ M-Sa. 528 Royal St (between St. Louis and Toulouse Sts). 523.7741 ﾕ

48 HISTORIC NEW ORLEANS COLLECTION

For a cool retreat from the French Quarter crowds, take a guided tour of the elegant **Louisiana History Galleries** to see exhibits that range from early propaganda paintings designed to attract settlers (New Orleans streets are paved with gold and the Mississippi River is bordered by mountains) to modern satellite photographs. Free exhibits in the street-level **Williams Gallery** change regularly. The late Kemper and Leila Williams purchased the 1792 **Merieult House** and the rear 19th-century brick cottage, which was their home, in the 1930s. This collection was established on the property in 1966. For serious study, closed stacks at the new, state-of-the-art **Research Center** (410 Chartres St, between Conti and St. Louis Sts, 598.7171) offer the city's most extensive collection of historic records—6,000 linear feet of documents and a total of 300,000 images. ♦ Williams Gallery free; admission for guided tours of the second-floor galleries and the Williams house. Tu-Sa. 533 Royal St (between St. Louis and Toulouse Sts). 523.4662; fax 598.7108 ﾕ

49 COGHLAN GALLERY

Vincent Nolte bought this property in 1819 and lived here while writing his autobiography, the basis for the novel *Anthony Adverse*. The house is known as "The Court of Two Lions," for the twin stone beasts that face each other atop the high green gate. Just beyond, a courtyard shop is filled with garden ornaments, softly gurgling fountains, and

little winged angels—all crafted by local artisans. The fountains are a favorite watering station for French Quarter pets. ♦ Daily. 710 Toulouse St (between Royal and Bourbon Sts). 525.8550

50 HOTEL MAISON DE VILLE

$$$$ One of the city's best small hotels surrounds a broad brick courtyard with banana trees, flowering plants, and a three-tiered fountain. The reception area and 23 guest rooms and suites are furnished in 18th- and 19th-century antiques, and the baths are rich with marble basins and brass fittings. Restored slave quarters dating from the 18th century (Tennessee Williams lived and wrote here in room **No. 9**) are incorporated into the main complex. A few blocks away are the hotel's seven **Audubon Cottages** (John James Audubon lived in cottage **No. 1** while working on *Birds of America* in 1821), each with two bedrooms, wide pine floors, exposed beam ceilings, period furnishings, and private or shared patios. An adjoining swimming pool is open to guests staying at either facility. Mornings bring orange juice, croissants, bran muffins, and a pot of coffee—along with a newspaper and fresh rose—on a silver tray; and Port and Sherry are served in the evenings. A nice additional touch is that complimentary VCRs and videos are available at the desk. ♦ 727 Toulouse St (between Royal and Bourbon Sts). 561.5858, 800/634.1600; fax 528.9939; www.maisondeville.com

Within Hotel Maison de Ville:

THE BISTRO

★★★$$$ This tiny Parisian-style bistro, lined with red leather banquettes and mirrored panels, showcases a seasonal menu, which could feature anything from crawfish fritters with sauce piquante to confit of duck with a wild-mushroom corn cake and apple/fennel compote. The crème brûlée is superb. The noise level is high, and tables are too close together, but the ultra-stylish food is worth a little discomfort. Highly recommended. ♦ International ♦ Daily lunch and dinner. Reservations required; jacket recommended. 528.9206

51 THE COURT OF TWO SISTERS

★★$$$ Tourists love the well-publicized daily jazz brunch with a massive spread of some 80 regional dishes (jambalaya, shrimp Creole, crawfish étoufée gumbo) and a band that strolls around the wishing well, fountain, banana trees, and tropical birds. The two sisters were Emma and Bertha Camors, whose *rabais* (notions shop) outfitted fashionable ladies with formal gowns, imported lace, and Parisian perfumes from 1886 to 1906. Today, the restaurant is operated by two brothers, Joe and Jerry Fein, whose father bought the

THE SKINNY ON FAT TUESDAY: A SURVIVAL GUIDE

It has been called the greatest free show on earth, but Carnival is one of the leading money makers for the New Orleans area. More than 17,000 active *krewe* members shell out an average of $400 each for throws alone, and overall spending approaches $500 million annually. Many hotels are booked a year in advance and restaurants are filled to capacity, so this is no time to hit town without reservations. If you want to enjoy the chaos, be prepared. Mardi Gras is a legal holiday and many city services come to a screeching halt as most of the populace takes to the streets. Crime rates are usually down, because even the bad guys take the day off to party. If you're looking for food, hotels are the best bet. And don't expect the few businesses which are open to respond hospitably to those in search of rest rooms only. Whether or not you choose to "mask," be sure to wear loose clothes and extremely comfortable shoes. A costume should be roomy enough to allow for layers underneath (depending on the unpredictable local climate) and plenty of jumping up and down. It should also be easy to put on and take off, as changing areas are nonexistent. Many tourists make the mistake of wearing suits or dresses, a dead giveaway to pickpockets. **MGM Costume Rentals** (1617 St. Charles Ave, between Euterpe and Terpsichore Sts, 581.3999) is the largest outfitter in town, but most locals shop the Salvation Army, Goodwill, and other thrift stores to create custom-designed originals. Float riders tend to be more generous to folks in costume, especially to scantily clad young women. To fuel just one season, the city's largest Carnival supply house has sold as many as 40 million strings of beads, the most common trinket tossed to the screaming crowds. From giant toothbrushes to G-strings, "throws" fly in and out of popularity at a dizzying speed. Of late, spectators compete fiercely for plastic cups emblazoned with *krewe* emblems. And colored aluminum doubloons, minted with insignia and parade themes, are most safely caught in mid-air. To retrieve any that clink into the street, follow local example and stomp on the coin before stooping, or risk valuable fingers. Don't be surprised to find yourself begging, flailing your arms, or even trying to yank worthless plastic toys away from small children (for best results, yank upward and twist).

In general, families and older people will be most comfortable spending Fat Tuesday along **St. Charles Avenue**. Some groups camp overnight to stake out prime viewing spots along the parade route from **Lee Circle** to **Napoleon Avenue**. Plan to start off around 7:30AM and get as close as you can by cab (parking is next to impossible), then walk until you find a good place to spread a picnic blanket. For grandstand seating and daylong access to indoor buffets and rest rooms, contact the **Hotel Inter-Continental New Orleans** (444 St. Charles Ave, between Poydras and Gravier Sts, 525.5566). Those who aren't offended by bare flesh, lewd behavior, and blasphemy (or the electronically enhanced street evangelists who hit town to cash in on the wholesale sin) will find plenty of amusements in the **French Quarter**. The city's most outrageously costumed revelers, primarily men in drag, compete for prizes at the corner of Burgundy and St. Ann Streets beginning at 1PM.

Bourbon Street is usually packed, so cruise Royal or Chartres Street, or the **Jackson Square** area for plenty of spectacle with room to breathe. Be prepared for anything: dominatrix nuns, square-dancing transvestites, anatomically correct mummies, or hard-core missionaries lugging life-sized wooden crosses. Above all, watch for the famous "Frog People," an anti-evangelist group that razzes the preachers. Pick up one of their "Get Out of Purgatory Free" cards—just in case you don't survive to straighten out the accounts on Ash Wednesday.

---

building in 1963. ◆ Creole ◆ Daily brunch and dinner. 613 Royal St (between Toulouse and St. Peter Sts). 522.7261; fax 581.5804 &

52 ROYAL BLEND COFFEE AND TEA HOUSE

Friendly birds hop in to steal crumbs from the floor of this quiet sanctuary, a secluded neighborhood coffee shop that opens off a courtyard at the end of a long carriageway—far from the crowds of Royal Street. Choose from more than 20 brewed and iced coffees and a large selection of teas (blend your own, if you're feeling creative). The pastries are very good, and light lunch items (croissant sandwiches, salads, and quiches) are available daily as long as

the supply lasts. ◆ M-Th, Su from 7AM; F-Sa 7AM-midnight. 621 Royal St (between Toulouse and St. Peter Sts). 523.2716. Also at: 222 Carondelet St., 529-2005; 204 Metairie Rd (between Friedrichs Ave and Stella St), Metairie. 835.7779

53 OLD TOWN PRALINE SHOP

Bypass the slick newcomers for this vintage confectioner that has been in business since 1935—and looks it. Visit the moody rear courtyard, where blossoms cascade from a large stand of ginger plants and towering elephant ears are almost as high as the roof thing. Inside walls are decked with portraits of 19th-century heartthrob Adelina Patti, who lived here in 1860 while she performed at the French Opera House. The 17-year-old diva attracted scores of young Creole gentlemen who paced the block hoping to

---

Restaurants/Clubs: Red | Hotels: Purple | Shops: Orange | Outdoors/Parks: Green | Sights/Culture: Blue

catch a glimpse of her. ♦ M-Sa. 627 Royal St (between Toulouse and St. Peter Sts). 525.1413

54 PRESERVATION HALL

Living legends perform for standing-room-only crowds in this dark and grungy space with a few hard benches and the world's greatest traditional jazz. The legendary bands rotate nightly, playing 20-minute sets with time in between to sell recordings and let the crowd shift around. No drinks or food are sold, but you can bring in drinks from one of the many bars along the block. Doors open at 8PM and, if you're in line by 7:30PM, you may be able to claim a seat. New Orleans's most famous music hall was established in 1961 by Pennsylvanian tuba player and jazz lover Allen Jaffe. When he lay on his deathbed in the 1980s, musicians traveled from all over the world to bid him farewell. Hundreds attended his jazz funeral, one of the biggest such events the city has ever seen. ♦ Admission. Nightly 8PM-midnight. 726 St. Peter St (between Royal and Bourbon Sts). 523.8939 &

Pat O'Brien's ®

55 PAT O'BRIEN'S

Established in 1933 (at this location since 1942), the celebrated bar's claim to fame is the original Hurricane, four-and-a-half ounces of dark rum mixed with fruit juices and served in a 29-ounce glass shaped like a hurricane lamp (half a million are sold annually). The whole block is usually jammed with whooping college kids and tourists waiting to get inside. In the liveliest of the three bars, two pianists belt out school rah-rah songs and an enthusiastic crowd joins in. The rear courtyard has a gargantuan lit fountain, a busy bartender, and a souvenir stand. ♦ Daily from 10AM 718 St. Peter St (between Royal and Bourbon Sts). There is also an entrance at 624 Bourbon. 525.4823, 588-2744 &

56 OLD COFFEE POT

★★$$ Here at one of the coziest old restaurants in town, you can order a luxurious Creole breakfast for a fraction of the tab at Brennan's. The omelette Rockefeller is stuffed with creamed spinach and oysters, *pain perdu* (literally, lost bread) is sautéed in egg batter and sprinkled with powdered sugar, and the now-rare traditional *callas* (Creole rice cakes) are served with real maple syrup and pecans. The menu also features a good selection of seafood dishes and Creole/Cajun specialties, such as gumbo and fried shrimp. ♦ Creole ♦ Daily breakfast, lunch, and dinner. 714 St. Peter St (between Royal and Bourbon Sts). 524.3500

57 RICHARD RUSSELL GALLERY

Among the highlights here are three-dimensional steel line drawings by Barrett DeBusk, which cast wild shadows on the wall, and the red cat paintings of Jim Tweedy. Todd Warner's whimsical animal sculptures are so inviting, you'll need to keep an eye on the kids—an uncontrolled burst of enthusiasm could be very expensive. ♦ M-Th, Su; F-Sa until 10PM. 641 Royal St (at St. Peter St). Phone/fax 523.0533, 800/536.0533

58 M.S. RAU ANTIQUES

Proprietor Bill Rau's grandparents, Max and Fanny Rau, established the shop in 1912, and Fanny worked in the family business continuously from 1913 until her death in 1989—just three weeks shy of her 100th birthday. Fine American antiques are the specialty, along with Victorian cut glass, Wedgwood, jewelry, French porcelains, music boxes, silver, European clocks, and English and French furniture. Concealed within walking sticks elegant and inventive enough to outfit an 18th-century James Bond are swords, blow darts, dog leashes, whiskey flasks, bayonets, and multiple slashing spikes. Tamer gentlemen might prefer the solid ivory model designed by Fabergé. ♦ M-Sa. 630 Royal St (between Toulouse and St. Peter Sts). 523.5660, 800/544.9440; fax 566.0057 &

GUMBO SHOP

59 GUMBO SHOP

★★$$ It's touristy, but the food is very good and the prices are fair. For a whirlwind tour of Louisiana cuisine, try the combination platter with ample portions of shrimp Creole, jambalaya, and red beans and rice. Tables on the courtyard are shaded by lush greenery, but those in the large dining room are surrounded by the best atmosphere—air conditioning. ♦ Creole ♦ Daily lunch and dinner. 630 St. Peter St (between Chartres and Royal Sts). 525.1486; fax 897.3454

60 ROYAL CAFÉ

★★$$ The corner of Royal and St. Peter Streets, where the 19th-century **LaBranche House** is filigreed with double galleries of lacy ironwork in an oak-leaf and acorn motif, is one of the most photographed spots in town. This cafe, which occupies the first two floors, offers balcony dining with one of the best views in the Quarter. Creole barbecued duck is served with sweet poblano jelly and smoked sausage jambalaya. Louisiana crab cakes are lavished with a butter cream sauce seasoned with smoked tomatoes. A jazz pianist performs nightly and a working fireplace is cozy in winter. ♦ International ♦ Daily lunch and dinner. 700 Royal St (at St. Peter St). 528.9086

61 FLEUR DE PARIS

Select a basic straw or felt hat, then choose from hundreds of ribbons, veils, flowers, and other frills to suit your fancy. Custom millinery can be completed in as little as one day. Other stock ranges from tailored suits and dresses to Belgian lace wedding gowns, with appropriately luxuriant prices. ♦ Daily. 712 Royal St (at Pirate's Alley). 525.1899, 800/229.1899

62 PIRATE'S ALLEY

Though Jean Lafitte had long since departed when this passageway was cut in 1831, the myth persists that the mysterious pirate conspired here with Andrew Jackson to plan strategy for the 1815 Battle of New Orleans. Nevertheless, the twin walks on either side of **St. Louis Cathedral (Pere Antoine's Alley** is the other) are among the most romantic in all of New Orleans, especially in the foggy early morning.

On Pirate's Alley:

FAULKNER HOUSE BOOKS

William Faulkner wrote his first novel, *Soldiers' Pay*, while living here. The house is now a charming shop specializing in works by the former tenant, including first editions. The stock also features other fine works of literature and a good selection of Louisiana and New Orleans histories. ♦ Daily. 624/524.2940; 522.9725

63 BOURBON ORLEANS HOTEL

$$$ The notorious Quadroon Balls, where well-heeled Creole gentlemen established formal alliances with the legendary mixed-race beauties, were held in the adjacent **Orleans Ballroom,** which was built in 1817 by entrepreneur John Davis and restored for special functions when the hotel was added in 1964. Accounts of the 19th-century balls vary considerably. Some historians claim they were highly sophisticated affairs, to which mothers proudly brought their daughters in hopes of sealing a lifetime arrangement; others insist they were little more than orchestrated brawls. All agree that the ballroom itself was quite grand, and it is now the glittering centerpiece of a stately peach complex encircled by balconies with fine views of the French

Quarter. The hotel's lobby is rich with white columns, crystal chandeliers, and Oriental rugs; Queen Anne–style furnishings grace 211 guest rooms and suites with big marble baths; and there is a restaurant. Avoid rooms that overlook Bourbon Street or the courtyard swimming pool, which can be very noisy. ♦ 717 Orleans St (between Royal and Bourbon Sts). 523.2222, fax 525.8166; www.bourbonorleans.com ᕦ

64 RODRIGUE GALLERY OF NEW ORLEANS

A nervous-looking blue dog stares out at her adoring public from the haunting bayou landscapes of George Rodrigue. Since the Cajun artist first depicted his late pet as a terrier-mix werewolf (to illustrate a ghost storybook in 1984), the moonstruck pooch with startled yellow eyes has become an international icon, earning millions for her ex-master through his galleries in New Orleans, Carmel, and Tokyo. To contemplate her wise gaze from afar, pick up the oversized art book *Blue Dog Man* (Stewart Tabori & Chang, $50). Daily. 721 Royal St (at Orleans St). 581.4244; fax 581.2708; www.bluedogart.com ᕦ ♦

65 IMPORTÍCOS

A wildly colorful flock of temple gods (flying mermaids, elephants, pigs, fertility angels), Balinese puppets, carousel horses, wall masks, and other handcrafted exotica from Indonesia and India are showcased here. ♦ Daily. 736 Royal (between Orleans and St. Ann) 523.3100, 800/BYE.HAND.

66 BOTTOM OF THE CUP TEA ROOM

This wonderfully creaky little shop has been dispensing tea and prophecy since 1929. "One man, a regular, used to claim he was with the spirit of Betty Grable or Sonja Henie," says owner Adele Mullen. "Another woman wanted us to read [tarot cards] for her cat. She brought the cat in a bag." Devoted customers can call for long-distance consultations and do-it-yourselfers can buy fortune-telling supplies, occult books, and voodoo charms. Staff psychics are stationed in curtained booths at the rear, poised to read

---

Restaurants/Clubs: Red | Hotels: Purple | Shops: Orange | Outdoors/Parks: Green | Sights/Culture: Blue

tea leaves, palms, cards, horoscopes, and handwriting. ♦ M-Sa until 9PM, Su until 7PM. 732 Royal St (between Père Antoine's Alley and St. Ann St). 523.1204, 800/729.7148. Also at: 616 Conti St (between Chartres and Royal Sts). 524.1997

67 VIEUX CARRÉ HAIR STORE

Owner Barry Saussaye's great-great-grandmother established the company in 1877 to create wigs for the **New Orleans Opera**. At this location since 1952, theatrical hairpieces are still a specialty, along with a wide-ranging inventory of masks and makeup. ♦ M-Sa. 805 Royal St (between St. Ann and Dumaine Sts). 522.3258

68 PLACE D'ARMES HOTEL

$$ Near Jackson Square, this hotel's nine adjoining 18th-century row houses share a courtyard shaded by magnolias and banana trees. Be aware that some of the 81 rooms are windowless—the only light comes from French doors left open. There's no restaurant but complimentary croissants, juice, and coffee are served in a cheerful brick-walled breakfast area. ♦ 625 St. Ann St (between Chartres and Royal Sts). Phone/fax 524.4531, 800/366.2743; www.frenchquarter.com &

69 HOVÉ PARFUMEUR, LTD.

Perfumes, colognes, bath oils, and other sweet luxuries are mixed in a quaint back lab, and you can see large amber jars filled with the different formulas as you shop the exclusive collection of scents, soaps, potpourris, sachets, decorative bottles, and Limoges accessories. Look for the romantic labaliers, meant to be filled with perfume and worn on a necklace. ♦ M-Sa. 824 Royal St (between St. Ann and Dumaine Sts). 525.7827

70 NEW ORLEANS HISTORIC VOODOO MUSEUM

If you're on the lookout for the jawbone of an ass, you'll find it here, along with a couple of human skulls and a petrified cat. Nothing is isolated behind glass, except the resident Burmese python. Owner/curator Charles Gandolfo claims the world's only private museum dedicated exclusively to voodoo. (Ask about regularly scheduled rituals and guided tours to spiritually charged sites.) The tiny rooms are crammed with shocking

artifacts, and the casually corrupt atmosphere may be way too authentic for some. Others will simply love the quirky practitioners, who custom blend charms and potions, and the freelance occultists who drift in to talk shop. Be sure to bring an offering for the mischievous spirit Exu (he likes cigars and candy bars) or there could be trouble later. ♦ Admission. Daily. 724 Dumaine St (between Royal and Bourbon Sts). 523.7685

71 CAFÉ HAVANA

Fancy cigars are easy to find these days, but this shop usually has genuine Cubans. The changing stock in the vintage section can go back as far as 90 years, long before the embargo. The atmosphere is very relaxed, with a cluster of wooden rocking chairs that invites intriguing conversation with an international clientele. Coffee is served, as well, but no food. ♦ Daily. 842 Royal St (at Dumaine St). 569.9006

72 MADAME JOHN'S LEGACY

Some historians insist that this house (rather than the **Old Ursuline Convent,** which was built in 1749) is the oldest existing structure in the Lower Mississippi Valley. Originally constructed in 1724, there is some dispute as to whether the simple raised cottage was repaired or completely rebuilt after a 1788 fire. In any case, it's a fine example of early Louisiana architecture, with pitched roof, dormers, and slender colonnettes. Due to frequent flooding in earlier days (prior to the addition of a modern and very sophisticated drainage system), lower levels were used for storage and the upper floors for living quarters. In the 1770s, the notorious Barataria smuggler René Beluche made his home here. The building's name comes from a short story by 19th-century writer George Washington Cable, about a beautiful quadroon (a person of one-quarter black ancestry) named Zalli, whose dying white lover, John, willed the house to her. It was reopened to the public in 1998 by the **Louisiana State Museum** system as a venue for Southern folk art, with permanent displays featuring prominent self-taught artists and one gallery devoted to changing exhibits. ♦ Admission; discounts available if visiting two or more buildings in the Louisiana State Museum system; children aged 12 and under free. Tu-Su. 632 Dumaine St (between Chartres and Royal Sts). 568.6968

73 THE GRACE NOTE

This distinctive shop is filled with a selection of vintage and contemporary apparel and accessories, one-of-a-kind clothing, bags, and hats, as well as an appealing variety of art and collectibles. Daily. 900 Royal St. 522-1513; theGNote@bellsouth.net

MOTLEY KREWES: THE UNBRIDLED EXCESS OF MARDI GRAS

Mardi Gras, French for "Fat Tuesday," is the last chance for a full-tilt bender before the bell tolls on Ash Wednesday, ringing in 45 somber days of Lent. The spring celebration is the crowning blowout of a rambunctious season of parades, balls, and assorted bacchanals known as Carnival, from the Latin *carne vale,* or "farewell to flesh."

Carnival officially begins with Twelfth Night, aka Epiphany, on 6 January, and ends at midnight on Mardi Gras. Like Easter, the date of Mardi Gras changes from year to year. It can fall anywhere between 3 February and 9 March, but it is always exactly 46 days before Easter.

Most of the parties are private affairs, but the parades that roll day and night are free for all. Elaborate floats are the main attraction, filled with costumed riders who toss beads and trinkets (called "throws") to the crowds. Marching bands, clowns, motorcycle drill teams, flashy show horses, stilt walkers, jugglers, and dancing girls add to the wild display. Buildings all over town are decked with lights and festooned with the traditional Carnival colors of purple (for justice), green (for faith), and gold (for power).

The mass hysteria really cranks up during the final two weeks of the celebration, when more than 60 parades stop traffic throughout the city and suburbs. Every hotel in town is filled for the five days (Friday through Tuesday) that comprise "Mardi Gras weekend." Since nobody gets much work done anyway, one of the newer traditions, Lundi Gras, crams "Fat Monday" with free outdoor concerts and fireworks on the riverfront at **Spanish Plaza**.

The folks behind the fuss are members of the nonprofit clubs, known as *krewes,* which sponsor the parades and balls that bear their intriguing names. The oldest and swankiest, the **Mystick Krewe of Comus,** was founded in 1857. Around a dozen old-line organizations, established in the 19th century, present the season's debutantes at exclusive *bal masques,* strictly formal, private events. More freewheeling and democratic, the newer *krewes* (**Bacchus** and **Endymion** are the biggest) sponsor celebrity-laden floats and paid-admission "supper dances" instead of private balls. In all, there are nearly 100 clubs for men, women, men and women, families, and gays—not counting the hundreds of informal groups who create the wild extravaganzas that chug along with the "truck parades."

When the big day finally dawns, more than one million people hit the streets for the world's greatest binge. Crowd lovers can swim through the mob on **Canal Street,** heading upstream on **St. Charles Avenue** for elbow room and family values, or downstream through the **French Quarter** for scandalous costumes and X-rated escapades. Parking regulations are strictly enforced, but nearly all other rules are suspended. Be reasonably discreet, and jaded police looking festive themselves in beads and fluorescent sunglasses) will be happy to glance the other way. Plan an early start to catch the famous marching clubs that wind from bar to bar, dispensing paper carnations to ladies who pay with a kiss. The oldest group, the **Jefferson City Buzzards,** was founded in 1890. Musician Pete Fountain is the pied piper for his star-studded **Half-Fast Walking Club.** Both trace (more or less) the designated Canal Street/Uptown route, preceding the **Krewe of Zulu** parade, which rolls around 8:30AM, and the **Rex** parade, at 10AM.

Zulu, the city's oldest black parading *krewe,* was founded in 1909 to satirize the pompous carryings-on of white society. The first king, William Story, mocked the pretensions of Carnival "royalty" by carrying a banana stalk scepter and wearing a lard-can crown. Louis Armstrong reigned in 1949. The club is now composed of black and white members who ride the floats together, and **Zulu**'s gilded coconuts are the most prized of all Carnival throws.

Although almost all *krewes* proclaim their own kings and queens each year, Rex and his queen are the undisputed monarchs of Mardi Gras. In fact, even visiting royalty have been known to bend a knee to the reigning "King of Carnival." He is chosen by the inner circle of **The School of Design,** the elite organization that sponsors the **Rex** parade, which is Carnival's main event. Protocol dictates that spectators switch from "Hey Mister! Hey Mister! Beads! Cup!" to "Hail Rex!" as his float glides by.

Keep an eye peeled for the African-American marching and singing clubs known collectively as the **Mardi Gras Indians**. Clad in spectacular costumes, famous tribes such as the **Wild Tchoupitoulas, Golden Eagles,** and **Ninth Ward Hunters** have performed around the world. Their rhythms rock the streets as they pass by. Although their origins are unclear, some theorize that the earliest members may have created the flamboyant headdresses to ridicule Reconstruction-era laws that forbade black men to wear masks. The party ends abruptly when the clock strikes midnight, as street cleaning crews are preceded by a double wedge of mounted policemen who sweep the mob out of the French Quarter for the traditional "reclaiming of Bourbon Street." In fact, official reports measure the success of each Mardi Gras in tons of garbage collected.

KEELY EDWARDS

74 CORNSTALK HOTEL

$$ The famous cast-iron fence, in a cornstalk-and-morning glory design, was an 1850 present from Dr. Joseph Biamenti to his wife, a native midwesterner who missed the rural scenery of her childhood; today it's one of the most photographed architectural details in the Quarter. The 14 guest rooms are furnished in Victorian style with antique canopy beds, marble-topped tables, and crystal chandeliers. Complimentary continental breakfast is served in the rooms, on the balcony, or on the deep front porch. Parking is available. ◆ 915 Royal St (between Dumaine and St. Philip Sts). 523.1515, 523.1516; fax 522.5558; www.travelguides.com/bb/cornstalk

75 QUARTER MOON

Quirky jewelry—both elegant and amusing—is individually cut, hammered, soldered, and polished on the premises. Their sterling silver "vicious fishes" make fun cuff links or tuxedo studs for lawyers and other ambitious friends. You'll also find millinery and handwoven accessories by local artists. ◆ Daily. 918 Royal St (between Dumaine and St. Philip Sts). 524.3208

76 SIGLE'S ANTIQUES AND METALCRAFT

Here's the place to put together your own authentic French Quarter balcony. Lacy ironwork is also available in individual pieces that have been converted into plant holders or wall brackets. Besides the large line of ornamental iron, check for china, glass, antiques, and gifts. ◆ M-Sa. 935 Royal St (between Dumaine and St. Philip Sts). 522.7647 &

77 URSULINE GUEST HOUSE

$ The 13 pleasant rooms here, each with phone and cable TV, are carefully maintained. The courtyard is small, but lovely, with a hot tub, and there's free wine each evening. The clientele is predominantly gay and lesbian, but this place welcomes straights as well. Limited off-street parking is available; be sure to request a space at reservation time. ◆ 708 Ursulines St (between Royal and Bourbon Sts). 525.8509, 800/654.2351; fax 525.8408 &

78 ROYAL PHARMACY

The third generation of the Tusa family will ring up your purchase on a 1940s cash register at their corner drugstore (a neighborhood fixture since the 1890s) with ancient glass cases, wooden shelves, pressed tin ceilings, and mosaic tile floors. Alas, the antique marble-topped soda fountain dispenses no more, but you can still order a canned soft drink and loiter on one of the stools. Free delivery in the French Quarter. ◆ M-Sa. 1101 Royal St (at Ursulines St). 523.5401

79 GALLIER HOUSE MUSEUM

Built in 1857 by architect **James Gallier Jr.** as a home for his family, it's one of the most carefully researched and best preserved historic houses in the Quarter. Gasoliers (gas-burning chandeliers) hang from 12-foot ceilings in stately rooms that are furnished with velvets and brocades, marble mantels, antique clocks, crystal, silver, and china. A vintage carriage is parked in the carriageway. ◆ Admission. M-Sa. 1118-32 Royal St (between Ursulines and Governor Nicholls Sts). 525.5661

80 MONA LISA

★★$ It must have taken more than a little imagination to look at these two skinny rooms and think, "restaurant," but the result is a solid success. Pizzas are the big draw in the noisy bohemian hangout, but the buttery fettuccine Alfredo and industrial-strength garlic bread are great, too. Finish up with homemade baklava. ◆ Italian ◆ Daily lunch and dinner. 1212 Royal St (between Governor Nicholls and Barracks Sts). Phone/fax 522.6746. Also at: 876 Harrison Ave (at Marshall Foch St). 488.0133

81 WHISNANT GALLERIES

The wildly eclectic—and expensive—inventory of unusual collectibles sold here comes from all over the globe. Middle Eastern and North African weaponry dates back to the 1500s; ethnic jewelry (silver, amber, antique ivory, coral, and glass) was handcrafted in Ethiopia and Morocco in the 19th century; and antique religious icons and *santos* come from Russia, Greece, and South America. The stock also includes 18th- and 19th-century paintings and furniture. ◆ M-Sa. 222 Chartres St (between Iberville and Bienville Sts). 524.9766; fax 524.9300

82 BOYER ANTIQUES & DOLL SHOP

The fine collectors' dolls at this shop are signed and dated by the artists, and their antique dolls and clothes, carriages, and tricycles also make appealing decorative accessories. ◆ M-Sa. 241 Chartres St (at Bienville St). Phone/fax 522.4513 &

83 OLD DOG, NEW TRICK

★★$ Black-and-white tile and large windows set a bright stage for vegetarian burgers, pizzas, sandwiches, and salads. Try Olivia's polenta, broiled with tomato sauce and mozzarella and served with grilled vegetables.

Umbrella-shaded sidewalk tables are scattered along the pedestrian mall. ◆ Vegetarian ◆ Daily lunch and dinner. 307 Exchange Alley (between Bienville and Conti Sts). 522.4569

84 THE PELICAN CLUB

★★★$$$ New York chic reigns in the dining room, with subdued lighting, plush carpeting, and tables set with fine china. Chef Richard Hughes, a New Orleans native, spent seven years polishing his style in the Big Apple. Try his roasted filet mignon with madeira demi-glace. Grilled whole baby rack of lamb comes with garlic mashed potatoes, and baby vegetables in a port sauce with mint pepper jelly. The white-chocolate bread pudding and chocolate pecan pie are crowd pleasers. Windows in the airy piano bar open onto Exchange Alley. ◆ International ◆ Daily dinner. Reservations recommended. 312 Exchange Alley (between Bienville and Conti Sts). 523.1504; www.pelicanclub.com ♿

85 LA BELLE GALERIE & THE BLACK ART COLLECTION

At over 6,000 square feet, one of the largest US galleries devoted to African-American culture features original works by national and regional artists, as well as serigraphs, lithographs, and etchings. Be sure to see the 19th-century engravings from *Harper's Magazine,* French posters of Josephine Baker, and intricately beaded voodoo flags. Antique African artifacts include fetishes, ceremonial masks, musical instruments, and ancestral figures. Louisiana festival posters and limited-edition prints by regional artists are also shown. ◆ Daily. 309 Chartres St (between Bienville and Conti Sts). Phone 529.5538; fax 529.3080 ♿

86 W HOTEL

$$$ Formerly Hotel de la Poste, W French Quarter, this 98-room boutique hotel blends old world French Quarter style with contemporary luxury and conveniences. Two suites and four historic carriage house rooms also available. The hotel is built around a traditional New Orleans Courtyard with an outdoor pool. Dine in or order room service from **Bacco,** a Brennan Family Restaurant next door. Amenities include AVEDA products, CD/VCR players and high-speed Internet access. ◆

316 Chartres St (between Bienville and Conti Sts). 581-1200; fax 522-3208♿

Next to the W Hotel:

BACCO

★★$$$ Vaulted ceilings, Italian artworks, and hand-painted Venetian silk chandeliers complement the regional Italian menu. Wood-burning ovens (one is large enough to roast whole pigs) turn out smoky free-range chickens, Tuscan-style duck, pizzas, and breads. **Bacco** is owned by the branch of the Brennan family which also created **Commander's Palace, Mr. B's Bistro,** and **Palace Cafe.** ◆ Italian ◆ Daily breakfast, lunch, and dinner. Reservations recommended for dinner. 310 Chartres St. 522.CIAO; fax 521.8323 ♿

A Great New Orleans Bistro

87 LOUISIANA SUPREME COURT BUILDING

Tall, glossy-leafed magnolia trees surround the Baroque marble-and-granite structure that occupies the entire block across the street from **Brennan's.** Built in 1907 as the **Civil Courts Building,** it was subsequently occupied by the Louisiana Department of Wildlife and Fisheries. Work began in 1992 to refurbish the stately landmark, abandoned for years, as a new home of the **Louisiana Supreme Court.** Following extensive renovation, the building is now open to the public. ◆ 400 Royal St (at Conti St)

88 OMNI ROYAL ORLEANS HOTEL

$$$$ Be sure to have a drink by the rooftop pool for the best views in the French Quarter. The more than 346 rooms and suites here are decorated in 19th-century style—no two alike—and the lobby is splendid with chandeliers, marble halls, gilt mirrors, and grand statuary. Gift boutiques and beauty and barber shops line the lower level. Other amenities include 24-hour room service, valet parking, fitness facilities, and a full business center with computers, fax, and secretaries. ◆ 621 St. Louis St (between Chartres and Royal Sts). 529.7010, 800/THE-OMNI; fax 529.7037; www.omnihotels.com ♿

Within the Omni Royal Orleans Hotel:

RIB ROOM

★★★$$$ This favorite of high rollers and politicos has a glowing rotisserie that turns out excellent roast chicken and beef dishes.

Restaurants/Clubs: Red | **Hotels: Purple** | **Shops: Orange** | **Outdoors/Parks: Green** | **Sights/Culture: Blue**

The pastry cart is infamous for its decadent creations. The dining room is formal and quietly elegant, with large windows overlooking the street. ♦ Continental ♦ Daily breakfast, lunch, and dinner. Reservations recommended for dinner; jacket required at dinner. 529.7045 ♿

89 K-PAUL'S LOUISIANA KITCHEN

★★★★$$$$ Superstar Cajun chef Paul Prudhomme's home base is a deceptively simple country-style cafe with old brick walls and plain wooden tables and chairs. The menu changes daily, but look for Prudhomme's world-famous gumbos, étouffées, and jambalaya—all highly recommended—as well as a colorful collection of specials that ranges from roasted duck with pecan gravy to bronzed salmon with sautéed crabmeat and dill hollandaise. Arrive by 11AM (service begins at 11:30AM) to beat long lunch lines. Parties of fewer than four people may be asked to share community tables in the downstairs dining room during lunch or dinner on busy days. At dinner, private tables can be reserved in the upstairs dining room (closed at lunchtime); note that if you reserve for four, no one will be seated until all are present. ♦ Cajun ♦ M-Sa lunch and dinner. Reservations (accepted for dinner only) recommended. 416 Chartres St (between St. Louis and Conti Sts). 524.7394

90 NOLA

★★★$$ Riding the raging success of **Emeril's** in the Warehouse/Arts District, this is the second of three restaurants opened by chef Emeril Lagasse. Dine at the food bar for front-row views of the action around the wood-burning oven that produces great pizzas, breads, chicken, and cedar-plank-roasted fish. The menu changes seasonally, offering such homegrown specialties as spinach salad with fried oysters and creamy Herbsaint dressing, Louisiana crab cakes with fire-roasted chile beurre blanc, or a grilled double pork chop with pecan-glazed sweet potatoes. A hefty selection of desserts ranges from deep-dish apple pie with cinnamon ice cream to a bananas Foster split drenched in warm caramel sauce. Contemporary sculptures and architect **Jim Farr's** splashy design draw an artsy crowd. ♦ International ♦ M-Sa lunch and dinner; Su dinner. Reservations recommended. 534 St. Louis St (between Decatur and Chartres Sts). 522.NOLA ♿

91 NAPOLEON HOUSE

★★★$ Fans of the little Frenchman once refurbished this 1797 building to create the perfect pied-à-terre for an emperor on the skids. When Mayor Nicholas Girod, pirate Jean Lafitte, and other loyal supporters offered the mayor's own residence as a New Orleans home for their hero, his empire had dwindled to the tiny island of St. Helena. Napoleon's untimely death in 1821 scotched that plan, but today the world-class bar and restaurant is still the favorite spot for locals to meet and hatch plots. Peeling sepia walls, classical music, creaky stairwells, and cranky waiters are luxuriantly Old World. On the second floor, **L'Appartement de l'Empereur** (525.2431) is reserved for private functions. Order a hot (broiled) muffuletta, dripping with chopped olive salad, and a cooling gin-based Pimm's Cup garnished with cucumber. Sit by the open French doors, watch the parade along the sidewalk, and soak up the atmosphere—you're in one of the best places in town. ♦ Creole/Italian ♦ Daily lunch and dinner. 500 Chartres St (at St. Louis St). 524.9752; fax 523.9570

92 NEW ORLEANS PHARMACY MUSEUM

Louis Dufilho Jr., who became one of the nation's first licensed pharmacists in 1816, owned this 19th-century shop that now houses a remarkable collection of antique apothecary jars, patent medicines, cosmetics, surgical tools—even live leeches—all displayed in hand-carved rosewood cases. Here you'll find the notorious Spanish Fly that was used for aphrodisiacs and hair tonics, Lydia Pinkham's famous vitamins that promised "a baby in every bottle," and the grisly trephine that bored a hole in the skull to relieve headaches caused by "demons" or "too much pressure." Cozier sights include an Italian marble soda fountain built in 1855 and a beautiful walled courtyard planted with medicinal herbs. The building, believed to have been designed by **J.N.B. DePouilly**, was restored and opened as a museum in 1950. ◆ Admission. Tu-Su. 514 Chartres St (between St. Louis and Toulouse Sts). 565.8027; fax 565.8028 &

𝕳arper's 𝕬ntiques

93 HARPER'S ANTIQUES

Continental and American antiques, furniture, silver, porcelain, objets d'art, and paintings of the 18th, 19th, and 20th centuries are superbly displayed in this stately shop. The interior design service here attracts international clients. Browsing is encouraged. ◆ M-Sa. 610 Toulouse St (between Chartres and Royal Sts). 592.1996; fax 523.9985; www.harpersantiques.com

𝕹ew 𝕺rleans 𝕾ilversmiths

94 NEW ORLEANS SILVERSMITHS

In addition to numerous serving sets, the lavish stock of sterling and silverplate includes such hard-to-find essentials as asparagus tongs, Tabasco holders, cigar cases, flasks, toothpicks, and even the perfect tussy-mussy (a Victorian flower holder that was used to keep a lady's gloves from getting soiled). ◆ Daily. 600 Chartres St (between Toulouse St and Wilkinson Row). 522.8333, 800/219.8333

95 LUCULLUS

Proprietor Patrick Dunne named his gallery after Lucius Licinius Lucullus, a Roman general (famous for his lavish banquets) who went to the great groaning board in the sky around 57 BC. The fascinating collection of culinary antiques includes European and American china, copperware, and silver. Cooking, feasting, and imbibing accoutrements, including everything absinthe, date from the 17th to early 20th centuries. ◆ M-Sa, or by appointment. 610 Chartres St (between Toulouse St and Wilkinson Row). 528.9620; fax 561.8030

96 LA MARQUISE PÂTISSERIE DU ROI

European pastries, quiches, hot mocha, and cappuccino are an elegant indulgence at this quaint and tiny Old World shop with scarred marble tables and an umbrella-shaded oasis in the rear courtyard. ◆ Daily from 7: 30AM. 625 Chartres St (between Toulouse and St. Peter Sts). 524.0420

97 LE PETIT THÉÂTRE DU VIEUX CARRÉ

The country's oldest continuously operating community theater began in a **Pontalba** apartment drawing room in 1916. The present two-story gray stucco building is a faithful 1922 reproduction of the former 18th-century house (designed by architect **Don Gilberto Guillemard**) that was once the residence of the last Spanish governor of Louisiana, Joseph Xavier de Pontalba. The balcony rail, made by local craftsman Marcellino Hernandez in 1796, is from the original structure. In the lobby, large wrought-iron chandeliers are suspended from high ceilings, and the inner courtyard has a tiered fountain and banks of greenery and flowers. The theater season runs from September through June and usually offers around six musicals and plays, as well as four colorful productions in the **Children's Corner**. ◆ Box office: M-Sa. 616 St. Peter St (between Chartres and Royal Sts). 522.2081 &

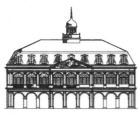

COURTESY OF FRIENDS OF THE CABILDO

98 CABILDO

With its colonnades, Spanish arches, dormers, and mansard roof, this famous landmark is nearly identical to the **Presbytere** (see page 39), which flanks the other side of **St. Louis Cathedral**. The Spanish governing council known as "The Illustrious Cabildo" was housed here from 1799 to 1803, hosting ceremonies in which Louisiana was retroceded by Spain to France on 30 November 1803. A mere three weeks later, on 20 December 1803, transfer papers for the Louisiana Purchase (from France to the US) were signed in a second-floor chamber. The historic building, now a property of the **Louisiana State Museum** (which also incorporates the **Presbytere**, the **1850 House**, the **Old US Mint**, and **Madame John's Legacy**), was severely damaged by fire in 1988. Miraculously, most of the important documents and artifacts (including a death mask of Napoleon) were saved, and the building reopened six years later. The permanent exhibition traces the early history of Louisiana from exploration through colonial days, Civil War, and Reconstruction. On display are artifacts from the Battle of New Orleans, and from the plantation and slavery

Restaurants/Clubs: Red | **Hotels: Purple** | **Shops: Orange** | **Outdoors/Parks: Green** | **Sights/Culture: Blue**

37

MUDBUG MANIA

Like it or not, when you visit New Orleans, you are very likely to encounter Cajun Country's most famous foodstuff. Despite its name, the humble crawfish is actually a lobsterlike crustacean—and only tourists pronounce it crayfish.

Though Louisiana is home to more than 30 different species of these "mudbugs," only two are commercially important: the red swamp crawfish (*Procambarus clarkii*) and the white river crawfish (*Procambarus zonangulus*). Live crawfish are usually most plentiful March through May, but the tail meat is frozen and sold throughout the year.

Whether fresh or frozen, the crawfish is an excellent source of protein, calcium, phosphorus, iron, and several B vitamins, including thiamine, riboflavin, and niacin. Not only that, but the fat content is very low—only 1.35 grams per 3.5 ounces of cooked meat.

Since it began in the early 1960s, crawfish farming has developed into the largest freshwater crustacean aquaculture industry in the US. Louisiana leads the nation, accounting for more than 90 percent of the domestic crop. According to figures from the Louisiana Crawfish Promotion and Research Board, more than 1,600 farmers oversee some 111,000 acres of ponds. Over 800 commercial fishermen harvest crawfish from natural wetlands, primarily the Atchafalaya Basin. The combined average annual yield ranges from 75 million to 105 million pounds. The total economic impact on the state economy exceeds $120 million annually, and more than 7,000 people depend directly or indirectly on the crawfish industry.

The typical crawfish farmer creates his ponds by building levees around low-lying swampland or by flooding high land, such as rice fields. Each pond is stocked only once with crawfish, which then survive on grasses and other natural feed to reproduce at a staggering rate.

It's hard to overharvest crawfish, as one female can produce up to 800 eggs each year. A well-managed pond will yield an average of 1,500 to 2,000 pounds of crawfish per acre each year; an extremely well-managed pond can yield up to twice that amount. When the season ends (in May or June), the ponds are drained totally dry by diesel pumps. The crawfish then burrow into the mud to lay their eggs. The ponds are refilled on 1 October and the season opens around 1 December, when the cycle begins anew.

As you're attacking a pile of boiled mudbugs, you may notice some of your fellow diners practicing an exotic Louisiana ritual: After they squeeze the meat from each tail (the only portion that's really edible), true aficionados suck the savory juices out of the head. *Bon appétit!*

---

systems, including a slave auction block.
♦ Admission; discounts available if you visit two or more buildings in the Louisiana State Museum system. Children aged 12 and under free. Tu-Su. 701 Chartres St (at St. Peter St). 568.6968 &

99 ST. LOUIS CATHEDRAL

A masterpiece of elegant simplicity, the oldest cathedral in the US replaced two even earlier churches (destroyed by hurricane and fire) named for Louis IX, France's saint-king. Dedicated as a cathedral when it was consecrated in 1794, the present structure was originally designed by **Don Gilberto Guillemard**. Architect **J.N.B. DePouilly** added the finishing touches circa 1849-51. The large mural behind the altar (which depicts St. Louis announcing the Seventh Crusade), as well as those on the ceiling, were painted in 1872 by Alsatian

Those fanciful trimmings that adorn French Quarter balconies were created by two different methods. The earlier wrought-iron ones were fashioned by hand via forge and anvil and featured simple, delicate scrolls and geometric patterns. For balconies made in later years, cast iron was poured into molds at foundries to produce lacy and intricate metalwork interwoven with oak leaves, nymphs, grape vines, and morning glories.

artist Erasme Humbrecht. Pope Paul VI designated the church a minor basilica in 1964, and the flagstone plaza in front was christened **Place Jean Paul Deux,** in honor of the 1987 visit of Pope John Paul II. ♦ Tours: M-Sa 9AM-5PM; Su 1:30-5PM. Chartres St. (between Pirate's and Père Antoine's Alleys). 525.9585 &

Behind St. Louis Cathedral:

ST. ANTHONY'S GARDEN

The official name is **Cathedral Gardens,** but parishioners long ago christened the beautiful tree-shaded yard in honor of Father Antonio de Sedella. The beloved Capuchin priest arrived in 1779 and served the colony for almost 50 years. He is best remembered for his generosity to the poor, including a system similar to modern-day food stamps that he created among neighborhood merchants. Be sure to notice the marble monument that was erected by order of Napoleon I's naval minister to commemorate the many French sailors who died during yellow-fever epidemics in New Orleans. The garden was not always so peaceful; in colonial days, it was often the scene of bloody duels.

100 PÈRE ANTOINE'S ALLEY

This flagstone walkway, cut in the mid-1830s, was named for Father Antonio de Sedella (see **St. Anthony's Garden** above), who was called Père Antoine by the French Creoles.

101 PRESBYTERE

A property of the **Louisiana State Museum**, this historic building hosts permanent and changing exhibits on regional culture, including a major new permanent exhibit on Mardi Gras. Much of the present structure (which stands on the site of a 1720 wooden monastery and its replacement, both destroyed by fire) dates from 1795, though it was not completed until long after the 1803 Louisiana Purchase. The city acquired the building in 1853, and for a time it was used as a courthouse. ◆ Admission; discounts available if you visit two or more buildings in the Louisiana State Museum system. Children aged 12 and under free. Tu-Su. 751 Chartres St (between Père Antoine's Alley and St. Ann St). 568.6968 &

trashy diva

102 TRASHY DIVA

Vintage clothing and accessories range from 1860 to 1960, but the flapper era is a specialty. The stock of wearable antiques includes beaded gowns, Titanic-era tea gowns, shoes, and a new line of vintage reproduction clothing. New corsets are imported from England. ◆ Daily. 829 Chartres St (between St. Ann and Dumaine Sts). 581.4555; www.trashydiva.com &

103 IRENE'S CUISINE

★★★$$ Tiny, but squeaky clean dining rooms scream "Italian," with walls cluttered by photos, decorative plates, wine bottles, and garlic strings. Servings are generous and attractively presented. Rosemary chicken is roasted with whole garlic and flamed with brandy. Soft-shell crab is pan sautéed and served over fresh linguine with herbs and crawfish tails. Tables are very close together, the crowd is noisy, and service can be uneven, but romance still reigns. ◆ Italian ◆ Daily dinner. No reservations. 539 St. Philip St (at Chartres St). Phone/fax 529.8811

104 HOTEL PROVINCIAL

$$ This hotel is actually a rambling complex of restored historic town houses, slave quarters, and commercial buildings winding around several lovely patios. Many of the 94 rooms are furnished with magnificent antique beds, carved armoires, and marble-top tables. There is a restaurant, and another added bonus is the free on-site parking. ◆ 1024 Chartres St (between St. Philip and Ursulines Sts). 581.4995, 800/535.7922; fax 581.1018; www.hotelprovincial.com &

105 CROISSANT D'OR

★★$ Newspaper boxes line the sidewalk, and the large back courtyard (complete with fountain and greenery) is a fine place to work the crossword puzzles and splurge on excellent European-style pastries and café au lait. Croissant sandwiches and quiches make good light lunches. The best indoor tables are set in cozy window alcoves. ◆ Daily 7AM-5PM. 615-17 Ursulines St (between Chartres and Royal Sts). 524.4663

Beauregard-Keyes House and Garden

106 BEAUREGARD-KEYES HOUSE AND GARDEN

Built in 1826 for wealthy auctioneer Joseph Le Carpentier, this raised cottage was home to Confederate General P.G.T. Beauregard after the Civil War, and in the 1940s the novelist Frances Parkinson Keyes lived there. Curved stairs lead up to the Greek Revival entry, where costumed docents begin tours of the house and manicured French garden. Check the gift shop for Keyes's books—she wrote *Dinner at Antoine's, Steamboat Gothic, Blue Camellia,* and *Chess Player* (about local master Paul Morphy). ◆ Admission. Tours hourly M-Sa 10AM-3PM. 1113 Chartres St (between Ursulines and Governor Nicholls Sts). 523.7257

107 OLD URSULINE CONVENT

The only extant example of pure French Creole architecture in the city, this large and sturdy three-story structure has a steeply pitched roof, rows of dormer windows, and a square portico. Designed in 1745 by **Ignace François Broutin,** it was completed in 1752 by builder Claude Joseph Villars Debreuil. Of national historic significance, the oldest building in the Mississippi Valley is the only undisputed survivor of the 18th-century conflagrations that destroyed much of early New Orleans. The Sisters of St. Ursula arrived in 1727 and occupied other quarters until completion of this building. Children of wealthy aristocratic Creoles obtained their early education here, and it was also the first school in the nation that held classes for black and Indian children. Included in the complex are **Our Lady of**

Restaurants/Clubs: Red | Hotels: Purple | Shops: Orange | Outdoors/Parks: Green | Sights/Culture: Blue

Old Ursuline Convent

KENNETH SNOW

Victory Church (known to many locals as **St. Mary's Italian Church**), a gatehouse, and formal gardens. The property can be seen only on a guided tour. ♦ Admission. Tu-F 10AM-3PM; Sa-Su 11:15AM-2PM. Guided tours hourly (except noon). 1100 Chartres St (at Ursulines St). 529.3040

108 SONIAT HOUSE

$$$$ More than 20 staff members provide excellent service for guests who stay in the 31 rooms and suites here in one of the best small deluxe hotels in New Orleans. Rodney and Frances Smith have furnished their two restored 1830s town houses with European and American antiques, Oriental rugs, and luxurious modern baths (most with Jacuzzis and telephones). The courtyard is lush with flowers, a fountain, and a fish pond. Other amenities include 24-hour concierge service and an honor bar in the First Empire drawing room, but there is no restaurant. Across the street, eight additional suites with private parlors surround a lavish courtyard. ♦ 1133 Chartres St (between Ursulines and Governor Nicholls Sts). 522.0570, 800/544.8808; fax 522.7208; www.soniathouse.com

Her father Jefferson may have been president, but Varina "Winnie" Davis, aka "The Daughter of the Confederacy," was a queen: She reigned over the Mystick Krewe of Comus during Mardi Gras 1892.

109 LE RICHELIEU

$$ Among the best bargains in town are the 86 lavishly decorated rooms and suites—with no two alike—overlooking a landscaped courtyard and pool at this hotel. So many celebrities have stayed here that live-in owner Frank Rochefort's office is papered wall-to-wall with autographed photos. Paul McCartney lived in one of the suites for over two months while cutting an album. Free and secure off-street parking is a rare and valuable perk. A small coffeeshop serves breakfast and grilled items until 9PM. ♦ 1234 Chartres St (at Barracks St). 529.2492, 800/535.9653; fax 524.8179; www.neworleansonline.com/richelieu.htm &

110 LOUISIANA MUSIC FACTORY

No Top 40 here, but you can get hard-to-find New Orleans music, R&B, zydeco, Cajun, and maybe the biggest selection of New Orleans jazz anywhere, including many out-of-print records. Call about Saturday afternoon concerts—primarily showcases for regional talent—by artists promoting new releases.

Well-informed staffers are a great source for info on obscure recordings as well as what's happening at local clubs. A much smaller branch that specializes in traditional jazz is located inside the museum at the **Old US Mint** (400 Esplanade Ave, at N Peters St, 524.5507). ◆ Daily. 210 Decatur St (between Iberville and Bienville Sts). 586.1094; fax 586.8818

NEW ORLEANS

111 HOUSE OF BLUES

"This joint is dedicated to the memory of Jake Blues," proclaims a sign over an ornate antique bar at the local branch of this national chain, which is owned by Dan Aykroyd, among others. A premium sound system and painstakingly scruffy atmosphere have attracted rare club appearances by Eric Clapton and Bob Dylan, as well as Taj Mahal, George Thorogood, Clarence "Gatemouth" Brown, the Dirty Dozen Brass Band, and other greats who fill the schedule nightly. Preferred seats are the old church pews that surround the balcony, but the music hall (which holds a maximum of 1,000 SRO) is small enough so performers' faces are visible from every corner. A second, smaller venue upstairs, **The Parrish,** accommodates more intimate music and comedy shows. The hall has five bars, and an adjoining restaurant and bar (no cover) are supplied with TV monitors for closed-circuit views of the stage. Food is also served on the back patio. The menu is surprisingly inexpensive, with a good selection of burgers, po-boys, gourmet pizzas, salads, and specialty sandwiches priced under $10. The backyard smokehouse turns out righteous Tennessee-style barbecue. Regional art lines the walls and the restaurant ceiling is plastered with sculptures of legendary musicians. Tables are set up inside the music club for the cramped—and overpriced—Sunday gospel brunch. A small shop sells souvenirs. The members-only **Foundation Room,** with its decadent Storyville-meets-Tibet ambiance, offers upscale dining, private meet-and-greets with performers and other special events. Members from other club locations are welcome. ◆ Cover in music club. Daily lunch and dinner until midnight (F-Sa until 1AM). Music club doors open at 8PM. 225 Decatur

St (between Iberville and Bienville Sts). 529.BLUE &

112 BECKHAM'S BOOKSHOP

Two floors house over 50,000 used volumes and 10,000 classical phonograph records at this creaky Dickensian store, a favored haunt of local booklovers for more than 30 years. The smaller original shop, Librairie (823 Chartres St, between St. Ann and Dumaine Sts, 525.4837), has less of the same. ◆ Daily. 228 Decatur St (between Iberville and Bienville Sts). 522.9875 &

113 TIPITINA'S

The French Quarter branch of the famous and well-loved music club is a funky, tourist-district cousin of the Uptown original. Top local talent plays here, including Allen Toussaint, Cyril Neville, Kermit Ruffins, George Porter Jr., and other internationally known musicians. Seating, on a first-come, first-served basis, is limited; otherwise it's SRO. Blues pianists perform daily during lunch. The reasonably priced (especially for the French Quarter), no-nonsense menu features local favorites such as po-boys, red beans and rice, jambalaya, gumbo, catfish, and fried chicken. ◆ Daily lunch and dinner until midnight. Music M, Su from 8PM; Tu-Sa from 10PM. 233 N Peters St (between Iberville and Bienville Sts). 566.7095. & Also at: 501 Napoleon Ave (at Tchoupitoulas St). 895.8477

114 PELIGRO FOLK ART

Local and regional folk primitives—everything from polished works by professionals to funkier pieces by self-taught artists—are the focus of this gallery/boutique. The colorful inventory also features ju-ju dolls (used by Louisiana voodoo practitioners), eerie Day of the Dead tableaux, and other exotica from Haiti and Mexico. ◆ Daily. 305 Decatur St (between Bienville and Conti Sts). 581.1706 &

115 BIENVILLE HOUSE

$$ Of the 83 rooms, those with balconies are best; some face Decatur Street and have great river views, and others overlook the pretty flagstone courtyard and pool. The rooms themselves are more motel than hotel in style, but they're comfortable. There is a restaurant, and secured off-street parking is available. ◆ 320 Decatur St (between Bienville and Conti Sts). 529.2345, 800/535.7836; fax 525.6079; www.bienvillehouse.com

116 KERRY IRISH PUB

Named after the West Coast county in Ireland, this friendly bar is a good place to hang out and enjoy *craic* (gossip and good times) with the Irish staff and a congenial crowd. Most nights, balladeers perform traditional folk songs; at other times there's a jukebox with lots of music selections from the Old Country. ♦ Daily from 2PM. 331 Decatur St (between Bienville and Conti Sts). 527.5954

117 SOUTHERN CANDYMAKERS

Mention New Orleans and the sugary pecan confections called pralines almost always come to mind. The award-winning candies sold here are made from the Tompkins' family recipe and sought after by locals and visitors alike. Variations are just as tantalizing—you'll want to try the almond toffee, cashew tortes, tiger bark, pecan log rolls, chocolate clusters, glazed pecans, and fudge, too. If you think it's too much sugar overload in one visit, the Tompkins have a thriving mail order business, including gift tins and holiday boxes. Ask for a catalog. ♦ Daily. 334 Decatur Street (at Conti St). 523.5544, 800/344.9773; fax 523.5540; www.southerncandymakers.com

118 BEVOLO GAS AND ELECTRIC LIGHTS

If you've fallen in love with the gaslights at the **Cabildo, Brennan's,** Jackson Square, or other historic sites, don't miss this shop, which has been producing the lamps by hand for over 50 years. Ask for a tour of the upstairs work-rooms, where one long workbench is a former bowling alley lane, and lamp tops are still spun on a 1920s lathe. Custom designs are available, too, sized for anything from cottages to castles (bring a photo of the place with you). ♦ M-Sa. 521 Conti St (between Decatur and Chartres Sts). 522.9485; fax 522.5563 ♿

119 NEW ORLEANS SCHOOL OF COOKING AND LOUISIANA GENERAL STORE

Three chefs lead highly entertaining regional cooking classes Monday through Saturday from 10AM to 1PM and 2 to 4PM. The class fee includes the meal prepared in class. The adjoining shop is packed to the cypress rafters with foodstuffs, cookbooks, skillets, and other kitchen gifts. ♦ Shop: daily; classes: M-Sa. Reservations required for classes. 524 St. Louis St (between Decatur and Chartres Sts). 525.2665, 800/237.4841; fax 525.2922

120 THE CENTURIES ANTIQUE PRINTS AND MAPS

Dig through the groaning bins for old maps of your hometown or ancestral land. Five centuries of documents, dating back to 1493, include architectural prints, astronomy charts, medical drawings, etchings, and lithographs. ♦ Daily. 517 St. Louis St (between Decatur and Chartres Sts). Phone/fax 568.9491

121 BOOKSTAR

Stairwell and balcony railings are trimmed in purple with a gold fleur-de-lis design at the massive New Orleans branch of this lively bookstore, a division of **Barnes & Noble.** Shelves are filled with general-interest books, but the specialty sections, including regional titles and gay and women's literature, are quite strong. It's also a good spot to pick up free local papers for entertainment listings and current events. ♦ Daily. 414 N Peters St (between Conti and Decatur Sts). 523.6411; fax 523.4617 ♿

122 HARD ROCK CAFÉ

★★$$ Crowds line up to view the guitar-shaped bar crowned by Fats Domino's piano; Dr. John's cape, top hat, and cane; Elton John's shoes; Professor Longhair's jackets; wildly exotic costumes of the Wild Tchoupitoulas Mardi Gras Indians; and memorabilia from other pop icons. Burgers, salads, fajitas, barbecue, sandwiches, and milk shakes are a fine excuse to sit and soak up the vibrant atmosphere. ♦ American ♦ Daily lunch and dinner. Gift shop: M-Th, Su until 10PM; F-Sa until midnight. 418 N Peters St (at Decatur St). 529.5617; fax 581.4960 ♿

123 SPORTS ART

This shop is possibly the only source in town for fossilized dinosaur dung (aka coprolite), but owner Don Weaver's first love is antique duck decoys, and he claims the world's largest private collection of more than 8,000. You'll also find rare hunting and fishing books, paintings, prints, and bronzes, as well as stuffed ex-wildlife, including rattlesnakes, tarantulas, scorpions, and alligator heads. A complete voodoo department for all your ritual needs stocks chicken-foot mojos, gris-gris bags, and dolls with pins. ♦ M-Sa; but call ahead as hours vary. 521 Decatur St (between St. Louis and Toulouse Sts). 525.3846

124 CRESCENT CITY BREWHOUSE

★★$$ The beer's the thing at this showy microbrewery, where glass walls on the first and second floors frame gleaming copper vats. Sample darks, lights, ambers, or one of the ever-changing special drafts created by German brewmaster Wolfram Koehler. Burgers, salads, and a good selection of finger foods can be carried out to balcony tables overlooking the Mississippi. Try the crawfish enchilada or the ribs—the best in town. ♦ American ♦ Daily lunch and dinner. 527 Decatur St (between St. Louis and Toulouse Sts). 522.0571 ⑤

IRISI) CHANNEL PUB
FRENCH QUARTER, NEW ORLEANS

125 O'FLAHERTY'S IRISH CHANNEL PUB

"Where the Celtic Nations Meet" is more than just a watering hole—you can take lessons in Irish dancing on Saturdays. The Celtic Folk perform nightly, and famed troubadours such as Tommy Makem and Andy M. Stewart take the stage when they're in town. You can order homemade Irish stew or shepherd's pie in the pub section and the gift shop sells imported bangers (sausages), rashers (bacon), black pudding (blood pudding), and white pudding (minus blood). ♦ Daily from noon. 514 Toulouse St (between Decatur and Chartres Sts). 529.1317

126 RALPH & KACOO'S

★★$$ Touristy yes, but all meals are prepared to order by up to 25 line cooks in this block-deep, 546-seat seafood house. A brilliant saltwater aquarium and boat-shaped oyster bar add color to an eclectic decor that could be described as Seafaring Olde English Country Kitchen with One Tiger. Start with marinated crab fingers or fried alligator. For unusual entrees, try the stuffed soft-shell crawfish sauced with hollandaise, or shrimp verde, broiled and brushed with garlicky lemon butter spiked with chopped oregano. And don't miss the hushpuppies. ♦ Seafood ♦ Daily lunch and dinner. 519 Toulouse St (between Decatur and Chartres Sts). 522.5226; fax 522.5253 ⑤ Also at: 601 Veterans Memorial Blvd (at Aris Ave), Metairie. 831.3177

127 CAFE MASPERO

★★$ Two-fisted sandwiches and thick-cut fries draw a crowd, so expect to stand in line. Hot pastrami, roast beef, smoked ham, and other thinly sliced deli meats are piled high on round French buns and charbroiled. Chopped-sirloin burgers, fried seafood, and red beans and rice are also very good. The wide brick arches, French doors, fan windows, and huge antique bar are rich and moody. ♦ American ♦ Daily lunch and dinner. 601 Decatur St (at Toulouse St). 523.6250

128 JACKSON BREWERY AND THE MILLHOUSE

This castle-like complex, on the site where Jax Beer was brewed from 1891 to 1974, debuted in 1984 as a spectacular marketplace filled with dozens of locally owned shops and restaurants, as well as national chains, including the **Bayou Country General Store, The Limited, Giorgio, Michael Ricker Pewter Museum and Gallery, Pato's on the River,** and the **Virgin Megastore** (with three floors of music, video, and books). The paddle wheeler *Natchez* (586.8777) departs from the Toulouse Street Wharf near here. ♦ M-Th, Su until 9PM; F-Sa until 10PM. 600 and 620 Decatur St (at St. Peter St). 566.7245, 586.8015; fax 596.1025 ⑤

Restaurants/Clubs: Red | Hotels: Purple | Shops: Orange | Outdoors/Parks: Green | Sights/Culture: Blue

129 PONTALBA APARTMENTS

Among the oldest apartment houses in the nation, the three-story redbrick structures that face each other across the expanse of Jackson Square were built between 1849 and 1851, thanks to the largesse (and even the occasional manual labor) of the colorful Baroness Micaela Almonester Pontalba. The handsome cast-iron work on the twin facades bears the initials AP in her honor. At the time of the buildings' construction, Americans were pouring into the city and establishing profitable businesses beyond Canal Street; the Baroness created this mixed-use commercial and residential project to help the French Quarter Creoles keep pace. Now, as then, shops line the ground level and highly coveted apartments are on the upper floors. ♦ The Lower Pontalba: St. Ann St (between Decatur and Chartres Sts); the Upper Pontalba: St. Peter St (between Decatur and Chartres Sts)

Within the Lower Pontalba:

LA MADELEINE FRENCH BAKERY & CAFÉ

★★$ Crusty baguettes, brioches, and other rustic breads are baked fresh daily in a wood-burning oven. European pastries and croissants are the best reason to dine here, but salads, quiches, and soups make a quick and healthy meal. Empty tables can be scarce, especially during the breakfast rush, so pack up a picnic and head for the levee. ♦ French ♦ Daily breakfast, lunch, and dinner. 547 St. Ann St. 568.0073 ♿ Also at: Numerous locations throughout the area

BOURBON FRENCH PARFUMS

Originally established in 1843 on Bourbon Street, the romantic shop retained its famous name after moving to Jackson Square. Try one of the house fragrances—such as Alessandra, Wildest Dreams, Narcisse, or Honeysuckle—or indulge yourself and commission a custom blend. ♦ Daily. 525 St. Ann St. 522.4480

1850 HOUSE

Part of the **Louisiana State Museum,** this three-story apartment is restored in the style of a mid-19th-century, middle-class Creole household. The kitchen is furnished with antique utensils; dolls in the nursery are dressed in lace; and the dining room table is set and waiting for the family to come in to dinner. A special first-floor display is accessible for visitors who can't climb the stairs to view the entire house. ♦ Admission; discounts available if you visit two or more buildings in the Louisiana State Museum system. Children aged 12 and under free. Tu-Su. 523 St. Ann St. 568.6972

Within the Upper Pontalba:

THE KITE SHOP

Vibrant fabric kites, wind socks, and flying toys flutter from the walls and ceiling of this tiny alcove. ♦ Daily. 542 St. Peter St. Phone/fax 524.0028

RENDEZVOUS, INC.

Elegant linen and lace clothing for infants and children is the specialty here. Vintage shelves are also stocked with delicate tablecloths, embroidery, and antique lace. ♦ Daily. 522 St. Peter St. Phone/fax 522.0225

OH SUSANNAH

Antique dolls for serious collectors seem right at home in this historic space, where you'll also find new reproductions and a small selection of children's play dolls. ♦ Daily. 518 St. Peter St. 586.8701; fax 522.0225

ARIUS ART TILES

Ceramic tiles handmade at a sister gallery in Santa Fe are decorated with traditional Southwest designs or regional Louisiana icons (which are not available at the New Mexican gallery). Custom tiles are available by special order. ♦ Daily. 504 St. Peter St. 529.1665; fax 529.1665

130 JACKSON SQUARE

The equestrian statue of Andrew Jackson, with **St. Louis Cathedral** looming in the background, is the signature image of New Orleans. Surrounded by a tall iron fence and filled with banana trees and flowering shrubs, the small green park was *Place d'Armes* to the French Creole colonists (*Plaza de Armas* to later Spanish colonials), a training field for the militia and military units. It was rechristened in the mid-19th century to honor the man who defeated the Brits in the 1815 Battle of New Orleans. Today, the French Quarter showplace is bordered by a flagstone pedestrian mall that's festive with sidewalk artists, vendors, magicians, and other entertainments by day, and placid and achingly beautiful late at night and early in the morning. Just remember to keep a lookout for dog droppings and mimes. ◆ Park: daily 6AM-9PM; mall: 24 hours daily. Bounded Decatur, Chartres, St. Peter, and St. Ann Sts

CARRIAGE STAND

Climb aboard here, if you must, for a mule-drawn jaunt through the Quarter. Enjoy the view, but ignore tall tales from your driver and exasperated glares from motorists stuck in your wake. If you prefer to be picked up at your hotel, call **Good Old Days Carriages** (523.0804) for a duded-up buggy, complete with cellular phone. ◆ Fee. Daily until midnight

131 WASHINGTON ARTILLERY PARK

Ⓟ Wide expanses of steps and ramps (an impromptu amphitheater for an ever-changing cast of street entertainers) lead up from Decatur Street for fine views of Jackson Square on one side and the Big Muddy on the other. The hard-surfaced park was named in honor of the 141st Artillery, which has fought in nearly every conflict since serving under Zachary Taylor in the 1845 Mexican War. The waterfront area between the ends of Canal Street and Esplanade Avenue was used as a military training ground in the earliest days of the colony. ◆ Decatur St (northeast of St. Peter St)

132 RIVERFRONT STREETCAR

Esplanade Avenue is the downtown terminus for the six vintage Perley Thomas cars, painted bright red, that stop at strategic points along the Mississippi in the French Quarter, the CBD, and the Warehouse/Arts District. Note that the proper term is "streetcar"—only tourists call them trolleys. ◆ Fee. Daily 6AM-11PM. 248.3900

133 MOONWALK

The wooden promenade on the levee behind **Washington Artillery Park** is a great place to stretch out on a bench and watch the traffic along the Mississippi. Stroll over after a midnight visit to **Café du Monde** and listen to the street musicians by moonlight.

134 TUJAGUE'S

★★★$$$ Pronounced Two-jacks, New Orleans's second-oldest restaurant (**Antoine's** is its senior) was established in 1856 and named for Madame Tujague, who was famous for the elaborate breakfasts she served to workers from the **French Market** across the street. Presidents Roosevelt, Truman, and Eisenhower (and France's de Gaulle) are among the hundreds of notables who have

eaten in this formal dining room with polished dark wood furnishings and white napery. All meals are served from a very simple table d'hôte menu, a five-course feast of shrimp remoulade, soup du jour, brisket of beef with Creole sauce (the succulent house specialty), a choice from three daily entrees, dessert, and strong coffee. If you don't have time for a meal here, at least stop in at the stately historic bar. ◆ Creole ◆ Daily lunch and dinner. Reservations recommended. 823 Decatur St (at Madison St). 525.8676; fax 525.8676 ⅃

135 FRENCH MARKET

Indians traded here more than 200 years ago, then French and Spanish colonials set up shop; the present structure began as a Gascogne butcher's market built in 1813. Today, the graceful colonnades frame an arcaded complex of shops and restaurants, the result of a multimillion-dollar renovation in 1975, that stretches from **Washington Artillery Park** to Barracks Street. The **Old Farmers' Market** (between Ursulines and Barracks Streets) is the nation's oldest, still lined with open-air sheds where area growers sell their produce around the clock. The adjoining community flea market draws a fun crowd during daylight hours. ◆ Free. Farmers' market: 24 hours; shop hours vary

Within the French Market:

CAFÉ DU MONDE

★$ The traditional last stop after a night on the town, the city's most famous sidewalk cafe has been open around the clock since the 1860s, closing only "for Christmas and some hurricanes." Always crowded—with locals as well as tourists—the tables are jammed close together in an awning-shaded pavilion, with a few scattered around a small inside room. Café au lait, hot beignets (heavenly pillow-shaped doughnuts draped in powdered sugar), orange juice, and milk are the only items on the menu—which is stamped on the napkin holders. ◆ Cafe ◆ Daily 24 hours. 800 Decatur St (at St. Ann St). 525.4544. Also at: Numerous locations throughout the city

---

Restaurants/Clubs: Red | Hotels: Purple | Shops: Orange | Outdoors/Parks: Green | Sights/Culture: Blue

Bella Luna

★★★★$$$ The sweeping river views and quietly elegant atmosphere are just right for a romantic moonstruck evening. Soft gray walls are trimmed in white and tables are well-spaced for quiet conversation. All pasta is made in house. Chef Horst Pfeifer's menu changes seasonally, but favorites include Bella Luna crawfish and crab cakes with homemade ancho remoulade, house-cured pork chop in New Orleans-style pecan crust, and savory osso buco. Housemade pastas, baked goods, and gourmet kitchenware are sold at the street-level **Bella Luna Pasta Shop**. ♦ International ♦ Daily dinner. Reservations recommended. 914 N Peters St (just northeast of Decatur St). 529.1583 ♿

136 Progress Grocery

Operated by the Perrone family since 1924, this colorful Italian market also offers foods, spices, and housewares imported from Greece, Spain, France, and the Caribbean. Ask for a mail-order price list to take home, including information on next-day air delivery of muffulettas. ♦ Daily. 915 Decatur St (between Dumaine and St. Philip Sts). 525.6627; fax 525.5454 ♿

137 Central Grocery Co.

Since 1906, the Tusa family's cluttered and aromatic Italian *alimentari* has marketed an exotic inventory of imported pastas, coffees, olive oils, spices, and more. Dried salamis, fish, and garlic dangle from the ceiling, and the help is authentically surly. This is the place to order the original muffuletta, a two-person feast of deli meats, cheeses, and spicy olive salad stacked between thick Italian bread. ♦ Daily. 923 Decatur St (between Dumaine and St. Philip Sts). 523.1620

137 The Crabnet Wildlife Art and Gifts

This wide-ranging collection features decorative woodcarvings of ducks (decoy, flying, standing), fish, birds, and other creatures; more than 90 percent of the represented artists are Louisiana-born. Don't miss Ken Picou's startling and colorful reproductions of antique fishing lures. This is also the only place in the state to buy oil paintings by internationally known wildlife artist Randy McGovern. ♦ Daily. 925 Decatur St (between Dumaine and St. Philip Sts). 522.3478, 800/424.3478; www.thecrabnet.com

138 Second Skin Leather

Purveyor of fine leather, as well as latex, sexual hardware, and erotica for men and women, the shop carries indescribably salacious inventory ranging from unmentionables to unfathomables. ♦ M-Sa noon-10PM; Su noon-6PM. 521 St. Philip St (between Decatur and Chartres Sts). 561.8167; fax 561.5662; www.secondskinleather.com ♿

139 French Market Restaurant and Bar

★★$$ Follow your nose to the huge cauldron of crabs, shrimp, or crawfish boiling just inside an open sidewalk-level window. Even the po-boys are stuffed with freshly shucked fried oysters. Sit on the balcony for good views of the historic **French Market**. The menu notes fudge a little—the building has been around since 1803, but the restaurant only opened in 1972. ♦ Seafood ♦ Daily lunch and dinner. 1001 Decatur St (at St. Philip St). 525.7879

140 Café Sbisa

★★★$$$ Museum-quality regional artworks, an antique marble bar, and mezzanine seating add plenty of grand style. In fine weather, the best tables are on the balcony overlooking Decatur Street. The seasonal menu makes good use of regional seafood and produce, including trout Eugene (with shrimp and oysters in a cream sauce) and grilled veal chop with caramelized shallot butter. Live entertainment is scheduled on Friday and Saturday nights and for the Sunday jazz brunch. ♦ International ♦ M-Sa

THE BEST

Marc J. Cooper
Director, Vieux Carré Commission

Eating anything cooked by Susan Spicer at **Bayonas**, although I truly love her rabbit.

I love the oysters *en brochette* at **Galatoire's**. They make them the old-fashioned way, wrapped in bacon.

Catching Kermit Ruffins at **Vaughn's** on a Thursday night in Bywater.

Taking the streetcar on **St. Charles Avenue**—I love our live oaks.

I'm proud to be one of the people who helped bring the Sidney Bechet statue to **Louis Armstrong park**—it's a great tribute to a great man.

I love **Esplanade Avenue,** the Creole version of what **St. Charles** is uptown.

---

dinner; Su brunch and dinner. 1011 Decatur St (between St. Philip and Ursulines Sts). 522.5565; fax 523.8095 &

141 MOLLY'S AT THE MARKET

If you're in the mood for a little hard-boiled company, lots of newspaper types hang out here—and local television personalities tend bar on widely publicized occasions. Neon beer signs glow between the ceiling rafters and the walls are plastered with mug shots, including an autographed portrait of Pope Pius XI, circa 1923. The legendary watering hole is also headquarters for one of the city's three St. Patrick's Day parades. ♦ Daily from 10AM. 1107 Decatur St (between Ursulines and Governor Nicholls Sts). 525.5169

142 JIMMY BUFFETT'S MARGARITAVILLE

★★$ Parrothead alert! This sprawling cave (previously occupied by the **Storyville Jazz Hall**) is an outpost of Buffett's celebrated Key West club. Live music is featured nightly beginning at 10:30PM, and the famous owner takes the stage himself when he blows into town. Better than the average bar fare, Bahamian conch chowder is spicy enough to please any Cajun (for extra island-hot zing, shake on a little Matouk's, a tongue-torching pepper sauce imported from Trinidad). Real Key lime pie is flavored with the native Florida fruit and piled high with meringue. An adjoining shop peddles Buffett parapher-nalia. ♦ American/Caribbean ♦ Daily lunch and dinner. 1104 Decatur St (between Ursulines and Governor Nicholls Sts). 592.2565

143 PALM COURT JAZZ CAFÉ

★★★$$ Serious jazz buffs must make the pilgrimage to **Preservation Hall,** but when the benches get too hard and you start longing

for table service, head here to catch many of the same musicians in more comfortable surroundings. World-famous local performers like Lionel Ferbos, Chuck Peter Badie, and Thais Clark are scheduled Wednesday through Sunday nights. The stylishly renovated old **French Market** warehouse is bright and airy, with off-white walls, mosaic tile floors, exposed brick, ceiling fans, and a vintage mahogany bar. Order red beans and rice with garlic chicken or a grilled shrimp salad with warm green onion dressing. Then browse the racks of rare records and CDs for outstanding Jazzology, Audiophile, and GHB labels. ♦ Creole ♦ W-Su dinner; music starts at 8PM. Reservations recommended. 1204 Decatur St (between Governor Nicholls and Barracks Sts). 525.0200 &

144 MASQUERADE FANTASY

Artist Jim Gibeault works only in leather to create traditional, fanciful, and mysterious masks—all hand-crafted and hand-painted. His walls are populated by sun gods, witches, spiders, tropical fish, birds, pigs, demons, and historic designs dating back to 14th-century Venice. Describe your own fantasy for a custom mask. ♦ M, Th-Su noon-6PM; and by appointment. 1233 Decatur St (between Governor Nicholls and Barracks Sts). 593.9269, 486.8854

145 LOUISIANA PIZZA KITCHEN

★★$ Wood-fired ovens produce crusty breads and exotic pizzas topped with smoked salmon, roasted garlic, barbecued chicken, pesto—even caviar. The Caesar salad and fresh Italian sausage are very good. Tall bottles of olive oil on every table are infused with herbs and peppers and the wine bar is well stocked. ♦ Italian/Provencal ♦ Daily lunch and dinner. 95 French Market Pl (at Barracks St). 522.9500. Also at: 615 S Carrollton Ave (between St. Charles Ave and Hampson St). 866.5900

Restaurants/Clubs: Red | Hotels: Purple | Shops: Orange | Outdoors/Parks: Green | Sights/Culture: Blue

Central Business District (CBD)/Riverfront

Bertrand St.

Bolivar St.

S. Roman St.

S. Derbigny St.

61

10

S. Villere St.

Cleveland Ave.

S. Liberty St.

LaSalle Ave.

Saratoga St.

Tulane Ave.

Elks Pl.

to New Orleans International
Airport and Baton Rouge

Gravier St.

1

Lafayette St.

S. Claiborne Ave.

Cypress St.

Clara St.

Magnolia St.

S. Robertson St.

Freret St.

Perdido St.

6

Duncan Plaza
Civic Center

22

Poydras St.

23

24

25

Earhart Blvd.

Lafayette St.

LaSalle St.

Main Post
Office

Girod St.

BR
90

Pontchartrain Expwy.

35
Union
Terminal

Loyola Ave.

S. Rampart St.

O'Keefe St.

Bacon Pl.

Julia St.

Baronne St.

S. Robertson St.

Freret St.

La Salle St.

S. Liberty St.

Clio St.

Erato St.

Simon Bolivar St.

S. Rampart St.

Howard Ave.

Melpomene Ave.

Thalia St.

Calliope St.

Terpsichore St.

Felicity St.

Baronne St.

Carondelet St.

Basin St.

N. Rampart St.

St. Louis St.

Conti St.

Orleans St.

St. Peter St.

St. Ann St.

Toulouse St.

Bienville St.

FRENCH
QUARTER

Jackson
Square

Jackson
Brewery

Burgundy St.

3

2
University Pl.

4

Dauphine St.

Iberville St.

Baronne St.

5

Carondelet St.

7

Bourbon St.

8

Royal St.

9

11

12

Chartres St.

13

14

10

Decatur St.

15

Canal St.

16

N. Front St.

Union St.

Carondelet St.

17 18

Common St.

Gravier St.

19

N. Peters St.

20

Woldenberg
Riverfront
Park
21

St. Charles Ave.

27

28

29 30

31

33

Aquarium of
the Americas

St. Charles Avenue Streetcar

37

38

Natchez St.

32

34

Canal
Street Ferry
Terminal

to Algiers

36

Poydras St.

39

40

42
Spanish
Plaza

Lafayette
Square

Lafayette St.

Pl. de France

41

Mississippi River

43

Girod St.

44

Church St.

Camp St.

Magazine St.

Julia St.

Commerce St.

S. Peters St.

Fulton St.

Convention Center Blvd.

WAREHOUSE/
ARTS DISTRICT

St. Joseph St.

Riverfront Streetcar

Howard Ave.

Constance St.

Tchoupitoulas St.

N. Diamond St.

45

N

km
mi

1/8   1/4   1/1   1/2

CENTRAL BUSINESS DISTRICT (CBD)/RIVERFRONT

The Central Business District is the commercial heart of New Orleans. Known to locals as the CBD, it begins where **Canal Street** meets the **Mississippi** and flows out to **Interstate 10** and the **Pontchartrain Expressway.** Here you'll find stately old banks and law firms, but if you think this means the CBD is a bit staid, just look to the river, where the **Riverwalk Marketplace,** cruising paddlewheelers, and other cargo of the tourism boom have launched a riverfront renaissance that has reawakened (some say with alarm) this drowsy area. The **Ernest N. Morial Convention Center,** built in 1984 for the World's Fair, was one of the CBD's first wake-up calls, opening the floodgates for chain hotels and tourist attractions—including the **Aquarium of the Americas** and clanging waterfront streetcars—that cater to the thriving convention industry.

Mainline Canal Street, as wide as Broadway and the great boulevards of Paris, spans an impressive 171 feet between opposite storefronts. The wide median is lined with palm trees and antique green lampposts, the base of each embedded with a bronze plaque that commemorates the city's four governments: France, Spain, the Confederacy, and the US. Once a year, during Carnival, a sea of masked revelers rocks from shore to shore, as enormous and gaudy floats lumber down this primary parade route.

Back in the late 18th century, when the French Quarter *was* New Orleans, the surrounding sugar plantations were gradually bought up and subdivided into lots to create suburbs, or *faubourgs,* such as Faubourg Marigny and Treme. The CBD was then known as **Faubourg Sainte-Marie,** and it was here that the first Americans made their homes when they came flatboating down the river after the 1803 Louisiana Purchase. Canal Street was the broad "neutral ground" separating the clannish French Quarter Creoles from the upstarts who filled the American Sector as it grew steadily upriver. Businessmen established trade between the two competing factions, and merchants set up stores staffed by both French- and English-speaking clerks. Canal Street is still the border between the French Quarter and the CBD, but it is also the line that separates the two major divisions of the city: everything below Canal Street, on the French Quarter side, is considered **Downtown** (or downriver); everything above is **Uptown** (or upriver). Today many shoppers have been diverted to the suburbs, while discount stores and long rows of sidewalk vendors have created a distinctly Third World atmosphere along the once-grand main street. But posh indoor malls such as **Canal Place** and old standbys like **Adler's** and **Rubenstein Bros.** continue to attract plenty of loyal customers to the CBD. And new waves of *les Américains* settle in the old Faubourg Sainte-Marie every day—at the massive convention hotels clustered along Canal and **Poydras** Streets.

1 NEW ORLEANS PUBLIC LIBRARY

In addition to lending books, the main branch maintains an extensive research facility dedicated to Louisiana and the City of New Orleans. ♦ M-Sa. 219 Loyola Ave (between Gravier St and Tulane Ave). 529.7323 &

2 ORPHEUM THEATRE

Directly across from the **Fairmont Hotel,** this historic theater, graced by a terra-cotta Beaux Arts facade, is the site of the **Louisiana Philharmonic Orchestra's** classical and pops concerts. Built in 1918, the original vaudeville house saw performances by Will Rogers, Milton Berle, Jack Benny, Fred Allen, and George Burns and Gracie Allen—among countless others. ♦ Box office open two hours prior to concerts. Tickets available from Ticketmaster, 522.5555; www.ticketmaster.com. 129 University Pl (between Common and Canal Sts). Business office 524.3285 &

3 THE RITZ-CARLTON NEW ORLEANS

$$$ Opened in October 2000, this is a much-awaited transformation of the historic Maison Blance building—a New Orleans landmark—into a luxury hotel containing 425 deluxe guest rooms, a private access club level with a dedicated concierge and private lounge. The more than $200-million renovation also includes the **Lobby Lounge** serving traditional afternoon tea, two restaurants, the **Library Lounge,** two spectacular ballrooms, conference facilities, and a business center. The 18,000-square-foot **Day Spa** is equipped with 15 private treatment rooms, state-of-the-art fitness equipment and styling salons. Rooms overlook the colorful French Quarter or Canal Street, a prime viewing spot for the Carnival parade during Mardis Gras. ♦ 921 Canal St (between Dauphine and Burgundy Sts). 524.1331, 800/241.3333

4 FAIRMONT HOTEL

$$$ One of the grandest of America's grande dame hotels celebrated its 100th birthday in 1993. The elegant old landmark, which debuted in 1893 as the **Grunewald** and was renamed the **Roosevelt** (in Teddy's honor) in 1923, was acquired by the prestigious Fairmont group in 1965. The long and colorful guest list has included eight US presidents, from Calvin Coolidge to Gerald Ford, as well as Emperor Haile Selassie and General Charles De Gaulle. Controversial Louisiana governors (and brothers) Huey and Earl Long were regulars. (Some say Huey built Airline Highway to connect the hotel with the capitol in Baton Rouge.) The block-long lobby, which runs from Baronne Street to University Place, is an opulent jewel box of gold leaf, crystal chandeliers, scarlet carpeting, and imported marble. The 700 guest accommodations, including 85 suites, are luxurious with goose-down pillows, large marble or tile bathrooms, electric shoe buffers, fax machines, and 24-hour room service; several huge suites also have a separate service entrance. A recent five-year, $41-million renovation brought guest rooms into the 21st century, while maintaining the Old World charm of this historic property. The **Sazerac Bar & Grill** (a separate entity from the more casual and traditional bar mentioned at right) serves breakfast, lunch, and dinner. The rooftop swimming pool (with a gazebo restaurant/bar that is open seasonally) overlooks a health club and two lighted tennis courts. ♦ 123 Baronne St (between Common and Canal Sts). 529.7111, 800/527.4727; fax 522.2303; www.fairmont.com &

Within the Fairmont Hotel:

SAZERAC BAR

Both Huey and Earl Long were regulars at this small and intimate watering hole, still a favorite haunt of the power drinking crowd. Paneled in dark African walnut, the walls are splashed with Paul Ninas's 10-foot murals of New Orleans scenes, formerly displayed at the 1939 New York World's Fair. Legend has it that the bar's namesake was the nation's first cocktail. In the 1800s, a Monsieur Peychaud concocted a tonic for stomach disorders at his apothecary shop in the French Quarter. He called the tonic "bitters," and flavored it with Sazerac-de-Forge Cognac and a dash of absinthe. Peychaud served his creation in *coquetiers,* and that French word for egg cups was soon Anglicized to cocktails. Today the celebrated Sazerac cocktail is still the specialty of the house and a dessert menu (with wines and Champagnes by the glass) is featured nightly. ♦ Daily from 11AM. 529.7111 &

5 CHURCH OF THE IMMACULATE CONCEPTION

Known to most locals as the **Jesuit Church,** the original (designed by the Reverend John Cambiaso and architect **T.E. Giraud** in 1851) was so loaded down by more than 200 tons of ironwork that it virtually collapsed of its own weight in 1857. It was replaced in 1930 by this nearly exact replica, designed by the architectural firm **Toledano, Wogan, and Bernard**. The exotic redbrick facade, with its twin onion domes and horseshoe arches, has flourishes of Moorish, Arabian, and Spanish detail. The elaborate cast-iron pews are from the first church, as is the bronze gilt altar (designed by local architect **James Freret** and built in Lyons, France), which won first prize at the Paris Exposition of 1867-68. The ethereal statue of the Virgin Mary was intended for the royal gallery at Tuileries Palace, a plan that was foiled by the 1848 French Revolution. The New Orleans congregation eventually purchased the statue in France for $5,000. ♦ 132 Baronne St (between Common and Canal Sts). 529.1477

6 HOLIDAY INN DOWNTOWN SUPERDOME

$$ Conveniently located for the Superdome and other CBD attractions, this high-rise sibling of the ubiquitous chain offers 300 newly renovated rooms, including three suites (each with a balcony), a landscaped rooftop terrace with heated pool, cable TV, a restaurant, and room service. VIPs check into the

top floor **Concierge Level,** where amenities include complimentary continental breakfast and afternoon hors d'ouvres. The building's distinctive high-rise painting of a vertical clarinet is a wonderful landmark. ♦ 330 Loyola Ave (between Perdido and Gravier Sts). 581.1600, 800/535.7830; fax 586.0833; www.basshotels.com/holiday-inn ♿

7 ST. CHARLES AVENUE STREETCAR

Write "streetcar" at the top of your must-do list. The moving National Historic Landmarks rumble from Canal Street in the CBD, through the Garden District and Uptown/University section, to **Palmer Park** in Carrollton. A major tourist attraction, but also workaday transportation for locals, the quaint green cars are part of the oldest continuously operating street railway system in the world. In 1835, they were powered by steam locomotives from Great Britain. Today's electric models are of 1923 and 1924 vintage, made by the Perley A. Thomas Company of High Point, NC. Board at Canal and Carondelet Streets (your best chance for an empty seat) and make the 13.3-mile, 90-minute round-trip; an additional fare is required for the return. (Note: Unless you want to advertise your status as a tourist, don't call the streetcars "trolleys.") ♦ Fee. Daily 24 hours. 248.3900

8 B. DALTON BOOKSELLERS

This full-service branch of the national chain sprawls over two floors, with especially good selections of regional, business, and African-American interest books. Shipping is available. ♦ Daily. 714 Canal St (between St. Charles Ave and Carondelet St). 529.2705 ♿ Also at: Numerous locations throughout the area

8 ADLER'S

New Orleans's answer to Tiffany's, **Coleman E. Adler and Sons Jewelers** was established in 1898. Today the fourth generation oversees a glittering collection of diamonds, colored stones, silver, china, crystal, and gifts. ♦ M-Sa. 722 Canal St (between St. Charles Ave and Carondelet St). 523.5292 ♿ Also at: Numerous locations throughout the area

9 RUBENSTEIN BROS.

Established in 1924, this landmark men's clothing store carries a full line of suits, overcoats, shoes, shirts, sportswear, and accessories. Labels include Polo/Ralph Lauren, Timberland, and Canali. ♦ M-Sa. 102 St. Charles Ave (at Canal St). 581.6666 ♿ Also at: Numerous locations throughout the area

10 HAMPTON INN

$$ A great value, this surprisingly attractive link in the chain occupies floors 4 through 14 of a National Historic Landmark building

dating from 1903. Furnished in modern style and comfort, the 187 rooms and suites are large, with tall windows (many boast fine views) and high ceilings. Amenities include valet parking, a fitness room, and complimentary continental breakfast (but there is no restaurant). ♦ 226 Carondelet St (between Gravier and Common Sts). 529.9990, 800/426-7866; fax 529.9996; www.hamptoninn.com ♿

11 COURTYARD BY MARRIOTT

$$ This comfortable hotel is an especially good value during Carnival because it's right on the main parade route. While the 17 balcony rooms are sometimes booked up to a year in advance for Mardi Gras weekend, any of the 140 guest rooms—many of which open onto the six-story atrium—are a good bet for a home base. The spacious accommodations have large work desks and coffeemakers. An exercise room, indoor whirlpool, and full-service breakfast restaurant provide additional creature comforts. The St. Charles Avenue streetcar stops just outside the front entrance. ♦ 124 St. Charles Ave (between Common and Canal Sts). 581.9005, 800/321.2211; fax 581.6264; www.courtyard.com ♿

12 LE MERIDIEN

$$$$ Streamlined all the way from the glassed-in waterfall in the marble lobby to the sleek penthouses on the 30th floor, Forte Hotels' local outpost adds a little style to Canal Street's convention row. The 494 standard rooms are furnished in soft beiges and grays; there are also seven suites, some of which are split-level with two-story windows affording spectacular views—especially at Carnival time. The business center offers fax, photocopying, telex, and secretarial services. Many locals join the **Meridien Health Club** for the Nautilus equipment, sauna, and temperature-controlled outdoor pool. ♦ 614 Canal St (between Camp St and St. Charles Ave). 525.6500, 800/543.4300; fax 525.1128; www.lemeridien-hotels.com ♿

Within Le Meridien:

MIDI SOUTH OF FRANCE

★★$$ This new bistro, formerly La Gauloise, focuses on the cuisine of the Provence region of France. Chef Emmanuel Bernard, a colleague of chef-consultant Michel Rostang, heads the restaurant. Expect flavorful French country cuisine, including bouillabaisse, sautéed escargots with Provencal sauce, and pan-seared Hudson Valley Foie gras. ♦ Daily lunch, and dinner. 525.6500 ♿

TALES OF THE CITY:
SPECIALTY TOURS OF NEW ORLEANS

When you first arrive in New Orleans, you will probably want to get your bearings via a general-interest tour, such as those offered by **Gray Line** (587.0861; fax 587.0742; www.grayline.com), **New Orleans Tours** (592.0560; fax 527.0093; www.visitnola.com), **New Orleans Steamboat Company** (586.8777; fax 587.0708; natchez@nosteamboat.com), or **New Orleans Paddlewheelers** (524.0814; fax 524.6265; www.visitnola.com). Such an introductory tour is a good way to get a quick overview of the city, but how do you get to know its quirky personality traits, its individual charms, its historical idiosyncrasies?

Well, short of spending the rest of your life doing research, the best way is to take one of the many offbeat tours led by individuals (and sometimes companies) with a specialized background and focus. They'll show you facets of New Orleans that you never knew existed.

For instance, have you heard the story about a "young man of negotiable affection" who confused Tennessee Williams with Tennessee Ernie Ford and asked him to sing "Sixteen Tons?" Dr. Kenneth Holditch, a research professor at the **University of New Orleans** and owner of **Heritage Tours**, tells that tale and many others during his literary walking tours, which visit the old haunts and hangouts of many local lions. In addition to Williams, the tour delves into the lives of William Faulkner, George Washington Cable, Sherwood Anderson, Katherine Anne Porter, Lillian Hellman, and Truman Capote.

An acknowledged expert on Williams, Holditch also offers a second walk devoted exclusively to Louisiana's most famous playwright. The itinerary and focus of either of Holditch's tours can be tailored for specialized groups. For further information or to arrange an excursion, contact **Heritage Tours** (949.9805; fax 948.7821) or **Faulkner House Books** (524.2940).

Music scholar John McCusker will take you past the birthplaces, homes, and performance sites of many great local jazz artists on his **Cradle of Jazz Tours** (282.3583; jazztour@aol.com). Among the musicians featured are "Kid" Ory, Buddy Bolden, and "King" Oliver.

You can visit New Orleans locales that have been captured on celluloid by taking Carolyn Kolb's **Film Site Tours** (861.8158), including many of the **French Quarter** locales from *Interview with the Vampire* (from the Anne Rice novel), the French Quarter drugstore seen in *Angel Heart,* the balcony immortalized in *Walk on the Wild Side,* and even the laundromat from *Panic in the Streets.* Kolb, a local writer and historian, knows the city intimately and can spin a good yarn; in addition to her film tours, she also gives excursions tailored to suit a wide range of other individual interests—from literature to politics.

Laid Back Tours shares the road less traveled with visitors interested in seeing New Orleans from a recumbent cycling point of view. **Unique Group Tours** include a "Bike & Blues Tour," which is a full day bike and music tour package, and "The Seafood Boil Ride," a park tour that includes a N'awlins style meal with boiled crawfish, shrimp and crabs. Prices start at $35 per person, five-person group minimum. 625 Hagan Ave. 488.8991, 800.786-1274, www.laidbacktours.com.

There's certainly no shortage of swamp tours in Louisiana, but **Turgeon Tours & Charters** (689.2911, 800/73.SWAMP) limits groups to six for their nature-based cruises, which are especially popular with bird-watchers and wildlife photographers. David and Valerie Turgeon, who lead the tours, are lifelong residents of **Bayou Barataria,** the home waters of pirate Jean Lafitte. They also are avid nature enthusiasts and have extensive expertise about fishing. Along the way, you'll see healthy freshwater marshes and swamps, coastal wetlands restoration projects, old fishing communities, historic cemeteries, shrimp boats, oyster beds, and wildlife, including different species of birds, turtles, muskrats, and (in warm months) alligators. It's quite a distance from town, so you may want to drive yourself out to Bayou Barataria; when you contact the Turgeons to set up a tour, ask about their special arrangements with local car rental companies for one-day packages.

With all the different nationalities that have made their home here throughout the years (Spanish, French, Canadian, American), New Orleans has some of the most varied architecture to be seen in any city in the US. The **Preservation Resource Center of New Orleans** (581.7032; fax 522.9275; www.prcno.org), which maintains architectural archives and often spearheads neighborhood restoration projects, custom-designs architecture tours for individuals or groups with 24 hours notice.

For the inveterate shopper with an eye for distinguishing antiques, historian and antiques expert Macon Riddle leads excursions to the shops and art galleries of the French Quarter, **Warehouse/Arts District, Garden District,** and **Uptown.** She'll also do advance research and arrange for shipping, as well as keeping track of measurements and other details. For an appointment, call **Let's Go Antiquing** (899.3027; fax 891.2703).

Voodoo-oriented tours abound in New Orleans, but the one led by writer and former **Jean Lafitte National Park** ranger Robert Florence emphasizes the practice's traditional heritage and history, rather than myths and tall tales.

Restaurants/Clubs: Red | **Hotels: Purple** | Shops: Orange | Outdoors/Parks: Green | Sights/Culture: Blue

For example, voodoo is actually a blanket term for a number of different religious sects, and it's also been the origin of several medically effective folk remedies. Among the sites visited are ancient cemeteries (one of Florence's particular areas of expertise) and a genuine voodoo temple. For more information, contact **Historic New Orleans Walking Tours** (947.2120; fax 947.2130; www.tourneworleans.com).

13 PALACE CAFÉ

★★★$$ The younger generation of Brennan cousins (that famous restaurateur family of **Commander's Palace, Bacco,** and **Mr. B's Bistro** fame) runs this grand Parisian-style bistro. Tables by the huge plate-glass windows (at sidewalk level) are the place to see and be seen; a sweeping staircase leads to a second-floor dining room for those who prefer quieter surroundings. The focus is on the freshest Louisiana seafood, with many dishes prepared in a ceramic-tile rotisserie from France. Start with oyster shooters (sauced raw oysters plopped in shot glasses) or traditional "oysters pan roast" accompanied by crusty bread to soak up the rich and creamy rosemary-scented juices. The signature white-chocolate bread pudding, scattered with dark chocolate shavings, is a welcome twist on the local mainstay. The stately Italianate/Baroque building, designed circa 1907 by the architectural firm **Toledano and Wogan,** was for decades the home of **Werlein's Music Company**. ♦ Creole ♦ M-F lunch and dinner, Sa-Su brunch and dinner. Reservations recommended for dinner. 605 Canal St (between Chartres and Royal Sts). 523.1661 ఉ

14 NEW ORLEANS MARRIOTT HOTEL

$$$ Two towers are divided by an enormous lobby and a busy area that corrals the outdoor pool, sun deck, and health club. Large suites in the 41-story **River Tower** are equipped with wet bars and bath phones; concierge service adds extra perks to the **French Quarter Tower**. In all, the 1,290 rooms (including 54 suites) are heavily trafficked by conventioneers. ♦ 555 Canal St (at Chartres St). 581.1000, 800/654.3990; fax 523.6755 ఉ

Within the New Orleans Marriott Hotel:

RIVERVIEW RESTAURANT

★★$$$ Expect lofty views—and prices—from the formal dining room on the 41st floor. But the elaborate buffet and live music at the Champagne jazz brunch (Sundays and holidays) is a good deal that draws local customers, too. ♦ Continental ♦ M dinner; Tu-Sa breakfast, lunch, and dinner; Su brunch and dinner. 581.1000 ఉ

The Mississippi River is 2,200 feet wide at Canal Street. The bankside depth ranges from 30 to 60 feet; the midstream depth from 100 to 200 feet.

15 SHERATON NEW ORLEANS

$$$ This behemoth is located directly across the street from the equally gargantuan **Marriott,** with which it wages a friendly but active rivalry in the convention business sweepstakes. A multistory glass wall in the **Sheraton** overlooks Canal Street—a great place to watch parades during Carnival—and a showy spiral staircase descends to the lounge where a jazz trio performs nightly. The hotel's 1,100 rooms and suites are large; those on the **Concierge Level** promise express check-in/-out, some baths with TV sets and telephones, and other amenities. Adjoining the main lobby, the **Waterbury Fitness Center** (592.5631) offers aerobics classes, strength training equipment, a pool, whirlpools, steam rooms, saunas, and massages. There are also two restaurants: an elegant dining room and a cafe, a lobby bar and a **Starbucks**. ♦ 500 Canal St (at Magazine St). 525.2500, 800/253.6156; fax 561.0178; www.sheraton.com/neworleans ఉ

16 US CUSTOMS HOUSE

Day-to-day customs business carries on in this important landmark, a rather forbidding conglomeration of Egyptian and Greek Revival architecture that occupies the entire 400 block of Canal Street. The ground was broken in 1848 for what was then the most expensive federal construction project ever undertaken. One of the most spectacular sights in New Orleans is the awesome **Marble Hall** on the third floor, where 14 massive marble columns support a skylight 54 feet high. ♦ Free. M-F. 423 Canal St (between N Peters and Decatur Sts)

17 INTERNATIONAL HOUSE

$$$ This classic Beaux Arts building has been converted into one of the city's most striking boutique hotels, with 119 rooms, including three Jacuzzi suites and eight penthouses with panoramic views. Guest accommodations are decorated in warm neutral colors and are graced by 12-foot ceilings, oversized bathrooms with aromatherapy cosmetics, CD players, original photographs by local artists, and two-line telephones with voice mail. Other amenities include complimentary continental breakfast, a fitness center, and valet parking. The lobby and candlelit bar are especially stylish, with 22-foot ceilings, ornate columns, and aromatic plants. ♦ 221 Camp St (at Gravier St). 553.9550, 800/633.5770; fax 553.9560; www.ihhotel.com ఉ

Within the International Hotel:

LEMON GRASS

★★★$$ Run by celebrated local chef Minh Bui, **Lemon Grass** offers an outstanding take on contemporary French/Vietnamese cuisine. Bui incorporates the freshest local ingredients meticulously prepared and presented with his signature flair, cuisine that is light and healthful, robust and zesty and full of big bold flavor. Try the spring rolls, Vietnamese bird's nest and Asian curried Gulf Shrimp. The restaurant's ambiance, designed with Feng Shui in mind, is dreamy and refreshing—just like the cuisine. ♦ Lunch M-F, Dinner M-Su. 221 Camp St (at Gravier St). 523-1200

18 OMNI ROYAL CRESCENT

$$$ Centrally located in the heart of the financial district, this boutique hotel is a well-feathered nest for high-flying business travelers. The 98 rooms (including seven suites with Jacuzzis) are furnished in traditional style with lavish prints, Egyptian cotton bedding, marble baths, and additional phone lines to accommodate fax machines or modems. The rooftop pool and full fitness center are designed in the style of a Roman bath. The lobby is small but jewel-box elegant, brightened by chandeliers, fresh flowers, and **Christino's** (a stylish restaurant that also provides room service). ♦ 535 Gravier St (at Camp St). 527.0006, 800/THE.OMNI; fax 523.0806, 527.0897 &

19 THE PELHAM

$$$ Although this stylish hotel opened only a few years ago, the building dates from the 1850s, when it was constructed on the site of the old Bienville Plantation. A first-class renovation makes good use of the 14-foot ceilings, elegant trim, and large windows (some interior rooms are windowless, but they are brightened by the fabric-covered walls). English-style furnishings and an emphasis on personal service add a formal touch to the 60 guest rooms and small lobby. The **Metro Bistro** is a warm and stylish retreat for breakfast, lunch, and dinner. ♦ 444 Common St (at Magazine St). 522.4444, 800/659.5621; fax 539.9010; www.neworleanscollection.com &

20 CANAL PLACE

Three levels of luxurious shops, taking up the entire block from Canal to Iberville and crowned by a soaring atrium with glass elevators, include **Saks Fifth Avenue, Brooks Brothers, Laura Ashley, Gucci, Betsy Johnson, Pottery Barn, Williams-Sonoma, Kenneth Cole,** and other swank outlets. A fast-food court, a four-screen cinema, the **Southern Repertory Theatre** (see below), and the **Downtown Fitness Center** (525.2956) round out the third level. And it's all topped off by the fabulous **Westin Canal Place Hotel**. All-day parking rates are reasonable in the complex's garage, which is right at the midpoint for exploring the French Quarter, CBD, Riverfront, and Warehouse/Arts District. Mall shops and area attractions (including the **Aquarium of the Americas**) will validate the tickets for discounted parking. ♦ Mall open daily until midnight; shops open M-W, Su 10AM-6PM; Th-Sa 10AM-7PM. Canal and N Peters Sts. 522.9200 &

Within Canal Place:

RHINO

A sleek gallery stocked with fine crafts doesn't fit the usual image of a nonprofit cooperative, but this one suits the 80 Louisiana artists who have banded together to market their work "Right Here In New Orleans." (That's RHINO—get it?) This is the place to visit for highly original sculpture, textiles, wood carvings, glass, jewelry, furniture, and more—both decorative and functional. ♦ Daily. 523.7945 &

MIGNON FAGET LTD.

One of the most celebrated homegrown artists draws shapes from nature and classical architecture for her chic handcrafted jewelry. ♦ Daily. 524.2973 & Also at: Numerous locations throughout the area

SOUTHERN REPERTORY THEATRE

A grand golden doorway leads into the intimate 150-seat theater devoted to works by Southern playwrights, both established (Tennessee Williams, Lillian Hellman) and rising stars (Robert Kornfeld, Rosary O'Neill). The season usually runs from September through June. ♦ Box office open M-F, 1-5PM. 861.8163 &

WYNDHAM NEW ORLEANS AT CANAL PLACE

$$$ Consider the various advantages of unpacking your bags here: panoramic views of the river and city, deluxe digs, and 50 or so shops (including a food court, a cinema, and a theater) right beneath your feet. The hotel lobby is on the 11th floor of Canal Place, and the accommodations climb up to the 30th floor. You can glide down the elevator for a spree at **Saks** or **Gucci,** and then shoot up to the rooftop pool for a cooling dip. The hotel

Restaurants/Clubs: Red | **Hotels: Purple** | **Shops: Orange** | **Outdoors/Parks: Green** | **Sights/Culture: Blue**

55

was renovated to the tune of $20 million in 1997; the 438 rooms and suites are now elegantly decked out in deep jewel tones, with such amenities as large marble baths, stocked mini-bars, dual-line phones, hair dryers, ironing equipment, in-room safes, and coffeemakers stocked with Starbucks coffee. The public spaces are rich with antiques (the grandfather clock is more than 300 years old), jardinieres, Oriental rugs, and rows of high-arched windows. Settle near one for afternoon tea (served in the lobby Thursday through Saturday from 2 to 4 PM, by reservation only) with panoramic views. Or, if you are so inclined, avail yourself of the 24-hour room service and the health club. ♦ Check in via the Iberville Street entrance to Canal Place. 100 Iberville St (southeast of N Peters St). 566.7006; fax 553.5120 &

Within the Wyndham New Orleans at Canal Place:

RIVERBEND GRILL

★★$$$ This sedate room with long-range views of the river far below provides the perfect atmosphere in which to savor grilled seafood, steaks, and fowl. The Sunday jazz Champagne brunch features live music and other indigenous treats, such as shrimp Creole, red beans and rice, eggs Benedict, and oysters Rockefeller. ♦ Creole/American ♦ M-Sa breakfast, lunch, and dinner; Su brunch and dinner. Reservations recommended for dinner. 566.7006 &

21 WOLDENBERG RIVERFRONT PARK

This 16-acre green space traces the Missis-sippi all the way from the French Quarter **Jackson Brewery** complex to the **Canal Street Ferry Terminal,** with lots of benches and street musicians to prolong the trip. Major sculptures include Ida Kohlmeyer's *Aquatic Colonnade* (a colorful row of 20 columns, each 25 feet high and topped with a fanciful underwater creature) and John Scott's *Ocean Song* (eight stainless steel pylons, 12 feet high, that support enormous rings hung with moving paddles). New Orleans sculptor Franco Alessandrini returned to his native Italy to carve the 21-foot-tall marble *Monument to the Immigrant*—with Lady Liberty standing guard above a young family of refugees—that honors the memory of the immigrants who built New Orleans. Extensive landscaping showcases an impressive variety of indigenous trees and shrubs. ♦ M-Th, Su 6AM-10PM; F-Sa 6AM-midnight

Within Woldenberg Riverfront Park:

AQUARIUM OF THE AMERICAS

More than 10,000 sea creatures swim through the one-million-plus gallons of water in this futuristic aquarium complex that's part of **The Audubon Institute**. Stand on a four-foot glass porthole to watch toothy six-foot-long sharks glide just beneath your feet, or climb down to the first floor for an eye-to-eye encounter as they slowly make the rounds of the 400,000-gallon tank. You can also stroll through the 30-foot-long acrylic tunnel in the Caribbean Reef display for a strange underside perspec-tive on cow nose rays, angelfish, parrotfish, and hundreds of other swimming specimens. Among the other highlights are the rare white alligator in the Mississippi River Delta exhibit, the world's largest collection of jellyfish, and the glass-enclosed rain forest: a spectacular climb past waterfalls, wild orchids, brilliantly colored tropical birds, and piranha. You can also see dazzling films on the towering screen of the **Entergy IMAX Theater** throughout the day. Like other IMAX theaters, this one presents larger-than-life movies about every-thing from the vanishing buffalo to the incredibly tenacious Rolling Stones, though underwater subjects predominate. The riverboat *John James Audubon* docks right out front for daily zoo cruises upstream to **Audubon Park** (ask about package rates). ♦ Admission; additional fee to the Entergy IMAX Theater. Daily. 861.2537 &

22 LOUISIANA SUPERDOME

Get ready for statistics about the largest indoor arena in the world. It occupies a total land area of 52 acres, and has on-site parking to accommodate 5,000 cars and 250 buses. It's 27 stories high; the roof area covers 9.7 acres; and the diameter of the dome is 680 feet. The air-conditioning equipment weighs 9,000 tons. The building contains 169,000 cubic yards of concrete, 20,000 tons of structural steel, 400 miles of electrical wiring, and 15,200 lighting fixtures. The 166,000-square-foot concrete floor is covered with 15-foot-wide strips of AstroTurf, which was rechristened Mardi Gras. The seating is rearranged according to the size of an event: capacity for a football game is 70,000, expandable to 76,791. Major concerts (the Rolling Stones, Paul McCartney) can accommodate 87,500. The **New Orleans Saints** of the National Football League play home games in the enormous facility, which also hosts the annual **Sugar Bowl** and the Thanksgiving weekend **Bayou Classic,** a grudge match between **Grambling** and **Southern Universities**. The **Dome Cafe** is a favorite lunch spot for locals working in the area. ♦ Admission. Tours daily on the hour from 10AM to 4PM. 1500 Poydras St (at LaSalle St). 587.3810; www.superdome.com &

23 NEW ORLEANS CENTRE

In this spectacular crystal palace, the one-hundred-foot-high central atrium is decked with marble and cascading greenery. Located in a modern pink skyscraper that connects with the **Superdome,** the three-level shopping mall houses some 60 shops and eateries, including **Macy's, Lord & Taylor, Victoria's Secret, The Gap, The Limited,** and **LaVanti.** ◆ M-Sa 10AM-8PM; Su noon-6PM. 1400 Poydras St (between Loyola Ave and LaSalle St). 568.0000 ♿

Within New Orleans Centre:

AFRO-AMERICAN BOOK STOP

This locally owned shop specializes in books by and about African-Americans, featuring a good selection of works by regional authors, as well as posters, prints, sculptures, and greeting cards. ◆ Daily. 588.1474. Also at: 5700 Read Blvd (at Lake Forest Blvd). 243.2436 ♿

24 HYATT REGENCY

$$$ The Hyatt hotel chain's trademark glass elevators glide up and down the 27-floor atrium past tropical landscaping, fountains, and a nouveau-posh lobby illuminated by massive chandeliers. The 1,184 guest rooms offer direct access to the vast **Poydras Plaza** complex that shelters the **New Orleans Centre** (connected to the hotel by a network of glass-enclosed ramps). The **Superdome** hunkers right next door. Key-access elevators sweep up to the concierge-level **Regency Suites** for special pampering. Each room in the **Lanai** section has a terrace or patio that faces the swimming pool. Other amenities include three restaurants (one is a revolving steak house), a casual dining room, and a sports bar; a health club; and free shuttle service to the French Quarter. ◆ Poydras St and Loyola Ave. 561.1234, 800/233.1234; fax 587.4141; www.hyatt.com ♿

25 SMITH & WOLLENSKY

★★★$$$$ A hit at branches nationwide, the stellar New York steak house opened this outpost in October 1998. Set in a 100-year-old landmark (once home to **Maylie's Restaurant**) and extending into the building next door, the 400-seat operation is a cosmopolitan retreat lined with dark woods and polished marble. One table is nestled in the old cast-iron elevator. The US prime beef, dry-aged on the premises, is superb (it can also be purchased at the in-house retail shop). You can order a sirloin strip, filet mignon, or 22-ounce bone-in rib steak. Or consider the crackling pork shank with firecracker applesauce, proclaimed number-one dish in America by *USA Today*. Those with lighter appetites may order mustard-crusted tuna, grilled Atlantic salmon, and other seafood. As in many northern steak houses, the dessert menu offers New York cheesecake and warm apple crumb tart. If you're determined to exert a little restraint, you can still have your seasonal sorbet or ice cream and eat it too. ◆ Steak house ◆ Daily lunch and dinner. Reservations recommended for lunch and dinner. 1009 Poydras St (between O'Keefe and S Rampart Sts). 561.0770; www.smithandwollensky.com ♿

26 LE PAVILLON

$$ A good choice for fans of overstated luxury, this hotel's lobby is lined with columns, crystal chandeliers, and a marble railing from the Grand Hotel in Paris. Four floors of bay windows distinguish the front facade, and the outrageously grand side entrance is flanked by two colossal semi-nudes who dwarf the cars that pull into their towering porte cochere. The architectural firm of **Toledano and Wogan** built the Renaissance/Baroque boarding palace in 1907 for a mere $2.5 million. The 219 standard rooms are identically decorated with traditional furnishings; but seven suites are fitted out with velvets and brocades, carved armoires, and canopied beds. There is also a restaurant and lounge. ◆ 833 Poydras St (at Baronne St). 581.3111, 800/535.9095; fax 522.5543; www.lepavillion.com

27 HOTEL INTER-CONTINENTAL NEW ORLEANS

$$$ Works by contemporary New Orleans artists distinguish the lobby, and the fifth-floor courtyard is landscaped with fine sculptures in this ultra-modern, rose granite hotel. A few blocks from the galleries of the Warehouse/Arts District, it offers 482 stylish accommodations on 14 floors. Suites located on the **Club Floor** are particularly elegant, with rich upholstery and a massive marble bath, Jacuzzi, full

---

Restaurants/Clubs: **Red** | Hotels: **Purple** | Shops: **Orange** | Outdoors/Parks: **Green** | Sights/Culture: **Blue**

kitchen, and maid's room. The hotel also offers a complimentary health club with a rooftop pool and 24-hour room service. Live entertainment is featured Wed-Sat. ◆ 444 St. Charles Ave (between Poydras and Gravier Sts). 525.5566, 800/445.6563; fax 523.7310; www.interconti.com &

Within the Hotel Inter-Continental:

VERANDA

★★★$$$ New Orleans's renowned chef Willy Coln presides over the luxurious dining room, where light filters through a glass canopy into an interior courtyard decked with lush tropical plants and decorative garden furniture. German by birth, Coln has created a menu that is a carefully arranged marriage of continental and New Orleans cuisines. Try his signature Louisiana crab cakes or Gulf shrimp with sweet-potato pancakes. To finish your meal with a flourish, choose the delicious Black Forest cake. Jazz buffet brunches on Sundays and holidays are sumptuous. ◆ Continental ◆ M-Sa breakfast, lunch, and dinner; Su brunch and dinner. Reservations recommended for brunch and dinner; jackets recommended for dinner. 525.5566 &

In the Heart of New Orleans

New Orleans

28 QUEEN & CRESCENT HOTEL

$$ This stellar renovation of the old home office building of the Queen & Crescent Railroad retains the architectural charm (including the tall ceilings) of the early 1900s, updated with soft warm colors and sleek traditional furnishings. The 196 rooms are fitted out with mini-bars and coffeemakers, plus fax and modem capabilities. A stylish lobby lounge, fitness center, and valet parking round out the amenities. ◆ 344 Camp St (at Natchez St). 587.9700, 800/205.7131; fax 587.9701; www.queenandcrescenthotel.com

29 LIBORIO CUBAN RESTAURANT

★★$ This local favorite, newly spruced up with new oak furnishings and chartreuse walls, still serves the same Cuban steaks and sandwiches that have attracted a loyal following for more than 20 years. Other good bets are *medianoche* (midnight bread) stuffed with roasted pork, ham, and swiss cheese and grilled on a sandwich press; and *ropa vieja*, thinly shredded beef spiked with red wine and seasonings and garnished with fried plantains. ◆ Cuban ◆ M lunch; Tu-F lunch and

dinner; Sa dinner. 321 Magazine St (between Natchez and Gravier Sts). 581.9680

30 CUVEÉ

★★★$$$$ This sleek, new dining establishment offers bold regional cuisine prepared by chef Richard "Bingo" Starr, formerly of the **Windsor Court Hotel, Emeril's,** and **Delmonico**. Standouts include smoked salmon tasso nestled on a potato galette with Creole mustard creme, sugar cane-smoked duck breast and bouillabaisse. The wine cellar is outstanding, with a fine selection of wine available by the glass. M-Sa breakfast, dinner; M-F lunch. 322 Magazine St (between Natchez and Gravier Sts). 587.9001

31 DOUBLETREE HOTEL

$$ Like its neighbors in the Central Business District, this hotel caters largely to conventioneers. The 363 guest rooms here are furnished with light woods and pastel fabrics—country French meets downtown skyscraper. Extra frills on the **Concierge Level,** as well as valet parking, an outdoor pool, restaurant, cafe, and sports bar, provide additional conveniences. ◆ 300 Canal St (at S Peters St). 581.1300, 888/874.9074; fax 522.4100; www.citinet.com/doubletreenworleans &

32 WINDSOR COURT HOTEL

$$$$ Sign the register at this luxury hotel and you'll be in good company with other illustrious guests, including Princess Anne, Margaret Thatcher, Rod Stewart, Kevin Costner, Kathleen Turner, and Julia Child. In the quiet and elegant lobby, Oriental rugs adorn green marble floors, potted plants fill giant jardinieres, and fresh flowers grace gold-encrusted tables. A gracious afternoon tea is served here. Displayed throughout the public areas is an $8-million art collection, featuring many pieces linked to Britain's House of Windsor. Of the 324 units, most are lavish 1- or 2-bedroom suites with four-poster beds, marble baths, and 3 phones (with 2 incoming lines and dataports for computers and fax machines). The health club adjoins an outdoor Olympic-size swimming pool. ◆ 300 Gravier St (at S Peters St). 523.6000, 888/596.0955; fax 596.4513; www.windsorcourthotel.com &

Within the Windsor Court Hotel:

THE GRILL ROOM

★★★★$$$$ Tall windows, hung with Austrian drapes, overlook the brick courtyard with its statue of St. George, and massive oil paintings (part of the hotel's multimillion-dollar collection) dominate the dining room walls. The menu changes monthly, but stellar offerings have included tempura soft-shell crab in a pecan-and-andouille crust with wild rice; roasted pork tenderloin in tequila and pineapple with sweet potato puree and grilled tomato relish; and baby spinach with crispy lobster ravioli and herbed goat cheese with blackberry vinaigrette. The "Chef's Tasting Menu" gives serious foodies the opportunity to sample the evening's best dishes in seven courses of tasting size portions. An excellent wine cellar includes many fine Bordeaux Grands Crus. The only five diamond, five star restaurant in New Orleans. ♦ International ♦ Daily breakfast, lunch, and dinner. Reservations recommended for dinner; jacket required for dinner. 522.1992 ⑤

LE SALON

The lobby lounge is the place for a cup of Earl Grey with all the trimmings: tiny sandwiches, dainty pastries, scones with clotted cream, and fresh strawberries. Cushioned chairs and chamber music attract ladies who lunch and a fashionable after-work crowd that meets here for power teas. ♦ Daily seatings at 2 and 4:30PM. Reservations recommended. 596.4713 ⑤

A Jazz Casino Company Property

33 HARRAH'S NEW ORLEANS CASINO

Located across the street from the French Quarter on Canal Street, this is the only land-based casino in Louisiana. There are five separate gaming areas, 100,000 sq. ft. in all, and a 250-seat buffet restaurant. With 2,900 slots and craps, blackjack and baccarat tables, you can win (or lose) your money any way you like. Valet and free parking make it even easier. Mardi gras parades take place daily. ♦ Canal St (between Pl de France and S Peters St). 800/VIP-JAZZ, 533.6000; www.harrahsneworleans.com

34 CANAL STREET FERRY TERMINAL

Here is where you pick up a ferry to take you on a picturesque glide across the Mississippi, past looming freighters, tugboats, barges, and paddle wheelers that crowd one of the world's busiest ports. The Canal Street ferry connects the East Bank of New Orleans with historic Algiers, an isolated West Bank city that can be dangerous, especially after dark. If you choose to stay on board, the round trip takes

about 25 minutes. The illuminated twin bridges and city skyline are spectacular at night, but remember that the ferry makes its last round-trip crossing to Algiers at 11:30PM. ♦ Free for pedestrians; cars pay for return trip only. Daily 6AM-11:30PM. Canal St (east of Pl de France). 364.8114 ⑤

35 UNION TERMINAL

Amtrak trains and **Greyhound** buses call this home. Splashy WPA-style murals trace Louisiana history to cushion the wait. ♦ Daily 24 hours. Loyola Ave (between S Rampart and Girod Sts). 528.1610

36 GALLIER HALL

One of the city's most brilliant examples of the Greek Revival style, this structure was designed by **James Gallier Sr.** and built between 1845 and 1850. Six Ionic columns support an ornate pediment, with figures representing blind Justice, Commerce (loaded down with barrels, bales, trunks, and other symbols of trade), and Liberty (sporting a Phrygian cap). In the mid-19th century, New Orleans's fractious factions divided the city into three separate municipalities: The French Quarter was the First Municipality, the American Sector was the Second Municipality, and Faubourg Marigny was the Third Municipality. This was the city hall for the governing body of the Second Municipality. In the 1950s, a modern structure was built to house New Orleans's City Hall and the government offices were relocated there. Now a private office building, **Gallier Hall** is not open to the public for tours, but the New Orleans Recreation Department (NORD) stages six productions (usually musicals) each year in a basement theater with a separate entrance at 705 Lafayette Street. ♦ 545 St. Charles Ave (between Lafayette and Poydras Sts). 565.7457, NORD theater schedules and tickets 565.7860

37 BEST WESTERN PARC ST. CHARLES

$$$ Centrally located on Lafayette Square, the hotel is within walking distance of the **Convention Center, Superdome,** and **Riverwalk Marketplace**. Each of the 120 comfortable guest rooms is furnished in a contemporary style and contains two queen-size beds. Executive level accommodations have in-room fax, data ports, printers and copy machines. Additional amenities include a fitness center, an outdoor pool, and a gourmet restaurant, **Gerard's Downtown** (see page 60). Guests are served a complimentary continental breakfast in the lobby lounge area. Valet parking is available for an additional fee. ♦

Restaurants/Clubs: Red | Hotels: Purple | Shops: Orange | Outdoors/Parks: Green | Sights/Culture: Blue

500 St. Charles Ave (at Poydras St).
539.9000; 800/272.4373; fax 522.9060
Within the Best Western Parc St. Charles:

GERARD'S DOWNTOWN

★★★$$$ After a 14-year stint as executive chef at **Mr. B's Bistro,** Gerard Maras now commands his own bistro in the **Parc St. Charles** hotel. Iron gates decorated with stained glass inserts grace the entrance, and stained glass is repeated in a wall separating the dining area from the kitchen. With mahogany accents, beautiful chandeliers, tables napped in linen, fine bone china, crystal and fresh flowers, it is one of the most romantic restaurants in the city. The innovative menu is grounded in classic French style. Start with baked oysters on the half shell with bacon and jalapeño cream sauce and wilted lettuce. Entrées such as lobster ravioli with homemade duram pasta, Maine lobster and sauce Americaine; herb-crusted lamb chops with satin potatoes and pear and chili chutney; and garlic roasted chicken aubergine with sage and natural juices are a few house specialties. Whatever precedes it, Gerard's signature dessert—Theobroma, or food for the gods, which combines chocolate-raspberry cake and a rich, bittersweet chocolate soup— must be sampled. ◆ Contemporary French ◆ Tu-F lunch and dinner, Sa dinner. 525-0200

38 THE BON TON CAFE

★★★$$$ The entrance to this urbane 1840s building is flanked by gaslights and canopy, but the (mostly) formal ambience is lightened by red-and-white checkered tablecloths and food that is pure bayou country. If you want to sample Cajun cuisine in a nontouristy setting, join the local crowd here for crawfish bisque, fried soft-shell crab, spicy turtle soup, or eggplant, shrimp, and crabmeat étoufée. Opened in 1953, this family-run spot has a long-standing tradition of doing things in *bon ton* (French for style). ◆ Cajun ◆ M-F lunch and dinner. Reservations recommended for dinner. 401 Magazine St (at Natchez St). 524.3386 &

39 MOTHER'S

★★$ Rich and famous guests of the swank **Windsor Court** (such as Kevin Costner, Kathleen Turner, and food critic Mimi Sheraton) sneak across the street to line up for breakfast with the local laborers, bluebloods, artists, and office workers who crowd one of New Orleans's favorite dives. Order grits and biscuits with

---

In the Louisiana Purchase—perhaps the greatest land deal in history—Napoleon sold the United States nearly 600 million acres for $15 million. That amounts to about four cents an acre.

"debris" (gravy thick with the bits of beef that shred off the roast) or "black ham" (burnt, sugary end pieces). The plate lunches are an inexpensive introduction to Creole cuisine and the po-boys are piled high. ◆ American/ Creole ◆ Daily breakfast, lunch, and dinner. 401 Poydras St (at Natchez St). 523.9656

40 W HOTEL

$$$ This New York-style hotel is raising plenty of eyebrows with the locals for its high-concept urban chic, modern styling and model-worthy staff. Convenient to the **Convention Center, Superdome,** and the Warehouse/Arts District, this concrete highrise has 443 rooms geared to the business traveler, with in-room Internet access and meeting rooms wired with the latest in telecommunications. There is a restaurant, and the dramatic lobby bar, **Whiskey Blue,** is a happening singles spot. ◆ 333 Poydras St. (at Tchoupitoulas St). 525.9444; fax 525.3156; www.whotels.com &

41 WORLD TRADE CENTER

Huge plate-glass windows at street level are filled with a colorful collection of flags from the many consulates and foreign agencies that are quartered in this riverside high-rise. The changing art exhibits in the lobby are worth a look. ◆ 2 Canal St (just east of Pl de France). 581.4888 &

Within the World Trade Center:

TOP OF THE MART

Sunset is the best time to watch the town light up from the 500-seat revolving cocktail lounge on the 33rd floor. The deck travels at a leisurely three feet per minute, making one revolution (past cityscape and river) every hour and a half. The tableside windowsill is stationary, though, so don't stash handbags or packages there. Even though this lounge could do with a little sprucing up, the view is top rate. ◆ One (expensive) drink minimum. M-F 10AM-midnight; Sa 11AM-1AM; Su 2PM-midnight. Patrons must be 18 or older. 522.9795 &

42 SPANISH PLAZA

This huge open expanse, paved in intricate mosaic tiles, was a 1976 bicentennial gift from Spain. A fountain splashes 50 feet into the air, its base inlaid with vibrant Iberian coats of arms. The sprawling front yard of **Riverwalk Marketplace,** this is the point of embarkation for several paddle wheelers (you'll see the ticket kiosk) and the scene of a rowdy masked ball, free to anyone in costume, on the eve of Mardi Gras. Outdoor concerts, fireworks, and other special events are scheduled year-round. ◆ Canal St (east of Pl de France) &

43 NEW ORLEANS HILTON RIVERSIDE

$$$ One of the interior stairways here leads directly into the **Riverwalk Marketplace,** so guests can cover the waterfront from Canal Street to the **Convention Center** with no breaks in air conditioning—a significant plus in summer. The hotel's 1,600 guest rooms (including 78 suites) sprawl around a soaring lobby atrium. A well-equipped business center offers fax, computer, and photocopying services, and the **Rivercenter Racquet and Health Club** (556.3742) is the city's best fitness facility, with an outdoor jogging track; indoor tennis, racquetball, and squash courts; a golf clinic; and a swimming pool, among other amenities. ♦ 2 Poydras St (east of Convention Center Blvd). 561.0500, 800/445.8667; fax 568.1721; www.neworleanshilton.com &

Within the New Orleans Hilton Riverside:

PETE FOUNTAIN NIGHT CLUB

The famous New Orleans clarinetist moved from his Bourbon Street club to this plush red room when the **Hilton** opened in 1977. Shows are Tuesday, Wednesday, Friday, and Saturday at 10PM when Fountain's in town; the club is closed when he's on the road. ♦ Cover. Reservations required. Third floor. 523.4374 &

KABBY'S

★★$$$ The big attraction is a 200-foot glass wall with smashing dockside views. Paddle wheelers embarking just outside create the strange sensation that the dining room backs away from the boats, rather than vice versa, and passing freighters fill the frame. The brunch buffet on Sundays and holidays is one of the best in town, patronized by locals, as well as visitors. The regular menu offers well-prepared regional seafood dishes and steaks. Mississippi Mud Pie is too appropriate to pass up. ♦ Seafood ♦ Tu-Sa lunch and dinner; Su brunch. Reservations recommended for dinner. 584.3880 &

44 RIVERWALK MARKETPLACE

More than 140 shops and restaurants line broad interior walkways alive with colorful vending carts and strolling entertainers. Floor-to-ceiling windows frame sweeping views of the Mississippi for a cool half-mile ramble from the foot of Canal Street to the **Convention Center**. The **Rouse Company,** which developed South Street Seaport in New York and similar complexes in other cities, built the marketplace in 1984. Chain outlets here include **The Sharper Image, Abercrombie & Fitch, Banana Republic, Crabtree & Evelyn, The Nature Company, Victoria's Secret, The Body Shop,** and **Eddie Bauer.** This complex made national headlines when it was side-swiped by a freighter in December 1996, resulting in 100 minor injuries, but no deaths. The *Bright Field,* bound for Japan with 128 million pounds of corn, lost power and demolished a section of the mall (along with several waterfront units of the **New Orleans Hilton Riverside**). The crippled freighter remained in its accidental berth until the first week of January 1997, when officials determined that it could be removed without further damage to the landside structures. The unaffected portions of the mall were back in business for the Super Bowl a few weeks later, and reconstruction has since restored this waterfront extravaganza to full service. ♦ M-Sa 10AM-9PM; Su 11AM-7PM. 522.1555 &

Within Riverwalk Marketplace:

DEVILLE BOOKS AND PRINTS

Strong on art books, this locally owned shop also stocks a good collection of works by local authors, as well as posters, prints, and maps. ♦ Daily. 595.8916. Also at: 344 Carondelet St (at Perdido St). 525.1846 &

45 ERNEST N. MORIAL CONVENTION CENTER

Paris got an Eiffel Tower for its World Exhibition; the Paris of the Americas got a convention center. But New Orleans wasn't short-changed from an economic standpoint. With a total enclosed space of nearly 3 million square feet in 18 separate halls, the sleek facade distinguishes one of the most sophisticated meeting facilities in the US. Designed by **Perez Architects** and **Billes/Manning Architects** and named for former mayor Ernest "Dutch" Morial, it was originally built for the 1984 World's Fair. Today the riverfront complex (an easy walk from most major hotels) helps New Orleans maintain its standing as one of the top six convention destinations in the country. ♦ 900 Convention Center Blvd (between Thalia and Julia Sts). 582.3000; fax 582.3088 &

R&B musician Dr. John got an early start in show business: He was an Ivory Snow baby.

WAREHOUSE/ARTS DISTRICT

Black turtlenecks have replaced blue collars in the Warehouse/Arts District, and the cocktail chatter of gallery hoppers tinkles along streets that once rang with "tote that barge" and "lift that bale." The SoHo of the South is still a bit sleepy compared to the New York original, but the picturesque 19th-century warehouses and office buildings are snapping wide awake at the hands of noisy and energetic young tenants. A first-class collection of art galleries is the major attraction, but visitors also flock to the rambunctious **Louisiana Children's Museum** and nightclubs like **The Howlin' Wolf** and **The Praline Connection Gospel and Blues Hall**, while serious diners make pilgrimages to **Emeril's** and **The Praline Connection.**

The first Saturday of each month marks the opening of new exhibits on **Julia Street's** Gallery Row, a festive opportunity to meet the latest arrivals on the local and national scene. And on the first Saturday in October, the entire district is transformed into one big block party for the annual event called Art for Arts' Sake, which draws thousands of artists, art lovers, and voyeurs to the streets.

The K&B Corporation could rightfully be called the angel of this ongoing renaissance. In 1973, when the corporate headquarters for the local drugstore chain moved to its present location at **Lee Circle**, the company donated its former home—an enormous old warehouse on **Camp Street**—to a group of contemporary artists who were struggling to mount an exhibit of their work. The enthusiastic response to that first show spurred the development of a vast multidimensional facility, which debuted in 1976 as the **Contemporary Arts Center (CAC).**

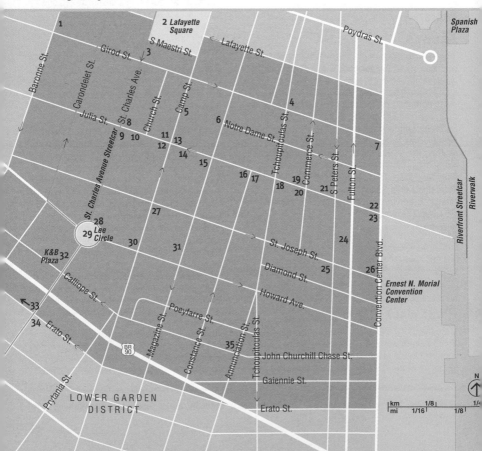

Meanwhile, escalating rents in the French Quarter had already forced many galleries to leave their quaint cottages and move uptown to **Magazine Street**. When the CAC exploded on the scene, pioneers like Arthur Roger and Simonne Stern relocated on nearby Julia Street. More and more dealers followed, and the pace really began to pick up with the advent of the 1984 World's Fair. In the early 1980s, as riverfront wharves were being razed to make way for pavilions and playgrounds, visions of zillions of visitors (and dollars) began dancing in the heads of shop owners and real estate developers. Chic condos sprouted in spruced-up buildings along **South Peters** and **Fulton Streets**, near the exposition site. (The World's Fair, incidentally, was what is known in theatrical circles as an artistic success and a financial disaster.)

Before all the fuss, what is now called the Warehouse/Arts District was merely a backwater region of the Central Business District. Even now the boundaries tend to blur and merge, but most of the action is concentrated in a pocket of the CBD bounded by the riverfront and **Baronne, Calliope**, and **Lafayette Streets**.

1 YA/YA

For once, you can feel good about where your tax dollars go. Funding from the National Endowment for the Arts (among other major sponsors) helps support the energy and creativity that abound in this studio/gallery. Owner and artist Jana Napoli works with the internationally acclaimed YA/YA (Young Aspirations/Young Artists), a private, nonprofit arts and social service organization for inner-city residents ages 14 to 24. Their bold images and designs transform ordinary wooden furniture and decorative objects into vibrant masterworks that have been exhibited in New York, Los Angeles, Paris, Milan, Tokyo, and Amsterdam. YA/YA students also paint murals and print fabric for original garments and upholstery. Sales proceeds are split as follows: 50 percent goes to the student and his/her family; 30 percent is placed in trust for college; and 20 percent goes back into the organization to purchase supplies and materials. ♦ M-F; Sa by appointment; summer hours vary. 628 Baronne St (between Girod and Lafayette Sts). 529.3306; fax 524.7432 &

1 ESTUDIO/GALLERY

Artists Zella Funck and Martin LaBorde occupy some 2,500 square feet above the YA/YA workshop. Abstract paintings and ceramics by Funck, an award winner in the Tokyo International Silk Screen Conference, are also exhibited at the World Trade Center in Hong Kong and the National Museum of Women in the Arts. Her new series of free-standing screens, embellished with everything from dancehall girls to Italian cathedrals, make glamorous and functional room dividers. LaBorde's intriguing "magic of the moment" paintings are populated with stars and wizards. You can see his fanciful murals splashed across the facade of **The Upperline Restaurant**. LaBorde also exhibits in Mexico and Germany and has received the Pushkin Medal of Honor of the Soviet Union. His works can be purchased through the **Martin LaBorde Gallery** in the French Quarter (see page 27). ♦ By appointment only. 630-B Baronne St (between Girod and Lafayette Sts), Second floor. 524.7982

Jana's B&B

1 JANA'S B&B

$$$ If you really want to dive into the local art scene, here's the perfect jumping-off point. Artist Jana Napoli rents three avant-garde apartments on the third and fourth floors of her 1840s town house, located above the working studios for YA/YA and **Estudio/Gallery**. You'll be surrounded by whimsical creations in the two-bedroom/two-bathroom front unit on the third floor, where the parlor is enlivened by surreal "music-scroll" chairs and other YA/YA furnishings, and one of the beds is made from the former altar of a local Carmelite mission. Indonesian shadow puppets, silk kimonos, and striking original paintings cover the walls. A smaller loft suite on the third floor, starkly modern, has large

operable skylights that overlook nearby rooftops and CBD skyscrapers. Both share a large and well-equipped kitchen. The kitchen's French doors open onto a landscaped back deck with nighttime views of the sparkling lights that outline the Mississippi River bridges and **St. Patrick's Church**. An interior window frames Napoli's working studio. A narrow stairway leads to the simple fourth-floor unit, with a microwave and small bathroom, plus great views from skylight windows. All units are supplied with (do-it-yourself) coffee, fruit, pastries, and yogurt. You can walk to the French Quarter, CBD, and Warehouse District by day, but be aware that the surrounding blocks are virtually deserted at night. ◆ 628 Baronne St (between Girod and Lafayette Sts), Third floor. 524.6473

2 LAFAYETTE SQUARE

Ⓟ The cool expanse of green grass, shade trees, and statuary was originally laid out in 1788, making it the second-oldest square in town, after Place d'Armes (now Jackson Square) in the French Quarter. In the 19th century, when New Orleans was a divided city, each square served as the center of religious and social activity: the Place d'Armes for the French Creoles and Lafayette Square for the Americans. This square was christened in honor of the 1825 visit of the Marquis de Lafayette, a great friend of New Orleans. At its center, in a spot once occupied by a statue of the king of Spain, stands a likeness of statesman Henry Clay. Originally erected in 1860 at the intersection of Canal Street and St. Charles Avenue, the statue was moved to this site in 1901. ◆ Bounded by Camp St and St. Charles Ave, and S and N Maestri Sts

On Lafayette Square:

STATUE OF JOHN MCDONOGH

Facing St. Charles Avenue, this affectionate tribute honors the philanthropist who left large endowments for several New Orleans public schools that still bear his name. Appropriately, McDonogh is depicted with young children at his feet. Until his death in 1850, he was regarded as an eccentric old miser (to save ferry fare, he regularly crossed the Mississippi in a rowboat) with radical ideas. He believed slaves should be educated, so he set up schools and a work-for-wages system to help them buy their freedom.

3 LAFAYETTE HOTEL

$$$ Here are some of the loveliest hotel rooms in New Orleans, overlooking the major parade route for Carnival and with views of the **St. Charles Avenue Streetcar** line and charming Lafayette Square the rest of the year. Built by the Wirth family in 1916, the small brick hotel also housed their pharmacy. During World War II, the hotel was leased to

the US Navy and the rooms were outfitted with bunk beds to quarter female enlistees. By 1946, the Waves were gone and, over the years, the building deteriorated. In 1991, developers Mickey Palmer and Patrick Quinn restored the property and, $6 million later, reopened it as a small and intimate hotel. Four-poster beds, upholstered easy chairs, and English botanical prints grace the 24 rooms and 20 suites. Marble baths have brass fittings, terry robes, hair dryers, and Swiss-milled soaps. All suites are furnished with marble wet bars; four have Jacuzzis. Full-length windows in some second-floor rooms open onto balconies—a premium luxury at Mardi Gras, which is reflected in the seasonal rates. ◆ 600 St. Charles Ave (at S Maestri St). 539.9000, 800/270.7542; fax 523.7327; www.neworleanscollection.com

Within the Lafayette Hotel:

ᴹᴵᴷᴱ DITKAS

New Orleans

MIKE DITKA'S

★★★$$$ The former Saints coach—not exactly beloved by the locals—is the name behind the incredible steaks served up at this companion restaurant to **Iron Mike's** in Chicago. Chef Christian Karcher offers a variety of oyster dishes along with signature slabs of beef and an incredible double-cut pork chop. A cigar bar is onsite. Live music is offered on weekends and sometimes during the week in an adjacent bar. Huge plate-glass windows overlook St. Charles Avenue and Lafayette Square. Valet parking is available. ◆ American ◆ M-Sa breakfast, M-F lunch and dinner; Sa-dinner. ◆ 569-8989

4 VIC'S KANGAROO CAFE

A friendly gang of neighborhood artists frequents everyone's favorite Aussie pub, a long skinny room with a scarred wooden bar and loads of down-under atmosphere. There's also a very limited menu, but food is a minor (and unappealing) sideline. Eat elsewhere, then stop here for good darts and great beer, plus live music every Saturday night. ◆ Daily. 636 Tchoupitoulas St (between Girod and Lafayette Sts). 524.4329

5 ST. PATRICK'S CHURCH

Irish immigrants established a parish here in the 1830s after French Quarter Creoles made it clear that God spoke only *en français* at **St. Louis Cathedral**. This tall, slender, Gothic Revival church (illustrated at right) was designed by Irish architects **Charles and James Dakin** who modeled it after England's York Minster. It was completed by **James Gallier Sr.,** who was responsible for most of the interior, with its high vaulted and ribbed ceilings in the nave and sanctuary. (Born **James Gallagher,** the famous Irish-American architect also designed **Gallier Hall,** which stands right across Lafayette Square.) The church is celebrated for its lovely stained-glass windows and the three large murals over the altar, painted in 1841 by Leon Pomerede. **St. Louis Cathedral** was being rebuilt in 1851, so it was here that Bishop Antoine Blanc became the first archbishop of the fourth archdiocese in the US. Services are still conducted here; traditionalists may enjoy the Latin Mass on Sunday at 9:45AM. ♦ 724 Camp St (between Julia and Girod Sts). 525.4413

6 NEW ORLEANS SCHOOL OF GLASSWORKS & PRINTMAKING STUDIO

The South's largest contemporary glassworking and printmaking facility, this is one of the few nonuniversity facilities in the US that teaches glassblowing, printmaking, and bookbinding to the general public. If you can't attend the regular six-week sessions, two-day classes and private lessons are available. Casual visitors are always welcome to watch the faculty and assisting artists in the work area. Masters demonstrate blowing and casting techniques in front of an 850-pound recycling furnace filled with molten glass. Finished pieces for sale are on display in the gallery and front windows. Shoppers/collectors may find anything from elegant Venetian-style goblets to hand-bound books to glass architectural models. The gallery is open year-round, but the hot shop is closed from June through September, when kiln-fired glassworks are created. ♦ M-Sa. 727 Magazine St (between Julia and Girod Sts). 529.7277

7 WYNDHAM RIVERFRONT HOTEL

$$$ Ornate gilded columns flank the entryway to the old rice mill that has been restored as the main entrance to this high-rise hotel. Two modern wings extend on either side. The facility's 202 guest rooms are tailored and sedate with muted taupe walls and drapes, dark wood furnishings, and beds dressed in neutral stripes. Coffeemakers, dataports and voice mail, hair dryers, irons, and other in-room comforts ease the stay. Just one block away from the **Ernest N. Morial Convention Center,** the hotel provides such amenities as exercise facilities, business services, lobby lounge, and restaurant. ♦ 701 Convention Center Blvd (at Girod St). 524.8200, 800/WYNDHAM; fax 524.0600; www.wyndham.com &

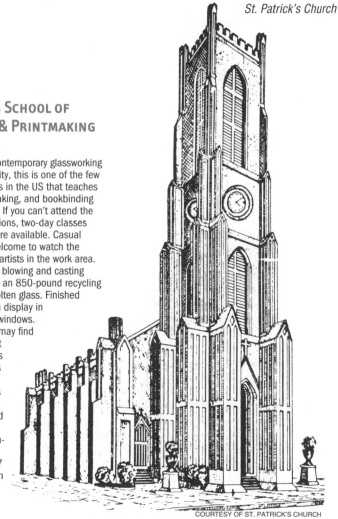

St. Patrick's Church

COURTESY OF ST. PATRICK'S CHURCH

Restaurants/Clubs: **Red** | Hotels: **Purple** | Shops: **Orange** | Outdoors/Parks: **Green** | Sights/Culture: **Blue**

CAUGHT ON FILM

If you believe the movies, New Orleans is a place where women spell trouble, city folks speak with an Alabama country drawl, and every day is Mardi Gras. Summer heat and spicy food spark passion instead of heartburn, and shopworn hookers and tap-dancing street urchins know all the city's secrets. When the Dixieland music swells, a hurricane is brewing and somebody's going to get chased through a dark warehouse filled with Carnival floats. For these and more sweet lies, check out:

Angel Heart (1987) Lisa Bonet is a modern voodoo princess, Mickey Rourke plays Mickey Rourke, and Robert De Niro may or may not be the devil in Alan Parker's steamy thriller set in and around New Orleans.

The Big Easy (1987) Former District Attorney Jim Garrison (see *JFK*, below) appears in a cameo role in this torrid crime romance that pairs homicide detective Dennis Quaid with assistant D.A. Ellen Barkin. The music's hot (and so are the sex scenes), but Quaid's accent is all over the regional map. Where y'at, cher?

Blaze (1989) Paul Newman plays maverick Louisiana governor Earl Long in this fact-based tale that focuses on Long's love affair with a young stripper named Blaze Starr.

The Buccaneer (1958) See Yul Brynner with hair—swashbuckling through the swamps of Barataria and romancing the governor's daughter—as pirate Jean Lafitte, comrade of Andy "Old Hickory" Jackson (Charlton Heston) at the Battle of New Orleans.

Cat People (1982) Nastassja Kinski slept at the **Lanaux House Bed & Breakfast** and worked in the gift shop of the **Audubon Zoo** in Paul Schrader's chic, violent, and sexy remake of the 1942 classic. Malcolm McDowell is a scream as her incestuous brother who preaches at a psychedelic storefront church.

Down by Law (1986) Blues singer Tom "I'd Rather Have a Bottle in Front of Me Than a Frontal Lobotomy" Waits is perfectly cast as a backstreet drifter in Jim Jarmusch's eerie portrait of Louisiana lowlife.

Easy Rider (1969) After they finally get to Mardi Gras, ill-fated bikers Peter Fonda and Dennis Hopper acquire a couple of professional dates, drop acid, dine at a grand Creole restaurant, and trip among the crumbling tombs of an aboveground cemetery.

Interview with the Vampire (1994) Local lion Anne Rice initially objected to the casting of Tom Cruise as her beloved Lestat, but she pulled in her claws after she saw his performance in this opulent production. **River Road** plantations and the **French Quarter** provide atmospheric backdrops, especially **Oak Alley,** which stands in for **Pointe du Lac,** ancestral home of the vampire Louis (Brad Pitt).

JFK (1991) Oliver Stone's film about the Kennedy assassination is almost as controversial as the conspiracy theories that obsessed former New Orleans D.A. Jim Garrison.

King Creole (1958) Elvis Presley plays a man's man who sings and gets into lots of fistfights and woman trouble. This time he's doing it in the French Quarter.

The Pelican Brief (1993) In this adaptation of the John Grisham bestseller, Julia Roberts plays a **Tulane** law student who solves the murder of two Supreme Court justices. Denzel Washington costars as the crusading reporter who helps her unravel the mystery.

Panic in the Streets (1950) Richard Widmark stars as a doctor who helps the New Orleans police scour the city for a killer (Jack Palance) infected with a contagious plague.

Pretty Baby (1978) Brooke Shields lost her anonymity in Louis Malle's scandalous, but gorgeous, film about a child prostitute sold to the highest bidder at a jazz-age brothel. Many of the scenes were filmed in the faded grandeur of the **Columns** hotel.

A Streetcar Named Desire (1951) Marlon Brando. Vivien Leigh. Tennessee Williams. Need we say more?

The Swarm (1978) Sorry to spoil the suspense, but we can't keep this to ourselves: The city is saved when a bee-encrusted Volkswagen is s-l-o-w-l-y driven through the French Quarter and into the Superdome, where maintenance guys crank up the air conditioner until the killer swarm goes dormant.

Suddenly Last Summer (1960) Based on Tennessee Williams's *Garden District,* an old-line matriarch (Katharine Hepburn) is doubly traumatized by revelations that her late son was a homosexual and that her niece (Elizabeth Taylor) appeared on a public beach in a white bathing suit.

Walk on the Wild Side (1962) In one of her early saucy roles, Jane Fonda plays a young girl sucked into the life of prostitution in a New Orleans whorehouse. Anne Baxter and Barbara Stanwyck also star.

Wild at Heart (1990) Laura Dern and Nicolas Cage take off on a cross-country crime spree in David Lynch's twisted travelogue that loops right through the Big Easy.

8 KINKO'S

This is a handy place to know about if you need to fax, photocopy, or rent computer time (Apple Macintosh or IBM) at 4AM, and it's also a great way for harried procrastinators to meet kindred spirits. ◆ Daily 24 hours. 762 St. Charles Ave (at Julia St). 581.2541; fax 525.6272

9 HUMMINGBIRD GRILL

★$ A seedy dive sitting under a flophouse, this unlikely wee-hours haunt draws an eclectic crowd: tipsy debutantes, cops, cab drivers, street people, and businesspeople in perfectly tailored suits. There is no cuisine here, just plain down-home food. Breakfast is served anytime and the portions are prodigious. Dig into bacon and eggs, buttery grits, and big biscuits. The Virginia ham and pork chops are great, but avoid the pancakes, which are bright yellow—a startling sight after a hard night on the town. Be sure to save room for pie. ◆ American ◆ Daily 24 hours. 804 St. Charles Ave (between St. Joseph and Julia Sts). 523.9165

10 MARGUERITE OESTREICHER FINE ARTS

Oestreicher's homegrown collection includes the estate of American master Milton Avery, along with paintings by his wife Sally M. Avery and daughter March Avery, who carry on the family tradition, and incredible works on found fabric, hand sewn by Gina Phillips. Be sure to notice the haunting faces painted by Margaret Witherspoon and ethereal abstracts by Raine Bedsole. The collection also features works by Alexander Stolin, John Geldersma, Edward Schmidt, Tom Woodruff, Gary Komarin, Joseph Cornell, and Balthus. ◆ Tu-Sa; hours vary in August. 626 Julia St (between Camp St and St. Charles Ave). 581.9253; fax 566.1946 &

11 WYNDY MOREHEAD FINE ARTS

Both the serious art collector and the casual browser are welcome at this friendly gallery. Morehead's international stable of artists includes anyone from emerging regional talents to nationally established stars. Organic surrealist pieces by Bernard Mattox, influenced by archaeological digs in Central and South America, are skewed miniatures of primitive architectural details. Don't miss Sandi Grow's

stylized elongated horses. Sculptures and paintings outside are displayed in the courtyard, and even the bathroom is filled with art. ◆ M-Sa. 603 Julia St (between Camp and Church Sts). 568.9754; fax 568.9755 &

12 PRESERVATION RESOURCE CENTER OF NEW ORLEANS

A driving force behind many of the New Orleans preservationist movements, including development of the Warehouse District, this organization is appropriately quartered in a historic 1832 town house. (The 600 block of Julia Street—known as **Julia Row** or the **Thirteen Sisters**—is lined with 13 such town houses that were posh private residences in the 19th century.) The center maintains extensive archives. It also spearheads the ongoing Operation Comeback program to revitalize the adjacent Lower Garden District. Walking and bus tours of city architecture are available to individuals or groups, but only by appointment with 24 hours notice. ◆ Fee for tours. M-F. 604 Julia St (between Camp St and St. Charles Ave). 581.7032; fax 522.9275

G·E·O·R·G·E S·C·H·M·I·D·T
G   A   L   L   E   R   Y

12 GEORGE SCHMIDT GALLERY

No middleman here. Established local artist and scholar George Schmidt runs his own gallery, offering etchings, oils, and drawings that explore themes from *Hadrian in the Office of Gaius the Jurist* to *Nick LaRocca at the Corner of Royal and Canal, 1915.* ("Peel back the veneer of New Orleans and you see ancient Rome," he says.) This fascinating character is also founder and lead singer of the city's beloved New Leviathan Oriental Fox Trot Orchestra. Seven of his murals depicting the history of Mardis Gras are on permanent display in Pete's Pub in the Hotel Intercontinental. ◆ M-Sa. 608 Julia St (between Camp St and St. Charles Ave). 524.8137; www.georgeschmidt.com &

13 ARIODANTE CONTEMPORARY CRAFT GALLERY

The gallery is small, but so are most of the contemporary fine crafts on display. Changing shows present exquisite handmade ceramics, glass sculptures, jewelry, and furniture. Available only between Thanksgiving and Christmas, ornaments (priced from $5 up) are created from porcelain, turned wood, handblown glass, and other distinctive materials. ◆ Tu-Sa May-Oct; M-Sa Nov-Apr. 535 Julia St (between Magazine and Camp Sts). 524.3233 &

---

14 GALERIE SIMONNE STERN

One of the oldest contemporary art galleries in New Orleans, this represents mid-career and nationally recognized artists. Regional artists include: George Dunbar, Richard Johnson, Simon Gunning, Hasmig Vartanian, Nicole Charbonnet, and Jeffrey Cook. Recent exhibits have featured the work of John Alexander, Fletcher Benton, Bryan Hunt, Margaret Evangeline, James McGarrell, Albert Paley. ♦ T-Sa. 518 Julia St (between Magazine and Camp Sts). 529.1118; fax 525.7030; www.sterngallery.com

15 NEW ORLEANS AUCTION GALLERIES, INC.

An all-woman staff of auctioneers creates an unusual atmosphere and fast pace (100 to 125 lots per hour) at estate auctions scheduled every seven to eight weeks. If you can't be in town but see something you like in the showroom, leave an absentee bid or make arrangements to bid by phone. Fine antiques, silver, paintings, works on paper, sculpture, glass, jewelry, rare books, and documents are shipped to clients worldwide. ♦ M-F. 801 Magazine St (at Julia St). 566.1849; fax 566.1851 &

16 HERIARD-CIMINO GALLERY

The minimalist point of view prevails in this stark white space that features the richly textured abstracts of Barcelona painter Joan Duran, the bold strokes and bright colors of Hunt Slonem's lush exotics, and New Orleanian Martin Peyton's sculptures that weld industrialized materials into African symbols. ♦ M-Sa. 440 Julia St (between Constance and Magazine Sts). 525.7300; fax 525.7333 &

ARTHUR ROGER GALLERY

16 ARTHUR ROGER GALLERY

Exhibitions here, mounted by nationally known curators, have included Bill Fagaly's *Preacher Art,* with works by Sister Gertrude Morgan and Reverend Howard Finster. Roger primarily represents well-established artists like Ida Kohlmeyer, whose paintings and sculptures are among the collections at New York's Metropolitan Museum of Art and the Smithsonian Institution; her exuberant *Aquatic Colonnade,* 20 painted metal sculptures on 16-foot columns, can be seen in New Orleans at the **Aquarium of the Americas.** Roger says he searches "for things that appeal to young collectors as well as connoisseurs." The

5,000-square-foot exhibit space, created by architect **Wellington Reiter,** received a prestigious Alpha Group award for excellence in interior design. ♦ M-Sa. 432 Julia St (at Constance St). 522.1999; fax 522.6999; www.heriard-cimino.com &

17 LOUISIANA CHILDREN'S MUSEUM

A sturdy old warehouse is the perfect home for this hands-feet-and-everything-else-on museum, geared for the young and inquisitive set. Here, if you blow a bubble so big you can stand in it, a sign reminds you to think about how things look and sound from inside. Climb on a stationary bike, and the mechanized Mr. Bones, in safety helmet and goggles, pedals alongside while you take your pulse and listen to your heartbeat. Strike a pose against a phosphorescent wall, and jump back to see your trapped shadow. At the child-size supermarket, little consumers make grocery lists, shop, and ring up their purchases on a real cash register. At the **Kidwatch TV** station, they take turns at a tiny anchor desk, complete with cue cards and weather map, and work the cameras themselves. **First Adventures** is a play space where the under-three crowd can tumble, jump, get messy, and even (fat chance) rest. A favorite with adults is **Recollections II,** kinetic video "painting" with your body on a larger-than-life screen. Gentle memos—see, hear, feel, think—are everywhere, because it's so easy to forget that it's all (yuck) educational. ♦ Admission. Daily June-Sept; Tu-Su Oct-May. 420 Julia St (between Tchoupitoulas and Constance Sts). 523.1357; www.lcm.org &

18 EMERIL'S

★★★★$$$ Emeril Lagasse, former chef at the estimable **Commander's Palace,** exploded on the restaurant scene with this one-man show in 1991; *Esquire* critic John Mariani promptly dubbed it Restaurant of the Year. A recent renovation by designer David Rockwell nixed the industrial look for a (thankfully) sound absorbing mix of exotic wood, a see-through spice wall, and brilliant sunflowers—a real Bam! Everything here, from Worcestershire sauce to ice cream, is made in-house. Start with savory cheesecake studded with lump crabmeat and wild mushrooms or opt for the New Orleans barbecued shrimp with tiny rosemary biscuits. For a main course try the grilled pork chop in a tamarind glaze, edged with roasted sweet potatoes and a green-chile mole sauce. Sweet Gulf shrimp—sautéed with tomato, basil, and garlic—are scattered over "pasta rags" tossed with truffle-infused oil. As for dessert, the exotic fruit sorbets are hardly a sacrifice, but take the plunge and order the famous banana cream pie—with banana crust, caramel sauce, and chocolate shavings. For the ultimate blowout try Emeril's Degustation, a seven-course tasting menu of the chef's latest creations (offerings change daily). A more casual option is to grab one of 10 seats at the **Chef's Food Bar**—a galvanized steel counter with a concrete top, bordering the open kitchen—where—if you get lucky—you can watch one of the nation's premier culinary stars at work. ♦ International ♦ M-F lunch and dinner; Sa dinner. Reservations recommended for dinner. 800 Tchoupitoulas St (at Julia St). 528.9393; fax 558.3925 &

19 CHRISTOPHER MAIER FURNITURE DESIGN

A spectacular cypress armoire, its doors carved with Egyptian-style wings shaded in bronze and gold leaf, is just one of the exotic treasures available from the studio/shop of this talented artisan, who recently opened a second gallery in Los Angeles. Maier's work has been featured in *Vogue, Metropolitan Home,* and *House and Garden,* among other national publications. Fine wood inlays decorate his leopard print table, linen-fold panel bed, coffee table with hand-carved weave design, sunburst mirrors, and dining-room chairs. Some chests and armoires resemble New Orleans cemetery vaults. Smaller gift-sized accessories are also on display. All pieces in the collection can be customized by choice of materials, finish, and dimensions. He also creates "body portraits" in wood. Special orders take around three weeks, and major commissions can take up to 16 weeks. ♦ M-F. 329 Julia St (at Commerce St). 586.9079; fax 586.9095; www.christophermaier.com

20 LEMIEUX GALLERIES

Both novice and experienced collectors flock to this "people's gallery" that represents a large number of Third Coast artists (those who live and work in the five Gulf states, especially Louisiana). Look for urban landscapes by painter Shirley Rabé Masinter and sculptures by Evelyn Menge. The pottery,

jewelry, and other contemporary crafts are affordable as well as aesthetic. ♦ M-Sa; Su by appointment. 332 Julia St (between Commerce and Tchoupitoulas Sts). 522.5988; fax 522.5682 &

20 STILL-ZINSEL CONTEMPORARY FINE ART

The bright white ceiling, walls, and floor add plenty of drama to the works shown here. Surrounded by all that white space, the art seems to float in mid-air. Among the artists represented are Gregory Saunders, also exhibited at the **New Orleans Museum of Art,** who creates double-take original drawings (powder graphite on paper) that resemble manipulated photographs; and Ronna S. Harris, assistant professor of art at **Tulane University's Newcomb College,** whose modern female nudes are equally realistic. ♦ M-Sa. 328 Julia St (at Commerce St). 588.9999; fax 588.1111 &

21 EMBASSY SUITES HOTEL

$$$ A contemporary high-rise that would be more at home next door to an airport, this is the only hotel directly on Julia Street's Gallery Row. The 226 suites are comfortably appointed, many with river views, and a full American breakfast is included in the rate. (The hotel's restaurant also serves lunch and dinner daily.) Registered guests are treated to free drinks from 5 to 7PM in the atrium, which is decorated in a Mardi Gras theme, with images of costumed revelers splashed across the walls. ♦ 315 Julia St (between S Peters and Commerce Sts). 525.1993, 800/EMBASSY; fax 525.3437; www.embassy-suites.com &

22 MULATE'S

★★$$$ The historic Cajun Country roadhouse out in Breaux Bridge (see page 167) is more picturesque, but this city outpost of the "World's Most Famous Cajun Restaurant" has the same great music and freewheeling atmosphere. Here you'll find a hardwood dance floor for foot-stomping, rafters for the raising, and two brands of hot sauce on every table. The food is kind of pricey but delicious, and if you factor in the portion sizes and live entertainment, it's still a good deal. The enormous and colorful zydeco salad is topped with andouille sausage, blackened catfish, shrimp, and quail eggs. A meal-sized appetizer of six crabmeat-stuffed mushrooms, deep fried and as big as golf balls, is a quick and inexpensive alternative. ♦ Cajun ♦ Daily lunch and dinner. 201 Julia St (at Convention Center Blvd). 522.1492 & Also at: 325 Mills St (southwest of Rees St), Breaux Bridge.

318/332.4648, 800/854.9149;
www.mulates.com

23 TRUE BREW COFFEE

★★$ Stop here for a quick shot of iced coffee in a cool, brick-lined cavern. Huge wood support beams, exposed ceiling joists, mismatched antique tables, and walls filled with original art (for sale) add to the bohemian atmosphere. An adjoining theater sometimes presents plays or holds readings on Thursday through Sunday nights. Baked goods (served all day) and salads and sandwiches (Monday through Friday, lunchtime only) are large and imaginative. For fine hot-weather fare, try the whole-wheat pita sandwiches stuffed with curried chicken. Another cool choice is cream cheese on seven-grain bread, spiked with fresh basil and sun-dried tomato relish. The chocolate-covered espresso beans are great, but for a stronger jolt, full bar service is available. ◆ International ◆ Daily. 200 Julia St (at Convention Center Blvd). 524.8441. Also at: 3133 Ponce de Leon St (between N Lopez St and Esplanade Ave). 947.3948 ﾐ

24 THE HOWLIN' WOLF

The live music heard here might be rock, R&B, blues, alternative, jazz, or something completely different. The emphasis is on originality—no oldies or cover bands. Roadhouse groups (Southern Culture on the Skids, The Chicken Wire Gang) are big draws. The young adult crowd is heavy on college students, but this is also a popular haunt of area musicians. Visiting international stars sometimes sit in with local groups. There's no cover on Monday nights, when acoustic performers and songwriters crowd the open mike. ◆ Cover (except Mondays). M, W-F from 3PM; Sa-Su from 5PM. 828 S Peters St (between St. Joseph and Julia Sts). 529.2341, recorded information 523.2551; fax 523.2551 ﾐ

25 THE PRALINE CONNECTION

★★$ Riding the wave of its Faubourg Marigny success, this clean and basic-looking Warehouse District outpost of **The Praline Connection** offers the same Creole soul food, and chefs regularly trade duty at both restaurants to keep the quality consistent. Chicken—baked, stewed, or fried—is simply perfect. Fried seafood, meat loaf, stuffed bell peppers, gumbo, and étouffées are other good bets. Most entrées come with corn bread and a choice of greens or beans. Don't forget to stock up on the namesake homemade candy. ◆ Soul food ◆ Daily lunch and dinner. 901 S Peters St (at St. Joseph St). 523.3973 ﾐ Also at: 542 Frenchmen St (at Chartres St). 943.3934; www.pralineconnection.com

25 THE PRALINE CONNECTION GOSPEL AND BLUES HALL

This 9,000-square-foot hall, formerly a steamboat engine factory, adjoins the Warehouse branch of the celebrated soul food restaurant of the same name. Legend has it that the huge 50-foot carved bar, imported by barge from Chicago, saw duty in a speakeasy owned by Al Capone. The 20-by-30-foot stage is flanked by the actual facades of two historic Uptown houses, and the club's exterior is splashed with exuberant murals of street scenes and jazz musicians. Sunday gospel brunch is a blast, an uptown version of a down-home church supper. ◆ M-Sa lunch and dinner, Su brunch and dinner; call for schedule of live music and special events. 907 S Peters St (between Diamond and St. Joseph Sts). 523.3973ﾐ

26 HOLIDAY INN SELECT

$$ Located just across the street from the **Ernest W. Morial Convention Center,** this six-story hotel fits right in with the 19th-century lofts of the Warehouse District, even though it was built in 1995. The simple graystone facade is trimmed with cornices and friezes and the entry is framed by the triple arches of a bronze-tinted canopy. The hotel's 170 guest rooms open onto elevated hallways that overlook a central atrium. All rooms are fitted with large desks with ergonomic chairs and strategically placed lighting. Other amenities include exercise and game rooms, guest laundry area, a restaurant with room service, and a lobby lounge with a 60-inch television

Confederate President Jefferson Davis died on 6 December 1889 in New Orleans at the home of a friend, cotton merchant Joseph Payne. He was buried in Metairie Cemetery, but several years later his wife decided to move his body to Richmond. A couple of days before the transfer, on 27 and 28 May 1893, Davis's body was laid in state at the Memorial Hall of the Confederate Museum. More than 50,000 people came to pay their respects—an all-time attendance record for the museum.

At the time of the Louisiana Purchase, the city of New Orleans consisted of 4,000 houses and 10,000 residents, which included 5,000 Caucasians, 2,000 free Negroes, and 3,000 slaves.

Lee Circle

KEELY EDWARDS

screen for sports enthusiasts. ♦ 881 Convention Center Blvd (at St. Joseph St). 524.1881, 888/524.1881; fax 528.1005; www.basshotels.com ♿

27 CONTEMPORARY ARTS CENTER (CAC)

The heart of the Warehouse/Arts District throbs within an enormous industrial skeleton, crisscrossed with catwalks and splashed with light. Both showcase and unofficial university, the CAC is staffed by practicing artists and accessible to just about anyone (a sense of humor doesn't hurt). Ever-changing exhibitions command more than 10,000 square feet of gallery space with works that are innovative and challenging, and there are two theaters with a lively schedule of productions by established and emerging playwrights. Integral musical programming pairs sights with sounds, sometimes presenting all-star jams by modern jazz greats who play together for the first—and perhaps only—time. In the early 1970s, a $5-million renovation by Concordia Architects converted the handsome turn-of-the-century warehouse into a 40,000-square-foot masterpiece, incorporating major works of art into the design. Sculptor Gene Koss created the front desk, a spectacular wave of glass plates; Steve Sweet, known for his Xerographic portraits, designed the lobby information board; Tina Girouard made the Lexan panels that frame the elevator shaft with images of Southwestern Louisiana; and architect/furniture designer **Mario Villa's** lighting sconces flank the front entrance. ♦ Admission; free on Thursday. Daily. 900 Camp St (at St. Joseph St). 523.1216, box

office 528.3800; fax 528.3828; www.cacno.org ♿

28 OGDEN MUSEUM OF SOUTHERN ART

Recently opened in a spectacular two-building complex around **Lee Circle,** this vast repository of Southern art is now housed in temporary space at 603 Julia St. The collection includes 18th-century water colors, 19th-, 20th- and 21st-century paintings and ceramics and sculptures. M-F 10-5. Free. ♦ 539.9600; www.ogdenmuseum.org

29 LEE CIRCLE

A stalwart statue of Confederate general Robert E. Lee stands here atop a 60-foot shaft, surrounded by green space and park benches. Lee died in 1870, during Reconstruction, when the political climate delayed any sort of tribute. A fund-raising committee drummed up the required sum by 1876, but various snags postponed completion until 1884. Ironically, New York sculptor Alexander Doyle was commissioned for the job. Ex-Confederate President Jefferson Davis and Confederate General P.G.T. Beauregard were among the dignitaries present at the dedication ceremony. Incidentally, this is about the only place in town where you can get a sense of direction: the general faces steadfastly north. Local wags claim the initials of the nearby YMCA stand for "Yankees May Come Again." ♦ St. Charles and Howard Aves

30 CONFEDERATE MUSEUM

Physically near but spiritually several light-years away from the **CAC,** the second-largest collection of Confederate memorabilia in the US (the largest is in the Museum of the Confederacy in Richmond, VA) is housed in a quaint Romanesque building with a cannon by the front steps. This is Louisiana's oldest museum, designed in 1891 by architect **Thomas Sully.** From the floor to the soaring

---

Restaurants/Clubs: Red | **Hotels: Purple** | **Shops: Orange** | **Outdoors/Parks: Green** | **Sights/Culture: Blue**

24-foot ceiling, the hall is lined in gleaming red cypress and framed by illuminated showcases. An adjoining fireproof room (circa 1900) shelters a collection of fully restored battle flags. In 1893 Confederate President Jefferson Davis's body lay in state in the **Memorial Hall** here before being taken to Richmond for burial. Mrs. Davis donated a large collection of her family's personal memorabilia, and the walls are studded with portraits of the South's greatest men of war. Other treasures include antique guns, swords, and even artillery. Civil War buffs will want to make a stop in the gift shop, where several rare books are for sale. ♦ Admission. M-Sa. 929 Camp St (at Howard Ave). 523.4522

THE NATIONAL
D-DAY MUSEUM
NEW ORLEANS

31 NATIONAL D-DAY MUSEUM

This $21 million living-history tribute to war veterans of World War II is a world-class military archive and the result of decades of work by local historian and writer Dr. Stephen E. Ambrose. The museum is located in New Orleans because Higgins Industries, the manufacturer of the landing craft that delivered US troops onto the beaches at D-Day, was based in New Orleans. Take in the powerful 45-minute film documentary before proceeding through the three floors of exhibits, organized as a chronological, self-guided tour through the war, from the first hints of Nazi aggression to America's mobilization and the sea and air assaults on the beaches of Normandy. The final gallery covers the Allied victory in Europe, ending with a huge mural of the US military cemetery at Omaha Beach, Normandy. Soldier's personal accounts, captured in text and on film, are relayed in mini theaters and oral-history booths throughout the galleries. Personal mementos—a worn bible, letters home, scuffed boots—are especially moving. ♦ 945 Magazine St at Howard Ave. 9-5 daily, except Thanksgiving, Christmas, New Year's Day and Mardi Gras. Admission fee. 527.6012; www.ddaymuseum.org.

During World War II, women all over the US became "Rosie the Riveters," working in factories and shipyards, and New Orleans women were no exception. One local manufacturer of torpedo boats encouraged his employees by playing "The Star Spangled Banner" over the public address system and hanging posters in the bathrooms of Hitler, Mussolini, and Hirohito with the caption: "Come on in. Take it easy. Every minute you loaf helps us plenty."

32 K&B PLAZA

Perhaps as reparation for those bright purple drugstores (since acquired by Rite-Aid) planted all over town, the indoor/outdoor sculpture gallery at the former K&B corporate headquarters is a beautiful addition to the cityscape. The plaza is anchored by *The Mississippi,* a monumental carved granite work by Isamu Noguchi, commissioned for this site and building. *The Virlane Foundation Collection* began with George Rickey's *Four Open Rectangles Excentric, Square Sections.* Since that acquisition, the collection has grown to include works by some of the most important 20th-century American and European contemporary artists. Among them are Frank McGuire's welded steel *Streetcar Stop,* British sculptor Michael Sandle's *The Drummer,* and bronze versions of hand and foot benches by Mexican artist Pedro Friedeberg, best known for his wooden sculptures. For more art, go to the seventh floor to see the world's strangest pendulum clock entitled *Blends of Self Interest* by Nancy Graves, or activate the motion sensor on Peter Vogel's *Sound Barrier* to trigger an electronic serenade. The building, completed in 1963, was designed by the Chicago office of **Skidmore, Owings & Merrill,** and won an Award of Merit from the American Institute of Architects. ♦ Plaza daily 24 hours; indoor gallery M-F 8:30AM-4:30PM. 1055 St. Charles Ave (between Calliope St and Howard Ave). 586.1234

33 UGLESICH'S RESTAURANT

★★★$$ New Orleanians are very snobbish about their dives (the scruffier the better), and here's the undisputed champion of that ongoing one-downsmanship contest. Nowhere in town will you find a worse neighborhood, a dowdier building, or greater food. And the tongue-twisting name (say *YOU-*gla-sitches) scores extra points for style. Order fried oysters and the live bivalves will be shucked before your eyes, dusted with cornmeal, and plopped into sizzling canola oil. Huge "angry shrimp" are spiked with hot chili paste; shrimp Uggie, marinated and smothered in a spicy tomato-based sauce, are heaped over rice; onion rings and fresh-cut fries are perfect; and the beer is extra cold. The dining room is cramped and the chairs are wobbly, but you could sit next to a movie star or famous chef—**Bayona**'s Susan Spicer is a regular. Jovial owner Anthony Uglesich, whose family opened the landmark restaurant in 1924, will probably be stationed behind the oyster bar, where he has worked since 1954. Even with the installation of a new exhaust system, some odor from the open kitchen will cling to your clothes for the rest of the day, but it will only bring back happy memories. Sidewalk tables are available in good weather. ♦ Seafood/Creole ♦ Cash only. M-F lunch. 1238 Baronne St (at Erato St). 523.8571

34 DELMONICO RESTAURANT AND BAR

★★★$$$$ The city was abuzz in 1998 when Chef Emeril Lagasse reopened this local institution, which, in its more than century-long former life, had attracted a daily following among New Orleans's power brokers. The subdued and sophisticated interior is a masterpiece of renovation—rich with wood paneling, Venetian chandeliers, and sumptuous draperies of embroidered taupe Ultrasuede, and accented with fresh, peach-colored roses. Lagasse's well-trained staff presents such reinvented classics as beef Wellington, grilled chicken Clemenceau, mayonnaise-enriched crabmeat Imperial, and the 20-ounce steak Delmonico lavished with marchand de vin sauce. The dapper bar, decorated with sepia photos of gentlemen boxers (who used to work off their lunchtime calories in the old gym formerly located upstairs), also serves an abbreviated menu of elegant hors d'oeuvres, including premium caviar at market cost. ♦ Creole/Continental ♦ M-F lunch and dinner; Sa dinner; Su brunch and dinner. 1300 St. Charles Ave (at Erato St). 525.4937; www.emerils.com

35 SPICE INC.

Susan Spicer, nationally known chef and owner of **Bayona** in the French Quarter, has opened her own gourmet grocery on the ground floor of this former cotton mill—converted to luxury condominiums. Here you'll find kitchenware, exotic ingredients, and international cheeses, as well as ready-made specialties such as Spicer's famous roasted garlic soup, and lavish sandwiches. The fully equipped kitchen doubles as a classroom for several weekly demonstrations by guest chefs and cookbook authors, as well as contemporary cooking seminars and hands-on dinner parties. ♦ Daily. 1051 Annunciation St (at John Churchill Chase St). 558.9995

THE BEST

Jeanne de la Houssaye
Illustrator

I love the FREE MUSIC my city offers! Street musicians in the **Quarter** range from dreadful to delightful, but they all ring with the funky sound of the streets. I can hear a plaintive harmonica player from my studio, and the calliope on the steamboat *Natchez*. One of the players is a virtuoso who renders operatic overtures. **Christ Church Cathedral** has free Sunday afternoon concerts, and the **Downtown Development District** sometimes sponsors Brown Bag concerts in front of **City Hall** and in **Lafayette Square**. And my absolute favorite is eavesdropping on the jazz brunch at **Commander's** from my own front porch.

Riding the STREETCAR is a real New Orleans experience anytime, but especially in the spring, when the yards and neutral grounds explode with azaleas, and at Christmas, when tree lights refract through the leaded glass doors.

Used bookstores are full of literary treasures. One of my favorites is **Beckham's** at 228 Decatur.

New Orleans is a place for WALKING. Some places should only be seen from street level. My favorite is my own neighborhood, the **Garden District**. The gardens in spring—and November, when the acorns are all crunchy and scrunchy underfoot—are especially nice, but any time of year the spreading live oaks, columned houses, and brick sidewalks bring back an era the neighborhood works hard not to forget. **PJ's** coffeehouse at **Washington** and **Prytania** is a good place to take a break, and **Garden District Book Shop**, in the same building, has a great selection of books on New Orleans and the South. The **Riverfront** offers an easy stroll along the levee from the **Aquarium** to the **French Market**. Of course, the **Quarter** can only be seen by foot.

One of the best sandwiches in the world, right up there with a fried oyster po-boy, is the muffuletta at **Central Grocery**, on **Decatur Street** across from the **French Market**. Italian cold cuts and antipasto are heaped on fresh bread, and only a real champ can eat a whole one.

I love to walk the boardwalk trails or paddle a canoe through **Jean Lafitte National Park,** across the river. It offers the startling contrast of a real Louisiana swamp with all the attendant water and wildlife (yes, snakes and maybe alligators) with a view of the New Orleans skyline above the treetops. Awesome!

And the best thing about New Orleans is living here!

Restaurants/Clubs: Red | Hotels: Purple | Shops: Orange | Outdoors/Parks: Green | Sights/Culture: Blue

GARDEN DISTRICT

The name Garden District conjures up an image of horticultural abundance, and there is indeed an Eden of oleanders, jasmine, and bougainvillea here, with added bushy splashes of scarlet, pink, and white azaleas in early spring. Looming above the flowers are banana trees with broad pale green leaves, tall palms, magnolias with snow-white blooms, and gnarled old live oaks trailing tangled shreds of Spanish moss, all providing a colorful backdrop for block after block of posh Greek Revival, Italianate, Victorian, Queen Anne, and Second Empire houses. Many of the large, rambling structures incorporate elements of several different styles, giving the impression that the architect just couldn't resist one last dab of icing on the cake.

The Garden District began to blossom a few years after the 1803 Louisiana Purchase—the transaction in which President Thomas Jefferson paid $15 million for the entire Louisiana Territory. At the time, New Orleans was a small town with a population of about 8,000. But it was an important port, and early in the 19th century there was money to be made in the developing city. Yankee entrepreneurs with fat wallets and Yankee architects with dreams of glory followed the action downriver. The newcomers were deeply hated by the French Creoles, who viewed them as not much better than barbarians. To the Creoles, not only did *les Américains* appear crude, but they bore the ignominy of not being French.

Ostracized, the new arrivals settled across Canal Street, just upriver from the French Quarter. More and more Yankees appeared, extending their "American Sector" farther

upriver. In 1833, the Yankees had established the City of Lafayette, two miles upriver from the uppity Creoles, on a portion of the vast plantation of Jacques François Esnould Dugue de Livaudais. Lafayette was annexed by New Orleans in 1852, and became today's Garden District.

Bounded by **Jackson** and **Louisiana Avenues**, and **Magazine Street** and **St. Charles Avenue**, this section of the city bears no resemblance to the French Quarter. Whereas the old Creole town houses in the Quarter are quietly elegant and reserved—with moody interior courtyards shut off from prying eyes—the mansions uptowners occupy in the Garden District are flashy cousins of those in Baltimore and Philadelphia. They were, after all, designed by Yankees, for Yankees. Now, as always, most of these private homes are closed to the public. However, if you happen to hit town during the annual Spring Fiesta (which always begins the Friday after Easter), you can join one of the many garden, interior, and patio tours that let you inside some of the city's finest residences.

Those who prefer an unguided rummage through the past will love the funky old antiques shops that line the lower reaches of Magazine Street—they house some treasures and lots of junk, but reasonable prices and quirky proprietors make the dusty expedition worthwhile.

1 THE PONTCHARTRAIN

$$$$ Although it's slightly beyond the official downtown boundary, this hotel is the place to stay in the Garden District. It isn't uncommon for parents to enroll one of their children in **Tulane,** then head straight for the stately hotel to reserve a room for graduation day. Ask about suites once occupied by Richard Burton, Yul Brynner, Charles Boyer, Mary Martin, Walt Disney, or Tennessee Williams. Whatever your name, the bed will be turned down nightly and you'll have valet, laundry, and 24-hour room service. Lyle Aschaffenburg built **The Pontchartrain** in 1927 as a residential hotel, and the property remained in his family until 1987. Conversion to a conventional hotel began in 1941, but some permanent residents hung on until 1990. A brick building with a Moorish facade and blue canopy, the posh European-style operation has neither a swimming pool nor swinging lounges. The lobby is rich with Oriental rugs, faux marble columns, and a barrel-vaulted ceiling; the hand-painted murals in the elevators are the work of Elizabeth Hadden. The 74 rooms and 29 suites all have exterior windows (front-facing rooms above the fifth floor command river views, those on the east side face the city skyline). All are elegantly furnished with antiques, and have 12-foot ceilings and striking white tile bathrooms. If you're planning to entertain, a pair of 2,000-square-foot penthouses can accommodate 40 guests for a cocktail reception. Several small pension-style rooms in the rear (shower baths only) are a good choice for gentility on a budget. ◆ 2031 St. Charles Ave (at Josephine St). 524.0581, 800/777.6193; fax 529.1165; www.pontchartrainhotel.com ও

Beyond his own impressive literary achievements (including winning the National Book Award for his 1961 novel *The Moviegoer*), local writer Walker Percy also played a major part in discovering a comic masterpiece. While he was teaching at Loyola University in 1976, a woman asked him to read a manuscript by her son, John Kennedy Toole, who had committed suicide in despair over his failure to get published. Percy was sure it would be a waste of time, but he reluctantly agreed. To his amazement, he loved the book, and he immediately volunteered to help Mrs. Toole find a publisher. As a result, the LSU Press published *A Confederacy of Dunces* in 1981, and the book received wide critical acclaim, including the Pulitzer Prize.

Louisiana's counties are known as parishes because the original divisions followed the ecclesiastical jurisdictions of the Roman Catholic Church.

Within The Pontchartrain:

CAFE PONTCHARTRAIN

★★$$ Portions of Anne Rice's *The Witching Hour* were set in this small cafe, but the atmosphere isn't the least bit ominous. Uptowners flock here for breakfast, and it's also a good place for salads and sandwiches. ◆ American ◆ Daily breakfast, lunch, and dinner. 524.0581 ও

BAYOU BAR

The **New Orleans Saints** signed their National Football League contract here in 1966. Decked with murals of Louisiana bayous and plush banquettes, the low-key piano bar draws a sedate local crowd. ◆ Daily from 11:30AM. 524.0581 ও

2 GARDEN DISTRICT HOTEL

$$$ This Garden District link in the Ramada chain boasts 133 rooms and suites, a restaurant (room service is available), and a lounge. Accommodations are standard motel issue, but they're clean and comfortable. The **St. Charles Avenue Streetcar** rumbles along right out front for picturesque transport to the Central Business District in about five minutes. A complimentary shuttle to the quarter is also offered every half-hour. ◆ 2203 St. Charles Ave (at Jackson Ave). 566.1200; 800.265.1856; fax 581.1352

3 DABNEY-O'MEALLIE HOUSE

The tall, Greek Revival mansion built around 1857 for Lavinia Dabney, was one of the last works of architect **James Gallier Jr.,** whose own home on Royal Street in the French Quarter was built around the same year. The Ionic columns and double galleries on the side of the house were added later. The house is a private residence. ◆ 2265 St. Charles Ave (at Philip St)

4 RUHLMAN-HACKETT HOUSE

This Greek Revival raised cottage, built in 1854 by architect **James Gallier Sr.** for Susan Hackett, is typical of a mid-19th-century Garden District home. It's a private residence. ◆ 2336 St. Charles Ave (between Philip and First Sts)

5 GRINNAN-REILLY HOUSE

Irishman **Henry Howard** designed this Greek Revival mansion for cotton broker Robert Grinnan in 1850. The architect for many other grand-scale Garden District homes, Howard also designed two of the most handsome plantations west of the city—**Nottoway,** on River Road near the town of White Castle, and **Madewood,** near Napoleonville (see pages 162 and 164). The house is a private residence. ◆ 2221 Prytania St (between Jackson Ave and Philip St)

6 THE JOSEPHINE

$$ Well situated for walking tours of the Garden District and easily accessible by streetcar, this 1870 Italianate guest house has been faithfully restored and furnished with French antiques, gilt mirrors, and original art (including several contemporary works). Each of the six guest rooms opens onto a balcony or gallery overlooking the surrounding gardens and private courtyard. A complimentary breakfast of fresh breads and café au lait is served with style. ♦ 1450 Josephine St (at Prytania St). 524.6361, 800/779.6361; fax 523.6484; www.travelbase.com

7 GRIMA HOUSE

The names of the architect and the original owner are unknown, but this Italianate-cum-Second Empire house, with exquisite plasterwork on the pediment, dates from around 1850. Alfred Grima purchased and renovated the house in the 1890s. The three landscaped gardens, designed for year-round flowering, are filled with azaleas, roses, camellias, jasmine, and blue-flowered jacaranda, and are shaded by cherry and mimosa trees. It's a private residence. ♦ 1604 Fourth St (at St. Charles Ave)

8 DAMERON HOUSE

The only thing certain about this structure is that it's a Greek Revival raised cottage. No two historians agree on the architect, date of construction, or occupants. According to some accounts, it was built as late as 1860 for James Dameron, a wealthy Virginia-born businessman. A more interesting version is that it was built much earlier as a home for Antoine Mandeville de Marigny and his Anglo-Saxon wife, Louise Claiborne. Antoine was the youngest son of Bernard de Marigny, a Crescent City legend. When his father died in 1800, 15-year-old Bernard became one of the richest Creoles in the state. He owned vast plantations, and his own estate was in Faubourg Marigny. But by the time he was 20, he had blown a million dollars, partly as a result of his passion for shooting craps—a game he is said to have introduced into this country. He died a pauper at age 83. The house remains a private residence. ♦ 2524 St. Charles Ave (at Third St)

9 LOUISE S. MCGEHEE SCHOOL

An exclusive school for girls since 1929, this elaborate French Second Empire-style mansion was the most expensive house in the area when it was built in 1872 for $100,000. It's also known as the **Bradish Johnson House,** after the wealthy sugar entrepreneur for whom it was built. Most historians attribute the

design to New Orleans-born **James Freret,** who studied at the École des Beaux Arts in Paris; dissenters say the architect was actually New Yorker **Lewis E. Reynolds.** The stables are now the school's cafeteria, and the carriage house is a gym. ♦ 2343 Prytania St (at First St)

10 TOBY'S CORNER

Neither the architect nor the exact date of its construction are known, but the home built for Philadelphian Thomas Toby is believed to be the oldest house in the Garden District, occupying this site since at least 1838. The simple raised cottage is surrounded by lush gardens—the large Livaudais Oak on the grounds (named after the plantation on which the Garden District was built) is a member of the Louisiana Live Oak Society, a prestigious group whose members are several hundred years old and wear shawls of Spanish moss draped on their swooping, gnarled boughs. The house is a private residence. ♦ 2340 Prytania St (at First St)

11 BUCKNER HOUSE

When wealthy cotton baron Henry S. Buckner moved from Kentucky to New Orleans during the city's mid-19th-century boom years, he hired New York architect **Lewis E. Reynolds** to build this immense white plantation-style house. Completed in 1856, it has 48 Classical columns on the wraparound double galleries and an interior measuring 22,000

Louise S. McGehee School

KENNETH SNOW

square feet. You have to view the house from both Jackson Avenue and Coliseum Street to fully appreciate its size. A half-century later, the house became the second home of **Soule College,** the city's first business college, which was founded on St. Charles Avenue in 1855. The Soule family closed the school in the early 1980s, and the house is once again a private residence. ♦ 1410 Jackson Ave (at Coliseum St)

12 THOMAS MANN GALLERY

Three blocks beyond the downtown border of the Garden District, but definitely worth the short walk, this stylish venue (formerly **Gallery I/0**) is still home base for Thomas Mann's "techno-romantic" jewelry, which is sold in galleries nationwide. Mann creates startling metal amulets that incorporate hearts, birds, fish, eyeballs, and other natural shapes. Other artisans' works are featured on a monthly basis. ♦ M-Sa.1812 Magazine St (between Hastins Pl and St. Mary St). 581.2113. Also at: 829 Royal St (between St. Ann and Dumaine Sts). 523.5041

13 CHRIST CHURCH CATHEDRAL

The Fourth Episcopal Cathedral of New Orleans, more familiarly known as **Christ Church Cathedral,** is a majestic Gothic-style church that dates from around 1887 and was designed by **Lawrence B. Valk** of New York. Most of the more than one hundred stained-glass windows were produced by the Willett Studio in Philadelphia between the 1950s and 1970s. New Orleans architect **Thomas Sully** designed the bull's-eye window in the transom, a chapel containing wood sculptures by New Orleans artist Enrique Alferez (who is also responsible for many of the bronze statues on park benches around town). Free concerts are held in the sanctuary some Sunday afternoons; call for schedule. ♦ Chapel services Su, 7:30AM; Cathedral services Su, 9AM and 11AM. 2919 St. Charles Ave (between Sixth and Seventh Sts). 895.6602

14 BRIGGS-STAUB HOUSE

This house was designed in 1849 for Charles Briggs by **James Gallier Sr**. With its pointed arches and shutters and bull's-eye window, it's one of a kind—the only Gothic Revival house in the Garden District.

Make that two of a kind: the little guest house on the grounds is a miniaturized copy. Both are privately owned. ♦ 2605 Prytania St (at Third St)

15 OUR LADY OF PERPETUAL HELP CHAPEL

Formerly home to a chapel of the Redemptorist Fathers, this elaborate Italianate confection of columns and cast-ironwork was built in 1857 for coffee broker Henry Lonsdale by the firm of **J.K. Collins & Co.** Now owned by novelist Anne Rice, the building is closed to the public. ♦ 2521 Prytania St (at Third St)

16 WOMEN'S OPERA GUILD HOUSE

With its Corinthian columns and turret, this home designed in 1858 by **William Freret** for Edward Davis marries the Greek Revival and Queen Anne styles. The octagonal turret was a late-19th-century addition, housing a music room, dining room, and additional bedrooms. The house was bequeathed to the **Women's Opera Guild** by its last inhabitant, Nettie Seebold, who died in 1955. The house isn't

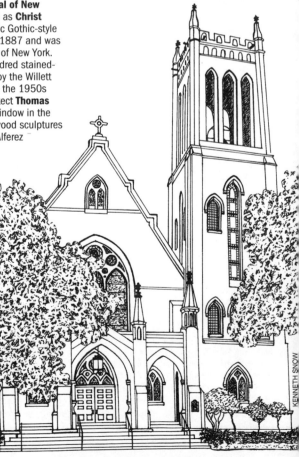

Christ Church Cathedral

KENNETH SNOW

CHEAP THRILLS

They don't call it The Big Easy for nothing—in New Orleans, the best things in life are cheap. We've got you started by listing 10 of the best cheap diversions in the city; all cost less than $10 for two people. To get more ideas, check the daily Times-Picayune newspaper and the *Gambit* and *Offbeat* weeklies; the theater, music, and sports departments at **Tulane, Loyola,** and the **University of New Orleans;** and bulletin boards at coffeehouses all over town.

1 Cruise across the **Mississippi** in one of the world's busiest ports. The round trip to **Algiers** aboard the **Canal Street Ferry** is especially wonderful at night, when the bridges and New Orleans skyline appear to shimmer in the moonlight. The ferry terminal is in the **CBD,** where **Canal Street** meets the river.

2 Hop the **St. Charles Avenue Streetcar** for a cool rumble through the oaks and past the downtown shopping area, the stately mansions of the **Garden District, Audubon Park,** and the **Uptown/University** neighborhood.

3 Marvel at the sweeping views of the Mississippi and cityscape from the 31st-floor observation deck of the **World Trade Center** (2 Canal St, just east of Pl de France, 581.4888).

4 Visit **City Park** in **Mid City,** where you can ride a historic carousel or miniature train at **Carousel Gardens** or take in the sights at the **New Orleans Botanical Garden,** a visual feast of Art Deco fountains, reflecting pools, tropical blooms, and Enrique Alferez sculptures.

5 Pick up a muffuletta and two root beers at **Progress Grocery** (915 Decatur St, between Dumaine and St. Philip Sts, 525.6627 &) and stroll to the **Moonwalk** for a picnic accompanied by a panoramic view of riverboat traffic on the Mississippi.

6 Enjoy café au lait and beignets *à deux* at historic **Café du Monde** (French Market, 800 Decatur St, at St. Ann St, 525.4544), a local institution that also happens to be located on one of the best people-watching corners in town.

7 Listen to living legends from the Golden Age of Jazz play at **Preservation Hall** (726 St. Peter St, between Royal and Bourbon Sts, 523.8939; www.preservationhall.com &) daily from 8PM to midnight.

8 Let your spirits soar at the 10AM Sunday Mass at **St. Louis Cathedral.** The service is complemented beautifully by music from a full choir and a pipe organ. **Christ Church Cathedral** (2919 St. Charles Ave, between Sixth and Seventh Sts, 895.6602) also hosts classical music concerts on selected Sunday afternoons; call ahead for the schedule.

9 Drop into the **Contemporary Arts Center** (900 Camp St, at St. Joseph St, 523.1216 &) on "Texaco Thursdays," when admission to the visual arts galleries is free. In addition, there are free musical concerts and reasonably priced theater productions throughout the year.

10 Take in an outdoor jazz concert at the **French Market** in the French Quarter. The schedule is erratic, but bands often play on Saturdays and Sundays from 1 to 3PM.

open to individuals, but groups of 20 or more can make arrangements for guided tours. ◆ 2504 Prytania St (at Second St). 899.1945

17 GARDEN DISTRICT BOOK SHOP

Here is Anne Rice's neighborhood bookstore, just six blocks from her house and a great source for limited, first, and signed editions of her work. Owner Britton Trice, a leader in the local literary scene, also hosts regular signings by regional and national authors.

He stocks an excellent selection of used and rare books on New Orleans and Louisiana, as well as a wide range of art and design books. ◆ Daily. 2727 Prytania St (between Fourth St and Washington Ave). 895.2266; fax 895.0111

18 COLONEL SHORT'S VILLA

The year 1859 was a busy one for architect **Henry Howard.** He completed this Italianate mansion for Kentucky-born colonel Robert Short, and built the palatial **Nottoway** plantation west of town on the banks of the Big Muddy. The cast-iron **Cornstalk Fence** around this villa is one of two originals; the other is at the **Cornstalk Hotel** in the French Quarter. Both were cast by the New Orleans branch of the Philadelphia foundry Wood & Perot. This is still a private residence. ◆ 1448 Fourth St (at Prytania St)

Restaurants/Clubs: Red | Hotels: Purple | Shops: Orange | Outdoors/Parks: Green | Sights/Culture: Blue

Robinson House

19 ROBINSON HOUSE

Built between 1859 and 1865 by **Henry Howard** for Virginia tobacco merchant Walter G. Robinson, this is one of the most elaborate houses in the Garden District. The two-story structure boasts white columns, cast-iron galleries, and porticoes; it's a private residence. ♦ 1415 Third St (between Coliseum and Prytania Sts)

20 MUSSON-BELL HOUSE

Creole Michel Musson, who was a New Orleans postmaster, had this frame Italianate house built in 1853. It originally had bay windows on the front. The lacy cast-iron galleries were added in 1884. Musson was related to French Impressionist painter Edgar Degas. The house is a private residence. ♦ 1331 Third St (at Coliseum St)

Many New Orleans houses were built of "barge board," which came from the thousands of keelboats and scows that were broken up and sold as lumber after floating down the Mississippi laden with pigs, whiskey, and animal hides. One typical piece of Louisiana antique furniture is the tester or half-tester bed, which featured either a tester (full canopy) or a half-tester (one that extended only a few feet beyond the headboard). These canopies were not just for show: In the days of yellow fever (from the beginning of the colony through the early 20th century), the use of effective mosquito netting often made the difference between life and death. The most sought-after pieces were crafted in the 19th century by Simeon Seignouret and P. Mallard.

21 MORRIS-ISRAEL HOUSE

Like **Henry Howard** and **James Gallier Sr.**, architect **Samuel Jamison** was an Irish citizen who came to New Orleans after apprenticing elsewhere. The Italianate mansion he built for Joseph C. Morris in 1869 is dressed in ornate swirls of cast iron. It's a private residence. ♦ 1331 First St (at Coliseum St)

22 CARROLL-CRAWFORD HOUSE

If this mansion built for Joseph Carroll seems to bear a striking resemblance to the nearby **Morris-Israel House,** it's because architect **Samuel Jamison** worked on both houses at the same time in 1869. The cast-iron galleries are identical. This house is also a private residence. ♦ 1315 First St (between Chestnut and Coliseum Sts)

23 BREVARD-MMAHAT HOUSE

Merchant Albert Brevard used part of his fortune to build this stately mansion, designed by architect **James H. Calrow** in 1857. It has been called the **Rose-Brevard House** because of the delicate cast-iron roses worked into the double galleries and the fence. Today it's the private residence of novelist Anne Rice, creator of *The Vampire Chronicles* series of books. Rice used the house as the setting for her best-seller *The Witching Hour.* ♦ 1239 First St (at Chestnut St)

24 LAFAYETTE CEMETERY

The burial grounds in the 1830s for the City of Lafayette, which was later incorporated into the City of New Orleans, this cemetery is surrounded by a brick wall, and the gate is often locked. Even if it isn't, don't wander in unescorted. (**Save Our Cemeteries** conducts tours of this and other area cemeteries; 525.3377.) The most famous of the cemetery's aboveground tombs is that of the Jefferson Fire Company No. 22, which incorporates a large bas-relief carving of a fire engine. This was the setting for some of the scenes in Anne Rice's novel *The Witching Hour.* ♦ Bounded by Washington Ave and Sixth St, and Coliseum and Prytania Sts &

25 COMMANDER'S PALACE

★★★★$$$$ This turreted turquoise-and-white Victorian mansion was first established as a restaurant in 1883 by namesake Emile Commander. (For a brief time in the Roaring Twenties, the family restaurant downstairs coexisted with a bordello upstairs, reached through a separate entrance around the corner.) However, it was the commanding Ella Brennan, who helped establish **Brennan's Restaurant** in the French Quarter, as well as **Mr. B's Bistro, Bacco,** and the **Palace Cafe,** who brought the restaurant to national prominence. The James Beard Foundation gave its seal of approval—a Lifetime Outstanding Restaurant Award. Today, Ella is semi-retired, and her daughter, Ti Martin, and niece, Lally Brennan, run the city's best and most famous Creole institution. A luxurious courtyard and garden-bright dining rooms create the warm atmosphere of an elegant private home. Enduring favorites include the sherried turtle soup, pan-seared foie gras with fresh citrus fruits and grilled homemade bread, shrimp remoulade, boned Mississippi quail stuffed with Creole crawfish sausage in a Port wine glaze, and pecan-crusted Gulf fish enriched with a lemony brown butter sauce. The bread pudding soufflé is famous. In New Orleans, jazz brunches have become a tradition at many fine restaurants, but they originated here. With festive balloons on the tables and cool sounds from a three-man combo, jazz brunch at **Commander's** is still the best in town.

Order Commander's eggs Benedict (served on herbed biscuits, topped with thin-sliced roast pork and hollandaise) or try the eggs Sardou (poached, on creamed spinach and fresh artichoke bottoms, topped with hollandaise). ♦ Creole/American ♦ M-F lunch and dinner; Sa-Su brunch and dinner. Reservations recommended for lunch and dinner; jacket required for dinner and Sunday brunch. 1403 Washington Ave (at Coliseum St). 899.8221 &

26 MONTGOMERY-HERO HOUSE

In 1868, when Reconstruction was in full force throughout the South, **Henry Howard** designed this house for fellow Irishman Archibald Montgomery, who made a fortune in New Orleans as president of the Crescent City Railroad. His house, decorated with brackets, arches, and swooping eaves, doesn't fit the typical Classical mold prevalent in the District. It is, like most of its neighbors, privately owned. ♦ 1213 Third St (between Camp and Chestnut Sts)

Payne-Strachan House

KENNETH SNOW

Restaurants/Clubs: Red | **Hotels: Purple** | **Shops: Orange** | **Outdoors/Parks: Green** | **Sights/Culture: Blue**

81

THESE OLD HOUSES

You don't need a working knowledge of lintels and dentils, porticoes and pediments, or turrets and bull's-eye dormers to enjoy New Orleans architecture. You just need an eye for beauty. The city is rich with Greek Revival, Italianate, Victorian, Queen Anne, and French Second Empire houses, as well as such indigenous designs as "shotguns" and "Creole cottages."

By all accounts, the first structures in the fledgling colony were more utilitarian than glamorous. The Creoles initially built simple thatch-topped palmetto huts that probably toppled with the first huff from the hurricanes that frequently hit the area. They quickly saw the need to construct buildings that could withstand the sometimes torrential rains and frequent floods without sinking into the alluvial soil.

To achieve maximum solidity, they combined two building methods, called *colombage* and *brique-entre-poteaux*. For the former, heavy timbers, arranged to form jambs and windows, were mortised and tenoned together, and broad horizontal boards were placed right on the ground. (Basements were, of course, out of the question, as the city is five feet below sea level.) Then, for even greater stability and insulation, bricks were used as infill between the frames or posts (hence the term *brique-entre-poteaux*, or "brick-between-posts"). Often, a rough plaster known as *bousillage* (made of mud, moss, and animal hair) was used for added support. A good example of these techniques is Lafitte's Blacksmith Shop (941 Bourbon St, at St. Philip St, 523.0066), a cottage whose existing ownership records date to 1772; it's now a popular bar.

Creole cottages, one of the most common styles in the city, were built flush with the *banquettes* (sidewalks). These square, hall-less houses have four rooms of equal size at the front and two cabinets (storage areas connected by an exterior porch or "gallery") at the rear. On **St. Peter Street** between **Bourbon** and **Dauphine Streets** are several Creole cottages decked out in a variety of finery, from simple Greek Revival details to showy gingerbread trim.

From these more simple houses evolved the "raised" plantation homes, picturesque blendings of French Colonial, European, and West Indian influences. The main living floor was placed upon an aboveground "basement" made of masonry, which served not only as storage space but as protection from the frequent floods. (The city now has an elaborate system of spillways that control flooding.) Living quarters above the main floor were built using the *colombage* method, with either weatherboard or plaster covering. West Indies-style double-pitched roofs extended out over the galleries, creating a shaded area so windows could be left open when it rained (so residents could enjoy the cool air). High ceilings allowed the hot air to rise and the heavier cool air to settle. Windows and doors had shutters, usually of vertical boards on the lower, or basement, level and louvered shutters on the principal floor. Fireplaces were located on interior walls, and chimneys poked up through the steep roofs to accompany the dormer windows that peered through the front and rear pitch. A perfect example of the West Indies-style raised cottage is **Madame John's Legacy** (632 Dumaine St, between Chartres and Royal Sts). Originally built in 1724, it is believed by many historians to be the oldest house in the **Lower Mississippi Valley**.

Just across **Canal Street** from the Southern Mediterranean town houses of the **French Quarter**, the region settled by *les Américains* (which now encompasses the **Central Business District (CBD), Warehouse/Arts District, Garden District,** and **Uptown/University area**) reflects entirely different architectural styles. This later building boom—the result of the population growth that followed the 1803 Louisiana Purchase, coupled with the worldwide infatuation with Greek Revival architecture—coincided with the Golden Age, a period of enormous growth and prosperity that stretched from the 1830s until the Civil War broke out in 1861. **Gallier Hall** (545 St. Charles Ave, between Lafayette and Poydras Sts, 565.7457), which dates from about 1845, is considered the city's most outstanding example of Greek Revival architecture; and the **Marble Hall** in the **US Customs House** (423 Canal St, between N Peters and Decatur Sts) has been designated one of the finest examples of late Greek Revival architecture by the American Institute of Architects. In addition to the Greek Revival school, a dazzling array of other styles is on display in the Garden District. The **Musson-Bell House** (1331 Third St, at Coliseum St) is a splendid example of an Italianate home; the **Louise S. McGehee School** (2343 Prytania St, at First St) is a magnificent Second Empire structure; and the district's only Gothic Revival home is the **Briggs-Staub House** (2605 Prytania St, at Third St).

The most ubiquitous architectural style in the city is the humble "shotgun house" so called because a bullet fired from the front room would zip straight through to the back. The boxcar-shaped structures (only one room wide, though some have side halls) are simply a long line of rooms that open onto one another.

27 PAYNE-STRACHAN HOUSE

Built for Judge Jacob Payne in 1849, this Greek Revival house, one of the first to incorporate ornamental ironwork, is known as the place where Confederate President

Legend has it that even though he has been dead since 1893, P.G.T. Beauregard still walks the halls at Beauregard-Keyes House in the French Quarter.

Jefferson Davis died while visiting Payne, his close friend, in 1889. ♦ 1134 First St (at Camp St)

28 GEORGE WASHINGTON CABLE HOUSE

Mark Twain was a frequent visitor to the home of 19th-century novelist George Washington Cable. Though not a native New Orleanian, Cable wrote short stories and novels that poked fun at the Creoles of the French Quarter. His raised cottage was built around 1874; today it's a private residence. ♦ 1313 Eighth St (between Chestnut and Coliseum Sts)

29 MORGAN-WEST STUDIO/GALLERY

Artist/owner Perry Morgan exhibits his own hand-painted furniture, silk ties, scarves, pillows, wall hangings, and lamp shades, as well as showcasing contemporary crafts and art created by local/regional artists. ♦ M-Sa. 3326 Magazine St (between Toledano St and Louisiana Ave). 895.7976

30 PRINCE & PAUPER

Prices are surprisingly low on the antiques and reproductions of 18th- and 19th-century European furnishings and accessories sold here. Bronzes, marbles, antique bamboo, Chinese stoneware, and whimsical *objets* come from around the world. ♦ Tu-Su. 3308 Magazine St (between Toledano St and Louisiana Ave). 899.2378, 899.2259; www.prince-pauper.com

31 SEMOLINA

★★$ Singles can dine comfortably at the "original international pasta bar," which is surrounded by art-filled walls and a casual scattering of tables. Multicultural noodles range from shrimp Bangkok (tossed with angel hair and mounds of bean sprouts in a soy broth) to pasta paella (saffron linguine studded with chicken, sausage, shrimp, mussels, and artichoke hearts). The dinner-time wait can stretch to 60 minutes at this very popular cafe. ♦ International ♦ Daily lunch and dinner. 3226 Magazine St (between Pleasant and Toledano Sts). 895.4260; www.semolina.com Also at: Numerous locations throughout the area.

32 THE BULLDOG

Choose from 50 drafts and over 250 bottled beers at this stylish pub with its dark wood ceilings, deep green walls, and impressive lineup of colorful signature taps. Sample brews from Africa, Austria, Bulgaria, China, Denmark, Jamaica, India, Thailand, and more. If you manage to try each available kind, you'll be awarded a commemorative T-shirt and your name will be added to a brass plaque on display. The bartender will give you a special key chain to help you keep track of the brews you've sampled; the key chains are honored indefinitely, though some people have been known to fill in all the slots in a single weekend. Great bar grub too, with the emphasis on Tex-Mex cuisine. ♦ M-Th, Su

from 1PM; F-Sa from 11AM. 3226 Magazine St (at Pleasant St). 891.1516

WILKERSON ROW

33 WILKERSON ROW

Stop here for cypress and pine furniture, along with a unique selection of shabby chic home accessories. Custom cypress kitchens and one-of-a-kind furniture are designed and built by award-winning designer Shaun Wilkerson. ♦ M-Sa. 3137 Magazine St (between Ninth and Harmony Sts). 899.3311; www.wilkersonrow.com

rue de la course

34 RUE DE LA COURSE

It has been said that New Orleans has more bars than churches, but the way things have been going lately, it won't be long before both are outnumbered by coffeehouses. Without question, this is one of the best, with some 50 tables inside and outside along the sidewalk. The pressed-tin walls, polished wood, dark green study lamps, and other decor elements evoke the comfortably worn look of the 19th-century coffeehouses of London and Paris. Choose from over 60 types of coffee, as well as various cakes, pastries, and bagels. A stack of games (chess, cribbage, backgammon, Scrabble) on the bar invites lingering and social interaction. ♦ Daily. 3128 Magazine St (at Ninth St). 899.0242, and multiple locations around the city

35 FUNKY MONKEY

Vintage clothing and accessories from the 60s and 70s make for a fun rummage. Anything from Hawaiian shirts to original psychedelic paintings might turn up. Most clothing items are used, but a new line features retro lingerie, dresses, and hot pants from Louisiana designer/seamstress D.C. Hargreaves. Halloween and Carnival costumes are a specialty. ♦ M-Sa; daily during Halloween and Carnival seasons. 3127 Magazine St (between Eighth and Ninth Sts). 899.5587 &

Restaurants/Clubs: Red | Hotels: Purple | Shops: Orange | Outdoors/Parks: Green | Sights/Culture: Blue

36 SABAI

This eclectic jewelry shop offers locally designed pieces at reasonable prices, with the emphasis on silver over gold. The gemstone rings are a knockout—a great place to do some Christmas shopping. ♦ M-Sa, 10-6, Su 11-5. 3115 Magazine St. (between Eighth and Ninth Sts). 891.9555; fax 891.8067. Also at 924 Royal. 525.6211. ♦

37 NEW ORLEANS CYPRESSWORKS

Don't want to pay the price for an antique farm table? Have a custom copy made from recycled 19th-century cypress and few people will know the difference. The number-one sellers here are beds made from vintage cypress doors. You can also place orders for kitchen cabinets, chests of drawers, entertainment centers, and other time-softened furnishings. Don't miss the century-old cypress forms once used to mold cast-iron foundry pieces, such as ship hatches, huge gears, or manhole covers. They make great tabletops or offbeat wall sculptures. ♦ M-Su. 3105 Magazine St (between Eighth and Ninth Sts). 891.0001; www.cypressworks.com

As You Like It
Silver Shop

38 AS YOU LIKE IT

Pick through tables piled with unmatched sterling silver flatware to find the pieces missing from your set, most stored in antique sewing machine drawers. Active, inactive, and obsolete silver patterns are the focus here, but you'll also see regal silver tea services, as well as water pitchers, candelabras, and vases. ♦ M-Sa. 3033 Magazine St (between Seventh and Eighth Sts). 897.6915, 800/828.2311; fax 897.6933; www. asyoulikeitsilvershop.com ♿

It was while watching the streetcars rumble through the French Quarter that Tennessee Williams, who first moved to New Orleans in 1939, wrote the lines that introduced one of the best-known characters in American theater, Blanche DuBois: "They told me to take a streetcar named Desire, and then transfer to one called Cemeteries, and ride six blocks and get off at Elysian Fields!"

39 MAGAZINE ARCADE

One of the most entertaining stops on the six-mile strip of Magazine Street is this multi-dealer mall. One room is filled with Victrolas, music boxes, crank organs, and other antique audio equipment. This fascinating jumble of shops also includes displays of medical instruments, antique tools, valuable Hendryx solid brass birdcages, old-fashioned dolls, dollhouses and dollhouse furniture, hobby horses, china, clocks, chandeliers, and hundreds of other collectibles. Mechanical items are rebuilt and guaranteed. ♦ M-Sa. 3017 Magazine St (between Seventh and Eighth Sts). 895.5451

40 RUBY ANN TOBAR-BLANCO, NEW ORLEANS

Tiny tombs, Creole cottages, gaslights, iron fences, and other local icons are referenced in the "New Orleans Collection" of handmade jewelry by talented artisan Ruby Ann Tobar-Blanco. Pins and pendants in her oddly beautiful "Abandonment Series" were inspired by dilapidated architectural details, while another series of regal necklaces, pins, and earrings are emblazoned with the fleur-de-lis. ♦ M-Sa; daily Oct-Apr. 3005 Magazine St (between Seventh and Eighth Sts). 800/826.7282, 897.0811

40 JOEY K'S RESTAURANT

★$ Stop here for lunch and you'll probably run into someone whose shop you've just left. Simple food and an easygoing atmosphere also attract a neighborhood crowd that drops in for beers and margaritas after work or for breakfast on Saturday morning. The sandwiches, fried seafood, and gumbo are just fine. ♦ American ♦ M-F lunch and dinner; Sa breakfast, lunch, and dinner. 3001 Magazine St (at Seventh St). 891.0997 ♿

Belladonna
Day Spa For Men and Women

41 BELLADONNA

At this exclusive day spa, you can pamper yourself with anything from a paraffin foot

THE BEST

Ronnie Kole
Jazz Pianist/Entertainer

If you have not made reservations for your hotel room, might I suggest our very favorite hotel, the **Royal Sonesta**. It's on **Bourbon Street,** right in the heart of the **French Quarter**. If you really want to do it up, check into the honeymoon suite. It's too much. Believe it or not, my wife and I spend at least one night a month there.

The first thing visitors should do after checking into their hotel is take a **Gray Line** tour of the city, so they get the feel of New Orleans and its history.

After that, go to the **Top of the Mart,** a revolving lounge on top of the **World Trade Center.** New Orleans is one of the most interesting cities to see from above. If you can go before the sun sets and watch the city as the lights come on, it's twice as interesting.

For dinner on your first night, I'd go to **Bella Luna**. It's on the river in the **French Market**. Great view, but more important, wonderful food. Ask chef Horst Pfeifer to make some recommendations. That's what I do.

A real must for dinner or lunch is **K-Paul's Louisiana Kitchen**. I'd recommend lunch, as it's not as crowded. Get there by 11AM and you won't have to stand in line, but it's worth the wait. The waitresses will explain the menu.

Commander's Palace is a place where you'll see as many locals as tourists. Paul Prudhomme is one of the great chefs who got their start here.

The **Court of Two Sisters** has a daily jazz brunch in a wonderful courtyard.

Bayona is where chef Susan Spicer was named 1993 chef of the year for the southeast region of the US.

In the **Riverband** area is **Brigsten's**. Chef Frank Brigsten was named one of the 10 top new chefs in the country a few years back. Great food in a shotgun house converted into an intimate restaurant.

My wife Gardner says I must include two special experiences. One is a visit to an **Yvonne La Fleur** fashion shop. The other is to visit the **Palace Café,** a Paris-type café on **Canal Street** owned and beautifully operated by the third-generation Brennans. Fascinating menu, good wines, and a life-size mural of every jazz musician that our city has produced, including me.

If you have a car, cross **Lake Pontchartrain** to the **North Shore** and visit **La Provence,** where chef Chris Kerageorgiou will blow your mind with his French cuisine.

---

treatment to a seaweed body wrap. A collection of packages is crowned by the "Total Transformation," which promises an exfoliating *gommage* body peel, Aroma Hydro massage, a deep-hydrating facial, a manicure and pedicure, as well as a spa lunch in the Japanese garden. Appointments can be hard to come by, so reserve well in advance. ♦ M-Sa by appointment only. 2900 Magazine St (at Sixth St). 891.4393 &

42 CHRISTOPHER'S DISCOVERIES
Imported exotica, antiques, gifts, fine linens, South American and African art are crammed into every corner of this fascinating shop. Partners David Marbella and Joe Christophers also operate a small B&B behind the store—an unnamed little gem that can sleep four $$. ♦ M-Su, 11-5. 2842 Magazine St (at Sixth St) 899.6226

43 CHARBONNET & CHARBONNET, INC.
Country pine antiques from England and Ireland are displayed alongside custom furnishings made on the premises in this

sprawling 8,000-square-foot showroom and workshop. The Charbonnets acquire gingerbread and jigsaw trim, cypress doors, and other "body parts" of razed houses, then fashion them into furnishings and kitchen cabinets. You'll also discover lamps and other decorative accessories, many created from old architectural details. ♦ M-Sa. 2728 Magazine St (between Fourth St and Washington Ave). 891.9948; fax 891.9952

44 CAFE ATCHAFALAYA
★★$ Traditional Southern food is surprisingly hard to find in New Orleans, where most down-home restaurants serve Cajun and Creole fare. Iler Pope's small cottage, simply furnished with tile floors and deep orange walls, is a comfortably worn setting for great fried green tomatoes, chicken and dumplings, country-fried steak with cream gravy, liver and onions, and fried catfish with hush puppies. Fresh fruit cobbler is topped with homemade vanilla ice cream. ♦ Southern ♦ Tu-F lunch and dinner; Sa breakfast, lunch, and dinner; Su breakfast and lunch. 901 Louisiana Ave (at Laurel St). 891.5271

Restaurants/Clubs: Red | **Hotels: Purple** | **Shops: Orange** | **Outdoors/Parks: Green** | **Sights/Culture: Blue**

Lake
Pontchartrain

West End
Park

Lakeshore Dr.

Lakeshore
Pkwy.

Lakeshore
Park

Stilt St.

Lake Terrace Dr.

Lakeshore Dr.

West End Blvd.

Jewel St.

LAKEFRONT

Wren St.

Lark St.

Killdeer St.

Boreas
Park

Orpheum Ave.

Robert E. Lee Blvd.

Dove St.

Gull St.

Hollyhock La.

Greek Orthodox
Cathedral of the
Holy Trinity

Bellaire Dr.

Fleur de Lis Dr.

Pontchartrain Blvd.

Mouton St.

General Haig St.

St. Bernard Ave.

Prentiss Ave.

Cartier Ave.

Filmore Ave.

General Diaz St.

Argonne Blvd.

Orleans Ave.

City Park
Stables

Bayou Oaks
Golf Courses

Wisner Blvd.

Filmore Ave.

Lane St.

Bayou Oaks
Driving Range

Mirabeau Ave.

Pratt Dr.

West End Blvd.

Milne Blvd.

Louisville St.

Canal Blvd.

Harrison Ave.

Polk St.

Kenilworth St.

Magnolia Dr.

Marconi Dr.

Scout
Island

Bayou St. John

1
City
Park

Harrison Ave.

Mandolin St.

Perlita St.

Paris Ave.

Virgil Blvd.

Woodlawn Pl.

Popp's
Fountain

Zachary Taylor Dr.

St. Bernard Ave.

Gibson St.

Dillard
University

Lake Lawn
Park Cemetery
Mound
Ave.

Navarre Ave.

Tad Gormley
Stadium

City Park
Track

Roosevelt Mall

Palm Dr.

Fredericks Dr.

Moss St.

Desaix Blvd.

610

Greenwood
Cemetery

Rosedale
Dr.

New Orleans
Botanical Garden

Victory Ave.

Lelong

Florida Ave.

2
Lake Lawn
Metairie
Cemetery

Cemetery

Wisner
Tennis
Center

Dreyfous Ave.

New Orleans
Museum of Art
(NOMA)

90

3

City Park Ave.

St. Louis
Cemetery
Number 3

Duels
St.

←4

Cemeteries

6

Moss St.

7

9

Mystery
St.

N Lopez
St.

N Rocheblave
St.

←5

For nos.
22-28, see
pg. 96

N Alexander St.

Dumaine St.

8

10
11
12

Ponce de
Leon St.

Gentilly Blvd.

N Galvez St.

S St. Patrick St.

N Carrollton Ave.

N Cortez St.

Orleans Ave.

N Lopez St.

St. Ann St.

Ursulines Ave.

Chazza St.

Esplanade Ave.

13

Canal St.

Cleveland Ave.

S Pierce St.

D'Hemecourt St.

S Banks St.

Bienville Ave.

N Dupre St.

16

N Tonti St.

N Miro St.

17

18

14

Ulloa St.

Jefferson Davis Pkwy.

15

N Broad St.

N Rocheblave St.

19

Bayou Rd.

10

61

Tulane Ave.

Gravier St.

Perdido St.

Criminal
District
Court

20

S Dorgenois St.

S Tonti St.

N Galvez St.

TREME

Louis
Armstrong
Park

Palmetto St.

Pontchartrain Expwy.

Earhart Blvd.

21

Poydras St.

90

10

Basin St.

N Rampart St.

Bourbon St.

N

km   1/2   1
mi   1/4   1/2

MID CITY

When some kind stranger directed Blanche DuBois to "take a streetcar named Desire, and then transfer to one called Cemeteries and ride six blocks and get off at Elysian Fields," he could have been routing her through Mid City. The catch-all name for a diverse collection of metropolitan neighborhoods, this large and colorful region is dominated by a historic thoroughbred racetrack, the infamous "dueling oaks" of City Park, the pretty residential district of Esplanade Ridge, and several of New Orleans's greatest neighborhood bars and restaurants. But lest you be tempted to overdo, it is also home to the criminal court complex on **Tulane Avenue** and what must be the world's largest concentration of cemeteries: Fourteen are clustered in an ominous mass at the very tip of **Canal Street**, creating a sea of whitewashed tombs that stretches for blocks in every direction.

Oak-shaded Esplanade Ridge, which soars just a few extra feet above sea level, is the best destination for Mid City walkers. The shops and restaurants at the upper reaches of **Esplanade Avenue** cater to the young professionals who have renovated the surrounding 19th-century cottages and Victorian shotgun houses. Ancient oaks line both sidewalks, forming a deep green canopy that shades the entire route. City Park is just across the **Bayou St. John** bridge, but if you turn left on **Moss Street** you'll see the landmark houses along the bayou's banks; now a quick 10-minute drive from the French Quarter, they were originally built as plantation manors and country retreats.

Bayou St. John was once a watery mainline for barges carrying cargo from the steamers of **Lake Pontchartrain** into town. French explorer Jean-Baptiste Le Moyne, Sieur de Bienville, traveled the natural canal in 1699 when he was searching out a site for the future town of New Orleans; and for centuries before European settlers arrived, the Biloxi and Accolapissa Indians fished and hunted along the bayou and camped under the ancient trees that shade modern-day picnics in City Park.

But this trip begins on Tulane Avenue and **Broad Street** in a much less glamorous neck of the woods, best explored by (locked) car. Drive past the **Criminal District Court** where attorney Jim Garrison led the conspiracy trials chronicled by Oliver Stone in *JFK*. This area has some good restaurants (**Genghis Khan, Bennachin**), some bad motels (which shall remain nameless), and little in the way of shopping, unless you are in the market for linoleum or bail bonds. But keep on going until you see the neon bowling pin that points the way to **Rock 'n' Bowl** heaven.

By the way, Blanche DuBois never should have depended upon the kindness of strangers in this instance: Those connections are impossible, unless the conductor has a poetic license.

1 CITY PARK

It is one of America's oldest public parks and (at 1,500 acres) the fifth largest, twice the size of New York's Central Park. Home to more than 80 plant species and 30,000 trees, this urban oasis is best known for its hundreds of ancient moss-draped oaks, the largest stand of mature live oaks in the world. The original property was drawn from the **Allard Plantation,** bequeathed to New Orleans by philanthropist John McDonogh, and pronounced a public park in 1854. In the early days, splendid iron gates facing the main entrances were supplemented by long stretches of barbed wire to discourage roaming cattle from the surrounding dairy farms. Hotheaded Creole gentlemen met to settle *affaires d'honneur* under the secluded oaks until dueling was outlawed in 1890. Outdoor concerts were all the rage in 1907 when the **Peristyle** (Dreyfous Ave) was built for the exorbitant cost of $15,000. Its columns framed the moon's reflection in the lagoon as elegantly clad couples waltzed past the orchestra. Today it's a great picnic spot. The Mission Revival-style **Casino** (Dreyfous Ave), which followed in 1912, now houses a snack bar, ice-cream parlor, and gift shop. Lumber magnate John F. Popp donated funds to build the Neo-Classical **Popp's Bandstand** in front of the casino. Dedicated on the Fourth of July in 1917, it showcased the Order of Moose Band, Professor Harry Mendelson's Loola Temple Band, and other crowd pleasers. Since then, it has hosted a mixed bag of performers ranging from John Philip Sousa to Charmaine Neville. More than 20,000 men and women took part in WPA building projects throughout the park during the 1930s. Several bridges built during the period are decorated with wrenches, mallets, and other icons designed by world-renowned sculptor Enrique Alferez to celebrate the working man. His chisels also helped shape the Art Deco style of the rose garden, **Popp's Fountain** and **Tad Gormley Stadium**. Dedicated by President Franklin D. Roosevelt, the stadium opened in 1937 with a game between **Loyola** and **DePaul** Universities. The stadium has since had its various uses: Dorothy Lamour sold war bonds here in 1942; Roy Rogers and Trigger led 15,000 schoolchildren inside for the annual March of Dimes parade in 1959; the Beatles played to a sold-out screaming crowd in 1964. Today, long lines of cars stretch beyond park entrances for the annual Celebration in the Oaks, from Thanksgiving through 4 January, when nearly a million tiny sparkling lights illuminate the trees each night. ◆ N Carrollton Ave and Wisner Blvd. 482.4888

Within City Park:

New Orleans Museum of Art

NEW ORLEANS MUSEUM OF ART (NOMA)

When Jamaican-born New Orleans philanthropist Isaac Delgado donated $150,000 to the city in 1910 for a museum in **City Park,** he envisioned a "temple of art for rich and poor alike." The Neo-Classical building, surrounded by lagoons, was designed by Chicago architect **Samuel Marx,** who had been selected in a national competition. Together the two men created a grand structure from Marx's design that he characterized as being "inspired by the Greek, but sufficiently modified to give a subtropical appearance." Improvements and expansions to the original building have continued over the years, and

today **NOMA** boasts an outstanding collection of more than 35,000 works valued at more than $200 million. In addition, there is one vast wing devoted to rotating exhibitions. Pick up a museum floorplan at the front desk to guide you through the maze of 46 galleries showing, just for starters, 17th-century Dutch paintings, Spanish Colonial art of South America, Italian Renaissance and Baroque painting, and a particularly fine photography collection. Other holdings include a collection of Japanese paintings of the Edo period, as well as works of Chinese, Indian, African, and Oceanic art. The **Art of the Americas** gallery highlights an extensive collection of pre-Columbian and Native American works. **NOMA**'s holdings of European and American decorative arts are equally impressive, including one of the largest glass collections in the US. There's an extensive collection of early Louisiana and American furnishings, French art of the 17th to 19th centuries, intriguing English and Continental portrait miniatures, and the treasures of Peter Carl Fabergé. Don't miss the exhibit of regional paintings, sculpture, and decorative arts from 1800 to the present, displayed in sequential order. This comprehensive survey begins with paintings of the 19th century. A selection of prime Newcomb pottery of the early 20th century features Art Nouveau works by masters of this school, as well as the eccentric ceramic creations of George Ohr, "The Mad Potter of Biloxi." Featured contemporary artists include Robert Gordy, Robert Warrens, Richard Johnson, Jim Richard, John Scott, Ida Kohlmeyer, Lin Emery, George Dureau, Randell Henry, Willie Birch, and Lynda Benglis. An exceptional collection of Southern self-taught artists includes Clementine Hunter, Sister Gertrude Morgan, Bruce Brice, David Butler, and Willie White.

Lunches, light snacks, and coffee are served in the sleek and stylish **Courtyard Cafe,** decorated with original works. Regional crafts, books, gift items based on the permanent collection, and fun arty clothing (don't miss the Van Gogh socks) are definitely worth a visit to the Museum Shop. ◆ Admission; free Thursday 10AM to noon for Louisiana residents. Tu-Su 10AM-5PM. 1 Collins Diboll Cir (at Lelong Dr). 488.2631; www.noma.com

FISHING

The park's lagoons contain all species found in the fresh or brackish waters of South Louisiana, including bass, catfish, and perch. Fishing permits are required; they can be purchased at the boat dock behind the **Casino.** ◆ Permit office, daily. Dreyfus Ave. 482.4888

WISNER TENNIS CENTER

One of the South's largest public tennis facilities boasts 36 lighted Rubico and Laykold courts. The complex offers individual and group lessons by **USPTA** pros, racquet rentals, and a pro shop. ◆ Daily 7AM-7PM Jan-Feb; M-Th 7AM-10PM, F-Su 7AM-7PM Mar-Nov; daily 7AM-5PM Dec. Victory Ave. 483.9383

NEW ORLEANS BOTANICAL GARDEN

WPA workers in the 1930s built this seven-acre garden and many of the Art Deco fountains, reflecting pools, and statues were designed by sculptor Enrique Alferez. Several major collections include bromeliads, begonias, ferns, seasonal floral and vegetable gardens, a water garden, and large tropicals from around the world. A garden shop vends supplies, seeds, gift items, and books. ◆ Admission. Tu-Su. Victory Ave. 483.9386&

STORYLAND

The first brave trip into the belly of the blue whale has been a rite of passage for local children since this charming fairy tale park was built in the 1950s. Kids can interact with 26 larger-than-life exhibits and attend weekend shows at the Puppet Castle. Don't miss the haunted house during the Halloween season. ◆ Admission. Sa-Su Jan-Feb; W-Su Mar-May and Sept-Dec; daily June-Aug; open 5:30-10PM for Celebration in the Oaks from Thanksgiving to 4 Jan. Victory Ave. 482.4888 &

CAROUSEL GARDENS

Known to generations of New Orleanians as "The Flying Horses," the antique carousel was built in 1906 on City Park Avenue and was moved to its present location in 1928. One of the few remaining carved wooden carousels in the country, it was placed on the National Register of Historic Places in 1989. Nearby you'll find one of three boarding stations for the miniature train, which has traveled through the park since 1898. Other rides in this quaint amusement area under the oaks include a small Ferris wheel, roller coaster, and antique cars. ◆ Admission. Sa-Su Jan-Feb; W-Su Mar-May and Sept-Dec; daily June-Aug; open 5:30-10PM for Celebration in the Oaks from Thanksgiving to 4 Jan. Victory Ave. 482.4888

CITY PARK TRACK

This 400-meter international track was designed for the 1992 Olympic Track and Field Trials and is now open to the public. The eight polyurethane lanes are designated for various levels of runners and walkers. ◆ Daily. Roosevelt Mall. 483.9496

BAYOU OAKS GOLF COURSES

This park has the largest municipal golf facility in the South, hosting 165,000 annually on four 18-hole courses. The facility offers electric carts, individual and group lessons by PGA pros, a pro shop, and the **Clubhouse Restaurant.** ◆ Greens fee. Daily. Filmore Ave. 483.9396

BAYOU OAKS DRIVING RANGE

This 100-tee, lighted, double-decker facility is staffed by PGA pros. ◆ Daily 9AM-10PM (last bucket 9PM). Filmore Ave and Wisner Blvd. 483.9394

CITY PARK STABLES

The staff gives individual and group lessons (by appointment only) and hosts a number of horse shows each year. ◆ Daily. Filmore Ave. 483.9398

2 LAKE LAWN METAIRIE CEMETERY

Welcome to one of the most remarkable attractions in town, crammed with bizarre photo opportunities. A little more than 120 years old, this relative latecomer is much more spacious than the crowded cities of the dead that served the densely populated French Quarter. Like the newer neighborhoods beyond its gates, this suburb of the dead has streets wide enough for cars and many of the magnificent crypts are surrounded by patches of green. Just as New Orleans's growing numbers of wealthy residents demanded gardens for their huge mansions, they also laid out bigger plots to build some of the most beautiful private funerary architecture in North America. **Metairie** is the one cemetery in town that is safe for individuals to explore on their own. Roam at will among tombs ranging from the sublime to the slaphappy. Gothic chapels, complete with elaborate stained-glass windows, stand side by side with Moorish temples and Oriental pagodas. You'll even see a pyramid guarded by a granite sphinx. One 60-foot-tall obelisk is situated on an 85-foot diameter plot. Another stately monument is modeled on the Tower of the Winds in Athens. On the National Register of Historic Places, this cemetery has 2,243 monuments, tombs, and buildings of historic interest. Stop by the flower shop at the entrance to the funeral home and trade your driver's license for a cassette player and tape that will lead you on a general tour (40 minutes), or one that visits Civil War soldiers and Louisiana statesmen (one hour), or great families of commerce (one hour). ♦ Free. Daily 7:30AM-5PM; tape equipment available 8:30AM-3PM. 5100 Pontchartrain Blvd (at Metairie Rd). 486.6331 &

3 PARKWAY TAVERN

When the satellite dish and cable connections deliver four or five games at once, the atmosphere can be more charged up than the real thing at a stadium. You'll certainly be closer to famous players' jerseys, shoes, hockey sticks, and other paraphernalia, which dangle from the ceiling and decorate the walls. But this is no theme-park sports bar; it's a funky old neighborhood hangout where you can tune in to several different events and get into as many arguments without leaving your chair. Not just for jocks, the most hotly contested games are scheduled every Thursday, for Ladies' Night, when the under-30 mob spills out onto the sidewalks. ♦ M-F from 2PM; Sa-Su from noon. 5135 Canal Blvd (between City Park Ave and Rosedale Dr). 488.2500 &

4 SEMOLINA

★★$ Singles can dine comfortably at the full-service pasta bar here, and the imaginative decor suits the casual atmosphere. Three-dimensional sculptures accent the hand-detailed walls, and large papier-mâché vegetables brighten the dark ceiling. Both food and wines are reasonably priced, which appeals to the youngish clientele. The menu is comprised of pastas of the world, with dishes ranging from curried-chicken linguine to pasta Chicago (spiked with sweet Italian sausage and garlic in red gravy). Entirely nonsmoking dining. Valet parking is free, but the lot can fill up during peak hours. ♦ Italian ♦ Daily lunch and dinner. 5080 Pontchartrain Blvd (at Metairie Rd). 486.5581 & Also at: Numerous locations throughout the area.

5 LONGUE VUE HOUSE AND GARDENS

A handsome estate that sits right smack on the border between Orleans and Jefferson Parishes, this was the home of the late philanthropists Edith Rosenwald Stern and Edgar Bloom Stern, she an heiress to the Sears fortune and he a wealthy cotton broker. Needless to say, money was no object in the building and furnishing of their Classical Revival home, designed in 1942 by New York architects **William and Geoffrey Platt.** Two sculpted American eagles atop brick pillars frame the entry court. They stand guard on either side of a long driveway, overarched by giant oak trees, which leads to the front door. Surrounding the house are spectacular gardens (the work of landscape architect **Ellen Biddle Shipman**), including the formal **Spanish Court,** patterned after the 14th-century Generalife Gardens of the Alhambra in Spain; the **Louisiana Native Garden,** which features delicate camellias and other indigenous blooms; and the **Portuguese Canal Garden,** showcasing a narrow canal graced with fountains and framed by azaleas and ferns. A **Discovery Garden** for children incorporates a historic greenhouse and mysterious bamboo tunnel. Within the house, the original furnishings and objets d'art remain. European, American, and Oriental antiques can be seen here, as well as displays of modern art and pottery, the latter including a collection of creamware made at Wedgwood and Leeds. The dining room walls are covered with intri-

Longue Vue House and Gardens

cately patterned Chinese rice paper, and the table is set with changing displays of fine crystal, china, and silver. The millwork and ornate cornices are also of particular note. ◆ Admission. Daily (last house tour starts at 4PM). 7 Bamboo Rd (between Palmetto St and Metairie Rd). 488.5488 &

6 TAVERN ON THE PARK

★★$$$ Polished brass fittings and gleaming dark woods create a warm and clubby atmosphere in this elegant restaurant overlooking **City Park,** housed in a building originally constructed as a coffeehouse in 1860. During a long and colorful past, it has hosted a bizarre spectrum of society. General Butler of the Union Army was a customer during the Civil War. Storyville's notorious "ladies of the night" came here with their gentlemen friends. Socialites were known to pop in for a risqué evening of slumming. Located near the infamous dueling oaks, legend has it that many a victorious gentleman stopped here to steady his nerves with a brandy-laced shot of caffeine. Today the menu offers traditional New Orleans fare, such as turtle soup, trout dishes, and barbecued shrimp. ◆ Creole ◆ Tu-F lunch and dinner; Sa dinner. Reservations recommended. 900 City Park Ave (at Dumaine St). 486.3333

7 SACRED HEART ORPHAN ASYLUM/CABRINI HIGH SCHOOL

Mother Cabrini lived in this building from 1905 until her death in 1917; Pope Pius XII, who declared her patroness of immigrants, signed her Decree of Canonization in 1946. The orphanage's beautiful chapel recently received a complete, careful restoration. The rich wood wainscoting and floors had been obscured by paint and carpeting for years. Mother Cabrini herself selected her favorite saints as the subjects for the chapel's stained-glass windows. She is depicted in the statue that stands by the altar, as well as in a canvas mural attached to the ceiling and a stained-glass window. Mother Cabrini's room, with its original furniture, is still dutifully maintained, and her bedspread from Italy still covers the bed. This is a working building so the chapel and restored room are only open by special request. ◆ By appointment only. 3400 Esplanade Ave (between Ponce de Leon and Moss Sts). 482.1193

7 PITOT HOUSE

James Pitot, first mayor of incorporated New Orleans, bought this house in 1810 from the great-grandmother of French Impressionist painter Edgar Degas. At that time, it was considered a country home. Erected in 1799, this stucco-covered brick structure was designed in the style of West Indies plantation manors. With wide covered porches all around, there was always shade somewhere. In the days long before hurricane tracking, solid wood shutters were ready to close at a moment's notice if a storm blew in. In 1904 the estate was purchased for a convent by Mother Frances Xavier Cabrini, the first US citizen to be canonized by the Catholic Church. In 1962, her missionary sisters donated the property to the Louisiana Landmarks Society, which moved the house from its original location at 1370 Moss Street to the present address. The house has been meticulously restored and furnished with authentic period furniture. ◆ Admission. W-Sa 10AM-3PM. 1440 Moss St (between Ursulines and Esplanade Aves). 482.0312 &

8 BAYOU ST. JOHN

Ⓟ Though the word comes from the Choctaw *bayuk,* which means river or creek, a bayou is actually a natural canal that has no current. Once barges traveled this important waterway into town, loaded with construction materials from the steamships that plied Lake Pontchartrain. These timbers and bricks, produced in St. Tammany Parish on the lake's north shore, were used to build **St. Louis Cathedral** and many of the other principal buildings of old New Orleans. In the 19th century, the banks of the bayou were lined with beautiful houses, and several still stand on what is now known as Moss Street. Only **Pitot House** (see above) is open for tours. The Greek Revival manor at 1342 Moss Street was built around 1834, and the old plantation house at 1300 Moss Street dates back to 1784. For a pleasant drive (or bike ride), begin at the corner of Orleans Avenue and follow Moss Street to the bridge at the entrance of **City Park,** then cross the bridge to Wisner Boulevard on the park side and continue along the bayou's edge to Lake Pontchartrain.

Restaurants/Clubs: Red | Hotels: Purple | Shops: Orange | Outdoors/Parks: Green | Sights/Culture: Blue

ALL THAT JAZZ FEST

Every year, on the last weekend in April and the first weekend in May, more than 4,000 musicians, singers, chefs, artists, and craftspeople flock to the **New Orleans Fair Grounds** in **Mid City** to create one of the world's premiere celebrations. The New Orleans Jazz and Heritage Festival (or Jazz Fest) is a feast for the ears, a major binge for connoisseurs of jazz (both traditional and modern), zydeco, gospel, blues, folk, world beat, and good old-fashioned rock 'n' roll. Top local and national artists (such as the Neville Brothers, Dr. John, and Fats Domino) perform at the festival, and music clubs all over town are booked solid with the overflow talent throughout the week. In fact, some of the audience members are even more famous than the acts on stage—Paul McCartney, Paul Simon, and Sting are just a few of the familiar faces that have been spotted in the crowd in recent years.

Jazz Fest is also the scene of a regional food extravaganza, where more than 50 cooks prepare and serve food for thousands of hungry music lovers. Competition is stiff for the spare 10-by-10-foot booths, and the chefs who make the cut must offer traditional dishes that represent one of the many ethnic groups that have settled in New Orleans. No funnel cakes here—belly up for gumbo ya-ya, crawfish étouffée, fried alligator, roast suckling pig, oysters *en brochette,* Cuban sandwiches, shrimp po-boys, pecan pies, and hundreds of other indigenous eats.

First-rate crafts and artwork by regional artisans include oak rockers, willow furniture, handmade jewelry, zydeco rub boards, hand-painted T-shirts, paintings, and sculpture.

Due to the festival's staggering popularity, hotel reservations need to be made well in advance (a year ahead isn't too soon), and restaurants fill up quickly, too. For schedules and details, contact the New Orleans Jazz and Heritage Festival office (1205 N Rampart St, New Orleans, LA 70116, 522.4786).

9 NEW ORLEANS FAIR GROUNDS

The historic grandstand and clubhouse (moved here from **City Park** in 1907) were destroyed by fire in 1993, but the restored facility recalls the style of the old building, with the clubhouse located right on the finish line. Racing season here at the third-oldest thoroughbred track in the US traditionally opens on Thanksgiving Day and runs until late March. Originally called the **Creole Race Course,** the facility was taken over in 1872 by the **Louisiana Jockey Club.** The main track is a one-mile oval of sandy loam soil, and the distance from the last turn to the finish line is 1,346 feet, making it the second-longest stretch in the nation. The turf course, approximately seven furlongs, is inside the main track. The fairgrounds got its name from early fairs held here by the Mechanics and Agricultural Association. Today, it is the (traditionally rain-buffeted and muddy) site of the New Orleans Jazz & Heritage Festival (522.4786), which takes over the complex every year for the last weekend in April and the first weekend in May. ♦ Admission. Post time M, Th-Su 12:30PM. 1751 Gentilly Blvd (between Ponce de Leon St and Desaix Blvd). 944.5515, clubhouse dining room reservations 943.2200, 800/262.7983

10 GABRIELLE

★★★★$$$ Nothing is ever frozen at this very popular restaurant, except the homemade ice cream. Chef Greg Sonnier and Mary Sonnier, his wife and pastry chef, have won a strong local and national following, including rave reviews in such publications as *Food and Wine, Bon Appétit,* and *Travel & Leisure.* The Sonniers have also been featured on *CBS Sunday Morning.* The menu changes weekly to take advantage of the freshest ingredients available at local markets. Treatments vary, but rabbit dishes and homemade andouille sausage usually feature prominently. Recent offerings have included seared foie gras on "pig's ear" pastry with huckleberry sauce and cracker-crusted rabbit Creole (with shrimp, rabbit sausage, and red sauce). Only the bread is made off the premises. The fresh style extends to the decor, which is a crisp ensemble of linen and lace, quiet colors, and plenty of flowers. Plate-glass windows overlook the trees of Esplanade Avenue. The tiny dining room only seats 40, but in fine weather guests happily move to outdoor tables on a landscaped deck. ♦ Contemporary Creole ♦ Tu-Sa dinner; open for lunch F Oct-May. Reservations recommended. 3201 Esplanade Ave (at Mystery St). 948.6233 ఉ

11 TRUE BREW COFFEE

Leave your suits in the closet if you want to dress for success with the friendly regulars who hang out at this tiny neighborhood shop. Each new day brings different hot and iced coffees and teas, and the pastries are simple but well prepared. Inside seating is pleasant, though cramped; the outdoor patio, also small, is quiet and pretty. Watch out for the chocolate-covered espresso beans; it's hard to stop at one or two, but more will have you bouncing off the walls. ♦ M-Sa 6:30AM-10PM; Su 7AM-10PM. 3133 Ponce de Leon St (between N Lopez St and Esplanade Ave). 947.3948 ఉ Also at: 200 Julia St (at Convention Center Blvd). 524.8441

11 WHOLE FOODS MARKET

A steady diet of New Orleans food can be a bit much after a few days. If you feel like your arteries will petrify at the sight of another fried shrimp, this local outlet of the national grocery chain is a good place to pack up a healthy picnic for nearby **City Park**. This market does carry the organically grown produce that the name promises, but it goes far beyond sprouted wheat bread and tofu. The stock also includes one of the city's largest selections of cheeses, good wines, and house-baked pastries. Belly up to the deli counter for spinach pie, whole baked chickens, vegetarian tamales, stuffed grape leaves, hummus, shrimp and hearts of palm salad, couscous, and much more. Specialty sandwiches include The Briez (brie, Black Forest ham, red onion, and lettuce on French bread) and Jim Bob (smoked turkey, swiss cheese, and coleslaw on honey-wheat bread). There are a few sidewalk tables, but no seating inside. To fortify yourself for several days, stock up from the huge selection of bulk nuts, trail mixes, and granolas. This is a blue-corn chip sort of place, but most of the exotica really tastes good. ♦ Daily 8:30AM-9:30PM. 3135 Esplanade Ave (at Mystery St). 943.1626; fax 947.7901; www.wholefoodsmarket.com ♿

12 CAFÉ DEGAS

★$ There's quite a story behind the name of this tiny Parisian-style cafe. French impressionist Edgar Degas lived and worked in the Esplanade Ridge neighborhood for a short time. His grandfather was a Louisiana cotton merchant, and Degas's painting of *The Cotton Market* in New Orleans was his first work sold to a museum. The Franco-Louisiana connection continues in the French menu (blessed by English translations), which offers a light selection of omelettes, appetizers, soups, and salads. Duck *à l'orange* and rack of lamb are good. The triangular building that just fits into the point of a sharp intersection used to be a barber shop, so there's not much elbow room. Sheltered outdoor tables are especially quaint and airy, cooled by ceiling fans. ♦ French ♦ Daily lunch and dinner. 3127 Esplanade Ave (at Ponce de Leon St). 945.5635 ♿

13 ROCK'N BOWL

One of the hottest music venues around is housed in a frumpy old bowling alley in a hideous shopping strip. Touristy this ain't, but the house is packed with natives Wednesday through Saturday nights when top local performers set the whole joint to howling. A single neon bowling pin and a faded sign that announces "**Mid City Lanes**, home of **Rock 'n Bowl**, since 1941" are the only exterior clues—and they don't look too promising—but take a deep breath and climb the stairs for what could turn out to be one of your favorite experiences in New Orleans. Bands play upstairs and down (at **Bowl Me Under**) for a revel without a pause, as rockers in bowling shoes shimmy on the approach lanes and everybody else crams the dance floors. Music can range from nasty old rhythm and blues to the latest world beat, sometimes on the same night, and usually minus a cover charge. Don't miss Boozoo Chavis, The Iguanas, Nathan & the Zydeco Cha Chas, or Marva Wright. There's full bar service at an ancient wooden island set in the center of the action, and the snack bar dispenses such unlikely fare as gumbo, fried alligator, po-boys, and dinner plates mounded with side orders of baked macaroni and salad. The walls are splashed with hand-painted murals that depict local street scenes, circa 1950. This is no place for finicky humorless types, but then neither is New Orleans. When you get home, you'll probably tell more people about **Rock 'n Bowl** than about **St. Louis Cathedral**. It's a true original. ♦ Mid-City Lanes: M-Th from 4PM, F-Su from noon; swing bands Tu 8:30-9:30PM, zydeco W-Th 9:30PM-2:30AM, various live music F-Su 9:30PM-2:30AM. 4133 S Carrollton Ave (between Tulane Ave and Ulloa St). 482.3133

13 BANGKOK CUISINE

★★$ Stop at this airy storefront space to heat up your senses for an evening of **Rock 'n Bowl** next door, since the snack bar food at

---

Restaurants/Clubs: Red | **Hotels: Purple** | **Shops: Orange** | **Outdoors/Parks: Green** | **Sights/Culture: Blue**

93

Mid-City Lanes is far too heavy for serious dancers. The curries are very good (especially the hot green curry), as are glass-noodle dishes and chicken soup flavored with coconut milk. Other house specialties are pad thai (panfried Siamese noodles with chicken, baby shrimp, bean sprouts, and green onions) and deep-fried eggplant wedges mounded with spicy jumbo shrimp. The service is friendly and super efficient. ♦ Thai ♦ M-F lunch and dinner; Sa-Su dinner. 4137 S Carrollton Ave (between Tulane Ave and Ulloa St). 482.3606

Genghis Khan

14 GENGHIS KHAN

★★★$$ Korean and other Asian fare at this elegant restaurant is accompanied by some of the best music in town: Owner Henry Lee, formerly a violinist with the **New Orleans Symphony Orchestra,** performs Tuesday through Thursday and Sunday nights (with a chamber group, pianist, or operatic singer). Friday and Saturday nights are especially festive, with a multi-course set menu and singing waiters and waitresses who belt out operatic and show tunes. For appetizers, try *bulgoki* (marinated charcoal-grilled beef), *mandu* (fried Korean dumplings similar to Chinese wontons but with more meat), and exotic "kim and caviar" (paper-thin sheets of dried seaweed, toasted and served with fried rice and caviar, eaten like a taco). The signature crispy whole fish is marinated in seasoned wine and fried in peanut oil. Marinated shrimp, beef, and vegetables are simmered with noodles and broth in a Korean hotpot that is brought to the table. For a night off from Cajun and Creole cuisine, this is one of the best quick getaways in town. ♦ Asian ♦ Tu-Su dinner. Reservations recommended. 4053 Tulane Ave (between S Pierce St and S Carrollton Ave). 482.4044

India House Backpackers Hostel

15 INDIA HOUSE

$ There are about 60 beds in this funky old hostel and its outbuildings, where the atmosphere is so casual that no one is quite sure of the exact number. Accommodations are dormitory-style; separate female and male dorms house singles, and couples are billeted in a limited number of private rooms and mixed dorms. There's no restaurant, but guests can bring in their own food and cook anytime in the community kitchen. They can also smoke or drink (within reason) in the common areas. A small aboveground pool is nicknamed "the Indian Ocean." To accommodate late checkouts and no curfew, the desk is staffed around the clock. A limited amount of free off-street

parking is available, too. This place is certainly rough around the edges, but the bohemian atmosphere is safe and friendly, and the international clientele seems to be mostly young and well-educated. ♦ 124 S Lopez St (between Cleveland Ave and Canal St). 821.1904; www.indiahousehostel.com

16 RUTH'S CHRIS STEAK HOUSE

★★★★$$$$ Owner Ruth Fertel's name now appears over a steak house empire that stretches from coast to coast. This dining room decorated with lots of dark wood, brass accents, plush upholstery, and deep green walls is the original restaurant. Join the local mob here for prime Midwestern beef that is aged, hand-cut, and served in a sizzling pool of butter (unless otherwise requested). It's a take-the-plunge spot where even the vegetables are fried, creamed, or sauced with hollandaise, and liquor is swirled into rich "dessert freezes." Prices are high, but so is the quality. Drive right to the door for valet parking. ♦ American ♦ M-F, Su lunch and dinner; Sa dinner. Reservations recommended. 711 N Broad St (at Orleans Ave). 486.0810 ♿ Also at: 3633 Veterans Memorial Blvd (at Hessmer Ave), Metairie. 888.3600

17 DEGAS HOUSE

$$$ French Impressionist Edgar Degas lived in this house from October 1872 to April 1873, when it belonged to his uncle, cotton merchant Michel Musson. The restoration of the 1852 structure received an award from the Louisiana Preservation Alliance, an affiliate of the National Trust for Historic

Preservation. Today it's an upscale bed-and-breakfast with seven guest rooms fitted out with 19th-century antiques and reproductions, crystal chandeliers, and Degas prints. Each of the rooms is named after a member of the Musson family; for example, the honeymoon suite (featuring a king-size bed and a private balcony that stretches the length of the house) is known as "Estelle's suite." Every morning, guests are served continental breakfast in the breakfast room, which is thought to have been the artist's studio. Tours of the property are available to nonguests. ♦ 2306 Esplanade Ave (between N Miro and N Tonti Sts). 821.5009, 800/755.6730; fax 821.0870; www.degashouse.com

18 THE HOUSE ON BAYOU ROAD

$$$ This small, West Indies-style plantation house was built for a Spanish Colonial diplomat in 1798. These days, it is a country-style inn set on two acres of gardens, ponds, and patios—and conveniently located just 11 blocks from the French Quarter. Guests are accommodated in four bedrooms in the main house, three bedrooms and a suite in a cottage, or a private one-bedroom cottage with a wet bar and Jacuzzi. All feature feather beds, robes, and slippers. A full breakfast, cooked by owner Cynthia Reeves, is served in a dining room furnished with Louisiana antiques. Though this place has the informal atmosphere of a bed-and-breakfast, it also offers such hotel-style amenities as a swimming pool, hot tub, limo service to and from the airport, secured parking, and workout privileges at a nearby athletic club. Reeves also operates a cooking school here, and packages which include classes are available. ♦ 2275 Bayou Rd (at N Miro St). 945.0992, 949.7711; 800/882.2968; fax 945.0993; www.houseonbayouroad.com

19 DOOKY CHASE

★★★$$ This bustling, comfortable New Orleans landmark was established in 1941 by Edgar "Dooky" Chase Sr. and his wife, Emily Tenette, and it soon became an important institution within the local black community. Today, the business is run by Dooky Chase Jr. and his wife, Leah Chase, who has an international reputation for her authentic Creole cuisine. She learned to cook from her mother, and her pots are still seasoned with the bay leaves and thyme that her sister grows at their childhood home in Madisonville. The filé for her gumbo is fresh, ground from the leaves of a sassafras tree that her father planted. Try her stuffed jumbo shrimp, crawfish étouffée, or redfish court bouillon (smothered with tomatoes, green peppers, and other seasonings). Breast of chicken à la Dooky is stuffed with oyster dressing, baked slowly in a wine sauce, and served with sweet potatoes. Mamere's crab soup and stuffed bell peppers are excellent as well. Take note of the changing exhibits of African art. This fine restaurant is located in what could be called an unsafe neighborhood, so take a cab to the door—it's worth the trip. ♦ Creole ♦ Daily lunch and dinner. Reservations recommended for dinner. 2301 Orleans Ave (at N Miro St). 821.2294, 821.0600

20 THE LION'S DEN

"The Queen of New Orleans," R&B legend Irma Thomas, is a regular here at her own club, a little down-home place with a rather forbidding exterior. The late-afternoon Happy Hour is popular with folks who work at nearby Parish Prison, and regularly scheduled live entertainment at night draws a mixed crowd with plenty of Europeans and other out-of-towners. If you're lucky, Miss Irma might cook her famous red beans, rice, and sausage (serve yourself a bowl), and she usually performs here nightly during Jazz Fest and Carnival. ♦ M-Sa from 3PM. ♦ 2655 Gravier St (between S Dorgenois and S Broad Sts). 822.4693

21 NICK'S BAR

Established by world-famous local mixologist Nick Castrogiovanni in 1918, this Mid City institution has packed in a hard-drinking university crowd for generations. Check the enormous sign on the wall for a l-o-n-g list of specialty concoctions that reads like the menu at an ice cream parlor, only much more risqué—some might even say offensive. And this is certainly no place for folks who are easily offended. The hard-surfaced floors are utilitarian, as are the coiled garden hoses that quickly dispose of the unfortunate side effects of mixing tropical cocktails with fraternity boys. It's an experience that those in their twilight years (over 25) might choose to avoid, but if you want to sample the truly remarkable range of intoxicants in peace, stop by weekdays between 3 and 10PM. ♦ M-F from 2PM; Sa from 4PM; Su from 6PM. 2400 Tulane Ave (at S Tonti St). 821.9128 ♿

22 PJ'S COFFEE & TEA CO.

Located in a renovated old house, this comfortable and understated oasis is a great place to recoup and fortify yourself for more sightseeing. Settle into one of the two inside rooms or a table on the shaded front deck. Tree-lined Carrollton Avenue offers pleasant long-range views if you're feeling a little claustrophobic from rambling the French

Quarter or old cemeteries. Newcomers wilt easily in hot weather and a stiff iced coffee is one of the quickest ways to cool down and perk up. The shop also carries bulk coffees (roasted in town), mugs, and other paraphernalia. ♦ M-F 6:45AM-8:30PM; Sa-Su 8AM-8:30PM. 637 N Carrollton Ave (at St. Peter St). 482.4847 & Also at: Numerous locations throughout the city

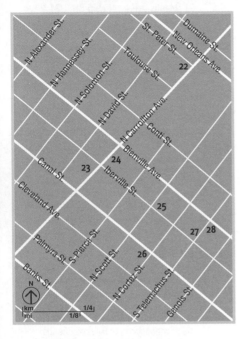

23 BENNACHIN RESTAURANT

★★$ Co-owners Alyse Njenge and Fanta Tambajang, natives of Cameroon and Gambia respectively, oversee the kitchen and two sparkling dining rooms enlivened by folk art and African music. Waitresses in traditional dress are congenial and easy on newcomers, correcting botched pronunciations with good humor as they answer questions about the menu. One star attraction is *akara* (crisp black-eyed-pea fritters) served with tomato stew as an appetizer or on French bread as a vegetarian sandwich. *Shipa-shipa* is a close cousin of shrimp Creole, stewed in a tomato sauce flavored with garlic and ginger. *Domoda* smothers beef chunks in a rich gravy

North America's only version of absinthe—minus the narcotic wormwood—is still produced by the Sazerac Company of New Orleans, which sells about 5,000 bottles of its Herbsaint annually, mostly to local fans. The anise-flavored liqueur is one of the main ingredients in the historic Sazerac, generally acknowledged as the world's first cocktail, which was created by a French Quarter druggist.

thickened with ground peanuts. *Bomok-chobi,* which must be ordered 90 minutes in advance, is a whole trout stuffed with ginger, garlic, and *nphebe* (an African spice similar to nutmeg), baked to a golden brown and served with fried ripe plantains and sautéed spinach. The regular menu is inexpensive, but lunch is a real bargain, with several specials priced under $5 until 4PM. ♦ African ♦ M-F lunch and dinner; Sa dinner. 133 N Carrollton Ave (between Canal and Iberville Sts). 486.1313

23 PALMER'S JAMAICAN CREOLE RESTAURANT

★★$ Local customers will recognize familiar flavors in these exotic-sounding dishes, as much of New Orleans Creole food is based on recipes that early cooks brought here from their Caribbean homelands. You'll almost hear that lilting island patois as you read the menu that features "Jamaican flatten chicken" (pounded thin, sautéed, and served over fettuccine with a tangy Spanish sauce), pepper pot soup, Bahamian chowder, and West Indian curried goat. Best bets are "jerked" fish (marinated in hot peppers, Jamaican pimiento, and lime juice, then sautéed, and served with a tomato/onion sauce), and marinated roast pork tenderloin (stuffed with onions). Chef/owner Cecil Palmer was born in Jamaica, and the two small dining rooms have a distinctly Caribbean atmosphere, full of bright colors and friendly chatter. It offers a cool respite on a hot summer day. ♦ Caribbean ♦ Tu-F lunch and dinner; Sa dinner. 135 N Carrollton Ave (between Canal and Iberville Sts). 482.3658

The Original

ANGELO BROCATO'S

ICE CREAM & CONFECTIONERY INC.

24 ANGELO BROCATO ICE CREAM AND CONFECTIONERY

More than a century ago, 12-year-old Angelo Brocato began an apprenticeship in a Palermo ice-cream parlor where he learned the special recipes for the sumptuous desserts of Sicily. As a young immigrant, Brocato worked on a sugar plantation until he earned enough money to start a tiny ice-cream shop, which was originally located in the French Quarter. Four generations later, his descendants still use his recipes to prepare colorful Sicilian cookies and pastries, as well as a full line of fresh fruit Italian ices and authentic gelati. Beautiful pastel wedges of spumoni are layered with pistachio, tutti-frutti, and lemon ice creams. *Cassata* has an additional layer of cake and chips of candied fruit. *Torroncino* is vanilla ice cream flavored with imported almond and cinnamon. The crisp pastry tubes that form cannoli are filled with sweetened ricotta cheese (chocolate on one end, vanilla on the other) and dipped in crushed pistachio nuts—great with cappuccino. The shop here in Mid City, now the only Brocato branch in town, remains true to the family tradition, with ceiling fans, glass-topped tables, and rows of apothecary jars filled with multihued candies. Just say yes. ♦ M-Th, Su 9:30AM-10PM; F-Sa 9:30AM-10:30PM. 214 N Carrollton Ave (between Iberville St and Bienville Ave). 486.0078 ♿

25 CHRISTIAN'S RESTAURANT

★★★★$$$ A small old church is the ideal setting for this formal and elegant restaurant. Dark woodwork and stained-glass windows add even more weight to the crisply dignified service, but hanging plants add splashes of color that keep the atmosphere from getting *too* somber. Appropriately enough, the church's former "crying baby room" is now a small but richly appointed bar. A fine indigenous spin on bouillabaisse Marseillaise is stocked with fish fillets, shrimp, oysters, and crabmeat simmered in saffron-flavored stock. Succulent signature dish beef fillet *farci* "Bayou La Loutre" is stuffed with a smoked oyster and garnished with more oysters in a demi-glace sauce. Baby veal Christian is sautéed and topped with fresh cream sauce, Port wine, and morel mushrooms. Ice creams, fresh fruit ices, and pastries are all made in-house. ♦ Creole/French ♦ Tu-F lunch and dinner; Sa dinner. Reservations recommended; jacket requested. Free parking. 3835 Iberville St (at N Scott St). 482.4924

26 MANDINA'S RESTAURANT AND BAR

★★$ These waiters can afford to affect an independent attitude—and they certainly do—when regular customers are lined up at the bar waiting for tables. A local hangout for generations, this unpretentious eatery is known for its turtle soup, trout (meunière or amandine), onion rings, fried oysters, and stuffed shrimp. Dinner specials (corned beef

and cabbage, spaghetti and meatballs, shrimp Creole, turkey with oyster dressing) change daily. Start with piquant shrimp remoulade or oyster-artichoke soup. Steaks, gumbo, and marinated crab fingers are good, too. The service is brisk and efficient, but don't expect to be coddled. ♦ Creole/Italian ♦ Daily lunch and dinner. 3800 Canal St (at N Cortez St). 482.9179 ♿

27 KATIE'S

★★$ Fried seafood and pasta dishes are especially good at this family-owned restaurant that draws a heavy lunch crowd from nearby hospitals and offices. Mama Mary's Italian Salad is loaded with egg, Genoa salami, chopped olives, artichoke hearts, mozzarella cheese, and mild Italian peppers. Don't miss the fried eggplant fingers served with a bowl of hot marinara sauce for dipping. ♦ Creole/Italian ♦ M-Sa lunch and dinner. 3701 Iberville St (at N Telemachus St). 488.6582

28 LIUZZA'S RESTAURANT & BAR

★★$ In a city known for casual neighborhood restaurants with wonderful food, this is one of the best. Little has changed since the grand opening in 1947, and devoted customers like things just the way they are. The mashed potatoes are real, and the 18-ounce fishbowl beer mugs are frozen before they're filled with the brew—in fact the restaurant won a prize for serving the coldest beer in town. Don't miss the onion rings, always freshly batter-dipped just before they're fried, and piled high and light. The fried seafood is excellent, as are *panéed* (breaded) veal with fettuccine Alfredo, eggplant casserole, stuffed crab, calf's liver smothered with onions, spaghetti, and the daily specials. Fried chicken is prepared to order and well worth the 30-minute wait. Don't even walk through the door if you're watching your cholesterol, though the dining room is packed with doctors from the hospital across the street who are certainly not heeding their own advice. They're smoking, too, which can be bothersome in this confined (and very noisy) space, although an exhaust system and separate nonsmoking area help to alleviate the problem. ♦ Creole/Italian ♦ M-Sa lunch and dinner. 3636 Bienville Ave (at N Telemachus St). 482.9120 ♿

Restaurants/Clubs: **Red** | Hotels: **Purple** | Shops: Orange | Outdoors/Parks: Green | Sights/Culture: Blue

THE ABC'S OF CRESCENT CITY CUISINE

For New Orleanians, food is not meant to be gobbled down in a race to get to the main attraction—it *is* the main attraction. A meal is lingered over, commented on, savored, and after it is (sadly) over, fondly remembered.

A luxurious binge at one of the grand Creole dining temples, such as **Galatoire's** (209 Bourbon St, between Iberville and Bienville Sts, 525.2021), **Antoine's** (713 St. Louis St, between Royal and Bourbon Sts, 581.4422; fax 581.3003; www.antoines.com &), or **Commander's Palace** (1403 Washington Ave, at Coliseum St, 899.8221; www.commanderspalace.com &), is an absolute must on any culinary pilgrimage to New Orleans. Tables worth gracing can also be found at **Bayona** (430 Dauphine St, between Conti and St. Louis Sts, 525.4455; www.bayona.com), **Emeril's** (800 Tchoupitoulas St, at Julia St, 528.9393; www.emerils.com &), Cuvée (322 Magazine St., 587-9001) and other stylish bistros where the city's younger chefs are cooking up international reputations for their cross-cultural cuisine. Diners on a strict budget can soak up plenty of atmosphere (and calories) at lunchtime, when most of these swank establishments offer reasonably priced table d'hôte specials. Meanwhile, the tab is always rock bottom at such neighborhood favorites as **Liuzza's** (3636 Bienville St, at N Telemachus St, 482.9120 &), **Uglesich's** (1238 Baronne St, at Erato St, 523.8571), and **West End Cafe** (8536 Pontchartrain Blvd, between W Robert E. Lee Blvd and Lake Ave, 288.0711).

For a quick primer on New Orleans and South Louisiana cuisine, consult the following list of dishes, ingredients, and dining lingo.

Andouille (On-*doo*-ee)
The very spicy Cajun sausage, stuffed with chunks of lean ham, is usually sliced and tossed into a gumbo, or grilled whole and served with piquant pepper jelly or other relishes.

Bananas Foster
Originally created at **Brennan's Restaurant,** this classic dessert now appears on many local menus. The bananas are sautéed in butter, brown sugar, cinnamon, and banana liqueur, then doused with white rum, flamed tableside, and heaped over vanilla ice cream.

Beignets (Ben-*yays*)
Pillow-shaped hot doughnuts, puffed with yeast and dusted with powdered sugar, have drawn the crowds to **Café du Monde** for more than a century.

Boudin (*Boo*-dan)
Rice, ground pork, and spices are stuffed into sausage casing and smoked; for crawfish or shrimp boudin, chopped shellfish is substituted for the pork.

Bread pudding
Made with crusty French bread and plenty of spice and raisins, then drenched with a buttery whiskey or brandy sauce, the New Orleans version of this dessert is anything but bland.

Café brûlot (Ca-*fay* broo-*low*)
At tony restaurants, strong coffee and various liqueurs are flamed tableside and ladled into cups with a great deal of fuss—and it usually looks better than it tastes.

Callas (*Cal*-iss)
As late as the 1930s, singing street vendors roamed the **French Quarter** toting baskets of hot rice fritters. Now hard to find, this authentic Creole breakfast dish, made with pecans and real maple syrup, is still served at the **Old Coffee Pot** restaurant.

Chicory coffee
Roasted chicory originally was used to stretch coffee rations during bad times, but the mellow blend lives on at **Café du Monde,** as well as in homes, coffeehouses, and restaurants throughout Louisiana. Waiters may ask if you want "chicory or regular," and custom dictates that the fragrant Creole brew be poured into the cup simultaneously with steaming hot milk for *café au lait*. Two good brands of chicory coffee available at most grocery stores are **CDM** and **Community**.

Court bouillon (*Coo* bee-yon)
A Spanish/Caribbean broth of tomatoes, onions, bell peppers, celery, bay leaves, and other spices that smothers fish or chicken and is served over rice.

Crab fingers
Peeled crab claws are either fried or marinated in garlicky olive oil for messy pick-up appetizers.

Crawfish bisque
The shells are cleaned and stuffed with a breaded crawfish dressing, then stewed with whole crawfish tails in a dark and rich gravy. (By the way, only Yankees say *CRAY*-fish; Southerners pronounce it the way it is spelled here.)

Crawfish pie
The freshwater critters in a peppery cream sauce are ladled into a prebaked crust or deep-fried like turnovers.

Creole mustard
Extra hot brown mustard is dense with flecks from the ground seeds. Look for **Zatarain's** brand in stores.

Dirty rice
Sometimes called "rice dressing," the spicy side dish tastes better than it sounds—it's flavored with ground chicken giblets and pork, onions, peppers, celery, and other seasonings.

Dressed
If you order a hamburger or sandwich "dressed," it'll come with mayonnaise, lettuce, and tomato.

Eggs Sardou (Eggs Sar-*doo*)
Poached eggs on a bed of creamed spinach and artichoke bottoms, topped with hollandaise.

Étouffée (*Ay*-too-fay)
Shrimp, crawfish, or chicken enveloped into a rich brown stew that is spooned over rice.

Filé (*Fee*-lay)
Powdered sassafras leaves used as a thickener in file gumbo.

Grillades (*Gree*-yods)
Thin slices of sautéed veal in spicy gravy are served with grits for this celebrated Creole breakfast delicacy.

Gumbo
If Louisiana has a signature dish, this is it. Seafood (or fowl) and sausage are simmered in a dark and complex broth flavored with onions, garlic, peppers, celery, and other seasonings, thickened with okra, roux, and filé, and ladled over rice.

Herbsaint (*Herb*-saint)
A locally produced legal version of absinthe, flavored with herbs, sometimes used in place of Pernod to spike seafood dishes.

Jambalaya (*Jam*-ba-*ly*-ah)
Spiced rice steamed with a combination of meats (shrimp, sausage, chicken) for a heated-up Cajun version of paella.

Maque choux (Mock *show*)
A side dish of seasoned corn.

Mirliton (*Mel*-ee-tawn)
Also known as a vegetable pear or chayote, the pale green squash is usually stuffed with a seafood or meat dressing.

Muffuletta (Muff-uh-*let*-uh)
A thick round of Italian bread layered with imported meats, cheeses, olive oil, and chopped olive salad, the hefty two-person sandwich originated at **Central Grocery** (923 Decatur St, between Dumaine and St. Philip Sts, 523.1620). The hot (broiled) version served at **Napoleon House** (500 Chartres St, at St. Louis St, 524.9752) is also very good.

Pain perdu (*Pan* pair-doo)
Literally "lost bread," the local version of French toast is made with thick slices of French bread, then dusted with powdered sugar.

Panéed meat (*Pon*-ayd meat)
Thin cutlets, usually veal or chicken, coated with seasoned bread crumbs, then deep-fried or sautéed.

Po-boy
Loaves of French bread are stuffed with roast beef and gravy, fried seafood, or other meats for the quintessential New Orleans sandwich, created in the 1920s as an inexpensive (but filling) meal for "poor boys."

Pompano en papillote (*Pom*-pa-no en pop-ee-yot)
In this famous dish that originated at **Antoine's**, the fish fillet is topped with either shrimp or crabmeat, then steamed in a balloon of white parchment.

Praline (Praw-*leen*)
The ubiquitous Creole candies—crisp rounds of sugar, cream, and pecans—are especially good crumbled over ice cream.

Red gravy
In the rest of the world it's known as marinara sauce.

Remoulade (*Rem*-a-laud)
Almost as many recipes exist for this as there are restaurants in New Orleans, but most combine mustard, oil, hard-cooked eggs, horseradish, and other seasonings for a piquant sauce that coats cold boiled shrimp as an appetizer.

Roux (*Roo*)
Flour browned in oil used to thicken gumbos, étouffées, gravies, and other smoky-rich flavored sauces.

Sauce piquante (Sauce pee-*kawnt*)
The dense and highly seasoned tomato sauce is used to flavor everything from alligator to wild game.

Shrimp Creole
A tomato-based spicy shrimp stew served over rice.

UPTOWN/UNIVERSITY

The St. Charles Avenue Streetcar rumbles upriver from Canal Street to reach this lofty district bounded by high society and deepest bohemia. Uptown New Orleans is alive with boutiques and bistros, thrift stores and greasy spoons, all patronized by the same unclassifiable clientele. Tattered mavericks dine at fashionable restaurants while bank presidents guzzle beer at waterfront dives. Residents are bedeviled by an active criminal underclass (burglars, mostly), as well as the most dreaded pack of grande dames to ever terrorize a southern town.

Without question the city's haughtiest neighborhood, this stronghold of the swells is vibrant with its own brand of local color. The dominant hue comes from the **Green Wave** teams of **Tulane University**, oak-lined avenues, **Audubon Park**, and old money. And by early March, the lawns and sidewalks are brilliant with azaleas. December brings dazzling, albeit tastefully restrained, holiday lights. But it's just before Lent that these posh streets are abloom with the ne plus ultra of local status: the flapping purple, green, and gold flags that adorn the doorways of past (and current) kings and queens of Carnival.

A round-trip streetcar ride is the easiest introduction to this once-a-year kingdom. First up, you'll pass some of Uptown's loveliest residential streets (disembark at **Jefferson Avenue, Nashville Avenue,** or **State Street** for a stroll). Next in line is **Audubon Park**, a spectacular and cooling retreat. Luxuriant with ancient moss-draped oaks and winding lagoons, it was created in 1884 for the Cotton Centennial and is now home to the **Audubon Zoological Garden**, one of the best zoos in the country. Just beyond the park, at the junction where the tracks—and the **Mississippi**—hang a sharp right, is the area known as **Riverbend,** bustling with smart

shops and excellent restaurants. The bars and coffeehouses of **Maple Street** cater to students from nearby **Tulane** and **Loyola Universities**. And don't miss unspoiled **Oak Street** for a nostalgic rummage through the dime stores and novelty shops that still crowd this 1940s time warp.

For a different point of view, board the **Magazine Street** bus and pick your stop from two miles of merchandise, ranging from museum-quality antiques to supplies for brewing your own beer. Browse the galleries for good buys on undiscovered masters of the local art scene, and linger a while in the old-fashioned bookstores and cafes. When the sun goes down, it's just a few blocks to **Tchoupitoulas Street** (take a cab) and the legendary **Tipitina's**.

creole
cuisine

1 ZACHARY'S CREOLE CUISINE

★★★$$ The late chef Eddie Baquet made the family's name at **Eddie's Restaurant and Bar,** and his son and grandson (Wayne Baquet Sr. and Jr.) continue the tradition at this big old cottage, painted a cheerful pink with blue-and-white trim. Soulful cuisine includes the famous Baquet gumbos, shrimp remoulade, red beans and rice, fried seafood, and crawfish pie. Fresh speckled trout is topped with either crawfish dressing or lump crabmeat in lemon butter sauce, and the inch-thick center cut pork chop is perfectly grilled. Polished oak floors, 15-foot ceilings, and piped-in jazz and R&B add plenty of atmosphere. ♦ Creole ♦ M lunch; Tu-Sa lunch and dinner; Su brunch. Reservations recommended for dinner. 8400 Oak St (at Cambronne St). 865.1559

2 RICCA'S WHITE PILLARS EMPORIUM

Everything from Victorian lampposts to weather vanes to mailboxes designed for iron fences can be found here, all reproduced in heavy-duty cast aluminum and sure to outlast the originals. Look up to see the collection of antique ceiling fans, which are not for sale. ♦ Tu-Sa. 8312 Oak St (between Dante and Cambronne Sts). 861.7113

Portrait of an Office: The New Orleans Cotton Exchange, which Edgar Degas painted in New Orleans, was purchased in 1873 by the Musée des Beaux Arts in Pau, France. It was the first Impressionist painting ever bought by a museum, and it was also Degas's first sale to a museum. It remains on exhibit there today.

2 MAPLE LEAF BAR

Named for the Scott Joplin rag, this storefront haven harkens back to 1920s jazz halls, with its rickety bentwood chairs, cozy bar, and intellectual/bohemian clientele. Truly one of the best watering holes in a town that's filled with them, this is a well-worn and well-loved spot to kick back and enjoy nightly live music (mostly Cajun, Zydeco, blues, and funk) and Sunday afternoon poetry readings. ♦ Daily from 3PM. 8316 Oak St (between Dante and Cambronne Sts). 866.9359 &

3 STREETCAR BARN

Technically known as the **Carrollton Station,** that tangle of overhead wires at the corner of Carrollton Avenue and Willow Street leads to a cavernous garage where craftspeople perform all services (electrical, woodworking, maintenance, and mechanical) on the historic streetcars. It's also the place where some of the working cars retire for the night. The facility is off-limits to the public. ♦ 8201 Willow St (at Dublin St)

4 JIMMY'S

The doors open when folks start gathering for the night's concert at this industrial-strength music club which offers no frills, no eats, and basic black walls. Most people stand or dance to the music, unless they've staked out a bar stool or seat on the large patio. There's just one continuous show each night, with a single cover charge, though as many as five bands might appear. The size is just about perfect: around 600 to 800 people can cram in, if you include the patio, making it large enough to attract decent acts, but small enough so there's not a bad standing spot in the house. A wide variety of musicians have performed here, including Junior Walker and the Allstars, the Fabulous Thunderbirds, The

Guess Who, Three Dog Night, Foghat, New Riders of the Purple Sage, Allen Toussaint, HooDoo Gurus, Graham Nash, Blue Oyster Cult, and the Ozark Mountain Daredevils. ♦ Tu-Sa from 8PM. 8200 Willow St (at Dublin St). 866.4982, 861.8200

5 CARROLLTON STATION

A bar doesn't have to be lowdown and spartan to put on great live music shows in Uptown New Orleans. Case in point, this small neighborhood hangout is actually kind of attractive, with a huge carved and paneled tiger-oak bar, antique white-tile floor, and decorator color scheme. But don't worry, it's still funky enough to escape any comparison to a 1990s theme joint. As with many local bars, this is a friendly place peopled with a wide range of characters. Live music is scheduled Thursday through Saturday nights, with acoustic sets occasionally scheduled on Sundays. (The schedule is heavier during Jazz Fest.) Choose from 12 beers on tap or order one of Uptown Shorty's margaritas (named for a loyal customer), never frozen and always made with fresh juice. ♦ Daily from 3PM. 8140 Willow St (at Dublin St). 865.9190

6 LEBANON'S CAFÉ

★★$ This cozy cafe offers a sense of place before your first bite of tabbouleh, just check out the mural of a Middle Eastern marketplace on the wall and Turkish water pipes lined up on the counter. The chef's special appetizer is more than enough for two, with its generous helping of garlicky hummus, baba ganuj, tabouleh, and falafel. The kabobs of lamb and beef are tasty, but vegetarians will find plenty of options as well, including vegetarian cabbage roll, veggie grape leaves, and an excellent yogurt salad with cucumber. ♦ Middle Eastern ♦ M-Su lunch and dinner. 1506 S. Carrollton (between Jeannette and Birch). 862.6200; fax 862.6900

6 CAFÉ NINO

★★$ Sicilian-born chef/owner Nino Bongiorno has been getting raves for his home-cooked Italian specialties like fettucine Alfredo, eggplant, and chicken parm and chicken marsala, plus some of the best pizza in town—and a genuine Philly cheesesteak, which he put on the menu after a Philly friend

complained that he couldn't get his fix in New Orleans. You're served on styrofoam, and the atmosphere is nonexistent, but Nino's food—now that's Italian! ♦ M-Su, lunch and dinner. ♦ 1510 S. Carrollton (between Jeannette and Hickory). 865.9200

7 RIVERBEND LEVEE

Walk across the railroad tracks (no fast trains this close to the end of the line) and climb to the top of the levee for a working man's view of the Mississippi. Here you can see plenty of industrial development and watch big ships round the bend.

8 DANTE'S KITCHEN

★★$$ Flowering vines and shrubs cling to the fenced patio at this pleasant riverside cafe. Guests are seated outdoors, in a glassed-in garden room, or in one of three small nonsmoking interior areas. Owner Lee Yates, who has worked at uptown restaurants including **Vaqueros** and **Commander's Palace**, has teamed up with chef Emanuel Loubier, former sous chef at **Commander's Palace**. Loubier's menu is organic regional cuisine, with standout dishes like poached salmon with caramelized fennel and double cut pork chop with stone ground grits. The trompe l'oeil is the work of Ivy Sherman, whose brother Jamie is in the kitchen at **Commander's**. ♦ American ♦ Tu-Sun lunch and dinner. 736 Dante St (at Maple St). 861.3634

9 LA BONBONNIERE

Hans Fink and Dieter Szembek create elaborate European pastries in their stately white-columned shop on the streetcar line. The harlequin slices, amandine tarts, napoleons, and chocolate rum cake are especially good. Some of the merchandise is almost too pretty to eat, but you'll cave in. ♦ Tu-Su. 1114 S Carrollton Ave (between Zimple and Oak Sts). 866.2760 &

10 BRIGTSEN'S

★★★★$$$ Frank Brigtsen was declared "Best Chef in the Southeast" by the James Beard Foundation at the 1998 awards ceremony. The most famous protégé of superstar chef Paul Prudhomme packs his homey cottage with locals who love his brilliant takes on South Louisiana standards. Oysters Rockefeller soup is a fresh version of that regional mainstay. Blackened yellowfin tuna is edged with smoked corn sauce, red bean salsa, and avocado sour cream. Crisp duck and dirty rice are sauced with pureed sweet potato, honey, and pecans. Brigtsen is particularly known for his rabbit dishes, and has received awards from Food and Wine and Travel Holiday, among others. The menu changes nightly, and a good selection of robust domestic wines complements the earthy cuisine. Be sure to save a spot for rich bread pudding or home-made ice cream. The Early Evening Special, offered Tuesday through Thursday nights from 5:30 to 6:30PM, is a great bargain, a three-course meal for $14.95. ♦ Cajun/Creole ♦ Tu-Sa dinner. Reservations recommended. 723 Dante St (between Leake Ave and Maple St). 861.7610

11 MIGNON FAGET LTD.

Original jewelry by talented homegrown artist Mignon Faget is sold in boutiques nationwide. Known primarily for her designs drawn from nature (Gulf Coast marine life, banana leaves, garden snails), Faget has won raves with her Schema line of architecturally inspired pieces. For chic souvenirs, the Louisiana Collection of pendants and charms includes Creole cottages, red beans, streetcars, even a gumbo necklace (rice pearls strung with sterling crabs, shrimp, and okra). Faget's studio and workrooms are on the second floor of this shop. ♦ M-Sa. 710 Dublin St (between Hampson and Maple Sts). 865.7361; www.mignonfaget.com. Also at: Numerous locations throughout the area.

11 CAFÉ VOLAGE

★★★$$ Chef/proprietor Felix Gallerani studied in Europe and honed his skills at several of New Orleans's well-known restaurants before opening his own. A native of Italy, Gallerani specializes in French Continental and Creole cuisines, but he will gladly accommodate any requests that can be filled from his exotic stock of ingredients. Good bets are quail à la Felix, stuffed with *pâté de campagne* and roasted in a rosemary glaze; red snapper Florentine; and grilled chicken Marzena (gypsy style), served on a bed of julienned ham, black olives, and shallots. The beautifully renovated cottage offers quiet dining rooms and outdoor seating in the courtyard. The scent from potted herbs along the entry walk should whet your appetite. ♦ Continental ♦ M-Sa lunch and dinner; Su brunch and dinner. Reservations recommended. 720 Dublin St (between Hampson and Maple Sts). 861.4227

12 YVONNE LA FLEUR

If froufrou feminine is your style, this celebrated local designer offers silks and laces that marry New Orleans charm to Continental elegance. Known worldwide for her custom millinery, La Fleur's marvelous hats have appeared in *The Great Gatsby*, *Pretty Baby*, *Chanel Solitaire*, and other films. Her exclusive YLF line includes sports, career, and evening wear, as well as a signature fragrance. European wedding gowns and mother-of-the-bride dresses are another specialty. Be sure to plan a stop here even if

you're short on time—but if you're short on money, keep walking. ♦ M-W, F-Sa; Th until 8PM. 8131 Hampson St (between S Carrollton Ave and Dublin St). 866.9666, 800/749.9666; fax 866.0165; www.yvonnelafleur.com

13 ON THE OTHER HAND

Bargain hunters will find haute couture and designer labels among the one-of-a-kind finery that crowds six rooms in these two Victorian shotgun houses. On consignment, the merchandise (sizes 0-26) comes from original owners as far removed as the West Coast, New York, and Paris. All items are marked one-quarter to one-third off the original price, but everything is subject to bargaining. The selection includes ball gowns, cocktail and dinner dresses, wedding dresses, shoes, hats, furs, and accessories, as well as men's formal wear. Fortify your search with complimentary cheese and wine or coffee and cookies. In warm weather, sip a glass of lemonade in the courtyard and watch the doves. ♦ M-Sa. 8126 Hampson St (between S Carrollton Ave and Dublin St). 861.0159

SYMMETRY
JEWELERS ● DESIGNERS

13 SYMMETRY JEWELERS

Choose *objets* from in-house artists or shop the changing exhibits that feature work by craftspeople from around the world. Take a look at the glass, metal, wood, and fabric art, and don't miss the display of antique pocket watches and vintage wristwatches. Rings can be sized while you lunch at one of the neighborhood restaurants. The jewelers here have created custom work for a long and eclectic list of notables, including Keith Richards, Pope John Paul II, and Rickie Lee Jones. ♦ Tu-Sa Jan-Oct; M-Sa Nov-Dec; or by appointment. 8138 Hampson St (between S Carrollton Ave and Dublin St). 861.9925, 800/628.3711; fax 861.0441; www.symmetryjewelers.com

14 CAMELLIA GRILL

★★$ Be prepared to wait in line and travel back in time. This white-columned diner, planted firmly at the corner where the **St. Charles Avenue Streetcar** hangs a right onto Carrollton Avenue, has changed little since the doors opened in 1946. When they're on the ball (not always these days), waiters clad in starched white linen offer service so snappy it's a floor show. There are no tables, but Uptown brahmins and scruffy students perch side by side on counter stools for old-fashioned grilled hamburgers and fries. You can get breakfast anytime (the omelettes and pecan waffles are especially good), and even Yankees will like the buttery grits. Pies made daily on the premises are another specialty. ◆ American ◆ Daily breakfast, lunch, and dinner. 626 S Carrollton Ave (between St. Charles Ave and Hampson St). 866.9573

15 DAIQUIRI'S

The New Orleans climate and high-octane alcoholic slush seem like a marriage . . . somewhere. This frozen daiquiri stand offers 20 different ways to forget the heat. Abstract names like Swamp-water and Sex on the Beach make choices hard, but that's the best part. Free samples are cheerfully doled out— after all, who'd order 12 ounces to a gallon of Triple Bypass without an introductory slurp? The quality is closer to **7-11** than **Trader Vic's,** but when the humidity hits one hundred percent, taste flies out the window. Stands like this one thrive all over town, including, believe it or not, several drive-thru outlets. We're not in Kansas anymore. ◆ M-Th, Su 10AM-midnight; F-Sa 10AM-2AM. 8100 St. Charles Ave (at S Carrollton Ave). 866.1846

16 LA MADELEINE FRENCH BAKERY & CAFÉ

★★$ The wood-burning ovens turn out crusty baguettes, the European-style pastries are sublime, and the dining area is reminiscent of a rustic French inn. Definitely stop here for dessert (strawberry napoleon, pecan tart, apricot croissant), but the salads, soups, quiches, and sandwiches are great, too. Choose a picnic and head for the levee or **Audubon Park**. ◆ Country French ◆ Daily breakfast, lunch, and dinner. 601 S Carrollton Ave (at St. Charles Ave). 861.8661 ᕤ Also at: Numerous locations throughout the area

17 COOTER BROWN'S TAVERN & OYSTER BAR

Try to sample even a fraction of the huge inventory at this local record holder (450 bottled beers and 40 drafts) and you'll end up drunk as you-know-who. This funky joint is big with college students, but they're just one faction of an extremely mixed crowd. The oyster bar is one of the best, and cheapest, in town. Play video poker for real money or try one of the pool tables. Recorded music is loud and fun. ◆ Daily from 11AM. 509 S Carrollton Ave (between Leake and St. Charles Aves). 866.9104; fax 865.7579

18 FIGARO'S

★★$$ The big draw here is Neapolitan-style pizza lightly brushed with garlic-herb butter instead of tomato sauce: the simple *bianca* topped with mozzarella; *margherita* (sliced fresh tomatoes, basil, fresh garlic, and parmesan); *spinaci e feta* (spinach, onions, fresh tomatoes, and feta); and *carciofi, pomodoro e salsiccia* (artichoke hearts, fresh tomatoes, Italian sausage, mushrooms, and mozzarella). The extravagant 15-inch Four Seasons pie is divided into quarters for a sampling of each of the four combinations listed above. The menu also features pasta dishes, salads, and sandwiches. Set in a renovated former gas station, the restaurant has a sleek look, with several outdoor tables along the front patio and a crisp white interior brightened by strings of garlic, herbs, and Italian meats. ◆ Italian ◆ Daily lunch and dinner. 7900 Maple St (at Fern St). 866.0100

19 JAMILA'S

★★★$$ This family-owned restaurant has quickly won a strong local following for its friendly and efficient service and excellent food. Set in a tiny storefront space, the dining room has an intimate charm, thanks to special touches like window boxes filled with flowers. The exotic Tunisian/Mediterranean entrées include a variety of couscous and pasta dishes, as well as skewered meats. The grilled homemade lamb sausage is great. Saturday diners are treated to a belly dancer for entertainment. ◆ Tunisian/Mediterranean ◆ Tu-F lunch and dinner; Sa-Su dinner. 7808 Maple St (between Burdette and Fern Sts). 866.4366

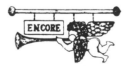

19 ENCORE

Find a bargain and support the Louisiana Philharmonic Orchestra at the same time. Symphony patrons donate (or consign) quality ball gowns and wedding dresses, as well as casual and after-five wear, to this nonprofit, volunteer-staffed organization. The farther you are from home, the slimmer the chance that anyone you know has seen one of these ensembles (and some of them are real doozies). ♦ Tu-Sa. 7814 Maple St (between Burdette and Fern Sts). 861.9028

20 STARBUCKS COFFEE COMPANY

The ubiquitous coffeehouse has finally managed to infiltrate New Orleans. Housed in a renovated filling station, the shop is fronted by a sheltered terrace filled with tables. ♦ M-Th, Su 7AM-11PM; F-Sa 7AM-midnight. 7700 Maple St (at Adams St). 864.0411 ♿ Also at: Numerous locations throughout the area

20 NAUTICAL

★★★$$$ You won't find nautical kitsch at this terrific new restaurant, named by *Bon Appétit* one of the best new eateries in the city. Instead, owner Eric Bay and chef Tommy Sapp have created an ambiance that is as crisp as a freshly furled sail, pale yellow walls accented with navy and streaming sunlight. Sapp, another fine chef to come out of Emeril's kitchen, offers eclectic American cuisine, including dishes like herb roasted duckling bathed in a sweet Merlot reduction and a duck and okra gumbo that is to die for. Every Sunday you can take a four-course, prix fixe culinary journey to ports like Mexico, Key West, and the Caribbean, There is also a chef's table just off the kitchen that delivers a show with dinner. ♦ 7708 Maple St. (between Adams and Burdette Sts). 866.7504

20 THE SUN SHOP

Look around this dusty little space carefully: A quick glance could bypass a real treasure. Owner Chester "Chick" Fortner specializes in native art from the Americas, and his searches range from Alaska to Bolivia and Peru. Anything handmade that catches his talented eye ends up on Maple Street. Spend a couple of dollars—or more than a thousand—on a decidedly eclectic inventory of masks, saints, pottery, baskets, jewelry, beadwork, and loose beads (for do-it-yourself artisans). The North American collection features items from the Sioux, Iroquois, Comanche, and other nations, and includes Native American audiotapes of war dances, stomp dances, and peyote songs. Of special note are the Zuni fetishes and Huichol beadwork. ♦ M-Sa Sept-June. 7722 Maple St (between Adams and Burdette Sts). 861.8338

21 PJ'S COFFEE & TEA CO.

Pale pink and cream walls, plenty of natural light, and a scattering of sidewalk tables create a sleek backdrop for a quick break or a long linger. This shop produces its own line of gourmet coffees, roasted in New Orleans and a great favorite with locals who hang out at the shops all over town. Try the mango iced tea, too. A large basket of newspapers and magazines encourages loitering, and the bulletin board is a great source for upcoming events and entertainment. Coffees and teas are also sold by the pound, along with brewing equipment and caffeine-related gifts. ♦ M-F 6AM-11PM; Sa-Su 7AM-11PM. 7624 Maple St (between Hillary and Adams Sts). 866.7031 ♿ Also at: Numerous locations throughout the area

22 BRUNO'S

Every city has its institutions, and to many Uptown New Orleanians, this tavern definitely qualifies. It's been a traditional meeting place since 1934, evidenced by the well-used but inviting interior. The college crowd can be rambunctious at night, but alumni business-people and other professionals dominate in the afternoons. Play pool, pinball, or video poker—or join one of the lively conversations and help solve the problems of the world. ♦ M-F from 3PM; Sa-Su from noon. 7601 Maple St (at Hillary St). 861.7615; fax 866.3816

23 MAPLE STREET BOOK SHOP

Housed in a quaint Victorian shotgun surrounded by a wrought-iron fence, this well-organized bookstore is crammed to the rafters with thousands of titles. The staff is knowledgeable and friendly, and owner Rhoda Faust is one of the city's literary leaders. The well-stocked New Orleans section includes a whole wall of regional cookbooks, works by more than 120 native authors (some signed, some first editions), and an extensive collection by Louisiana lion Walker Percy. ♦ Daily. 7523 Maple St (between Cherokee and Hillary Sts). 866.4916. Also at: 701 Metairie Rd (at Focis Ave), Metairie. 832.8937; www.maplestreetbookshop.com

23 MAPLE STREET CHILDREN'S BOOK SHOP

Right next door to the parent store, the quaint kids' version is bright, charming, and well stocked. Call to ask about regularly scheduled Saturday readings. ♦ Daily. 7529 Maple St (between Cherokee and Hillary Sts). 861.2105

BELLES LETTRES: NEW ORLEANS FROM A TO Z

A Confederacy of Dunces by John Kennedy Toole (Louisiana State University Press, 1980). The perfect introduction to New Orleans is the outrageous story of Ignatius J. Reilly, modern Medievalist and self-appointed guardian of proper geometry and theology." The comic masterwork, which won the 1981 Pulitzer Prize for Fiction, was published posthumously (the author committed suicide in 1969 at the age of 32).

Dinner at Antoine's by Frances Parkinson Keyes (Simon & Schuster, 1948). The murder mystery that begins with a meal at the venerable restaurant is just one of many novels Keyes wrote during her years of residence in the **French Quarter**. Her **Steamboat Gothic** (Messner, 1952) follows the ups and downs of a River Road plantation family, and **Blue Camellia** (Messner, 1957) is a pioneer epic set in Cajun country, circa 1880.

Feast of All Saints by Anne Rice (Simon & Schuster, 1979). Though better known for her supernatural sagas, Rice is at her best in this fascinating exploration of the complex social world of free people of color during the 19th century. Other books by this local lion (all published by Knopf) include **Interview with the Vampire** (1976), **The Vampire Lestat** (1985), **The Queen of the Damned** (1988), **The Witching Hour** (1990), **The Tale of the Body Thief** (1992), **Lasher** (1993), **Taltos** (1994), **Memnoch the Devil** (1997), and **Vittorio the Vampire** (2001).

Frenchmen, Desire, Goodchildren by John Churchill Chase (Macmillan, 1979). The stories behind these and other picturesque street names are an enchanting introduction to the history and folklore of New Orleans, plus a great way to get your bearings.

Gumbo Ya Ya by Lyle Saxon, Edward Dreyer, and Robert Tallant (Pelican, 1987). Originally published in 1945 as part of the WPA's Louisiana Writers' Program, the colorful encyclopedia of regional folklore and customs is still the greatest single source on the subject.

Keepers of the House by Shirley Ann Grau (Knopf, 1964). The homegrown author won the Pulitzer Prize for this Delta family epic. Her novel **The Hard Blue Sky** (Knopf, 1958) is a chronicle of Cajun life on **Isle aux Chiens**.

Lives of the Saints by Nancy Lemann (Louisiana State University Press, 1997). A native of **Uptown**, Lemann is a fun and trustworthy guide to the tangled web of New Orleans society. Her novel of modern manners, originally published in 1986, ranges from the mansions of the Garden District to the downtown dives on **St. Claude Avenue**.

Louisiana Hayride by Harnett Kane (Pelican, 1990). First published in 1941, Kane's clear-eyed and ironic account exposes the scandalous regime of Governor Huey Long. Though the truth was stranger than fiction, several novels were also inspired by Long's life and career, including **All the King's Men** by Robert Penn Warren (Harcourt Brace Jovanovich, 1946), **Sun in Capricorn** by Hamilton Basso (Scribner, 1942), and **Number One** by John Dos Passos (Houghton Mifflin, 1943).

The Moviegoer by Walker Percy (Knopf, 1960). The psychiatrist-turned-author, who set many novels in New Orleans, won the 1962 National Book Award for this story of a ruling-class misfit.

Music for Chameleons by Truman Capote (Random House, 1975). Society's darling shocked the beau monde with his caustic memoirs, including several unflattering revelations about his hometown of New Orleans.

New Orleans Stories edited by John Miller (Chronicle Books, 1992). An engaging survey of "Great Writers on the City," featuring excerpts from works by William Faulkner, Tennessee Williams, Louis Armstrong, Ishmael Reed, Kate Chopin, Zora Neale Hurston, John James Audubon, Mark Twain, and many others.

Pentimento by Lillian Hellman (Little, Brown and Company, 1973). Within her collection of autobiographical sketches, the playwright draws a rich portrait of her childhood in the **Uptown** New Orleans boarding house that was operated by her mother.

Zombification by Andrei Codrescu (St. Martin's Press, 1994). Observed through European eyes, the wild local culture seems even more irrational than ever. The author of this collection of wry essays is a transplanted Romanian, professor of English at **Louisiana State University,** and a regular commentator for NPR's "All Things Considered."

24 PHILLIP'S RESTAURANT AND BAR

★$ Larger than most neighborhood bars, there's plenty of space here for long-term regulars, as well as for the strong student contingent. Serious pool and big-screen TV sports are the main attractions; the red room offers a darker and quieter getaway. The walls are lined with original student art, and the giant salads and specialty pizzas are good. ◆

American ◆ Daily from 4:30PM. 733 Cherokee St (at Maple St). 865.1155

25 TULANE UNIVERSITY

Known to some as "The Harvard of the South," Louisiana's largest private university was founded in 1834 as the **Medical College of Louisiana**. It became the **University of Louisiana** in 1847, and in 1884 was named for Paul Tulane, a Princeton, New Jersey merchant who had given the state $1 million

Restaurants/Clubs: Red | Hotels: Purple | Shops: Orange | Outdoors/Parks: Green | Sights/Culture: Blue

to establish a private university. The 11 schools and colleges currently enroll more than 11,000 students from all 50 states and 75 foreign countries. The 900-member faculty includes a Nobel Prize–winning scientist. Almost one-third of the alumni continue to live and work in the New Orleans area. **Tulane Green Wave** teams excel at football, basketball, baseball, tennis, and track and field. ♦ 6823 St. Charles Ave (between Calhoun St and Audubon Pl). General information 865.5000, sports ticket office 861.WAVE, drama and dance department box office 865.5106, TUCP concerts, performances, films, and lectures 865.5143

Within Tulane University:

AMISTAD RESEARCH CENTER

A dip into these vast holdings can arouse feelings of love, outrage, and humor. The name of the archive is derived from the Amistad defense committee—a group of Northern abolitionists who championed the cause of enslaved Africans jailed for mutinying while on board the schooner *Amistad* in 1839. More than 10 million articles—letters, diaries, photographs, oral history tapes, rare books, and pamphlets, documenting the history of African-Americans and other minority, ethnic, and religious groups—are housed here. Scholars and writers from around the globe come to study the personal papers of hundreds of civil rights leaders, educators, writers, musicians, artists, and politicians. Notable are collections from the Louisiana Coalition Against Racism and Nazism, Free Southern Theater, poet Countee Cullen, and civil rights attorney A.P. Tureaud. The public has free access to the collection, but

> Playwright Lillian Hellman grew up in an Uptown boarding house. Her childhood years are vividly sketched in her autobiography, *Pentimento*, which was the basis for the 1977 film *Julia*.

> Many of the ancient herbal remedies used in voodoo actually worked, and modern medical research subsequently proved their effectiveness. For example, voodoo practitioners used molded bread to treat venereal diseases long before the discovery of penicillin.

only within the quiet and comfortable **Reading Room**. The cataloging system is easy to understand and archivists will bring requested books or documents to the front desk for anyone who presents a driver's license. Don't miss the paintings and sculptures lining the walls. The collection includes more than a hundred pieces of African art and more than 250 works by noted African-Americans such as William H. Johnson, Henry O. Tanner, Ellis Wilson, and Richard Barthé. The cavernous three-story facility is housed in **Tilton Hall,** a gray stone building that faces St. Charles Avenue at the entrance to **Tulane**. ♦ M-Sa 9AM-4:30PM, 865.5535; www.tulane.edu\~amistad

WOLDENBERG ART CENTER AT NEWCOMB COLLEGE

A recent expansion of **Tulane**'s original art building added the **Newcomb Art Gallery**, which features changing exhibits of the works of nationally known artists, shows of faculty and student works, and a permanent collection of the celebrated American art pottery that was produced at **Newcomb College** from 1895 to 1940. ♦ M-Sa. Newcomb Pl (between Freret and Willow Sts). 865.5327

26 AUDUBON PLACE

Two stone gatehouses are connected by the lacy ironwork arch that marks this imposing private street. A Texas real estate developer created the millionaires' row of stately houses in the early 20th century.

27 PARK VIEW

$$ It may look like a private home, but this ornate Victorian was actually built as a hotel for the 1884 World Cotton Exchange Exhibition held in nearby **Audubon Park**. Though a bit worn around the edges at press time, several of the 22 guest rooms boast balconies with views of the park or St. Charles Avenue. Fifteen have small private baths, and all on the first floor are brightened by chandeliers, wood floors, and Oriental-style rugs. Begin with croissants and coffee in the sunny **Audubon Room,** then catch the streetcar at the front door. This guest house is often booked up, so make reservations at least two to three months in advance, especially during graduation or other special events at nearby **Tulane** and **Loyola**. ♦ 7004 St. Charles Ave (at Walnut St). 861.7564; www.parkviewguesthouse.com

28 LOYOLA UNIVERSITY

In 1837, seven Jesuit priests arrived in New Orleans to establish a boarding college in the nearby community of Grand Coteau, at the request of Governor Bienville and the city's leaders. In 1847, the priests opened the **College of the Immaculate Conception** at the corner of Baronne and Common Streets in the **CBD**. Church superiors soon recognized the need to locate the school in a less congested area, so they acquired the Foucher Plantation, a large site directly across from what is now **Audubon Park,** for the sum of $75,000 in 1886. Edward Douglass White, a Jesuit alumnus and chief justice of the US Supreme Court from 1910 to 1921, aided in the purchase. When the doors opened in 1904, classes were held in a house behind the **Most Holy Name of Jesus Church** on what is now Marquette Place. Stately **Marquette Hall** was built in 1910 to keep pace with the growing number of students. **Loyola** was chartered as a university in 1912; the enrollment totaled a not very grand 69. Today, **Loyola** is a medium-size university with an enrollment of approximately 5,500 students representing all 50 states and 50 foreign countries. The 20-acre main campus overlooks **Audubon Park,** and a few blocks away, at 7214 St. Charles Avenue, the four-acre **Broadway Campus** houses the **Loyola School of Law.** By the way, the statue that appears to be running with arms stretched overhead (at the entry drive to the main campus) has been known to generations of students as "the touchdown Jesus." ◆ 6363 St. Charles Ave (between Calhoun St and Audubon Pl). University information office 861.5888, Loyola ticket booth for drama department productions 865.3824, Loyola ticket office for music department productions 865.2074, details on visual arts exhibits 861.5456, sports information 865.3137

29 DUNBAR'S

★★$ A comforting dish of smothered chicken with rice or perfectly fried chicken with red beans (seasoned with chunks of ham) is especially appealing when you've been on the road too long. College students and folks from the neighborhood frequent this unpretentious cafe for Creole soul food. It's a friendly place, the food is great, and the prices are l-o-w. ◆ Soul food ◆ M-Sa breakfast, lunch, and dinner. 4927 Freret St (between Upperline and Robert Sts). 899.0734

30 AUDUBON PARK

Thousands of people pour into this oasis each week to jog, bicycle, walk, or loaf. Graced by lagoons and shaded by a canopy of ancient oaks and magnolia trees, the sprawling 385-acre showplace was designed in the 1890s by John Olmsted, whose father, Frederick Law Olmsted, laid out New York's Central Park. The Classical entrance at St. Charles Avenue is a stately marriage of French and Italian Renaissance influences. Cars are banned in the front section of the park, from Magazine Street to St. Charles Avenue. A fitness course is located

next to the main road and an 18-hole golf course lies within its loop. Bridle paths skirt the perimeter, and picnic shelters, benches, and gazebos are scattered about the landscape. The **Newman Bandstand** hosts outdoor plays and concerts, and the nearby **Heymann Memorial Conservatory** shelters a fine collection of tropical plants. The mid-section of the park, from Leake Avenue to Magazine Street, is home to a public pool, **Cascade Riding Stables,** soccer and softball fields, and the 58-acre **Audubon Zoological Garden.** Beyond Leake Avenue, the area known as **River View** offers picnic grounds and sports fields framed by the Mississippi. Note: Although the park is open well into the evening, we recommend visiting during the daytime only—the area becomes very dangerous after dark. ◆ Daily 6AM-10PM. Golf course 865.8260, Cascade Riding Stables 891.2246, conservatory 891.2419, playing field reservations 861.2537

Within Audubon Park:

Audubon
Zoological Garden

AUDUBON ZOOLOGICAL GARDEN

New Orleans's world-class zoo, consistently rated among the nation's finest, winds through the heart of the park. More than 1,800 animals, many rare or endangered, live in natural habitats surrounded by 58 moody acres of oak trees draped with Spanish moss. The **Mombasa Tram** makes for an easy safari, stopping at major sights. Tops on the list is the award-winning **Louisiana Swamp Exhibit,** a 6.5-acre tract reclaimed from the world's largest metropolitan swamp and home to the only known collection of rare white alligators. Visitors travel a complex of raised boardwalks for a close-up view of nature's creepiest creatures. Regular daily feedings bring out the baby alligators, otters, alligator snapping turtles, garfish, and water snakes. Keepers roam the grounds inviting adventurous types to handle some of the more harmless varmints. Human feedings are at the **Cypress Knee Cafe,** where an inexpensive menu of gumbo, crawfish pie, and other indigenous eats may be the best food ever peddled in a park. **Jaguar Jungle** debuted in 1998, a mini-Mayan civilization in a rain forest setting populated by spider monkeys, scarlet ibis, Jabiru storks, sloths, anteaters, and the namesake cats. Also added in 1998, the **Diefenthal Earth Lab** is an environmental fun house where visitors play games, talk with scientists via video monitor, wander through a manufactured colony of giant doodlebugs and beetles, even interact with animatronic litter bins in "Talkin' Trash Theater." Other zoo highlights include the **Butterflies in Flight** exhibit and **Tropical Bird House,** which beautifully display dozens of rare and colorful species, many flying freely through the lush foliage. The **Sea Lion Pool,** built in the 1920s, is especially popular during daily feedings, usually scheduled at 11AM, 1PM, and 4PM. An underwater viewing area offers a fun glimpse of the animals as they swim below the surface. Zoo cruises leave **Audubon Park's River View** dock regularly, terminating at the Canal Street entrance to the **Aquarium of the Americas**. ◆ Admission. Daily. (between West and South Aves). 581.4629, 800/774.7394; www.auduboninstitute.org

31 GAUTREAU'S

★★★★$$$ There's no sign on the late 19th-century former pharmacy located on an obscure side street, but the busy valet parking attendants are a clue that something big is afoot inside. This elegant neighborhood restaurant has won international raves for its innovative French/Mediterranean menu. You may find appetizers such as warm crisp duck confit with dried figs or escargot with traditional garlic butter. Entrées might include braised lamb shanks with spinach and goat cheese, roasted chicken with garlic mashed potatoes and wild mushrooms, or seared salmon with roasted baby vegetables and Pommery mustard beurre blanc. The downstairs area is rich with paneled walls, pressed-tin ceilings, and photographs of old New Orleans. The original pharmacy showcases now hold liquors and wines. Some patrons prefer the much quieter upstairs dining rooms; one has only three tables. ◆ French/Mediterranean ◆ M-Sa dinner. Reservations recommended. 1728 Soniat St (between Dryades and Danneel Sts). 899.7397

32 DIVE INN

$ For the adventurous traveler with an offbeat sense of humor, here is a true original. A wildly eclectic conglomeration of six rooms and suites surrounds a large indoor pool lined with English china tile, which was built in the 1920s when the building served as a recreational facility for the Mexican consulate. The decor of the guest rooms is as off-the-wall as the rest of the place: In one room, the toilet

is housed in a phone booth from the movie *Kingfish;* in another it's set in the center of the shower. You could sleep on a Murphy bed or a loft accessible only by ladder. The most conventional suite, which opens onto the pool and an exterior patio, has a private living room, two bedrooms, and one bath. A continental breakfast, served each morning at the poolside bar, is included. Quality and comfort vary, but the atmosphere is friendly and uninhibited and the price is definitely right. This is where rocker Eric Burdon (of the band The Animals) stays when he's in town. ◆ 4417 Dryades St (between Napoleon Ave and Jena St). 488.4640, 800/729.4640; fax 488.4639

33 PASCAL'S MANALE

★★★$$ If you're watching your cholesterol, there are a few benign dishes on the menu, but why waste a trip to one of the city's cathedrals of high-fat cuisine? The famous, huge barbecued shrimp come unshelled in a bowl of peppery butter sauce—messy, but worth the effort. Chicken bordelaise and fried eggplant are other local favorites. Fried oysters Francesca on a bed of grilled ham are slathered with hollandaise. Don't expect anything remotely nouvelle from this veteran of the local restaurant scene (established in 1913) and you won't be disappointed. This is no place for clock-watchers either; even those with reservations may have to join the crowd in the bar for up to 30 minutes. A tray of half-shells at the marble-topped oyster counter should help the time pass pleasantly. ◆ Italian/Creole ◆ M-F lunch and dinner; Sa dinner; Su dinner Labor Day–Memorial Day. 1838 Napoleon Ave (between Baronne and Dryades Sts). 895.4877

34 MARTIN WINE CELLAR

One of the South's largest selections of wines and gourmet imports is available here, with the goods stacked to the ceiling of the warehouse-size space. A huge inventory of hot sauces, seasoning mixes, Creole coffees, and other Louisiana foods is priced for local consumption (much less expensive than the tourist shops in the Quarter). Overstuffed deli sandwiches will sweeten a trip to **Audubon Park.** ◆ Daily. 3827 Baronne St (between Peniston and General Taylor Sts). 899.7411; fax 896.7370 ᗱ Also at: 714 Elmeer Ave (between Demosthenes St and Veterans Memorial Blvd), Metairie. 896.7300; fax 896.7350; www.martinwine.com

35 THE LEFEVRE HOME BED & BREAKFAST

$ A short walk from **Tulane** and **Loyola Universities** and **Audubon Park**, this small bed-and-breakfast is popular with students' visiting families. The simple, but spacious, private home offers four guest rooms that share two-and-one-half baths and a communal living room with TV. The atmosphere is casual; you might hear beautiful sounds and five harps. Continental breakfast is included, and the **St. Charles Avenue Streetcar** line is a short four blocks away. ♦ By reservation only. 6022 Pitt St (between State and Webster Sts). 488.4640, 800/729.4640; fax 488.4639

36 LATTER PUBLIC LIBRARY

The Neo-Italianate stone mansion, designed by the architectural firm of **Favrot and Livaudais** in 1907, was home to a series of wealthy Uptowners before it was donated to the city in 1948. Its most famous tenants were aviator Harry Williams and movie star Marguerite Clark, the chic young couple who lived here during the 1920s. Since 1948 it has housed the most glamorous branch of the **New Orleans Public Library**, a luxurious spot to check out the latest best-seller beneath crystal chandeliers and opulent ceiling murals. Be sure to notice Doug McCash's playful puzzle-piece mural of zoo animals catching the streetcar in the children's room. ♦ M-Th, Sa-Su. 5120 St. Charles Ave (between Soniat and Dufossat Sts). 596.2625 ᴆ

37 ACADEMY OF THE SACRED HEART

Les Soeurs du Sacré Coeur have been educating the daughters of New Orleans's Catholic upper class since 1887. The Classic Revival brick structure, built in 1899, is accented by tall arched windows flanked by dark wooden shutters. The French Gothic chapel was added in 1906. ♦ 4521 St. Charles Ave (between Jena and Cadiz Sts)

38 TOURO SYNAGOGUE

Home to one of the city's most prominent Reform Jewish congregations, this 1909 building was named for Judah P. Touro, an impoverished Rhode Island native who moved to New Orleans in 1801 and became a successful businessman and philanthropist. His gifts also benefited nearby **Touro Infirmary** and the now-defunct **Touro-Shakespeare Home** for indigents. ♦ 4330 St. Charles Ave (between General Pershing St and Napoleon Ave). 895.4843 ᴆ

39 THOMAS SULLY HOUSE

This Queen Anne–style house was designed by and home to **Thomas Sully,** the founder of the city's first full-scale architectural firm. Between 1880 and 1905, the influential architect built 34 other houses along the avenue (many of which are no longer standing). This is a private residence. ♦ 4010 St. Charles Ave (between Constantinople and Marengo Sts)

40 THE COLUMNS

$ Massive pillars supporting the cavernous, two-story front porch give this **Thomas Sully**–designed mansion its name. Built in 1883 by a wealthy tobacco merchant, these days it's a comfortably worn and affordable hotel run by the friendly Creppel family. The 20 guest rooms are furnished in heavy Victorian furniture and the bathrooms are the deep clawfoot tub variety; some rooms share baths. The lobby is old-fashioned, with a mahogany stairway illuminated by a square, stained-glass skylight, and amenities include a restaurant and a lounge. You may experience a little déjà vu, as the building has been the location for a few films, most notably Louis Malle's *Pretty Baby*. ♦ 3811 St. Charles Ave (between Peniston and General Taylor Sts). 899.9308, 800/445.9308; fax 899.8170; www.thecolumns.com

Within The Columns:

THE VICTORIAN LOUNGE

Esquire has rated this place the best bar in New Orleans, and the locals who fill the three comfortable rooms agree. Dark milled wood, pressed-tin ceiling, lace curtains, velvet club chairs, and a (working) fireplace lend plenty of British pub atmosphere. Waitresses also serve drinks on the porch and side patio. ♦ M-Th from 3PM; F from 2PM; Sa-Su from 11AM. 899.9308

41 LA CREPE NANOU

★★★$$ Be prepared to have a drink and wait for a table at this popular spot, where you can pass the time watching the French owner prepare orders on the crepe grills at the end of the bar. The crepes are reasonably priced, salads are large, and the menu also features poultry, meat, and fish entrées. A separate bill of fare lists after-dinner Champagnes, coffees, *digestifs,* and—best of all—dessert crepes. ♦ French ♦ Daily dinner. 1410 Robert St (between Prytania and Pitt Sts). 899.2670

VAQUEROS

42 VAQUEROS

★★★$$ The haute Southwestern decor gives this restaurant an earthy, yet ultra-stylish look. The wide-ranging menu offers a number of unusual Mexican and Southwestern dishes, including New Mexico dry rub venison in a dried cranberry demi-glacé served with garlic mashed potatoes and a poached pear tartlet spiked with habanero, and ancho-glazed (pepper-glazed) shrimp with wilted spinach and a black bean, goat cheese, and cornbread tower. The same adventurous spirit extends to Sunday brunch, which adds exotic entrées like deep-fried turkey and beef tenderloin roulade stuffed with spicy chorizo sausage, spinach, and pine nuts to the usual array of egg dishes, grilled items, and pastries. ♦ Mexican/Southwestern ♦ M-F lunch and dinner; Sa dinner; Su brunch and dinner. 4938 Prytania St (at Robert St). 891.6441

43 UPPERLINE RESTAURANT

★★★★$$$ Be sure to introduce yourself to owner JoAnn Clevenger, usually stationed at the door, and ask for menu suggestions and a guided tour of her colorful collection of local art. This is one of the friendliest fine dining spots in town, where Uptown Republicans and rakish bohemians pull up at adjoining tables, and patrons are dressed in everything from evening wear to blue jeans. Comfortable is the operative word in this 1877 town house graced by flowers, lace curtains, and service that is competent but never pretentious. The eclectic and unstuffy menu ranges from a salad of watercress with stilton cheese and pecans to bronzed Mississippi catfish with barbecued crawfish. The most popular dishes with locals are the roast duck and any kind of seafood. Visitors should enjoy the "tasting dinner," featuring generous samples of seven

different house specialties, such as fried green tomatoes with shrimp remoulade, spicy shrimp with jalapeño corn bread, and duck étouffée. The award-winning wine list includes several good selections under $30. Clevenger calls her elegant down-home food "classic New Orleans with adventure." ♦ Contemporary Creole ♦ W-Sa dinner; Su brunch and dinner. Reservations recommended. 1413 Upperline St (between Prytania and Pitt Sts). 891.9822

44 BLUEBIRD CAFÉ

★★$ Twangy truck-stop music, *huevos rancheros,* and the scruffy 1960s atmosphere draw hordes of young bohemians to this tiny storefront diner where an empty table is a rare find. "Powerhouse eggs" (fortified with yeast, tamari, and cheese) are nutritionally correct, but thick malt waffles (drenched with butter, syrup, and roasted pecans) are more fun. The coffee is great, the pies are homemade, and the walls are decked with original art. ♦ American ♦ Daily breakfast and lunch. 3625 Prytania St (between Foucher and Antonine Sts). 895.7166

45 THE CHIMES BED & BREAKFAST GUEST HOUSE

$ Leaded- and stained-glass windows, French doors, and cypress staircases give plenty of character to this lovely old Victorian home, where guests are lodged in the converted carriage house and servants' quarters. Each of the five rooms has a private entrance from the brick courtyard, as well as a coffeemaker, spring water, cable TV, private telephone, and daily housekeeping. The carriage house, formerly an artist's studio, is especially attractive, with a slate floor and loft bedroom. A refrigerator located off the courtyard is stocked with beer, wine, soda, and juice, and operate

THAT OLD GRAY MAGIC: VOODOO IN NEW ORLEANS

:all it mojo or juju, gris-gris or voodoo—ancient religions and herbal medicine still thrive in modern New Orleans. nner-city practitioners hold court in housing projects and country folks pass along tales of secret rites in the swamp- ands. Even suburban moms show their kids how to pour salt over crossed matchsticks to make rain go away. For enturies, local religious customs have been so tangled up with candles and charms, icons and oaths, that it's ometimes hard to tell where Catholicism ends and voodoo begins. (Gris-gris, French for "gray-gray," is one of the nore common forms of voodoo and is a mix of white and black magic.)

lever mind the shops that cater to tourists; check the shelves in most local drugstores and supermarkets for "Money louse Blessing" spray, "Lucky Bingo" candles, "Away All Evil Spirits" furniture polish—even "Unseen Enemies" and Law Stay Away" incense. This one-stop shopping is nothing new. Newspapers from the mid-1800s carried adver- sements from local pharmacies for powders, potions, and other voodoo paraphernalia. Pharamacists' brown bottles ith crude paper labels, and journals filled with handwritten gris-gris formulas, are part of the collection at the **New rleans Pharmacy Museum** (514 Chartres Street, between St. Louis and Toulouse Sts, 565.8077).

luseum director Clara Baker says several of the ancient herbal remedies actually worked, and their effectiveness as been borne out by modern medical research. "They used moldy bread to treat syphilis and other venereal iseases long before the official discovery of penicillin. Garlic and vinegar, now touted as new natural miracle drugs, vere commonly used."

oodoo probably came to New Orleans in the late 1700s with refugee slaves from Santo Domingo. Published ccounts of the Sunday rituals in **Congo Square** began appearing in the early 1800s, during the reign of the most ifamous priestess of them all, Marie Laveau. Some historians believe this popular figure may have actually been vo different women. The first Marie was widowed and the mother of 15 children. She is remembered by some as a ilented nurse who cared for yellow fever victims and provided food for prisoners, by others as a scandalous heretic ho presided over secret orgies. It has been theorized that a second Marie, who resembled her mentor, carried on in er place when she died. There is also disagreement about Laveau's burial site, **St. Louis Cemetery Number 1** or **umber 2**. Modern followers visit both and festoon the tombs with fetishes and red X's. Neither site is safe for indi- dual travelers to visit on their own.

ne of several guided groups that tour these historic cemeteries (for further information, see "Tours" on page 9) is :d by the **New Orleans Historic Voodoo Museum** (724 Dumaine Street, between Royal and Bourbon Sts, 23.7685). The staff also presides over regularly scheduled voodoo rituals at the gravesites, Congo Square, and ther spots. The exotic legacy of Louisiana's African and Caribbean settlers is faithfully displayed at this small, ensely packed museum. Fascinating artifacts crowd the walls, and nothing is isolated behind glass except the esident 11-foot Burmese python. In-house practitioners mix customized gris-gris to order. This place is not for young hildren or fundamentalists, but if you don't mind brushing up against a few loose skulls or a mummified cat, it's uite an experience. Just be sure to bring along a cigar or candy bar for the altar of the spirit Exu, who may make lischief for those who forget to honor him.

on the honor system. A sit-down continental breakfast is included in the rate, and the **St. Charles Avenue Streetcar** is just four blocks away. The hosts, Jill and Charles Abbyad, are particularly welcoming and well informed about local happenings. This is a real find, and has plenty of repeat customers. ♦ By reservation only. No smoking. 1146 Constantinople St (at Coliseum St). 488.4640, 800/729.4640; fax 488.4639; www.historiclodging.com

46 CLANCY'S

★★★$$$ This noisy bistro is crammed with Uptown politicos, and the walls are lined with sketches of prominent residents who have served as "guest maitre d'." The dining rooms and bar are minimally attired in gray and white, with red trim and dark green ceilings. Try fried oysters with brie or crab cakes with roasted tomato salsa to start, followed by filet mignon with béarnaise, smoked duck, or grilled baby drum (a smaller cousin of the Louisiana redfish) with smoked salmon. The service can be kind of snooty, but this crowd doesn't scare easy, and neither should you. ♦ Creole ♦ M, Sa dinner; Tu-F lunch and dinner. Reser- vations recommended. 6100 Annunciation St (at Webster St). 895.1111

47 TAQUERIA CORONA

★★$ Almost from the day it first opened, the Mendez family's tiny and colorful restau- rant has been packed with fans; the lines at lunchtime sometimes stretch down the sidewalk. The main draw is soft tacos—a choice of meats (even tongue) sizzled on the

estaurants/Clubs: Red | Hotels: Purple | Shops: Orange | Outdoors/Parks: Green | Sights/Culture: Blue grill, then stuffed into flour tortillas with *pico de gallo* (fresh tomato salsa). The gazpacho and salads are other big sellers. Don't miss the Mexican rice pudding called *arroz con leche*. ◆Mexican ◆ Daily lunch and dinner. 5932 Magazine St (between Eleonore and State Sts). 897.3974. Also at: Numerous locations throughout the area

48 SCRIPTURA

If you take your writing seriously, stop here for a lavish selection of handmade papers, fountain pens, wax seals, letter openers, French inks, hand-blown Venetian glass pen rests, and other stationery products imported from around the world. Leather-bound journals, travel logs, and atlases are especially handsome. ◆ M-Sa. 5423 Magazine St (between Jefferson Ave and Octavia St). 897.1555; fax 897.0810

48 MELANGE STERLING

If you are looking to replace a missing or damaged piece of antique sterling silver, this place may be able to help. It stocks hollowware and flatware in hundreds of American and European patterns. In addition, the shop sells complete services, candelabras, coffee and tea sets, and trays. ◆ M-Sa. 5421 Magazine St (between Jefferson Ave and Octavia St). 899.4796, 800/513.3991

49 BEAUCOUP BOOKS

Walk through the door of this independent neighborhood bookstore and pass into a gentler era. Soft jazz plays as you browse through the large collection of local and regional works. Foreign-language editions are another specialty, particularly Spanish and French. Children's books are housed in a separate room popular with young sidekicks. Ask about signed copies. ◆ Daily. 5414 Magazine St (between Jefferson Ave and Octavia St). 895.2663, 800/543.4114; fax 895.9778; www.booksense.com&

49 U.TOPIA

Just when you think you've seen every crazy combination on Magazine Street, up pops a women's sportswear/designer furniture store. This is the only Louisiana shop that carries furnishings created by David Marsh, who hand paints the one-of-a-kind pieces for retailers in Aspen, Boston, and the San Francisco Bay area, among others. Several quality clothing

lines are also on hand, including a large collection of linen sportswear. ◆ Daily. 5408 Magazine St (between Jefferson Ave and Octavia St). 899.8488; www.utopianola.com

50 CC's GOURMET COFFEE HOUSE

Now you don't have to wait until you get home to try the best-selling coffee in South Louisiana. The full-bodied brew, in traditional dark roast, has been a regional favorite since 1919, and now the family-owned Community Coffee Company has transformed a former pharmacy building into its flagship store. The pressed-tin ceiling remains, but now the walls are lined with display cases that show off terrific pastries created by nationally known chef and television personality John Folse (the jambalaya quiche and the bourbon-pecan-fig tart are particularly good with the coffee). ◆ M-Th 6:30AM-11PM; F-Sa 6:30AM-midnight; Su 7:30AM-10PM. 900 Jefferson Ave (at Magazine St). 891.4969 & Also at: Numerous locations throughout the area

51 LE BON TEMPS ROULÉ

★$ This scruffy bar and short-order restaurant with no off-street parking looks like a place for neighborhood walk-ins, but it pulls customers citywide. You never know who might wander through the door next—a wino or a bank president—while at night, college students make up about half of the crowd. Try the HOT homemade chili, cheeseburgers, grilled chicken salad, or alligator po-boy. Raw oysters are free on Friday afternoons. Wash 'em down with one of the many varieties of imported and domestic beers. Shoot pool, play video poker, or shout over the 1,000-CD jukebox. Check the "Fool of the Week" blackboard for the latest winner of that unpopularity contest. If you're around in May, sign up for the Barathon, a 10-K race that starts here, with contestants running from bar to bar, guzzling 12-ounce drafts at each stop. The shortest time on record is 35 minutes, and the longest, 18 hours. ◆ American ◆ Daily lunch and dinner; bar: daily 11AM-3AM. 4801 Magazine St (at Bordeaux St). 895.8117

52 JON ANTIQUES

You needn't be adept at furniture refinishing to shop here. In fact, nothing even needs dusting in this immaculate store. The directly imported stock is dominated by English, French, and European antiques from the 18th and 19th centuries. Furnishings are complemented by porcelains, tea caddies, mirrors, and brass fireplace accessories. ♦ M-Sa. 4605 Magazine St (between Cadiz and Valence Sts). 899.4482; fax 899.4435

53 THE BEAD SHOP

In this shop set in a renovated 19th-century cottage, artisans and designers will find a dazzling inventory of beads and jewelry-making tools, as well as ethnic jewelry, pillows, pottery, and instructional books. Don't miss the beaded Haitian voodoo flags. Custom beading of bridal headpieces is a specialty. ♦ Open Daily. 4612 Magazine St (between Cadiz and Valence Sts). 895.6161

54 CAROL ROBINSON GALLERY

Visitors who limit themselves to the works on display around Jackson Square might get the idea that local art consists of dancing musicians, swamp scenes, or crawfish playing poker. Instead of settling for something to grace your refrigerator door, check out the excellent—and affordable—contemporary collection of regional and local art here. A new exhibition opens on the first Saturday of each month from September through June. Several different mediums are represented, with the emphasis on painting, ceramics, and sculpture. Color and black-and-white photography are also featured. See paintings by Jere Allen, *trompe l'oeil* sculptures by ceramicist Richard Newman, and lithography by Masahiro Arai (who has studios in New Orleans and Japan). The low-key, friendly atmosphere makes browsing enjoyable. ♦ Tu-Sa. 840 Napoleon Ave (at Magazine St). 895.6130

55 CASAMENTO'S

★★★$$ The quest for perfectly fried oysters leads some pilgrims all over town. For many, the search ends at this little hole in the wall across the street from the Second District Police Station. The no-nonsense oyster lover's menu includes oysters on the half shell, oyster stew, fried oysters, and oyster loaves. Holdouts can choose shrimp, trout, spaghetti, seafood platters, or sandwiches. The squeaky clean, ceramic tile-lined dining room has great service, but all those hard surfaces give it the acoustics of an indoor swimming pool. ♦ Seafood/Italian ♦ Tu-Su lunch and dinner; closed June–15 September. 4330 Magazine St (between General Pershing St and Napoleon Ave). 895.9761

56 TALEBLOO ORIENTAL RUGS

With all of the art and antiques available along Magazine Street, this might be the best place to design a new room from the ground up. The store specializes in antique and semi-antique Persians and Orientals, in sizes ranging from 2-by-3-foot mats to 15-by-30-foot "palace-size" rugs. All are handmade of wool or silk. ♦ M-Sa. 4130 Magazine St (between Marengo and Milan Sts). 899.8114; fax 899.8800

57 THE PRIVATE CONNECTION/PIECES

Step into this small gallery to view one of the most colorful and unusual displays on Magazine Street, featuring items that have all been made in Indonesia. Be sure to see the shadow puppets from Bali and Java (the ornate leather figures were not meant for an audience to view directly, but the artists decorated them anyway for the enjoyment of the puppeteers). And don't miss more traditional (three-dimensional) puppets. Hand-carved and -painted mobiles and "flying" temple guards (whimsical winged wooden figures) flutter from the ceiling. Bright wooden tables are shaped like animals. Most of the antique Dutch Colonial furnishings here are made of teak, with some mahogany and Burmese rosewood. Architectural details come from homes in East and Central Java. The stock also includes flower sculptures, baskets, jewelry, and batiks. ♦ M-Sa. 3927 Magazine St (at Austerlitz St). 899.4944. Also at: 1116 Decatur St daily (between Ursulines and Governor Nicholls Sts). 593.9526

58 KELSEY'S

★★★$$$ Owner/chef Randy Barlow worked with Cajun guru Paul Prudhomme for eight

Restaurants/Clubs: Red | Hotels: Purple | Shops: Orange | Outdoors/Parks: Green | Sights/Culture: Blue

years before opening his own critically acclaimed restaurant (named after his daughter) on the suburban West Bank in 1991. Five years later, he moved the operation to this bright yellow storefront on a busy Uptown corner. The dining room is decorated with framed posters and prints of Louisiana scenes, track lighting, and an antique wooden bar. Here he continues to turn out lusty fare with a South Louisiana flavor, including braised pork T-bone with gingersnap gravy, blackened rib-eye steak, panéed (breaded) rabbit, and pecan-crusted fish topped with shrimp or crawfish. The signature eggplant Kelsey is a fried eggplant pirogue overflowing with sautéed shrimp and oysters. ♦ Cajun/Creole ♦ Tu-F lunch and dinner; Sa dinner. 3923 Magazine St (at Austerlitz St). 897.6722

58 CASEY WILLEMS POTTERY

Other than special orders for the Guggenheim Museum Gift Shop, self-taught potter Casey Willems sells exclusively through this studio/shop. One of his most popular items is a European-style berry bowl with drainage holes and a basin below. Willems, a friendly man who obviously loves his work, chats while at his wheel and will gladly take interested customers on a guided tour of the glazing and kiln rooms. Be sure to check the walls for unique and humorous plates, decorated by Willems's animator son. ♦ M-Sa. 3919 Magazine St (between General Taylor and Austerlitz Sts). 899.1174

59 DAVIS GALLERY

This gallery offers more than the limited visual aesthetics of a traditional museum setting: visitors are invited (with the assistance of an employee) to touch and smell the fine examples of African ethnographic art on open display. All pieces are imported from West and Central Africa and have been used by members of the original cultures. Among the items are masks, basketry, textiles, jewelry, household objects, cooking implements, figures, cult items, and prestige symbols used to denote rank and social status. Great care is taken in presentation, as the gallery owners feel that the pieces are so powerful they need an appropriate backdrop to be fully appreciated. There's something here for collectors at every level, from $45 baskets to museum-quality treasures. The gallery has sold works to the Smithsonian and other prestigious institutions. ♦ Tu-Sa. 3964 Magazine St (at Constantinople St). 895.5206; fax 897.0248

60 MARIO VILLA

Celebrated local furniture designer Mario Villa's work is featured in private collections around the globe, and *Metropolitan Home*

named him among the top 100 designers in the world. The Nicaraguan-born artist graduated from **Tulane** with a degree in architecture, a strong background that is reflected in the Neo-Classical forms of his steel, brass, and copper furnishings. Each piece is constructed and finished by hand. The gallery also features a limited collection by other carefully selected local artists. With an inventory of furniture, accessories, and sculpture that changes regularly, the gallery is worth a stop on every visit to the city. ♦ M-Sa. 3908 Magazine St (between General Taylor and Austerlitz Sts). 895.8731; fax 895.7431

61 SULLIVAN STAINED GLASS STUDIO

If you fall in love with the stained-glass windows in historic New Orleans mansions, you could order one for your own house (and have it shipped home) at this bright gallery, which also does restoration work for local homes and churches. You'll also find a limited number of ready-made gift items, such as suncatchers and stained-glass crosses. ♦ M-Sa. 3827 Magazine St (between Peniston and General Taylor Sts). 895.6720

61 SHADYSIDE POTTERY

Watch master potter Charles Bohn at work in his studio at the back of the showroom. He's usually at the wheel all day on weekdays and until 2PM or 3PM on Saturdays. The shelves are stocked with such handmade items as lamps, bowls, vases, and ginger jars in a pleasing variety of textures and colors. One especially attractive display features copper matte glaze pieces. Bohn served an apprenticeship in Japan, and his work is influenced by the Classical style of the Greeks, Romans, Chinese, and Egyptians. The shop also carries a limited number of hand-blown glass items by other artists. Handmade Japanese kites by Mitsuyoshi Kawamoto usually decorate the walls—unless they're sold out. ♦ M-Sa. 3823 Magazine St (between Peniston and General Taylor Sts). 897.1710

62 LE WICKER GAZEBO

A collection of antique and new wicker furnishings includes settees, rocking chairs, sofas, headboards, and tables. You'll also find miniature chairs and rockers for children, a large number of antique quilts and throw pillows, and old jewelry and gift items. ♦ M-S . 3715 Magazine St (between Amelia and Peniston Sts). 899.1355

63 DIDIER, INC.

Located in a 19th-century raised Creole cottage, the elegant collection here could be mistaken for a small museum. There is no clutter, no furniture piled against the walls.

Each room is carefully laid out with high-style mahogany and rosewood American furniture, accessories, and prints circa 1800 to 1850. The owners are frequently away on buying excursions, so it's best to phone before making a special trip. ♦ Usually open M-Sa, or by appointment. 3439 Magazine St (at Delachaise St). 899.7749

64 STAN LEVY IMPORTS

Antiques lovers will find one of the area's largest collections housed in this 19th-century building. The company specializes in French and English furniture and accessories, but also stocks a limited inventory of Italian and American pieces. Thousands of items are displayed in the maze of showrooms. ♦ M-Sa. 1028 Louisiana Ave (between Constance and Magazine Sts). 899.6384; fax 899.6421

65 F&M PATIO BAR

Don't let the scuzzy atmosphere fool you. This dive is crawling with Uptown blue bloods. The riverfront institution began as a dance hall in 1943 and was a biker bar for a few years before it was bought in 1979 by the late Jed Palmer, a colorful local entrepreneur. Since then, the bar has attracted an eclectic late-night crowd with its large courtyard, funky atmosphere, and two of the best jukeboxes in town. Palmer's son Trevor now runs the place. A huge charbroiler at the edge of the patio turns out half-pound hamburgers, chicken breasts, and quesadillas. Fajitas, stuffed with steak, chicken, fish, or alligator sausage, are the house specialty. Service goes beyond casual, but it suits the atmosphere and clientele very well. ♦ M from 5PM; Tu-F from 1PM;

Sa-Su from 3PM. 4841 Tchoupitoulas St (at Lyons St). 895.6784

66 TIPITINA'S

Though a second branch has opened in the French Quarter, the original **Tipitina's** remains the acknowledged frowsy old queen of New Orleans music clubs. It's the required first stop on every serious cat's circuit of the city. Dr. John, the Neville Brothers, Taj Mahal, Otis Clay, Bo Diddley, Junior Walker, Bonnie Raitt, and Jerry Lee Lewis are just a few of the names that have shivered these walls. **Tip's** is named for a song by the legendary Professor Longhair, who is now immortalized in bronze near the front entrance of this raucous but intimate (capacity 700) dance hall. Top local bands open for some of the headliners, a great introduction to the as-yet-unknown talent that crowds the town. If the first floor is packed, elbow through to the balcony, where there might be a bit more room to stretch. Since the mid-1980s, Sunday evenings are reserved for Cajun *fais-do-dos*. If you'd like to take home a souvenir, there's a choice inventory of T-shirts, CDs, and tapes—many recorded on the club's own label. Advance tickets are now available at the box office here or through **Ticketmaster** (522.5555), but only for the big-name performers; you'll still need to show up early and wait in line to see the smaller local acts. And be sure to get your hand stamped for freedom to come and go. ♦ Th-Sa from 10PM; Su 4-9PM. 501 Napoleon Ave (at Tchoupitoulas St). 895.8477, concert line 897.3943 ♿ Also at: 233 N Peters St (between Iberville and Bienville Sts). 566.7095; www.tipitinas.com

THE BEST

Greg and Mary Sonnier
Co-owners/Chefs, Gabrielle Restaurant

Rent a sailboat at **Murray Yacht Sales/Boat Rentals** at **West End Harbor** and sail on **Lake Pontchartrain** for great views of the city skyline.

Picnic in **City Park**—you can rent a rowboat at the **Lagoon;** then visit the **New Orleans Museum of Art** or **Storyland;** take a ride on the flying horses at **Carousel Gardens**. Don't forget to visit the **New Orleans Botanical Garden**.

Eating seafood at **Brunings** on the lake.

Aquarium of the Americas or the **Louisiana Children's Museum** on rainy days; the **Audubon Zoo** on sunny days. You can walk to the zoo from **St. Charles**.

An all-day rider pass on the **St. Charles Streetcar** line. You will always see a beautiful home that you've somehow missed before!

Breakfast at the **Cameila Grill** or the **Bluebird Café**.

On Saturday, visit the corner of **Grand Route St. John** and **Moss Street** (on **Bayou St. John**); it has the oldest operational fire hydrant in the city. The **Pitot House,** then Vigil Mass at **Our Lady of the Rosary Catholic Church,** and, finally, an early dinner at **Gabrielle**!

Oysters at **Uglesich's**!

Antique shopping on **Magazine Street**.

We love to watch the people coming in and out of Jazz Fest (our restaurant is situated at the **Mystery Street** entrance to the **Fairgrounds**).

The train known as *Smoky Mary* no longer chugs out to the private fishing camps where notorious parties raged for days. Gone too are the legendary musicians, like Buddy Bolden and Louis Armstrong, who jammed while wealthy patrons jittered to rhythms that would later be called jazz. Before land reclamation projects began in 1926, the area now known as the Lakefront was mostly underwater. *Smoky Mary* terminated near the end of **Elysian Fields Avenue** at **Milneburg,** where sporting folk would cross long wooden piers that stretched over marsh and mud flats to reach the rickety camps on the shoreline. Along the way they would leap across breaks in the boardwalks, where a few inches of open space made the shacks technically independent of dry land and, consequently, of city laws prohibiting gambling and other popular vices. That sort of fancy footwork continued through the 1940s at **West End,** where the line dividing New Orleans from suburban **Jefferson Parish** runs right through the cluster of seafood houses perched on pilings over the water. Jefferson Parish did not enforce the antigambling laws, so restaurants that were over the line rang with pinballs and slot machines, while those inside the city limits were clean.

From West End, it's a short walk across the **17th Street Canal** footbridge to the tiny fishing community of **Bucktown,** which has been hopping for at least 140 years. Some say it was named for Wild Buck Wooley, who kept a tavern there in the 1800s. Others blame it on "bucking," 19th-century slang for the brawls that were common among the rough-and-tumble dancehall girls. The early bars drew a rowdy clientele from downtown New Orleans, and the area flourished during Prohibition. During the 1960s, restaurants such as **Sid-Mar's** and **Deanie's** moved in and helped make Bucktown a prime destination for great seafood presented in colorful and unpretentious surroundings.

Although the Lakefront has changed dramatically through the years, it is still the first resort for New Orleanians in search of cool breezes and good times. The saloons and bawdy cabarets have been replaced by noisy seafood houses and family restaurants. Showboats and floating circuses have given way to flashy yachts and Jet Ski races. The sedate north shore resort of **Mandeville** (see "Additional Highlights," page 154), once

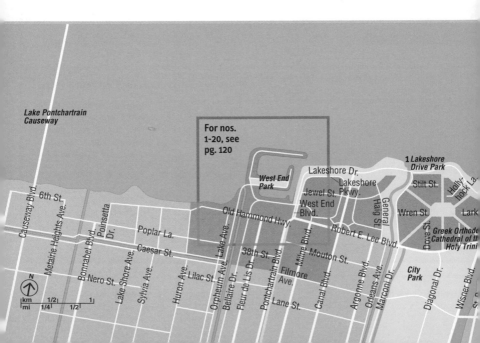

accessible only by passenger steamer, is now a cool 30-minute drive across the world's longest continuous over-water bridge. Milneburg, where Buddy and Louis blew their horns, has become the **University of New Orleans (UNO),** home to an internationally recognized jazz studies program directed by pianist Ellis Marsalis. The campus fronts **Lakeshore Drive,** a winding five-mile parkway that traces **Lake Pontchartrain's** edge from the marinas and restaurants of the West End to **South Shore Harbor** in eastern New Orleans where, like history repeating itself, state laws legalizing gambling on the water have resulted in the presence of modern gaming boats like **Bally's Casino.**

BUCKTOWN

If you want to chow down on fresh Louisiana seafood with the natives or cart an ice-chest–full back home, this small fishing village provides the opportunity. Casual and inexpensive family restaurants line a four-block stretch of **Old Hammond Highway,** which hugs the grassy **Lake Pontchartrain** levee. Turn south onto **Lake Avenue** to shop a cluster of seafood markets supplied by the independent fishermen who dock at tiny **Bucktown Harbor.** Seafood hasn't always been the area's main draw. In the 19th century, taverns and dance halls attracted a raucous crowd from downtown New Orleans, and Sunday picnickers would rent skiffs to paddle around the waterfront. During Prohibition, folks came here to buy illegal booze and hoochie-cooch the night away.

1 BRUNING HOUSE

From here, you can see **Brunings Seafood Restaurant,** founded by Theodor Bruning, across the harbor. This white wood-frame charmer was the family home, built around 1893 by his son, Captain John C. Bruning. In those days, the Bruning family operated two boathouses where they rented skiffs to New Orleanians who were vacationing or picnicking at Bucktown. When the waters got rough, Cap

would man his post in the widow's walk and watch for signs of boaters in trouble. He and his brother are credited with saving hundreds from drowning. Eventually the open widow's walk was replaced by the enclosed lookout. Known to neighbors as "the big house," this private residence (still owned by Brunings) has become a familiar local landmark and film location. It was the backdrop for a *fais-do-do* (sort of a Cajun hoedown) in the 1987 movie *The Big Easy*. ♦ 1870 Orpheum Ave (north of Old Hammond Hwy)

KENNETH SNOW

2 SID-MAR'S

★★$ If you're in the mood to relax over a pile of crustaceans and a pitcher of beer, dress down and stop here. This eatery has

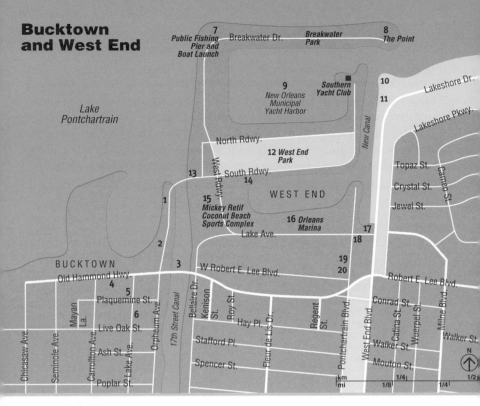

Bucktown and West End

7 Public Fishing Pier and Boat Launch   Breakwater Dr.   Breakwater Park   **8** The Point

Lake Pontchartrain

9 New Orleans Municipal Yacht Harbor   Southern Yacht Club   **10**   **11**   Lakeshore Dr.   Lakeshore Pkwy.

New Canal

North Rdwy.

12 West End Park

Topaz St.   Cameo St.

13   South Rdwy.   **14**   West Rdwy.

Crystal St.

15 Mickey Retif Coconut Beach Sports Complex   WEST END   Jewel St.

1   **16** Orleans Marina   **17**

Lake Ave.   **18**

2

BUCKTOWN   **3**   **19**   **20**

Old Hammond Hwy.   W Robert E. Lee Blvd.   Robert E. Lee Blvd.

4

5 Plaquemine St.   Bellaire Dr.   Kenison St.   Roy St.   Hay Pl.   Conrad St.   Catina St.   Wuerpel St.   Milne Blvd.   Walker St.

6 Live Oak St.   17th Street Canal   Stafford Pl.   Fleur de Lis Dr.   Regent St.   Pontchartrain Blvd.   West End Blvd.   Walker St.   Mouton St.

Chicasaw Ave.   Seminole Ave.   Mayan La.   Carrollton Ave.   Orpheum Ave.   Ash St.   Lake Ave.   Spencer St.

Poplar St.

km / mi   1/8   1/4   1/2   N

been a sentimental favorite since the 1960s, and the atmosphere is reminiscent of a ramshackle fishing camp. Natives love to kick back on the narrow screened porch and admire the little boats that brought in their dinner. ◆ Seafood ◆ Tu-Su lunch and dinner. 1824 Orpheum Ave (north of Old Hammond Hwy). 831.9541 ⑤

3 BUCKTOWN HARBOR

Generations of anglers have chugged out of the 17th Street Canal before dawn to harvest

Since the 19th century, the Feast Day of St. Joseph has been celebrated in New Orleans every 19 March by Sicilian immigrants and their descendants. They erect spectacular food-laden altars in homes, churches, and businesses all over town. The food is usually donated to the poor, though everyone shares in the festivities and goes home with a lucky fava bean to tuck inside a wallet or purse, a protection against going broke in the coming year.

Two of the world's most famous pen names were born right here in New Orleans. Riverboat pilot Samuel Clemens occasionally contributed to the *Crescent* between 1857 and 1861, and it was in that local newspaper that his alter ego, Mark Twain, first appeared. And, on the lam from embezzlement charges in Texas, William Sydney Porter came home for a short time in 1896 and adopted his lifelong literary alias, O. Henry.

the catch that's on the tables at neighboring restaurants by noon. The brick-and-metal pedestrian bridge over the canal connects with **West End Park** (see page 122) for a picturesque circuit—a great way to walk off some of those calories.

4 R&O PIZZA PLACE

★★$ There are three topics that are sure to spark an argument in New Orleans: religion, politics, and food. And one of the timeless, unanswerable questions is: Who has the best roast beef po-boy in town? One name that surfaces in every slugfest is **R&O,** where the toasted French bread is soaked with gravy so dark it's nearly black, and the beef, lettuce, tomatoes, and mayonnaise are piled high and sloppy. It's a mess—and the benchwarmers out front can hardly wait for a table to open up so they can get a chance to ruin their shirts. The pizzas and fried seafood are great, too. ◆ American ◆ M, W-Su lunch and dinner. 216 Old Hammond Hwy (between Lake and Carrollton Aves). 831.1248 ⑤

5 SCHAEFER & RUSICH

The closest thing to a frill in this no-nonsense seafood market is the rack of numbers that maintains some order in the aggressive rush-hour crowd. Pick up boiled shrimp or crabs anytime, crawfish from November through July. Don't forget corn on the cob and new potatoes boiled in the same kettles as the critters. Add ready-made pasta salad, French bread, and soft drinks for a complete picnic to go. If you want to get fancy, ask them to heat up a stuffed artichoke for you. Napkins aren't up to the task, so be sure to buy a large roll of paper towels before you come. ♦ Tu-Su. 1726 Lake Ave (at Plaquemine St). 833.3973

6 DEANIE'S SEAFOOD

★★$$ There's no lake view, but the clean, spartan dining rooms are packed with fiercely loyal locals who drive miles to dig into gargantuan seafood platters and po-boys. Instead of crackers or bread, bowls of spicy boiled new potatoes keep idle hands entertained until the real food arrives. Stuffed soft-shell crabs are fried and sauced with hollandaise. The barbecued shrimp are actually sautéed in peppery butter and served with plenty of hot French bread for dunking. ♦ Seafood ♦ Daily lunch and dinner. 1713 Lake Ave (between Live Oak and Plaquemine Sts). 831.4141 ♿

6 DEANIE'S SEAFOOD MARKET

The same boiled and fresh seafood that has people lined up three deep next door is available for quick pick-up at this adjoining market, which also packages for travel. A crate of blue claw crabs is sure to please the folks back home *mo' bettuh* than alligator key chains and pralines (which they also sell, by the way). ♦ M-Th until 8PM; F-Su until 9PM. 1713 Lake Ave (between Live Oak and Plaquemine Sts). 835.4638 ♿

WEST END

This Lakefront neighborhood dates back to 1871, when railroad service to the city's extreme western corner (edged by **Lake Pontchartrain** and the **Jefferson Parish** line) created a festive resort area that grew to include a hotel, several restaurants, amusement rides, picnic grounds, and marinas. Today the oak-shaded square of **West End Park** is bordered by boisterous waterfront seafood houses, the **Municipal Yacht Harbor,** private boathouses, and the very private **Southern Yacht Club** (the country's second oldest, established in 1840).

7 PUBLIC FISHING PIER AND BOAT LAUNCH

These unsupervised facilities in West End Park are free and open year-round. On Saturdays and Sundays, the parking lot is full of brightly clad windsurfers and Jet Ski jockeys who cast off from here. It's also a good place to sit and watch the late afternoon sun disappear into the lake. ♦ Breakwater Dr (north of N Rdwy)

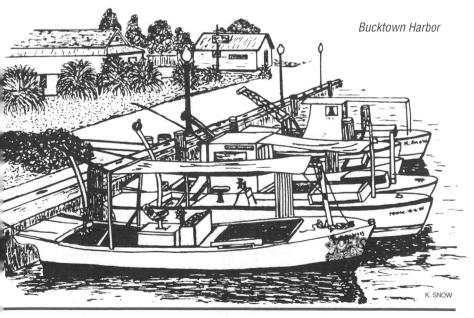

Bucktown Harbor

K. SNOW

Restaurants/Clubs: Red | **Hotels: Purple** | **Shops: Orange** | **Outdoors/Parks: Green** | **Sights/Culture: Blue**

8 THE POINT

A bumpy drive past the boathouses lining Breakwater Drive terminates at this turnaround, which is best known locally as the spot where generations of teenagers have parked after dark to "watch the submarine races." Old-timers may prefer to explore the rocky shoreline or sit on the wall and watch boats sail into the marina. The small circular lot is set on a man-made peninsula with fine views of the **New Canal Lighthouse** and **Municipal Yacht Harbor**. Save your dinner scraps to feed the flock of ducks, but wait until you're ready to leave or they will give you no peace. ◆ Breakwater Dr (north of North Rdwy)&

9 NEW ORLEANS MUNICIPAL YACHT HARBOR

If you have a boat in tow, the busy marina usually has around 25 transient slips available. The complex includes 610 slips and 135 boathouses, as well as the private **Southern** and **New Orleans Yacht Clubs**. Boatyards, bars, and restaurants are all within walking distance. Just across the street is **Sea Chest Marine Distributors** (7385 West Rdwy, at South Rdwy, 288.1250), a full-service ship's store that sells engines, parts, rigging, foul weather gear, boating clothes, and more. The harbormaster's office is open daily from 9AM to 5PM, but security officers will assist boaters who arrive after hours. ◆ North Rdwy (east of Breakwater Dr). 288.1431

10 NEW CANAL LIGHTHOUSE

One of only four wooden lighthouses left in the Gulf Coast region, this beacon (pictured below) also provides bunk space for the search-and-rescue crew of the local Coast Guard. The first lighthouse to mark the entrance of New Canal began operation in 1838, and the present wood-frame building was erected in 1905, then restored in 1976. An 1866 survey shows that the lighthouse was originally located 1,000 feet north of the shoreline at the end of a jetty. Because of modern landfill projects, the site now projects only slightly into the lake. The station is manned around the clock by crew members who monitor VHF Channel 16 for marine distress. The lighthouse makes a fine photograph, but it is never open to the public. ◆ Lakeshore Dr (north of Lake Ave)

11 JOE'S CRAB SHACK

★★$$ At this lively restaurant (formerly **Bart's on the Lake**) with a prime waterfront location, tables on wraparound decks overlook the Coast Guard's picturesque lighthouse station and the comings and goings of marina traffic. Part of a Texas-based chain of scruffy seafood eateries, the place has a fun, funky atmosphere, with rowdy lakehouse decor, freewheeling (but reasonably efficient) service, and a sign out front that always promises "free crabs tomorrow"—it proudly bills itself as "an embarrassment to any neighborhood." Boaters can tie up their craft at the lowest level for a casual feed. Although the nearby **Brunings** and **West End Cafe** do a better job with fried seafood, **Joe's** offers a wider variety of crabs (blue, stone, giant Dungeness, Alaskan king) and cooking styles (boiled, steamed, garlic, barbecue). The tables here have wide center holes that hold galvanized buckets where diners can deposit shells and other debris. ◆ Seafood ◆ Daily lunch and dinner. 8000 Lakeshore Dr (north of Lake Ave). 283.1010 &

12 WEST END PARK

This green space anchoring West End has Art Deco picnic shelters and WPA-era fountains. It's a prime destination for joggers and walkers who take their exercise comfortably in the shade of the live oaks that surround the square. ◆ West and South Rdwys &

New Canal Lighthouse

K. SNOW

13 BRUNINGS SEAFOOD RESTAURANT

★★★$$ Despite damages to the back wall by hurricane Georges (renovation is well underway and expected to be complete by press time), service continues in temporary quarters in the front of the establishment. The food is as great as ever. This has always been the place to splurge on a mound of fresh Louisiana shellfish fried, boiled, or broiled to perfection. The granddaddy of New Orleans seafood houses is the city's third-oldest restaurant (**Antoine's** was established in 1840, **Tujague's** in 1856). When German immigrant Theodor Bruning opened his doors in 1859, a separate ladies' entrance routed proper Victorians around the lounge area. No more. Men and women alike pass the antique oak-and-marble bar where waitresses shimmied in the 1920s and pinballs clanged through the 1930s and 1940s. The spittoons and slot machines are long gone, but there's still plenty of racket from the beer drinkers and crab pounders. Ceiling fans cool the casual dining room, which is set on pilings over the water to catch the lake breezes and spectacular sunset views. Fried seafood platters and stuffed whole flounder are the star attractions. Ask for spicy boiled new potatoes instead of french fries and get one (huge) order of onion rings for the table. ♦ Seafood ♦ Daily lunch and dinner. 1924 West End Pkwy (just west of West Rdwy). 282.9395 ৬

13 JAEGER'S SEAFOOD BEER GARDEN

★★$ It's possible to drop quite a few bucks here, but it can also be inexpensive if you choose the trademark family-style service. "Big A's Serious Seafood Platter" feeds six with a heap of fried shrimp, oysters, trout, crab cakes, soft-shell crabs, stuffed shrimp, oysters bordelaise, onion rings, french fries, and garlic bread. The kitchen staff will even deep-fry a whole marinated turkey—a bizarre local indclicacy with 24 hours' advance notice. Less ambitious diners can create their own mix from hot boiled shellfish and vegetables (sold by the pound) or assorted baskets of fried seafood. Fans of the raw stuff can order traditional half-shells or a line of raw oysters plopped in shot glasses. This is a loud spot that's fine for rowdy groups, and the noise level increases when an oldies R&B band performs (most nights). The best seats are on the back deck, where boaters dock for dinner and casual diners have great sunset views. ♦ Seafood/Italian ♦ W-F dinner; Sa-Su lunch and dinner. 1928 West End Pkwy (just west of West Rdwy). 283.7585 ৬

14 MURRAY YACHT SALES/BOAT RENTALS

If you want to spend a day on Lake Pontchartrain, this established dealer rents a 26-foot Pearson, with or without a captain. Sailors whose skills are just rusty can arrange a three-hour refresher course, and beginners can sign on for a full weekend of lessons to earn certification from the American Sailing Association. Groups of six or less can charter a three-hour sundown cruise with a captain. The office isn't always staffed, but an answering machine stands watch. ♦ 402 South Rdwy (east of West Rdwy). 283.2507.

15 MICKEY RETIF COCONUT BEACH SPORTS COMPLEX

As many as 1,200 barefooters show up every night from March through November to play volleyball on these deep sand courts. The park is open to the public and admission is free, except during tournaments and league play. It's usually easiest to get in on an afternoon game. The adjacent bar/grill lends volleyballs and other equipment, but they'll hold your driver's license hostage until you return. The park, a star of the New Orleans Recreation Department system, hosts several pro volleyball competitions during the year, most of them in May. Weekend tournaments attract sun worshipers, who spread out their beach towels on the levee to watch the games. Others come to watch the sun worshipers. ♦ Daily noon-11PM. 7340 West Rdwy (between Lake Ave and West End Pkwy). 286.0333 ৬

General Benjamin "The Beast" Butler, leader of the Union troops that occupied New Orleans during the Civil War, was given the derisive nickname "Spoons" by the many Southern ladies forced to surrender the family silver.

Restaurants/Clubs: **Red** | Hotels: **Purple** | Shops: **Orange** | Outdoors/Parks: **Green** | Sights/Culture: **Blue**

CHILD'S PLAY

New Orleans has a well-earned reputation as a playground for adults, but parents can find plenty of amusements that are suitable for kids, and fun for grown-ups, too.

1 **Immortalize** your face or hand at the **New Orleans School of GlassWorks & Printmaking Studio**. It takes about one hour to case a mold, and the finished sculpture can be picked up the next day. Visitors may also observe the glassblowing action at the fascinating working gallery.

2 **Paint** colors and images with your body movements on a huge video screen at the **Louisiana Children's Museum**.

3 Visit the **Aquarium of the Americas** in the **CBD** and **Uptown's Audubon Zoo** (which are connected by a fun riverboat cruise).

4 **Handle** a real-life fossil at the **Louisiana Nature Center**.

5 **Relive** the festivities of Carnival time at **Blaine Kern's Mardi Gras World** on the **West Bank**.

6 **Take** a guided tour of the **Superdome**.

7 **Listen** to a reading of a classic children's story on Saturdays at **Maple Street Children's Book Shop**.

8 **Ride** the antique carousel at **Carousel Gardens** in **City Park** (and while you're there, you can also feed the ducks and go fishing).

9 **Visit** such Louisiana historical figures as Andrew Jackson, Jean Lafitte, Louis Armstrong, and voodoo priestess Marie Laveau (well, their statues anyway) at the **Musée Conti Historical Wax Museum**.

10 **Board** a boat for a swamp tour in **Barataria,** land of the buccaneers, to see alligators, turtles, water birds—even a real pirate burial ground.

16 ORLEANS MARINA

It's best to make advance reservations for transient slips at this busy marina, especially for vessels over 40 feet or for those needing special disability accommodations. More than a dozen good restaurants are within walking distance, as are a supermarket, a mailing service, dry cleaners, hairdressers, drugstores, an ice-cream parlor, and a mainline bus stop. Some 50 tenants live aboard their moored vessels full-time, and a pair of well-fed otters make a good living patrolling the area. Other residents include a flock of wood ducks and several pelicans. Among the amenities here are 24-hour security, laundry facilities, and cable television. The harbormaster's office is open Monday through Friday from 8AM to 4PM, but boaters with reservations can tie up

Because it's surrounded by water, New Orleans depends on extraordinary measures for flood control. The city is protected not only by the best levees on earth, but also by a diversion system that includes the Bonnet Carré Spillway, which can redirect 250,000 cubic feet of water per second—much greater than the flow over Niagara Falls.

after hours and register the next day. ◆ 221 Lake Ave (between Pontchartrain Blvd and West Rdwy). 288.2351 &

17 ACME OYSTER HOUSE

★★$ This waterfront branch of the French Quarter institution debuted in October 1998, featuring the same superior raw oyster bar, as well as fried and broiled seafood, and specialty dishes such as oyster/artichoke soup and gumbo *poopa* (a hollowed-out French bread bowl filled with gumbo or red beans and rice). Boaters tie up at the adjoining bench-lined dock to enjoy the harbor views. ◆ Seafood ◆ Daily lunch and dinner. 7306 Lakeshore Dr (just north of Lake Ave). 282.9200 &

17 AMBERJACKS

On the second floor above **Acme Oyster House,** saltwater aquariums, bubbling water-filled columns, and strong tropical drinks will drown your sorrows in no time. There's a cover charge during comedy shows on Wednesday nights and for live bands on Friday and Saturday. Drink specials are featured daily. Cover W, F-Sa. ◆ M-F, Su from noon; Sa from 5PM. 7306 Lakeshore Dr (just north of Lake Ave). 282.6660

18 RUSSELL'S MARINA GRILL

★★$ Imagine a casual restaurant similar to **Denny's,** but with calm decor, good food, and a full bar, and you have this classic diner. This is the place to go when you have a late-night craving for a burger or fried seafood, and is a good bet for old-fashioned soda fountain sprees or breakfast anytime. The fresh crab-meat omelette is topped with hollandaise, and the giant seafood platter is piled with catfish, shrimp, oysters, and crab claws. The kitchen is open until 11:30PM during the week, and until 12:30AM on Friday and Saturday. ♦ American ♦ Daily breakfast, lunch, and dinner. 8555 Pontchartrain Blvd (at Lake Ave). 282.9980 ♿

19 WEST END CAFÉ

★★$ The friendly bar, trim dining room, and snappy service provide a sterling example of the New Orleans institution known as a neighborhood restaurant. Their fried and boiled seafood can compete with the best in town, while heretics can order a perfectly grilled hamburger steak with smothered onions and real mashed potatoes. The menu ranges from meatball sandwiches to trout meunière, so this is a good pick for groups with mixed tastes and budgets. Kids will enjoy racking up the spoils at the most generous claw machine in town. ♦ Seafood/Creole/Italian ♦ M-F lunch and dinner; Sa-Su breakfast, lunch, and dinner. 8536 Pontchartrain Blvd (between W Robert E. Lee Blvd and Lake Ave). 288.0711

20 ROSE MANOR

$$ East meets west in this large 1910 residence, which has been converted to a comfortable bed-and-breakfast with five guest rooms, including one private suite with a balcony, all with private baths. Owners Ruby and Peter Verhoeven collect hand-carved Chinese furnishings and European antiques, as well as old radios, jukeboxes, and other musical equipment. The marble insets on a Chinese sofa in the main parlor were designed to cool your back, a welcome amenity in this sunny marina neighborhood. The decor may be too busy for some, but the friendly atmosphere and fun variety of casual seafood restaurants are as appealing as the fresh lake breezes. Other perks include a complimentary full breakfast, cable TV, and guest membership privileges at the **West End Tennis and Fitness Club** two blocks away. ♦ 7214 Pontchartrain Blvd (between W Robert E. Lee Blvd and Lake Ave). 282.8200, 877/886.ROSE; fax 282.7283; www.rosemanor.com

LAKESHORE DRIVE

This parkway extends along the southern shore of **Lake Pontchartrain,** all the way from **New Canal** to **Lakefront Airport.** The breezy, landscaped road is definitely the scenic route; don't even think of speeding here.

21 LAKESHORE DRIVE PARK

Ⓟ Some call the stepped seawall (illustrated below) that leads into Lake Pontchartrain from this five-mile-long public park the world's longest grandstand. Engineers who transformed the former marsh into a protective barrier for the city carved an ever-changing landscape of curves and inlets to enhance the beauty of their man-made shoreline. The entire stretch of park is well stocked with picnic areas, shelters, and rest rooms. Pollution has made swimming impossible since the 1960s, but locals still make good use of the seawall for fishing, crabbing, and smooching. Thousands flock here on Saturday and Sunday afternoons,

Lakeshore Drive Park

K. SNOW

SANTA FLIES SOUTH

Created in 1986 to stimulate sluggish December tourism, the month long festival now known as "Christmas, New Orleans Style!" presents a full schedule of concerts, parades, children's programs, walking tours, riverboat cruises, cooking demonstrations, and other family fare. Many of the events are free, and special "Papa Noël Rates" at hotels citywide begin at $50 a night.

If you're in New Orleans anytime in December, the crisp weekends are perfect for driving Louisiana's great **River Road,** which traces both sides of the **Mississippi** from New Orleans to Baton Rouge. The graceful plantation manors and deep-roofed Arcadian cottages are all decked out for the holidays. Located in the same area is **Madewood** (4250 Hwy 308, southeast of Napoleonville, 369.7151; www.madewood.com), a stately Greek Revival manor that hosts the Christmas Heritage Celebration, a gala evening of wassail, feasting, and caroling in grand style that is usually held on the second Saturday in December.

Naturally, food is also part of the celebration. *Reveillon* (Christmas Eve) menus offered at many **French Quarter** restaurants throughout December are adapted from the elaborate banquets that were served in 19th-century Creole households after midnight Mass. Today's multicourse dinners promise the customary "fish, fowl, and flesh," along with *lagniappe* ("a little something extra") of *café brûlot* or eggnog.

At **City Park,** horse-drawn carriages and miniature trains offer an open-air journey through two miles of ancient oaks aglow with holiday lights. The gardens surrounding the park's antique wooden carousel are alive with puppet shows, gospel choirs, and storytellers. Creole kids even get a rare glimpse of a white Christmas on 26 December, when a sympathetic local company pumps in truckloads of real snow.

But the flaming finale of holiday events takes place at 7PM each Christmas Eve, when fire chiefs give the signal to torch the more than 100 bonfires that line the east and west banks of the Mississippi, an annual ritual in **St. James Parish** since the 1880s. Some claim the towering blazes light the way for Papa Noël as he paddles his pirogue to deliver gifts to good Cajun children. Others say they began as navigational signals that guided steamboats through the dense December fog. Or they may have illuminated the path for parishioners walking to midnight Mass.

Preparations for the Christmas Eve vigil begin soon after Thanksgiving, when River Road communities join forces to prepare bonfires. Typically shaped like tepees and filled with logs, more creative conflagrations resemble houses, oil platforms, fire engines—even four-wheel-drive vehicles. After sundown on Christmas Eve, both banks of the river are crowded with revelers as the flames light up the sky for miles. Passing cargo ships, paddle wheelers, and tugboats slow down to admire the view—some even chug merrily in circles—adding their signal flares and foghorns to the wild display.

For a complete listing of events, a schedule of hotel rates, and special restaurant menus, contact **"Christmas, New Orleans Style!"** at 100 Conti St, New Orleans, LA 70130 (800/673.5725).

when there can be traffic congestion and boom box intrusion. But during the week it is peaceful, and you'll be able to enjoy plenty of elbow room and long-range views. Walk, bike, or drive—there are no stop signs or traffic lights to spoil the view—but do remember that the Levee Board Police will strictly enforce the 35-mph speed limit (not that you would want to hurry, anyway).

22 UNIVERSITY OF NEW ORLEANS (UNO)

Founded in 1958 as part of the **Louisiana State University** system, this college has grown into the state's second-largest school (the largest university is in Baton Rouge), with an enrollment of approximately 16,000 students. The 420-acre Lakefront campus is one of Louisiana's youngest and best located universities. The school offers 53 undergraduate and pre-professional programs and 46 graduate programs through the doctoral level. Ninety percent of the alumni remain in the New Orleans area to live and work. Just 15 minutes from the French Quarter and Central Business District, the faculty here advises on urban planning and design, economics, finance, and

marine engineering. Graduates of the school of hotel, restaurant, and tourism go on to staff one of the city's main industries. And internationally known pianist Ellis Marsalis, father of Wynton and Branford, heads the music department's jazz studies program.
♦ Lakefront campus: Elysian Fields Ave (between Leon C. Simon and Lakeshore Drs). East campus: Franklin Ave (between Leon C. Simon and Lakeshore Drs). General information 280.6000, student and faculty concerts 280.6381, drama department productions 280.6317, box office 280.SHOW, sports 280.6100, campus activities 280.6349 ♿

On UNO's east campus:

KIEFER U.N.O. LAKEFRONT ARENA

This 10,000-seat auditorium is one of the city's main venues for a broad range of concerts and sporting events. The peculiar field ornament that looks like a huge steel gazebo has been the site of diverse outdoor events, including a visit by Pope John Paul II in 1987 and rock concerts by such trendy acts as the Red Hot Chili Peppers. The arena

THE BEST

Britton E. Trice
Owner, Garden District Book Shop/President, B.E. Trice Publishing

Food—a New Orleans obsession. Everyone is always talking about their last great meal. I order several appetizers so I can taste more things. Some of my favorites are barbecued shrimp and homemade biscuits at **Emeril's** (sit at the Chef's Food Bar and watch the master at work), the turtle soup at **Commander's Palace,** the grilled shrimp with black bean cake and coriander sauce at **Bayona,** the duck étouffée at the **Upperline.**

Other food favorites—boiled seafood on **Sid-Mar's** screen porch, family dinners at **Joey K's,** a Pimm's Cup on a hot summer evening at the **Napoleon House,** fresh oysters on the half shell at **Casamento's,** and Sunday morning *beignets* and *café au lait* at **Café du Monde.**

The river—We locals tend to take it for granted, but I'm always amazed at its power and grandeur when I do see it. Most of us live below sea level so we have to head to high ground to see the river. Best places to view it: The **Moonwalk** in the **French Quarter** and the butterfly-shaped building known as **River View** in **Audubon Park.**

Walking in the **Garden District**—Every time I walk through the Garden District, I discover a wonderful old house, architectural detail, or new plant that I never noticed before. Don't miss the **Lafayette Cemetery** with its aboveground crypts, or Anne Rice's manse where her book *The Witching Hour* is set. The free walking tour given by the **National Parks Service** starts at 2PM.

box office is located on the west side of the building, directly facing Franklin Avenue. As a **Ticketmaster** outlet, the box office also sells seats for any events represented by that statewide service, including ones held at other locations. ♦ Box office: M-F. 280.7171; www.ticketmaster.com ♿

SOUTH SHORE

For more than 60 years, this section of the lakeshore had been home to New Orleans's first airport and not much else. Recently, though, it has been under development as a recreation area and boasts a new marina and gambling boat.

23 NEW ORLEANS LAKEFRONT AIRPORT

The landing field juts out over the water at this complex, which was commissioned in 1934 as the first New Orleans airport. These days it's mostly private flyers who take off above the fishing camps that line the shore, but three on-site firms charter planes and helicopters (call the director of aviation for referrals). Enrique Alferez created the *Four Winds Fountain* on the front lawn as a WPA project in 1936. The celebrated sculptor (and former member of Pancho Villa's Mexican army) stood guard for three nights with a shotgun when a WPA official threatened to demolish the concrete nudes because the penis of the North Wind figure was exposed. The penis later disappeared in a mysterious accident city officials described as an act of vandalism. In 1991, Alferez was invited to supervise renovation of the fountain (including the removal of dozens of coats of paint that made the statues appear to be cavorting in long underwear) and to replace the long-missing member. Also worth a peek is the Art Deco architecture of the terminal building. The soaring lobby ceiling is circled by a bronze frieze that details great moments in aviation. Plaster pliers and wrenches decorate the doorways and balcony, and a terrazzo compass on the lobby floor points to cities around the world, setting out the distances from New Orleans (center of the known universe). ♦ Leon C. Simon Dr and Downman Rd. Director of Aviation, Randy Taylor, 243.4010 ♿

24 SOUTH SHORE HARBOR

Built in 1987, the city's newest harbor adjoins **New Orleans Lakefront Airport.** Transient dockage is usually available at the marina, with 447 slips (26 covered) located just 15 minutes from the French Quarter. ♦ 6701 South Shore Harbor Blvd (east of Downman Rd). 245.3152 ♿

At South Shore Harbor:

BALLY'S CASINO, LAKESHORE RESORT

The glitzy, Las Vegas–style emporium is quartered on a replica of an old-fashioned riverboat that cruises the lake (in good weather) or operates dockside. It's open around the clock, so gamblers can play the slot machines, craps, blackjack, roulette, video poker, and other games of chance any time they want. The casino also has live entertainment, cocktail lounges, and buffet dining. Admission and valet parking are free. ♦ Daily 24 hours. 248.3200, 800/572.2559 ♿

Restaurants/Clubs: Red | Hotels: Purple | Shops: Orange | Outdoors/Parks: Green | Sights/Culture: Blue

FAUBOURG MARIGNY/TREME/BYWATER

Faubourg Marigny bumps up against the downtown side of the French Quarter, where escalating rents and burgeoning tourism have driven many hip businesses and residents over the border into this funky *faubourg,* or "suburb." From **Esplanade Avenue** to **Elysian Fields Avenue,** and from the river to **Rampart Street,** the sidewalks are crowded with clean-lined 19th-century cottages, storefronts, and cafes. The original **Praline Connection** is here, as is the wonderful **Santa Fe** restaurant and the multi-cultural newcomer, **Marisol.** Nearby **Snug Harbor Jazz Bistro** and **Cafe Brasil** are prime destinations for music lovers, as is the historic jazz museum housed in the **Old US Mint** complex.

The bohemian atmosphere of Faubourg Marigny would have pleased its namesake, the homegrown aristocrat Bernard Xavier Philippe de Marigny de Mandeville. At his father's death in 1800, Marigny was the richest 15-year-old in America. He was also a profligate and rebellious youth who returned from his schooling in England with a taste for grand living and a serious dice habit. The sight of Marigny and his friends huddled over their dice became so common, in fact, that the Americans who lived across Canal Street referred to it as "Johnny Crapaud's game" (from *crapaud,* a variation of "frog," the derogatory name for the French). Later the jibe was further shortened, *et voilà*—"craps" was born.

According to local author John Churchill Chase, "everyone whom Marigny taught his game beat him playing it. And Marigny taught everybody in town." By the time he was 20 years old, he was forced to subdivide part of his plantation, which adjoined what is now the French Quarter, and sell lots. The names he chose for the streets of his subdivision are among his more colorful legacies, although some survive only in legend. What is now **St. Claude Avenue** he originally called **Good Children Street** *(Rue des Bons Enfants)* because it ran beside a cypress swamp where local children spent their days crawfishing. He also christened Elysian Fields Avenue in the vain hope that it would someday resemble the Champs-Elysées of Paris. Some of Marigny's other fancies—most notably **Love Street** *(Rue d'Amour)* and **Craps Street** *(Rue des Craps)*—did not sit too well with city tastemakers. Eventually Craps was tacked onto **Burgundy Street,** Love onto **Rampart,** and Good Children was renamed St. Claude in honor of Claude Treme, owner of a nearby plantation.

That land, acquired by the city in the early 19th century for the sum of $40,000, is the historic neighborhood still known as Treme (say Tre-*may*). It forms the other downtown border for the French Quarter and was once the site of the infamous red-

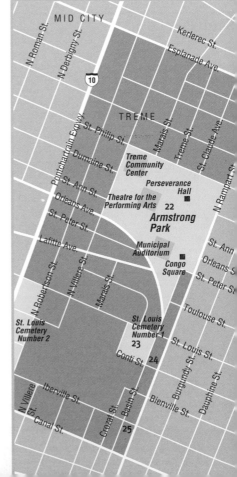

light district of **Storyville**. That area was named (to his chagrin) after Alderman Sidney Story, who proposed the 1897 ordinance that restricted all bordellos to this single controlled area. The houses operated until 1917, when the threatened withdrawal of an outlying US naval base shut down the district. Today, the **Iberville Housing Project** stands in its place.

The glory days of Storyville saw performances by Louis Armstrong, Buddy Bolden, and other great musicians who jammed at the clubs around **Basin Street**. They were part of a long tradition that began in the 1700s with Sunday slave dances in nearby **Congo Square** and continues with free concerts in **Armstrong Park**. Treme, known to some as the birthplace of jazz, is still home to a thriving community of musicians and, unfortunately, more than a few mean streets. The region bounded by **Rampart Street** and **I-10**, and **Iberville Street** and **Esplanade Avenue** can be extremely risky for tourists on the hoof. It's best to join a guided group to visit this fascinating area; one good tour company is **Cradle of Jazz Tours** (282.3583).

Adjacent to Faubourg Marigny, **Bywater** is a scrappy mix of industrial buildings, ramshackle Victorians and Creole cottages, with several excellent cafes, nightspots, and attractions making it worth a visit. Bordered by the railroad tracks along **Montegut Street** to the west, **St. Claude Avenue** to the north, Bywater is aptly named—it is surrounded by water on two sides, the Harbor Navigation Canal is to the east, and the Mississippi is to the south.

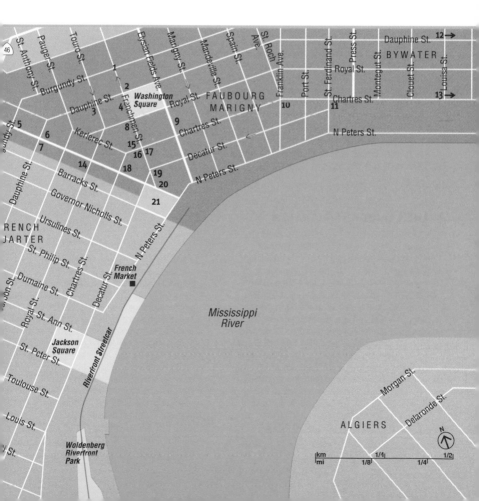

1 THE JOHN

Kay Vareen and her husband David Jaurequi, who plays guitar for Rockin' Dopsi, co-own this funky bar in the Marigny, a spacious watering hole with an excellent jukebox, pool tables, and seating on golden commodes—hence the name. Stop by for 99-cent Bloody Marys on Sundays from noon until midnight. 2040 Burgundy Street (Corner of Frenchman and Burgundy). 942.7159

2 SANTA FE

★★★$ German-born chef/owner Mark Hollger adds his Continental know-how to his love of Mexican and Southwestern cuisine. The result is lively fare that has had a large following for years. Seafood fajitas combine flash-fried shrimp, monkfish, oysters, mussels, soft-shell crab, and crawfish tails with onions, mushrooms, and peppers; the seafood combination serves up an enchilada, chile relleno, and chalupa filled with crawfish, crabmeat, and shrimp, topped with poblano-tomato sauce and cheese; and creamy crab and corn soup is seasoned with chilies. Begin with Hollger's signature nachos Santa Fe, topped with a piquant mixture of raisins, nuts, and cheeses, and end with traditional Mexican flan, or a purely European chocolate mousse that's served in a chocolate shell with strawberry sauce. The Friday-only lunch buffet is a terrific bargain. Every October, Hollger tips his toque to his homeland and adds several German favorites to the regular menu. The restaurant's three dining rooms are about as eclectic as the bill of fare (rattan armchairs are comfortable, but they don't exactly conjure images of the arid Southwest), but all are cheerful and bright. ♦ Southwestern ♦ W-Sa dinner. Reservations recommended. 801 Frenchmen St (at Dauphine St). 944.6854 ও

2 THE CLAIBORNE MANSION

$$$ Built in 1859 by W.C.C. Claiborne II, the son of Louisiana's first American governor, this opulent Greek Revival home overlooking Washington Square has been meticulously renovated in Neo-Classical style. Fred Astaire would feel right at home in the most lavish suite, with double parlors graced by a grand piano, 14-foot ceilings, two white marble fire-places, and a four-poster bed draped in white linen. In fact, the sophistication and privacy of the seven rooms and suites has attracted many visiting celebrities (but the highly discreet hotel staff won't say who). Other amenities include oversized marble bathrooms, fresh flowers, a lush tropical courtyard with a heated pool and vegetable garden, a large public kitchen, complimentary breakfast and evening snacks, and gated off-street parking. This is a nonsmoking house; pets are welcome. ♦

2111 Dauphine St (between Elysian Fields Ave and Frenchmen St). 949.7327; fax 949.0388 ও

3 LA PÉNICHE

★★$ When you crave an omelette at four in the morning, this homey restaurant is a welcome sight (except on Wednesdays, when it's closed). Located in a one-time neighborhood corner grocery, it's a comforting blend of natural wood, bright print tablecloths, and lots of flowers and greenery. Try for a window table to watch the late-night parade along the sidewalk. The fried seafood and half-pound burgers are good, as are eggs Benedict, waffles, and nightly dinner specials. ♦ American ♦ Th-Tu 24 hours; closed W, 1940 Dauphine St (at Touro St). 943.1460

4 PARKVIEW MARIGNY BED AND BREAKFAST

$$ Formerly an artist's studio/gallery and now a pleasant inn, this 19th-century Creole townhouse is nicely complemented by traditional furnishings and chic accessories. There are five stylish, high-ceilinged guest rooms, including one with a great dormer view of Washington Square and another with a shower that's big enough for two. In the morning, guests gather in the dining room for the complimentary continental breakfast. Knowledgeable hosts Christopher Liddy and Larry Molaison offer insider advice about the area. ♦ 726 Frenchmen St (between Royal and Dauphine Sts). 945.7875, 877/645.8617; fax 945.7886; pmarigny@aol.com; www.neworleansbb.com

MELROSE

5 THE MELROSE MANSION

$$$$ If you want to sample the grand life as it was enjoyed by the Creoles who first settled stately Esplanade Avenue, this is the hotel for you. The splendidly restored 1884 mansion was stripped to its bare timbers in some places, then carefully put back together in a painstaking operation that stretched over two years (after all, you can't match 19th-century plaster moldings at the local hardware store). An international clientele respects the beauty of the finished product so much that there are few signs of wear and tear. According to current owners, the Torres family, most visitors treat this beautiful inn as if it were their own, relaxing in the parlor—where wine and cheese are served during the cocktail hour—or on the veranda overlooking a landscaped pool. The nine rooms and suites are individually decorated with 19th-century reproductions and antiques; and each suite boasts a whirlpool tub. A workout facility is located on the third

HIGH NOTES

Dixieland lives, and well-worn institutions like **Preservation Hall** are definitely worth a listen, but traditional jazz is not the only sound in town. On any given night, at stellar venues all over New Orleans, you can get a fix of modern jazz, blues, rock 'n' roll, zydeco, folk, gospel, and even classical music. The places listed below are only a starting point; for even more suggestions, check the club listings in the weeklies *Gambit* and *Offbeat* and the Friday entertainment section *(Lagniappe)* of the *Times-Picayune*.

Unlike other manufactured theme bars, **House of Blues** (225 Decatur St, between Iberville and Bienville Sts, 529.BLUE; www.hob.com ♿) lives up to its hype, following through with a full schedule of top international and homegrown talent—from Eric Clapton to Buckwheat Zydeco—in a cavernous **French Quarter** building plastered with regional art and perfumed by the barbecue pit out back. However, true cats still join the lines **Uptown** at **Tipitina's** (501 Napoleon Ave, at Tchoupitoulas St, 895.8477 ♿), an avant-funk original that helped launch local legends like Dr. John and the Neville Brothers. **Tip's** has opened a French Quarter branch at 233 North Peters St (between Iberville and Bienville Sts, 566.7095; www.tipitinas.com ♿).

Another must for great music with indigenous eats on the side is **Snug Harbor Jazz Bistro** (626 Frenchmen St, between Chartres and Royal Sts, 949.0696; www.snugjazz.com), which bills itself "New Orleans's Premiere Jazz Club." The ballyhoo fits: The ambience is funky and kicked-back intimate; the food is hearty and informal (charbroiled burgers, fried seafood, baked potatoes); and the entertainment is world class (regulars include Ellis Marsalis, Charmaine Neville, and the Astral Project). You can even avoid paying the cover charge if you don't mind listening from the dining area, which doesn't have a view of the stage.

Just up the block, **Cafe Brasil** (2100 Chartres St, at Frenchmen St, 947.9386 ♿) is at the center of one of the most vibrant street scenes in town. The coffeehouse/bar is a meeting ground for young bohemians and a sounding board for fresh talent—anything from the **University of New Orleans Jazz Ensemble** to los Babies del Merengue. Best of all, there's no cover for the warm-up bands, and only a small cover charge when the main act fires up at about 10:30PM.

Classical music fans can get an earful at **Genghis Khan** (4053 Tulane Ave, between S Pierce St and S Carrollton Ave, 482.4044, 484.6552), a Korean restaurant in **Mid City**. Owner Henry Lee, who used to be a violinist with the **New Orleans Symphony Orchestra**, performs Tuesday through Sunday nights with a chamber group, pianist, or opera singer. His neighbors at **Mid-City Lanes** (4133 S Carrollton Ave, between Tulane Ave and Ulloa St, 482.3133) have set up the strangest mix of all: a vintage 1941 bowling alley that also presents live music for **Rock 'n' Bowl,** Tuesday through Saturday nights from 9:30PM to 2:30AM. Cajun, zydeco, blues, and swing are favored, but the schedule is a mixed bag that suits the wild and crazy atmosphere.

One final grace note: You can check out one of the city's greatest music outlets without even leaving your car or hotel room (as long as it has a radio). Broadcasting from **Treme,** the musical heart of New Orleans, **WWOZ 90.7-FM** is a listener-supported, volunteer-staffed, 24-hour community godsend. Tune into 'OZ to hear the best of jazz, blues, R&B, brass band, reggae, Brazilian, Cajun, African, Latin American, Caribbean, and worlds of other sounds.

floor with massage services available. On arrival guests are welcomed with complimentary mimosas; a continental-style breakfast is served each morning in the parlor. In the unlikely event you find something wanting, a concierge is on duty 24 hours. ♦ 937 Esplanade Ave (at Burgundy St). 944.2255; fax 945.1794; www.melrosemansion.com

6 GIROD HOUSE

$$$ A sister operation to **The Melrose Mansion,** New Orleans's only all-suite guest house is set in a town house that was built in 1833 by the city's first mayor, Nicholas Girod, for his son. Lofty ceilings and period furnishings distinguish the six suites, each featuring a living room, a bedroom, and a full kitchen stocked with fresh orange juice, muffins, and Creole coffee. Two of the suites are duplexes with balconies. A tropical patio is splashed

with colorful tropical flowers. There is no restaurant, but guests are welcome to take continental breakfast a block away at **The Melrose,** where they may also use the pool and workout facility. ♦ 835 Esplanade Ave (between Bourbon and Dauphine Sts). 522.5214; fax 945.1794; www.girodhouse.com

7 PORT OF CALL

★★$ Fat charbroiled burgers, accompanied by baked potatoes with the works, and excellent old-fashioned pizzas (no goat cheese here) keep the locals coming back to this favored watering hole. The prime steaks are very good, too. The nautical theme is perfect for a funky port city, with ceiling ropes, ship's wheel, bamboo, straw mats, and sailing prints. Polynesian concoctions served in ceramic tiki heads are fun; try Neptune's Monsoon, The

Restaurants/Clubs: Red | Hotels: Purple | Shops: Orange | Outdoors/Parks: Green | Sights/Culture: Blue

Red Turtle, Goombay Punch, or Huma Huma ("the drink of a Maui chieftain. One sip and... huma huma nuka nuka a pau"). The bartenders pour hard, and the service and atmosphere attract a good crowd, especially in the late afternoon and wee hours. ♦ American ♦ M-Th, Su lunch and dinner until 1AM; F-Sa lunch and dinner until 3AM. 838 Esplanade Ave (at Dauphine St). 523.0120; fax 947.7678

Snug Harbor

8 SNUG HARBOR JAZZ BISTRO

★★★$ Snug Harbor bills itself as "New Orleans's Premiere Jazz Club," and there is no better spot in town to hear top local talent in an intimate and suitably funky setting. World-famous pianist Ellis Marsalis, father of Wynton and Branford, usually performs here at least once a week. And don't miss the Victor Goines Quartet, Astral Project, and singers Charmaine Neville and Germaine Bazzle. The entertainment definitely rates four stars. Most people will feel right at home in the comfy old bar that attracts a decidedly mixed audience. You can't see the stage from the adjoining dining room, but all of the tables are well within earshot of the brilliant noise from next door. The reasonably priced and usually crowded eatery charbroils ultra-thick, juicy burgers and perfectly grilled chicken breasts. The simple menu also features a good (but more pricey) selection of seafood (the fried shrimp are especially big and light) and large baked potatoes accompany all sandwiches and entrées. ♦ Burgers/Seafood ♦ Cover charge in the bar. Daily dinner; shows at 9 and 11PM. 626 Frenchmen St (between Chartres and Royal Sts).949.0696; www.snugjazz.com

9 AMERICAN AQUATIC GARDENS

Even landlubbers with brown thumbs will enjoy a browsing ramble through this spectacular complex devoted to water gardening. The spacious store houses an ever-changing and beautifully displayed stock of accessories and kits for building indoor and outdoor ponds. Fountains are populated by stone carp, ducks, frogs, whales, and other spouting creatures; and lifesize bronze goddesses pour water from bottomless urns. Everything is shippable, except the largest concrete fountains. The live plant inventory includes many unusual specimens, which travelers usually pick up just before the flight home. The staff will pack the plants in damp plastic bags to carry on the plane. ♦ Daily. 621 Elysian Fields Ave (between Chartres and Royal Sts). 944.0410; fax 944.3951 ♿

10 FEELINGS

★★★$$ Don't let the name scare you off. Current owners Jim Baird and Dale de Bruyne inherited it, along with an enthusiastic following and a hefty stack of rave reviews from local and national publications, and decided not to tamper with success. The original opened on Royal Street in 1979 and moved to its present location one year later. This charming and sedate restaurant is located in the carriage house/slave quarters of the former D'Aunoy (say Dun-wa) Plantation. Bricks from its massive fireplace now surface the courtyard, an ideal place to enjoy cool spring and fall evenings under the luxuriant banana trees. A stone alligator, spitting water into the fountain filled with huge goldfish, provides a quirky regional touch. Top choices from the menu are also regional: oysters en brochette, wrapped in bacon, deep fried, and served with a sour cream and Creole (hot) mustard sauce; medallions of veal D'Aunoy, lightly prepared with herb-and-lemon butter, and topped with sliced mushrooms and hollandaise; and red snapper moutarde, sautéed in lemon butter and topped with Dijon mustard, hollandaise, and roasted almonds. The peanut butter pie is famous. Enjoy live music (and great martinis) at the piano bar on Friday and Saturday nights; at other times, listen to the stellar collection of recorded music, ranging from old jazz to Doris Day. ♦ International/Creole ♦ M-Th, Sa dinner; F lunch and dinner Su brunch and dinner. Reservations recommended. 2600 Chartres St (at Franklin Ave). 945.2222; fax 945.7019

11 NOCCA

The New Orleans Center for the Creative Arts, formerly housed in a warehouse uptown, has relocated to the edge of **Bywater**. The school that provided a launching pad for both Harry Connick Jr. and Wynton Marsalis offers top-rate talent in a series of music and dance recitals and film screenings that are open to the public. Recent performers include Rodney Mach on trumpet, a NOCCA alumnus now with the Barcelona Symphony, and Donald Harrison, an alto sax player and jazz master who also attended the school. Student recitals, often held on Sunday afternoons, offer a chance to catch a rising star before he or she makes it big. ♦ 2800 Chartres St (at the river). 940.ARTS; www.nocca.com

12 CLUB VAUGHAN'S LOUNGE

This friendly little dive hosts live music on most weekends, but Thursday is the biggest night of the week, with a performance by local trumpet player Kermit Ruffins & the BBQ Swingers. Ruffins has risen to national prominence in recent years, compared by many to a young Louis Armstrong. Although his star is rising, Ruffins still loves the old neighborhood—seeing him at **Vaughan's** is a highlight of any visit to New Orleans. ♦ 4229 Dauphine (at Lessups), Bywater 947.5502

Elizabeth's
Real Food
Done Real Good

13 ELIZABETH'S

★★$ Real food, done real good—the sign says it all. Owner Heidi Trull (her given name is Elizabeth but she goes by her middle name), cooks up huge plates of comfort food for a mix of local tradesmen, tourists, and even the occasional uptown gentlewoman. Prices are rock bottom and everything is good—save room for dessert, Trull has learned a thing or two from her husband, a pastry chef at **Emeril's**. American/Regional breakfast and lunch, Tu-Sa ♦ 601 Gallier St. (at Chartres) Bywater 944.9272

14 GAUCHE VILLA

An unfortunate name for this gorgeous landmark, the Italianate villa was built in 1856 for John Gauche, a wealthy merchant and importer of china and crockery. The spectacular cast-iron ornamentation, imported from Germany, features a dancing Cupid believed to have been copied from a drawing by Renaissance engraver Albrecht Dürer. The villa is a private residence. ♦ 704 Esplanade Ave (at Royal St)

15 FAUBOURG MARIGNY BOOKS

This specialty bookshop stocks a large inventory of gay, lesbian, and feminist literature, as well as cards, posters, calendars, and gift items. Mail order is also available. ♦ Daily. 600 Frenchmen St (at Chartres St). 943.9875

16 THE PRALINE CONNECTION

★★★$ The prices can't be beat and the food is the real article at this local favorite for Creole soul cuisine, delivered by a staff of natty dressers clad in black slacks, white shirts, and snappy black fedoras. They complete a festive scene of crisp

downtown style as they scoot around the black-and-white dining room. The chicken is great—baked, stewed, or fried—as are fried fish, stuffed bell peppers, home-style meat loaf, and crawfish étouffée. Most entrées come with corn bread and a choice of greens (mustard, collard, or cabbage) or beans (red, white, green, lima, or crowder peas with okra). Start with the gumbo, end with the sweet potato pie, and leave via the adjoining candy shop to stock up on pralines, fudge, and other homemade treats to sweeten the walk home. ♦ Soul food ♦ Daily lunch and dinner, F-Sa until midnight. 542 Frenchmen St (at Chartres St). 943.3934; fax 943.7903. Also at: 901 S Peters St (at St. Joseph St). 523.3973 ♿

17 CAFÉ BRASIL

★$ This alternative club/coffeehouse pointedly avoids any sort of format, but mobs of young and sometimes unruly people gather here for the art shows, plays, poetry readings, and music, music, music. Though the crowd is predominantly young and strenuously hip, featured artists range in age from 15 to 70. Musicians may be long-seasoned veterans or new ensembles from the jazz studies program at the **University of New Orleans;** you might hear bands from New York, Haiti, South Africa, or right around the corner. One of the best things about this place is the fact that there's no cover for the bands that play in the early evening, and only a small charge for the main act (which usually begins at 10:30PM). Excellent cappuccino, iced coffee, and espresso can be a bit of a problem for younger customers who have not yet learned to hold their caffeine—you'll see them boinging off the walls. Although this is primarily a coffeehouse, you can also order beer, wine, and mixed drinks. Several tables are scattered about the stage in the large room, but most people think the show is better outside along the sidewalk, where the management has parked a '58 DeSoto and other classic cars for your leaning pleasure (a creative response to complaints about patrons sitting on cars parked in front of the club). ♦ Cover. M-Sa from 6PM; Su from 5PM. 2100 Chartres St (at Frenchmen St). 949.0851 ♿

18 LANAUX HOUSE BED & BREAKFAST

$$$ This grand old mansion with a frilly ironwork balcony provided one of the settings for the 1981 remake of the movie Cat People. Built in 1879 as a two-bedroom house with the astonishing dimensions of 11,000 square feet, it's now home to owner Ruth Bodenheimer and visitors who stay in one of the three lovely suites. Each of the units has a

private entrance, original antique furnishings, a kitchenette, a phone, and a TV set. The grandest of them is graced by Oriental rugs and the original Mallard furniture. In addition, there's a very private cottage with its own tiny garden and fountain. Continental breakfast is laid out for guests to enjoy at their leisure. Bodenheimer claims that a ghost occupies the attic, but she doesn't like to share him with anybody. None of her guests have ever met him. ◆ By reservation only. Strict no-smoking policy. 547 Esplanade Avenue (at Chartres St). 488.4640, 800/729.4640; fax 488.4639; www.historiclodging.com

19 THE FRENCHMEN

$$ Two adjoining 1850s town houses have been converted into a 27-room hotel. The renovation preserved many of the old features, but the new furniture and finishings in some rooms won't exactly overwhelm you with 19th-century ambience. (Ask for room 200, which boasts a private balcony and a fine French Quarter view.) A small courtyard pool and Jacuzzi are landscaped with tropical plants. Limited off-street parking is available for seven or eight cars, but a vehicle is undesirable in this densely packed neighborhood. Complimentary continental breakfast is served in the lobby. All things considered, the price is reasonable for such a good location. ◆ 417 Frenchmen St (between Esplanade Ave and Decatur St). 948.2166, 888/365.2877; fax 948.2258; www.french-quarter.org &

Marisol

20 MARISOL

★★★$$$ Chef/owner Peter Vazquez is creating quite a buzz at this charming Faubourg Marigny restaurant with his dynamic, multicultural creations. Feast on specials like seared Hudson Valley Foie Gras, steamed mussels, and the fiery Thai crab and coconut soup. Patio dining available. Continental ◆ lunch Fr, dinner everyday, 437 Esplanade Ave., Faubourg 943.1912

The humble shotgun house gets its name from the speculation that a bullet fired through the front door would zip right out the back. The boxcar-shaped structure (usually only one room wide, though some have side halls) is simply a long line of rooms that open onto one another.

According to the memoirs of the famous madam Nell Kimball, the nickname "hooker" was inspired by Civil War General Joe Hooker, a notorious whoremonger who was a regular client in the red-light district of New Orleans.

---

21 OLD US MINT

Built by Philadelphian **William Strickland** in 1835 at the urging of President Andrew Jackson, the hero of the Battle of New Orleans, this Greek Revival–style facility minted the money that helped develop the West. Operations began in 1838 and ended in 1909, interrupted only by the Civil War. From 1861 to 1862, the Confederacy stamped coins here until they ran out of bullion. The old mint is now part of the system known as the **Louisiana State Museum,** which includes the **Presbytere, Cabildo, 1850 House,** and other historic sites. Today's visitors will see only a few remnants of the building's past, as all machinery was transferred to Philadelphia when production stopped. (Only around two dozen New Orleans–minted coins remain on display, so this is not a hot spot for numismatics enthusiasts.) The museum is, however, a must-see for anyone who wants to learn more about jazz. The galleries of the musical history section are devoted to ragtime, early jazz, big bands, and modern jazz. One prized artifact is the cornet that Louis Armstrong learned to play at the municipal boy's home in 1913. A photograph captures his ecstatic expression when he reigned as King of Zulu (a black Mardi Gras *krewe*) in 1949. Buddy Bolden, Jelly Roll Morton, and other home-grown prodigies are well represented, too. Be sure to swing by the *Women in Jazz* display to see the joyous portraits of Lizzie Miles, Blanche Thomas, Blue Lu Barker, and Sweet Emma Barrett. In the **Coin Vault and Gift Shop,** visitors can choose from a large selection of silver dollars and other coins that were produced here and elsewhere. Across the hall the **Louisiana Music Factory** offers a wide selection of traditional jazz, Louisiana music, and books. ◆ Admission; discounts available if you visit two or more buildings in the Louisiana State Museum. Children aged 12 and under free. Tu-Su. 400 Esplanade Ave (at N Peters St). 568.6968 &

22 ARMSTRONG PARK

This rather sad public square, which was supposed to commemorate the huge contributions made to the city by the musicians and residents of historic Storyville and Treme remains uncompleted to this day. The 32-acre park first opened in 1980 after seven years of construction and contention. On the park grounds are **Perseverance Hall** (the first Masonic Temple in the South), architecturally significant cottages called the **Reimann** and **Rabassa** houses, the **Theatre for the Performing Arts**, and **Treme Community Center.** The 12-foot statue of Louis Armstrong was funded by more than 1,000 donations from 26 countries, but he looks down on a very sticky situation. In 1997, a second statue, this one a bronze bust of the great Sidney Bechet, a native of N'Awlins who pioneered the jazz soprano sax, was added to the site. A system of lagoons was created, but the promised gondoliers never showed (many considered this a blessing). The brilliantly lighted arch, meant to evoke Tivoli Gardens, mainly drew unsuspecting tourists into the deserted park at night, when it is seldom patrolled and never safe. And many neighbors had reason to resent the high fences, which effectively excluded them from what had traditionally been their public meeting ground. The park has had its problems, but community activists have been working hard to change that image. Occasional Sunday afternoon free concerts, sponsored by **WWOZ-FM** radio and other neighborhood groups, attract good crowds. And there is still talk of revitalizing **Congo Square** with the sort of Sunday afternoon gatherings that made this historic spot come alive in the past. Meanwhile, it's still a bad idea to walk through the park alone day or night. ♦ N Rampart St (between St. Ann and Dumaine Sts)

Within Armstrong Park:

CONGO SQUARE

Many people believe that modern popular music, particularly jazz, sprang from this very spot, where slaves once gathered on Sundays to sing and dance. It is said that the puritanical Americans who lived beyond Canal Street disapproved of the practice, but pragmatic French and Spanish Creoles hoped this small safety valve would help prevent a rebellion. As many as 2,000 people attended the weekly market—dancers, spectators, merchants, voodoo priestesses, soldiers, and others all joined the lively mix. The rhythms grew more spirited and frenetic as the day wore on, until a cannon fired in the Place d'Armes signaled curfew time, when all slaves had to return home. According to legend, the Choctaw held their markets and religious ceremonies in this same area before the slaves began gathering here in the 1700s. Local voodoo practitioners consider it a spiritually charged site, and some still meet at Congo Square for formal rituals.

WWOZ 90.7-FM

Manager Dave Freedman encourages visitors to stop by this community radio station, located in the former kitchen building of Perseverance Hall, to pick up a program schedule and soak up a little atmosphere. The city's lifeline for jazz, blues, and worlds of other indigenous music, **'OZ** is listener supported and staffed by volunteers. You just might run into one of the jazz greats who drop by for interviews or live broadcasts. ♦ Daily. 568.1239; fax 558.9332

23 ST. LOUIS CEMETERY NO. 1

The first aboveground tombs in New Orleans are located in this historic spot, which opened in 1788. Louisiana governor W.C.C. Claiborne was buried here until 1906, when his remains were moved to a tomb in Metairie. Other celebrated residents include chess champion Paul Morphy and Etienne de Boré, the first mayor of New Orleans and the man who developed sugar refining in Louisiana. Although there is some dispute, many believe that voodoo's highest priestess, Marie Laveau, is here, too. The well-tended tomb is engraved (in French): "Here lies Marie Philome Glapion, deceased June 11, 1897, aged 62 years. She was a good mother, a good friend, and regretted by all who knew her. Passersby, please pray for her." Laveau's followers still mark the stone with red X's and crude fetishes. But don't attempt to find it on your own. This is one of the most dangerous cemeteries in town, and the only way to see it safely is with a group tour, such as those offered by **Save Our Cemeteries** (525.3377). ♦ Basin and St. Louis Sts

24 OUR LADY OF GUADALUPE CHAPEL

Once known as the **Church of the Dead**, this is holy ground to many New Orleanians. It was built in the 1820s to service yellow fever victims, after funerals were prohibited at **St. Louis Cathedral** in order to contain the spread of infection. Today, it is the official chapel for the New Orleans Police and Fire Departments, and the national shrine of St. Jude. ♦ 411 N Rampart St (between Conti and St. Louis Sts). 524.JUDE

25 SAENGER THEATRE

In recent years, this ornate historic theater has mounted national touring productions of *Phantom of the Opera*, *Cats*, and *Grand Hotel*. The annual season usually includes five to seven plays, musicals, and variety programs. The Italian Renaissance interior is a show in itself: stars twinkle in the midnight blue ceiling and backlit statues gaze down from on high above the loftiest balcony. ♦ Box office M-F 10AM-5PM; Sa 10AM-2PM. 143 N Rampart St (at Iberville St). 524.2490; www.ticketmaster.com &

Restaurants/Clubs: Red | Hotels: Purple | Shops: Orange | Outdoors/Parks: Green | Sights/Culture: Blue

By far the most sensual of US cities, New Orleans has always had a wickedly skewed take on life that can make the rest of America seem like another country. Mere mention of the name conjures up the bacchanalian abandon of Mardi Gras, sultry jazz, steamy streets, too much rich food and drink—not to mention that shameless old sybarite swathed in iron lace, the **French Quarter** herself. In 1819 Englishman Henry Bradsher wrote, "To all men whose desire only is to live a short life but a merry one, I have no hesitation in recommending New Orleans." It's been this way almost from the beginning, and, as gays and lesbians who have experienced the city—especially during Southern Decadence or other gay blowouts—will tell you, not much has changed.

Founded in 1718 in a cypress swamp teeming with snakes, alligators, and mosquitoes, the settlement was named **La Nouvelle-Orléans** in honor of the French regent, the duke of Orleans, a notorious libertine with a reputed penchant for wearing ladies' clothing. The town's tone was set by its first colonists—a motley crew of soldiers, fortune hunters, and drifters, along with petty thieves, miscreants, whores, and other social misfits, courtesy of King Louis XIV's efforts to empty the Paris jails. Not surprisingly, prostitution and public drunkenness were rampant.

When the puritanical Yankees took over after the Louisiana Purchase of 1803, they were at first appalled by the locals' pursuit of pleasure, a lifestyle of endless balls, soirées, and opera galas—not to mention the excesses of Mardi Gras. Eventually, of course, they joined the party, and by 1840 this was one of the world's great ports and the country's fourth-largest city. Opera, ballet, and theater flourished alongside gambling, cockfights, and dueling as the "Paris of the Swamps" cemented its place as one of the pleasure capitals of the globe.

By less than a century later, though, the French Quarter had deteriorated into a crumbling slum. But for the efforts of early preservationists, it would have been bulldozed; instead, new life blew in during the 1940s as gays, artists, musicians, writers, and assorted eccentrics were drawn by its raffish charms, laissez-faire attitude, and dirt-cheap rents. Nightspots flourished once again, like the **My-Oh-My Club,** with its scandalous revue of female

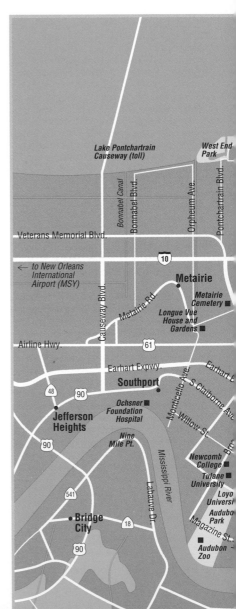

impersonators; the notorious **Club Rendezvous;** and **La Casa de los Marinos,** popular with foreign sailors and their local admirers.

Unfortunately, official discrimination and harassment persisted into the 1960s, much of it spearheaded by homophobic district attorney Jim Garrison (the same one who hounded gay businessman Clay Shaw for supposedly plotting against JFK). After a fatal fire at a gay bar in 1973 was met with official indifference, however, gays and lesbians finally organized and fought back. Today, the climate for gay rights in New Orleans has never been better: an anti-discrimination ordinance was passed in 1991; under current Democratic Mayor Marc Morial, domestic partner benefits were extended to city employees in 1997 (neither Morial nor any city politician would dream of running without courting the gay and lesbian vote); and gay presence in the French Quarter (also called the "Vieux Carré," locally pronounced "voo-ka-*ray*") is unmistakable with over 40 bars, restaurants, shops, and inns, and scads of rainbow flags flying from balconies

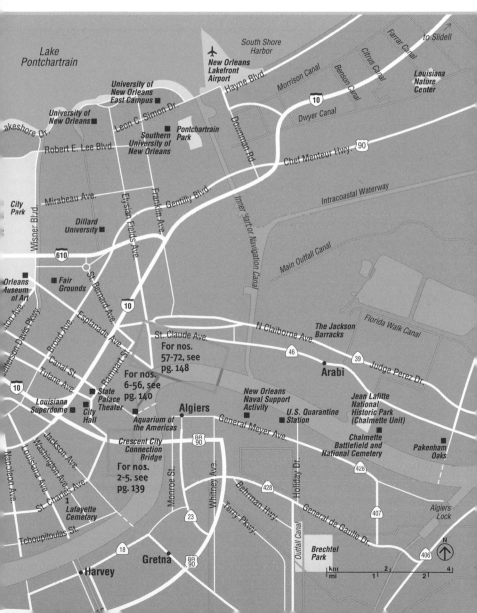

everywhere. The gay locals are not exactly the pumped attitude queens of South Beach, Chelsea, or West Hollywood, but they are mighty welcoming to visitors.

The old riverfront Quarter is quite compact, roughly 6 by 13 blocks. With its grillwork balconies and galleries, lush courtyards, French doors and shuttered facades, the neighborhood oozes charm, even as it sags and trembles when a truck rumbles by. The very heart of the action is the so-called Fruit Loop, bounded by world-famous **Bourbon Street,** and **Dauphine, St. Ann,** and **Dumaine Streets.** Here it's perfectly legal to carry alcoholic drinks on the sidewalk—and most everyone does, which on busy nights can turn the streets into one big outdoor party.

Certainly New Orleans boasts other charming neighborhoods: the **Faubourg Marigny** (funky and fairly gay, but quieter than the Quarter), the **Bywater, Mid City,** and the architecturally splendid **Garden District,** whose leafy serenity is preferred by a certain type of affluent gay. But most gay and lesbian denizens of the French Quarter wouldn't dream of living anywhere else.

Symbols

While all of the establishments in this section are gay-friendly and popular with gay visitors and locals, those that are specifically gay-oriented are identified with the following symbols:

♂ predominantly/exclusively gay-male-oriented

♀ predominantly/exclusively lesbian-oriented

♂♀ predominantly/exclusively gay-oriented with a male and female clientele

1 LAFAYETTE CEMETERY

In a city famous for its above-ground cities of the dead, this is the oldest (established in the 1830s), and among the most atmospheric (read Anne Rice's *The Witching Hour*). On All Saints' Day (1 November), when the living gather to tend the graves and remember their dearly departed, gay men traditionally assemble at the **Orphaned Homeless Boys' Tomb** to sip Champagne and pay their respects. A brick wall encloses the necropolis, and the front gate is often locked; even if it isn't, though, don't wander in alone, as muggers have been known to lurk behind the sarcophagi. It's best to take a tour; contact **Save Our Cemeteries** (525.3377) for information. ♦ Bounded by Washington Ave and Sixth St, and Coliseum and Prytania Sts; the gates are on Washington Ave (between Coliseum and Prytania Sts). 525.3377 &

2 ELMWOOD FITNESS CENTER

♂♀ This clean, modern facility not only has one of the best arrays of pumping and cardio equipment in town, but is also very popular with local gays of the sort who don't mind the constant high-energy sound track. The two-floor gym also has racquetball courts, a sauna, Jacuzzi, massage service, and classes in aerobics, spinning, and martial arts. ♦ M-F 5:30AM-9PM; Sa. 701 Poydras St (at St. Charles Ave). 588.1600

3 MIDTOWNE SPA

♂ Sleek and squeaky-clean, this five-story bathhouse draws a mixed crowd of black and white, young and not so young. They don't even make a pretense of having workout facilities here; instead, there's a steam room, popular "changing rooms" with cots and multichannel XXX monitors, and a constantly changing roster of activities including safer sex parties, free pizza on Wednesday, and Bear Nights (call for current details). A free continental breakfast is served daily. ♦ Admission. Daily 24 hours. 700 Baronne St (at Girod St). 566.1442

4 CONTEMPORARY ARTS CENTER (CAC)

The heart of the Warehouse/Arts District throbs within a 40,000-square-foot industrial skeleton, crisscrossed with catwalks and splashed with light. Ever-changing exhibitions feature innovative and challenging works; there are also two theaters with a lively schedule of productions by established and emerging playwrights. Recent offerings have included such frankly gay works as *Jeffrey* and *Angels in America*. ♦ Admission; free on Thursday. Daily. 900 Camp St (at St. Joseph St). 523.1216; box office 528.3800 &

5 THE GREENHOUSE

$$ Right on the edge of the Warehouse/Arts District, this gay-owned six-room inn is a world unto itself. The 1840 house and slave quarter have been transformed into a lavishly landscaped, clothing-optional Key West-style compound complete with year-round pool,

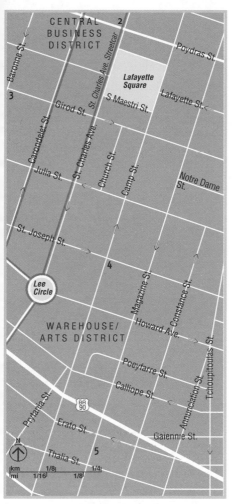

Jacuzzi, waterfall, cabanas, spa, even a grand piano in the hospitality room. For warm lazy nights, there's also a video library including both classics and adult flicks. Continental breakfast is served in the dining room, and off-street parking and a free shuttle to the French Quarter help make up for the fact that it's 12 blocks away. ◆ 1212 Magazine St (between Thalia and Erato Sts). 525.1333, 800/966.1303; fax 525.1306

6 MAMA ROSA'S

★$ Another French Quarter legend and big supporter of local AIDS fund-raisers, this place serves world-class pizza. But don't overlook the pasta, salads, and bodacious *muffuletta* sandwich. Check out the walls covered with paintings and photos of New Orleans. ◆ Italian ◆ Daily lunch and dinner. 616 N Rampart St (between St. Peter and Toulouse Sts). 523.5546

7 FOOTLOOSE

♂♀ A portrait of *Mommie Dearest* presides over the bar at this neighborhood hangout. Some of the friendliest bartenders in town welcome a diverse clientele (including a strong transgender contingent). Saturday night's cabaret shows are but a mere warm-up to the real hootenanny, which gets going around 2AM. ◆ M-F 2PM-2AM; Sa-Su 24 hours. 700 N Rampart St (at St. Peter St). 523.2715

8 BUCKAROO'S

♂ This smallish corner spot awash in stuffed animal heads draws a butch Levi's/country-western crowd. Sit at the front bar and you'll get a nice view of **Armstrong Park**'s ancient live oaks; for a closer tête-à-tête with that handsome cowboy, try one of the tables in the cozy room in the rear. ◆ M, W, Th 3PM-closing; Tu, Su noon-closing; F-Sa 24 hours. 718 N Rampart St (between Orleans and St. Peter Sts). 566.7559

9 NEW ORLEANS GAY-MART

♂♀ You won't hear "Attention, Gay-Mart shoppers!" over the P.A., but you will find a friendly, helpful staff and lots to choose from at the city's only full-service supplier of gay products and memorabilia. There are rainbows everywhere, from flags and towels to jewelry, decals, and T-shirts; there's also a good collection of gay-oriented greeting cards, videos, and erotic gadgets. **The Dungeon** upstairs offers a wide range of kinky accoutrements, including, for those so inclined, cattle prods and other disciplinary aids. ◆ Daily noon-7PM. 808 N Rampart St (between Dumaine and St. Ann Sts). 523.6005

10 TT'S

♂ Check out the painting to the right as you enter this ancient one-room saloon—yup, that's an honest-to-goddess, bonafide bullet hole. You can almost smell rough history here (along with hustlers sniffing for money). Male dancers liven things up on Friday night, drag comics do their thing on Saturday, and Wednesday evening's buffets are popular with the regulars. On the way out, take a peek at the **Voodoo Spiritual Temple Cultural Center** next door. ◆ Daily 11AM-3AM. 820 N Rampart St (between Dumaine and St. Ann Sts). 523.9521

Restaurants/Clubs: Red | Hotels: Purple | Shops: Orange | Outdoors/Parks: Green | Sights/Culture: Blue

10 WOLFENDALE'S

♂ Packed on weekends into the wee hours, this place lures a fun crowd (which tends to be heavy on African-American guys) who come to boogie on the small but busy dance floor, or to chat under the stars and banana trees in the courtyard. Live entertainment might include Connie Marcelle and the Climbers or D.L. Broadway and the Vamps. Monday night's feast of traditional New Orleans red beans and rice (courtesy of Connie) are a particular fave. ♦ Cover for shows. Daily 5PM-6AM. 834 N Rampart St (between Dumaine and St. Ann Sts). 596.2236

11 FRENCH QUARTER B&B

$ Despite the name, this gay-run but orientationally mixed bed-and-breakfast sits a block out of the Quarter in the Faubourg Treme, which can be iffy at night. Sporting a raffish charm, the property has four rooms with microwave kitchenettes, as well as a leafy tropical garden adjoining a pool and deck where guests can sunbathe in the altogether. ♦ 1132 Ursulines St (between N Rampart St and St. Claude Ave). 525.3390

12 FRENCH QUARTER SUITES

$$ Though technically outside the French Quarter, this gay-owned ex-apartment building is just a three-block stroll from Bourbon Street. It attracts mostly gay men, and each of the 17 roomy suites has a private entrance, full kitchen, and living room with sleeper sofa. Continental breakfast is served beneath a chandelier in a dining room graced with Audubon prints. A swimming pool and hot tub add to the experience. ♦ 1119 N Rampart St (between Gov. Nicholls and Ursulines Sts). 524.7725, 800/457.2253; fax 522.9716

13 BURGUNDY STREET OUTBACK

♂ The walls and ceiling of this cruise bar bristle with colorful painted scales, and the Aussie croc motif even spills over into the john— stopping mercifully short of the small outdoor patio. Nine-to-fivers from the nearby business district stop off for owner Wayne Cummings's sing-along organ, but on weekends it's the video poker machines (and the cheap drinks) that lure a decidedly mixed, somewhat seedy crew. ♦ Daily noon-2AM. 1000 Bienville St (at Burgundy St). 525.9793

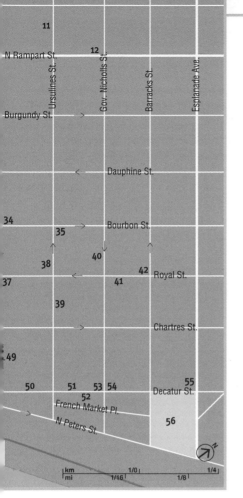

the Bourbon Street bars and back. If the cruise factor is too high, try the pool tables or the video poker for a change of pace. On Mardi Gras afternoon, the club sponsors the Bourbon Street Awards, the most phantas-magorical costume competition this side of Rio de Janeiro. ◆ Daily 24 hours. 740 Burgundy St (at St. Ann St). 525.8106

16 1014 DUMAINE STREET

This was the only property Tennessee Williams ever owned in New Orleans. At the time (1971-83) the building was divided into two apart-ments. Williams lived on the second floor and his bedroom opened onto the upper gallery. ◆ Between Burgundy and N Rampart Sts

17 DOUBLE PLAY

♂ The former **Wild Side** is a mixed bag indeed, with everything from hustlers and transvestites to the occasional straight couple looking for kink. Video poker and video darts are among the few amenities in this otherwise nondescript neighborhood hangout—in addition to the friendly hostess, Miss Do. ◆ Daily 24 hours. 439 Dauphine St (at St. Louis St). 523.4517

18 AUDUBON COTTAGES

Named for naturalist John James Audubon, who lived here in the 1820s, these houses were part of nine local properties restored by gay entrepreneur Clay Shaw (1913-74). Never heard of him? Check out Oliver Stone's film *JFK*, in which Jim Garrison, the homophobic New Orleans district attorney, accuses the man of conspiracy in a plot to assassinate the prez, and pretty much ruins his life. The cottages are now part of the **Maison de Ville Hotel** on nearby Toulouse Street. ◆ 505-11 Dauphine St (between Toulouse and St. Louis Sts)

19 GOOD FRIENDS

♂
♀ "Girlfriends," as some witty (or not) locals call this fun, friendly, and very popular neigh-borhood spot, mixes locals and tourists of all ages around an elegant carved mahogany bar. Downstairs, there's pool, video games, and a cozy fireplace for cool winter nights; upstairs, the piano keeps the regulars crooning show tunes. Check out the Mardi Gras paintings and photos of bygone Carnival queens in their fabulous gowns. ◆ Daily 24 hours. 740 Dauphine St (at St. Ann St). 566.7191

20 ST. ANN CAFÉ & DELI

*$ Tasty hot and cold sandwiches, daily specials, and a convenient location on the "Fruit Loop" make this a low-budget favorite for table or takeout—especially for hungry late-night party animals. ◆ Deli ◆ Daily break-fast, lunch, and dinner. 800 Dauphine St (at St. Ann St). 529.4421

14 CORNER POCKET

♂ Squeaky clean and staffed by super-friendly bartenders, this cornerstone of the Quarter's notorious "Wall Street District" is best known for the hustlers (and the admiring older gentlemen) in attendance. The pool table's always busy, but on Saturday and Sunday nights, all eyes turn to the "Boys on the Bar," go-go dancers who push much more than the envelope. ◆ Daily 24 hours. 940 St. Louis St (at Burgundy St). 568.9829

15 RAWHIDE 2010

♂ Drawing a good mix of locals, tourists, and the merely curious, the Quarter's only real leather/Western place nails the upper end of an established traffic pattern flowing to

---

Restaurants/Clubs: Red | Hotels: Purple | Shops: Orange | Outdoors/Parks: Green | Sights/Culture: Blue

GAY MARDI GRAS KREWES

New Orleans's Mardi Gras extravaganza is not only the biggest event of the year, but one of the gay Big Easy's most outrageous blasts, with a stream of party-minded homosexuals flowing from **Lafitte's** to the **Oz/Bourbon Pub** corner, then up **St. Ann Street** to **Good Friends** and **Rawhide**. The pitch rises all week, until everyone and everything goes totally bonkers on the final weekend, a time when anything can (and usually does) happen in the bars and on the pretty porch galleries, safely shored up to accommodate the frenzied overflow crowds.

But while New Orleanians happily welcome the world to the greatest free show on earth, they also quietly celebrate traditions few outsiders see. One is the fabulous balls given by private—gay and straight—clubs called *krewes*, whose members take the concept of costuming to unbelievable heights, literally and figuratively.

The creation of the gay krewes was largely a satirical response to the uptown society balls. Gay men were often called upon to escort dateless damsels to these time-honored but, for them, deadly dull functions. One day a lightbulb went off over their finely coiffed heads, and the boys realized they'd have lots more fun if *they* called the shots. The answer was elaborate Lido-style entertainment, a naughty sense of humor, and, of course, high camp and drag.

The first such organization, the **Krewe of Yuga** (or KY), debuted in 1958, staging a small private party at a time when public drag could mean arrest, even in laid-back New Orleans. Indeed, four years later the ball was raided and krewe members thrown into jail. Yuga subsequently bit the dust, but their courage paved the way for others before the gay movement finally ended further harassment. Some 30 krewes have come and gone since, many decimated by AIDS; today, four survive: **Petronius, Amen-Ra, Armeinius,** and **Lords of Leather**.

Rising costs and declining membership have forced the balls to charge admission in recent years, but at $25 these strictly black-tie events are still a bargain. Curious straights pack the balconies, while on the floor, gays and their guests enjoy phantasmagorical pageantry comparable to anything strutted in Las Vegas or Rio. The members appear harnessed into theme-related costumes made of thousands of plumes and faux jewels, some towering almost two stories. These tableaux are interspersed with singers, dancers, and other entertainment before the climactic arrival of the Queen and King, usually bedecked in the most elaborate outfits of all.

Competition is understandably ferocious as the krewes vie to mount the grandest extravaganza. The balls can be bankrolled for as little as $20,000, but the price tag usually spirals much higher with themes like Xanadu, the Tarot, Follies, and Birds of Paradise. People still talk about Petronius's Fairy Tale Ball, when the Queen of the Fairies outdazzled everyone in an $8,000 mechanical gown smothered in thousands of tiny lights and wing-flapping butterflies. Mounted on wheels and powered by two car batteries, it weighed over 200 pounds and had a skirt 18 feet wide. Now that's DRAG.

Unfortunately, the future of the balls is shaky. In addition to perennial financial woes, more than a few Gen-Xers and queer militants scoff at a tradition they consider passé—disregarding the hard battles that were fought for the right to celebrate. Priorities change, too: In 1993 the **Krewe of Polyphemus** folded with a membership that had declined from 50 to 21, choosing instead to throw their efforts behind AIDS projects.

Hard-working members, higher admissions, and the remaining krewe captains' enthusiasm may not be enough to save the balls. At current membership levels, they will last a few more years, but unless fresh interest is generated, Mardi Gras' most outrageous excesses may disappear forever. See them before they're only a glamorous memory.

21 QUARTER SCENE RESTAURANT & CATERING

★★$ Vibrant murals by local artist Marc Marino preside over two small dining rooms in this renovated Creole cottage, once a favorite of Tennessee Williams (whose preferred seat faced Dumaine Street). Currently under gay ownership, the restaurant offers some of the Quarter's best and freshest meal bargains, with a knockout catfish pecan, seafood po'boys, jambalaya, a diet-destroying chicken-fried steak breakfast, and 31 kinds of burgers. The menu is a hoot, too, with copious references to *A Streetcar Named Desire* and meal-sized salads named for Mardi Gras krewes. ◆ Creole/Cajun ◆ M, W-Su breakfast, lunch, and dinner until midnight. 900 Dumaine St (at Dauphine St). 522.6533

22 THE ROUNDUP

♂ The dreariest queer watering hole in the Quarter may also have its best jukebox—which is just fine and dandy, if you don't mind the druggies, hustlers, and other fiercely loyal locals who wouldn't dream of getting sloshed anywhere else. As Blanche DuBois once said, "Only Mr. Edgar Allan Poe could do it justice!" ◆ Daily 24 hours. 819 St. Louis St (between Bourbon and Dauphine Sts). 561.8340

22 PETUNIA'S

★★$$ Two intimate period rooms in a 19th-century Creole town house offer a splendid setting to enjoy the fresh seafood and local specialties (some of which, like the red beans and rice, are way overpriced). Sunday brunch is especially popular with lesbians and gays for the variety of delectable crepes served, plus some of the best grits and *grillades* in town, making the typical half-hour wait for a table worthwhile. Petunia's success has spawned a branch in Miami's South Beach. ♦ Southern/Creole ♦ Daily breakfast, lunch, and dinner. 817 St. Louis St (between Bourbon and Dauphine Sts). 522.6440

23 LUCKY CHENG'S

★★$$ The look is fin-de-siècle Shanghai bordello, and the service is lovely, lithe, and very feminine—until a closer look reveals the waitresses to be Asian guys in drag. Once you get past the gimmick, the Asianoid food is better than at Manhattan's Lucky Cheng's (sic) or at the branch in Miami—the crawfish curry here will make a believer out of you. The location across the street from world-famous **Antoine's** has raised more than a few eyebrows, even in a town used to wild excess. ♦ Asian/Creole ♦ M, Su dinner; Tu-Sa lunch and dinner. 720 St. Louis St (between Royal and Bourbon Sts). 529.2045 &

24 GAE-TANA'S PLACE PIGALLE

The quintessential Bourbon Street sex shop titillates gay and straight alike with a risqué mix of thingies to tickle, prod, or otherwise arouse your love object with. ♦ Daily 9AM-1AM. 605 Bourbon St (between St. Peter and Toulouse Sts). 523.6834

25 CAT'S MEOW

Now a straight joint, this was once the site of **Miss Dixie's,** the most venerable of the early gay bars. Miss Dixie herself is a living legend, beloved for her generosity to the gay and lesbian community—when bar patrons got busted during the witch-hunts of the 1950s and 1960s she would empty her cash registers to bail them out. ♦ 701 Bourbon St (at St. Peter St)

26 POPPY'S GRILL

★★$ The cheap and cheerful sister ship to the **Clover Grill** (see page 144) on Bourbon Street offers the same menu—plus cocktails, courtyard dining, and a wait staff that's lots of fun. This spot, which claims to make the best burgers on the planet, comes pretty damn close (the bacon, cheese, and mushroom special is divine). Unfortunately, the uncomfy

booths don't make for a lingering meal. ♦ Diner ♦ Daily 24 hours. 717 St. Peter St (between Royal and Bourbon Sts). 524.3287

27 BOURBON ORLEANS HOTEL

$$$ The notorious Quadroon Balls, where well-heeled Creole gentlemen met the legendary mixed-race beauties, were held in this grand property's **Orleans Ballroom,** built in 1817 by entrepreneur John Davis and restored for special functions when the hotel was added in 1964. It's the glittering centerpiece of a stately peach complex, encircled by balconies with fine views of **St. Louis Cathedral.** The lobby is rich in white columns, crystal chandeliers, and Oriental rugs, while Queen Anne-style furnishings grace the 211 guest rooms and suites with big marble baths. Avoid rooms overlooking Bourbon Street or the courtyard swimming pool, which can be very noisy. There's a restaurant. ♦ 717 Orleans St (between Royal and Bourbon Sts). 523.2222, 800/521.5338; fax 525.8166 &

28 OZ

♂ The crowd is young, buffed (for New Orleans, anyway), and more than ready to party at this world-class dance club. The throb of music coupled with the dazzling light shows—not to mention the hordes of shirtless dudes working the cavernous dance floor—can be awesome. So can the hunky dancers who work the upper levels. If the place looks familiar, it may be because Jeff Stryker filmed a Mardi Gras video here. ♦ Daily 24 hours. 800 Bourbon St (at St. Ann St). 593.9491

29 BOURBON PUB/PARADE DISCO

♂ Don't miss the **Pub,** a joint that's always jumping with a preppy/guppy/twinkie bunch of locals and a smattering of tourists, women, and daddies. The crowd flows practically nonstop around the enormous square bar, out the French doors onto the street, and back in. On weekends, the throngs here and at **Oz** across the street turn this intersection into one giant cocktail party. Upstairs, the **Parade** is the city's largest gay dance club, with DJs, a glitzy light show, and lots of bare, sweaty pecs. ♦ Cover for disco. Bourbon Pub: daily 24 hours. Parade Disco: Tu-Su 9PM-3AM. 801 Bourbon St (at St. Ann St). Parade entrance at 803 St. Ann St (at Bourbon St). 529.2107

30 BON MAISON

$$ A small gay owned inn sharing a lush courtyard with the **Bourgoyne Guest House,** this 1833 Creole town house enjoys a superb location for the gay and lesbian stretches of Bourbon and St. Ann Streets. There are five

units, including two suites with queen-size beds and full kitchens (one is also graced with period Eastlake furnishings). All the rooms have cable TV, a microwave, coffee maker, and refrigerator; some beds have conveniently mirrored headboards. No meals are served. ♦ 835 Bourbon St (between Dumaine and St. Ann Sts). 561.8498; fax 561.8498

BOURGOYNE
GUEST·HOUSE

SUITES & STUDIOS

30 BOURGOYNE GUEST HOUSE

♂ $$ As with the neighboring **Bon Maison**, there's simply no better location. This gay-owned inn offers three suites and three studios in a converted three-story 1830s Creole mansion. To stay in style, take the graceful cypress staircase to the third-floor **Green Suite**, where antiques abound and a balcony over-looks Bourbon. To stay on a budget, colorful host Jay Bourgoyne will happily point you to the no-frills studios at the rear of the lovely court-yard. Head somewhere else for sustenance. ♦ 839 Bourbon St (between Dumaine and St. Ann Sts). 525.3983, 524.3621

31 CAFÉ LAFITTE IN EXILE/THE CORRAL

♂ In one of the city's most popular gay bars, you can feel the living history in the old walls and in the glow of the eternal flame burning in memoriam of the original club's ousting from **Lafitte's Blacksmith Shop** a block away. The wall-to-wall (and verrry cruisy) crowd, running the gamut from daddies and Quarter clones to Levi's/leather boys and tourists, really gets into the campy sitcom and movie clips, mixed in with music videos and the spins of a live DJ. Upstairs, **The Corral** bar has a pool table and

In 1890 Herbert Asbury wrote of a "great influx of these [homosexual] men" and of an all-male bordello on Lafayette Street which threw lively balls and provided young men for fun and profit. "The mister of this establishment," Asbury wrote, "was a man who called himself Miss Big Nellie, and the permanent roomers included Lady Richard, Lady Beulah Toto, Lady Fresh, and Chicago Belle." In sharp contrast to their straight counterparts, the joint welcomed blacks and whites on a somewhat equal basis.

wraparound gallery for escaping the noise, smoke, and crowds below. ♦ Daily 24 hours. 901 Bourbon St (at Dumaine St). 522.8397

31 ALTERNATIVES

♂♀ Cards, sex novelties, skimpy bathing gear, and the usual queer accoutrements are the thing at this Bourbon Street shop resembling a large, bright closet. The staff is polite and helpful—so much so that some employees have been known to give condom/lube demonstrations. ♦ M-Th, Su 11AM-7PM, F-Sa 11AM-9PM Jan-mid-June, mid-Aug-Dec; M, Th, Su 11AM-7PM, F-Sa 11AM-9PM mid-June-mid-Aug. 907 Bourbon St (between St. Philip and Dumaine Sts). 524.5222

32 CLOVER GRILL

★★$ One of the zaniest eateries in a neigh-borhood where eccentricity is a way of life, this cozy and very gay little diner is a time trip-and-a-half. Cases in point: a jukebox filled with Connie Francis and Patsy Cline records, waffles with a clover imprint, and an outra-geous collection of wall clocks. For better or worse, the waiters are every bit as entertaining and the famous burgers (cooked under a hubcap) are superb. It's a favorite stop for the bartenders at **Lafitte's Blacksmith Shop** across the street, and for anyone with a case of the early-morning munchies. ♦ Diner ♦ Daily 24 hours. 900 Bourbon St (at Dumaine St). 523.0904

33 LAFITTE'S BLACKSMITH SHOP

Another haunt of Tennessee Williams, this bar is no longer gay but worth a look for the unique brick-between-post architecture common during the early French days. The scene of frequent photo shoots, it's one of the few build-ings (1772) surviving two disastrous French Quarter fires. Local lore insists it was a front for pirate Jean Lafitte's contraband, but there's no historical proof. ♦ Daily noon-early morning. 941 Bourbon St (at St. Philip St). 523.0066

34 LAFITTE GUEST HOUSE

$$ The Quarter's most lavish gay-friendly inn, this 1849 mansion dazzles right from the foyer with an original staircase sweeping grandly up a full three stories. The high-ceilinged Victorian parlor is a symphony in reds, while each of the 14 rooms is appointed with antiques and quality reproductions (one boasts a four-piece Eastlake bedroom suite). The garden is rich with subtropical plants and statuary, and the

many balconies offer stunning views of the Quarter and city skyline. The complimentary continental breakfast may be taken in the guest rooms, parlor, balcony, or courtyard, and afternoon wine and hors d'oeuvres are served in the parlor to encourage mingling. The clientele mixes gay and straight with comfort, but on Halloween and Mardi Gras it's a homo takeover. ♦ 1003 Bourbon St (at St. Philip St). 581.2678, 800/331.7971

35 Quartermaster Deli

★★$ Also known as the "Nellie Deli," this small joint is famous for its overstuffed 10-inch po'boys and *muffuletta* sandwiches. Try Scott's late-night snack package: cheese-and crab-stuffed jalapeño peppers, mozzarella sticks, hot Buffalo wings, corn dogs, and other greasy goodies. ♦ Deli ♦ Daily 24 hours. 1100 Bourbon St (at Ursulines St). 529.1416

36 French Quarter Postal Emporium

♂♀ A gay "mini post office" may sound like an odd establishment, but on the other hand, the helpful staff will cheerfully pack and ship those funky souvenirs and kinky sex toys, no questions asked. They also stock a fun selection of cards, miscellaneous gifts, and silly tourist T-shirts. ♦ M-F; Sa 10AM. 940 Royal St (at St. Philip St). 522.6651

37 Rue Royal Inn

$ Set in a handsome 1830s structure, this four-story hostelry has 17 rooms ranging from small units with queen-size beds to roomy suites with galleries overlooking the courtyard or historic Royal Street. They're all furnished with period reproductions, and most have exposed brick walls, wet bars, and kitchenettes. A few even have their own private hot tubs *à deux*—though there's also a communal clothing-optional Jacuzzi in the small courtyard. Although this establishment is gay-owned, most of the clientele tends to be straight except during Mardi Gras. Complimentary continental breakfast is included. ♦ 1006 Royal St (between Ursulines and St. Philip Sts). 524.3900, 800/776.3901; fax 558.0566

38 Ursuline Guest House

$ This late-18th-century Creole cottage has catered to gay men and straights for more than two decades, offering 13 cozy, well-maintained rooms with private entrances. Most open right onto a typical New Orleans courtyard complete with palms, wrought-iron furniture, and a tiled (and clothing optional) hot tub. A continental breakfast is included, and complimentary wine is served every evening. Limited parking is available on a first-come basis. ♦ 708 Ursulines St (between Royal and Bourbon Sts). 525.8509, 800/654.2351; fax 525.8408 ♿

39 Croissant D'Or

★★$ Cheat on your diet at one of the French Quarter's most charming coffeehouses, which bakes pastries worth dying for right on the premises. There's also a delightful lineup of quiches and sandwiches that keeps the gay boys and girls (and heteros too) coming back for more. The decor is best described as New Orleans funky, with carousel horses and Mardi Gras memorabilia tucked here and there. A small courtyard out back, particularly popular with students, harbors a fountain reproduction of the *Manneken-Pis*, Belgium's notorious peeing toddler. ♦ Coffeehouse ♦ Daily 7AM-5PM. 617 Ursulines St (between Chartres and Royal Sts). 524.4663

40 Spanish Stables

Dating from 1834, these twin structures were refurbished by gay businessman Clay Shaw in the late 1950s before restoration was fashionable. Shaw's achievements are honored with a bronze plaque, which includes a map of the properties he helped save. Today the complex houses apartments surrounding a handsomely landscaped pool and courtyard. ♦ 716-24 Gov. Nicholls St (between Royal and Bourbon Sts)

41 Moore Magic

♀ Catering to a clientele of spiritual lesbians, this fragrant shop carries herbs, oils, and incense, along with tarot cards and some woman-themed books and memorabilia. Karmic readings are available for a fee. ♦ Daily noon-7PM. 1212 Royal St (between Barracks and Governor Nicholls Sts). No phone

41 Mona Lisa

★★$ These two dark, skinny dining rooms have packed in the locals for years despite a frankly blah decor (mostly, endless variations on—you guessed it—the *Mona Lisa*). The reason, of course, is the food, though some have complained of late that the pasta and famous pizzas aren't as good as they used to be. It's still worth a try, though, and vegetarians and waist-watchers will find the generous salads are more than a meal. ♦ Italian ♦ Daily

THE UNTAMED TENNESSEE WILLIAMS

Unquestionably the **French Quarter's** most famous gay resident, Thomas Lanier (Tennessee) Williams is also New Orleans's most celebrated nonnative son. His name is closely linked with the city via works that have helped shape the world's picture of New Orleans—*Vieux Carré; A Streetcar Named Desire;* and *Suddenly, Last Summer.*

Hoping for economic relief through the city's Federal Writers' Project, Williams fled St. Louis for New Orleans in 1938, taking up residence at 722 Toulouse Street in the French Quarter. Here the naive 27-year-old was shocked and thrilled by the unbridled decadence of the neighborhood, which he quickly set about exploring. In doing so, he discovered a new side of himself, so that some 40 years later he would happily confess that the Quarter had exposed "a certain flexible quality in my sexual nature." His metamorphosis deepened as he chose the pen name "Tennessee," and, after only a few months, he ran off to California with a clarinet player.

He returned in 1941 flat broke, bumming cigarettes, and living from hand to mouth and place to place. During this period, he stayed for three months with close friends at **Bultman House** at 1521 Louisiana Avenue (between Prytania St and St. Charles Ave). Legend says the **Garden District** setting of *Suddenly, Last Summer* was inspired by the Bultman's grandiose two-story conservatory, which is clearly visible from Prytania. Eventually, though, he hocked everything (including his typewriter!) before fleeing again. When he returned four years later, it was on the triumphant coattails of *The Glass Menagerie;* this time he stayed briefly at the historic **Ponchartrain Hotel** at 2031 St. Charles Avenue (at Josephine St). It wasn't long before he was lured back to the Quarter, though, to 710 Orleans Street (directly behind **St. Louis Cathedral**), where he worked on *Camino Real.* In late 1946 he moved again, this time to 632 St. Peter Street where, from his upstairs window, he could see and hear a certain streetcar named *Desire.*

For the next 12 years Williams was in and out of the city he always acknowledged as his favorite, a place which gave him "a kind of freedom I had always needed. And the shock of it against the Puritanism of my nature has given me a subject which I have never ceased exploiting." He was clearly seduced by New Orleans's inherent romance and observed that he'd "never known anybody who lived in, or even visited the Quarter who wasn't slightly intoxicated— without booze!"

The writer was mostly rootless in the 1960s, but he often stayed in **Room 9** at the exclusive **Maison de Ville** at 727 Toulouse Street. No doubt he felt a twinge of nostalgia, as it was almost directly across the street from the garret where he had lived during his early impoverished years. Tourists may not visit the room, of course, but they're welcome to stroll back and explore the lush courtyard.

In 1971 he moved into an apartment at 909 St. Louis Street, and a year later bought his first New Orleans property, Apartment B at 1014 Dumaine Street. His new upstairs home had a bedroom facing the street and a rear gallery overlooking a courtyard, swimming pool, and the old slave quarters. In his autobiography Williams wrote, "I hope to die in my sleep, when the time comes, and I hope it will be in the beautiful brass bed in my New Orleans apartment"—the same bed in which, he also remarked, he'd spent 14 of his happiest years. In January 1983, Williams sold the house on Dumaine. He died six weeks later, not in his "beautiful brass bed," but in a New York City hotel room.

---

lunch and dinner. 1212 Royal St (between Barracks and Gov. Nicholls Sts). 522.6746

42 GOLDEN LANTERN

♂ The main claim to fame of this bare-bones gay-bar-with-pool-table: the annual Southern

Nelly author Truman Capote was born and raised in New Orleans and set many of his short stories here, including "Dazzle," in which a little boy yearns for a sex change. In "Music for Chameleons" he describes the denizens of the Vieux Carré: "Sailors and dock workers, cops and firemen and hard-eyed gamblers and harder-eyed floozies." The place overflows with entertainers from the Bourbon Street tourist traps. Topless dancers, strippers, drag queens, B-girls, waiters, bartenders, and the hoarse-voiced doormen-barkers who so stridently labor to lure yokels into Vieux Carré sucker dives."

Decadence celebration was born right in its bowels. In tribute, the Grand Marshal launches the extravagant parade from its historic portal every year. Otherwise the place attracts a set of regulars that doesn't mind (or perhaps prefers) the dim lighting. ♦ Daily 24 hours. 1239 Royal St (between Barracks and Gov. Nicholls Sts). 529.2860

43 604 IBERVILLE STREET

On 24 June 1973, patrons of the **Up Stairs Lounge** were celebrating Gay Pride Day when an arsonist struck, setting a blaze that left 32 dead. It was the worst toll of its kind in city history, but local police, fire, and government officials (as well as most religious leaders) reacted with cool indifference. This response galvanized the gay and lesbian community to form the Gay People's Coalition (GPC), so that many regard this tragic event as New Orleans' own Stonewall. Today the site is unoccupied. ♦ At Chartres St

NEW ORLEANS

44 HOUSE OF BLUES

Gay folks show up en masse on Thursday night at the mostly straight local branch of the national chain that's partly owned by Dan Aykroyd (of *Blues Brothers* fame). With five bars, church pews for seating, and a state-of-the art sound system, this joint has showcased the likes of Eric Clapton, Bob Dylan, Arlo Guthrie, and the Subdudes. The Sunday gospel brunches are especially popular—and have been part of recent Halloween AIDS fund-raisers and circuit parties. For no-cover, closed-circuit views of the show, check out the adjacent bar/restaurant, which serves salads, sandwiches, and some knockout barbecue, all surprisingly priced under $10. ♦ Cover in club. Restaurant: M-Th, Su lunch and dinner until midnight; F-Sa lunch and dinner until 2AM. Club show: Daily 8PM. 225 Decatur St (between Bienville and Iberville Sts). 529.2583; concert line 529.1441 &

45 OMNI ROYAL ORLEANS HOTEL

$$$$ No two of the 300-plus rooms are alike at this splendid gay- and lesbian-friendly property—and all are done up in grand 19th-century style. So Is the lobby, awash In marble, gold leaf, and chandeliers. If staying here Is beyond your budget, at least have a drink by the rooftop pool for the best views in the French Quarter. Amenities include 24-hour room service, valet parking, fitness facilities, and a barber and beauty salon. There is also a business center and the jacket-requiring **Rib Room**. ♦ 621 St. Louis St. (at Royal St). 529.5333, 800/843.6664; fax 529.7089 &

46 POSTMARK NEW ORLEANS

Starkey Kean and Earl Joyner have amassed some wonderful things at their eclectic, fun-filled boutique, including jewelry, candles, picture frames, even lamps. There are plenty of gay-oriented goodies, and absolutely the best selection of cards in the Quarter. ♦ M-Tu, Th-Sa; W, Su noon-6PM. 631 Toulouse St (between Chartres and Royal Sts). 529.2052, 800/285.4247

47 632 ST. PETER STREET

Tennessee Williams could see and hear the streetcars clanging down Royal Street in 1946 from his third-floor apartment in this building. It was here that he wrote much of *A Streetcar*

Named Desire, which won the Pulitzer Prize a year later. ♦ Between Chartres and Royal Sts

48 THE CLUB NEW ORLEANS

♂ Part of a chain with branches in Dallas, Denver, Houston, and Los Angeles, this immaculate gay men's club has five floors for both serious workouts and decadent frolicking. Personal fitness trainers are available along with free weights, and Universal and Nautilus equipment. And a steam room, dry sauna, and whirlpool offer excellent opportunities to meet that special someone before retiring to a private chamber. Twelve-hour passes are available. ♦ Daily 24 hours. 515 Toulouse St (between Chartres and Decatur Sts). 581.2402

49 SECOND SKIN LEATHER

♂ ♀ A mind-boggling array of sex toys and fetishistic goodies from the unmentionable to the unfathomable is on sale here. This is also a good place to shop for top-quality leather jackets, vests, harnesses, and chaps. Especially around gay holidays the place is jammed with boys and girls seeking that perfect last-minute touch. ♦ M-Sa noon-10PM; Su noon-6PM. 521 St. Philip St (between Decatur and Chartres Sts). 561.8167 &

49 MRB/THE PATIO

♂ Quarterites young and old have been hanging out for ages at the "Mississippi River Bottom" (pun possibly intended)—which may partly explain why owner Andy Boudreaux is a legendary fixture on the New Orleans gay scene. The large, high-ceilinged space and the two outdoor patios are always popular for drinking, cruising, and the occasional barbecue, but the crowds are at their peak for the MRB Dancers; just how much they take off depends on the mood of the audience and the lateness of the hour. ♦ Daily 24 hours. 515 St. Philip St (between Decatur and Chartres Sts). 523.7764

50 CAFÉ SBISA

★★★$$$ Almost a century old and still going strong, this two-story eatery must be

---

Restaurants/Clubs: **Red** | Hotels: **Purple** | Shops: **Orange** | Outdoors/Parks: **Green** | Sights/Culture: **Blue**

147

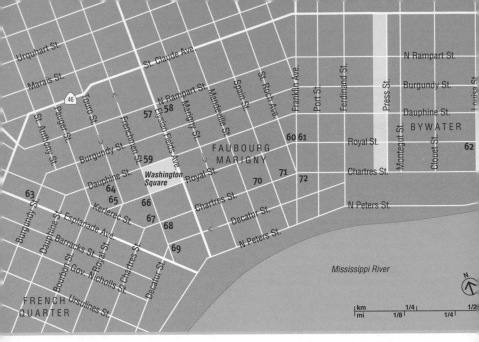

doing something right. An outside gallery offers sweeping views of the world-famous **French Market**, while the indoor mezzanine seating lends an airy ambience. The diners are a mix of local and tourist, straight and not, but there's a decidedly gay ambience at Sunday brunch. The grits and *grillades*, the crab cakes topped with poached eggs and hollandaise, and the eggs Lafourche served atop flavorful jambalaya are faves, and the bottomless Champagne glass is a real bargain. ♦ Creole/International ♦ M-Sa dinner; Su brunch and dinner. 1011 Decatur St (between Ursulines and St. Philip Sts). 522.5565 &

51 G&E Courtyard Grill

★★★$$ Imagine a succulent roasted duck, glazed with a Thai ginger barbecue sauce and served with shiitake-stuffed Asian dumplings and a stir-fry of bok choy and Napa cabbage. No wonder chef Michael Uddo's been getting national attention, or that his truly lovely courtyard restaurant has become a hit with discerning homosexuals. It doesn't hurt, of course, that everything's prepared with fresh, organically grown ingredients, or that the frescoes in the dining room look straight out of Tuscany. ♦ International ♦ Tu-Su lunch and dinner. Reservations recommended for dinner. 1115 Decatur St (between Gov. Nicholls and Ursulines Sts). 528.9376

FIORELLA'S CAFE

52 Fiorella's Cafe

★$ Try not to giggle at the faux nautical decor in the front room at this no-frills (but gay-beloved) Quarter institution that's been around forever. The fare is equally basic but

solid and one of the best deals in the Quarter with seafood, po'boys, and pasta dishes cooked up with an Italian touch. Service can be pokey, but at least it's earnest, and regulars swear the fried chicken is unbeatable. ♦ American/Italian ♦ M-Sa breakfast and lunch. Entrances at 45 French Market Pl and 1136 Decatur St (between Gov. Nicholls and Ursulines Sts). 528.9566

53 Vera Cruz

★★$ This joint may be officially straight, but it ain't nicknamed "Very Cruisy" for nothing (especially on Thursday, often the gayest night). The cavernous space, dominated by a dazzling mural complete with Latina streetwalkers, offers huge windows for watching the passing action on Decatur. The nicely varied Mexican menu takes some decidedly local twists on the order of crawfish *flautas*, though the standard chimichangas, roast pork, and fajitas are just as delish. ♦ Mexican ♦ W-F dinner; Sa-Su lunch and dinner. 1141 Decatur St (at Gov. Nicholls St). 561.8081

54 Gargoyles

A crazed amalgam of naughty 1990s and retro 1960s stuff, this gay-popular boutique specializes in wild clothes and even wilder accessories. Leather goodies for master and milady make for an especially fun browse. ♦ M-Th 11AM-6PM; F-Su 11AM-7PM. 1205 Decatur St (between Barracks and Gov. Nicholls Sts). 529.4387

55 The Mint

Named for the **Old US Mint** across the street, this show bar has a high tin ceiling, handsome tile floors, and a stage at one end. Pianist Roddy Barnes tickles the proverbial ivories on Monday and Friday, and other local entertainer drop in from time to time. It's still lots of fun, but things have never been the same since the departure of longtime performers Becky Allen and Ricky Graham and their much-loved *Hot Stuff: New Orleans Style* revue. ◆ Cover. Daily noon-3AM. 504 Esplanade Ave (at Decatur St). 525.2000 ♿

56 OLD US MINT

If you missed Mardi Gras, you can still get the flavor of the blowout in the jazz exhibits, costumes, and memorabilia on permanent display here. A collection of flamboyant getups from the gay Mardi Gras krewes rustled up some controversy a couple of years back, showing that even in this capital of sin, some sins are worse than others. ◆ Admission. Tu-Su. 400 Esplanade Ave (at N Peters St). 568.6968 ♿

57 CHARLENE'S/OVER C'S

♀ Dark and dingy, this serious girlz' dive draws all ages and types for its music and dancing, but it's especially popular with a butcher crowd. ◆ Tu-Th 5PM-closing; F-Su 3PM-closing. 940 Elysian Fields Ave (at N Rampart St). 945.9328

58 PHOENIX/MEN'S ROOM

♂ A major base of operations for the local Lords of Leather, the Leather Alliance, and the Knights d'Orleans, this loud, smoky, and seriously cruisy multi-room bar teems with harnesses, tattoos, and torn jeans. Upstairs from **Phoenix** is the infamous **Men's Room**, a nearly pitch-black magnet for the raunchiest action in town—almost anything can happen here and usually does. The neighborhood can get even rougher in the wee hours, so ask a bartender to call a cab. Ring the bell to get in. ◆ Phoenix: daily 24 hours. Men's Room: daily 9PM-5AM. 941 Elysian Fields Ave (at N Rampart St). 945.9264

59 CLAIBORNE MANSION

♂
♀ $$$ Drawing more men than women, this handsome manse dating from the 1850s is easily the grandest of the gay/lesbian-owned bed-and-breakfasts. The five well-appointed suites feature huge marble baths, fireplaces with original mantels, iron and mahogany queen-size beds, and hand-painted carpets; one suite even throws in a grand piano, and a

small unit has a double bed swathed in toile. Shaded by ancient live oaks, the lavish grounds include a pool with water-spewing lions, a cabana and arbor, and a garden that provides fresh fruit and vegetables for the complimentary breakfast taken poolside or in your room. Off-street parking is also available. ◆ 2111 Dauphine St (between Elysian Fields Ave and Frenchmen St). 949.7327, 800/449.7327; fax 949.0388 ♿

60 BIG DADDY'S

♂ You may or may not meet any actual big daddies, but it's practically guaranteed you'll run into a local or three (and a woman or two) at this old reliable Marigny hangout. There isn't much else to say about the nondescript space, but there must be a reason for the loyalty of the fun and friendly regulars. ◆ Daily 24 hours. 2513 Royal St (at Franklin Ave). 948.6288

61 BEARS & BOOTS

♂ The name says it all: this watering hole is for the leather/Levi's/bear crowd. It's also the official hangout of the New Orleans Bear & Bear Trapper Social Club and all that implies. So if beefy, furry animals are your thing, do your hunting here. Downstairs, **Another Corner** is just another place for friendly regulars to wet their whistles. ◆ Daily 11AM-3AM Sept-Mar. 2601 Royal St (at Franklin Ave). 945.7006

62 THE COUNTRY CLUB

♂ A kind of gay guest house without the rooms, this Victorian manse tucked away in the quiet neighborhood of Bywater hosts all sorts of boys-will-be-boys shenanigans. Walled grounds and dense banana groves surround a very private pool and sundeck where you can bare it all for tanning or swimming; it doesn't take much to imagine that things can get pretty frisky here after dark. Other amenities include a cabana, a poolside bar, and a workout room; the pool is heated, too, but this local phenomenon is best experienced in warmer months. ◆ Daily 10AM-9PM. 634 Louisa St (between Chartres and Royal Sts). 945.0742

63 BUFFA'S

★$ They've apparently never heard of cholesterol at this dark, unpretentious neighborhood joint, but when was the last time you paid $3.95 for a full dinner? The colorful local crowd is mostly straight, but there's something of a gay and lesbian following as well. Everyone flocks here for the basic fare, with meat loaf, spaghetti and meatballs, smothered pork chops, and Southern-fried veal cutlet leading the favorites. ◆ American ◆ Daily lunch and dinner. 1001 Esplanade Ave (at Burgundy St). 945.9373

64 La Péniche

★★$ This corner grocery store-turned-restaurant does a solid business throughout the day and late at night when folks head home from the bars. The look is natural wood, bright tablecloths, and plenty of flowers and greenery—and the big windowside tables make for fun people watching. The grub is mostly down-home stuff, with very reasonable daily specials. Service and quality can be erratic, but the enormous "Katherine burgers," the crawfish or crab omelettes, and the fried seafood dishes are usually safe bets. ♦ American ♦ M-Tu, Th-Su 24 hours. 1940 Dauphine St (at Touro St). 943.1460

65 Cafe Marigny

★$ Popular with gays and lesbians, this java spot has a nice lineup of gourmet coffees and desserts, and a limited selection of soups, salads, and sandwiches. The outside tables are great for checking out the crowds that go by, and the iced hazelnut coffee is perfect on a steamy New Orleans afternoon. ♦ Coffeehouse ♦ Daily 7AM-11PM. 1913 Royal St (at Touro St). 945.4472

66 Rubyfruit Jungle

♂♀ This stylish club is definitely where the girls are—though the high-tech dance floor, 80-foot copper bar, pool tables, and (occasionally fabulous) live music also bring in some gay guys and a few hip straights. On Tuesday nights, the boys predominate for the Big Easy's only weekly country and western dance. ♦ M-F 4PM-closing; Sa-Su 2PM-closing. 640 Frenchmen St (at Royal St). 947.4000 &

67 Faubourg Marigny Bookstore

♂♀ Founded in 1977, the South's oldest gay, lesbian, and feminist bookstore stocks the latest titles as well as older, hard-to-find material. A small selection of queer-catering cards, posters, music, and gift items makes this homey little corner shop a fun browse. It's also a popular stop for signings by local and visiting authors. ♦ M-F 10AM-8PM; Sa-Su. 600 Frenchmen St (at Chartres St). 943.9875

Tennessee Williams's friend Gilbert Maxwell once observed that one does not "remain to any degree puritanical in the French Quarter." At least not for long.

68 Frenchmen Street

What's arguably the hippest two-block strip in town draws collegiates, Gen-Xers, alterna-queers, the pierced, the grunged, and plenty of other boho and artsy sorts who happily defy categorizing. Love of music is a major common denominator, though many are drawn by the amalgamated art/poetry/music scene. The street offers an endlessly colorful, sometimes raucous but easy blend of cocktailers and caffeine-heads gay and straight, along with some of the best people watching in a town that's raised it to an art form. ♦ Between Decatur and Royal Sts

68 Café Brasil

★$ One of the hot spots on the Frenchmen strip, this alternative club/bar/coffeehouse draws a young and strenuously hip crowd, gay and straight. Though it's now far too popular to ever again be considered underground, it still operates from day to day, pointedly avoiding any formal format. The music is wildly disparate but rarely dull: You might hear jazzmen in their seventies, a band from South Africa, or a brand-new group put together the night before. ♦ Cafe ♦ M-Sa 5PM-3AM, Su 6PM-3AM. 2100 Chartres St (at Frenchmen St). 947.9386 &

69 The Frenchmen

$$ Small but comfortable, this 25-room hotel set in two adjoining 1850s town houses is handsome enough outside; once past the front door, however, the 19th century gives way to two-tone pile carpeting and other modern schlock (the dining room is an exception). All things considered, location, price, and the small swimming pool and Jacuzzi in the tropical courtyard make it a worthwhile option—keeping in mind that the rooftop sundeck is a barren concrete launching pad, and none of it is clothing optional. Some rooms have balconies with views of the firehouse, and an honor bar is available in the evening. ♦ 417 Frenchmen St (between Esplanade Ave and Decatur St). 948.2166, 800/831.1781; fax 948.2258 &

70 B&W Courtyards

$$ Don't be fooled by the modest facade of this 19th-century Creole cottage: inside, the renovated luxury and attention to detail of owners Rob Boyd and Kevin Wu keep gay and straight coming back. Outside, the namesake courtyards are lush with palm, orchid, and bamboo; there's also a lotus pond, fountains, and a Jacuzzi perfect for relaxing under the sun or stars. All four bedrooms have private entrances, and there's also a two-story detached cottage in the back. Breakfast and afternoon sherry are included in the rates. ♦ 2425 Chartres St (between Spain and Mandeville Sts). 945.9418, 800/585.5731

THE BEST

Rich Magill

President & CEO/Research Assistant, Bette & Co., Inc

Mardi Gras and the four days of Carnival just before—this continent's best and most amazing party. Arrive Friday, depart Wednesday, **and not before.**

Strolling through the lower (downriver) **Quarter** and the **Faubourg Marigny** along quiet streets, seeing the rainbow flag again and again—yes, these are queer neighborhoods.

Partying all night at **Oz**, the **Bourbon Pub**, and **Cafe Lafitte in Exile**, ending up on **Moonwalk** to watch the sun rise over the **Mississippi River**. Follow that with an early cup of coffee and **beignets** at **Café du Monde**. It's nearly nine and time for bed.

Alan Robinson

Bookseller/Owner, Faubourg Marigny Bookstore

The courtyard at **Feelings**. This black-tie to blue jeans restaurant is a short cab ride out of the **French Quarter**. Enjoy Friday lunch or sit on the balcony over the courtyard in the evenings.

Tea dance, Sunday or holidays at the **Parade Disco, Oz**, and **Cafe Lafitte in Exile**. Simultaneous parties turn the 800 block of **Bourbon** into a gay street party. You must go out on their balconies for a real New Orleans experience.

Mardi Gras day in the back of the Quarter. You'll have seen enough parades by then. Get up in time to see the walking krewe Society of St. Ann follow their brass band down **Royal** from the **Faubourg** to **Canal Street**. Then wander the back Quarter watching for the gay krewe members as they bring their incredible ball costumes to the street.

Southern Decadence—It is not for the faint at heart, the prim and proper, or anyone lacking a sense of humor. The parade, loosely described, is Labor Day Sunday.

Gay Pride Week—Annual gay pride festival beginning with a parade on Saturday followed by a fair at **Washington Square** Saturday and Sunday.

Douglas Weiss

Chief Operating Officer, NO/AIDS Task Force

Take a walk up **Royal Street** from **Esplanade Avenue** to see some of the most beautiful balconies in the **French Quarter** and antiques stores to die for!

Jack Gentry

Property Manager

Jackson Square—Street artists and music.

Oz—Gay strip bar.

Bourbon Pub—Gay bar.

Rubyfruit Jungle—Lipstick lez bar.

Remember the bars and action go on 24 hours a day. As we say here "Pace yo'self, cher."

NEW ORLEANS

71 LIONS INN

♂ $$ Five blocks from the Quarter nightlife, Jon Weber and Earl Clapper have created the best gay bed-and-breakfast bargain in town in the rear half of their home. The 1850s Edwardian duplex is guarded by lazing lions, and swarming with palmetto, lantana, and hibiscus. The four guest rooms are handsomely appointed, with beamed ceilings, stained glass windows, and private entrances (one has its own kitchen, another has no private bath). The clothing-optional tropical grounds offer water in many forms, with a fish pond, a water hyacinth/papyrus pool, a Jacuzzi, and a swimming pool. ♦ 2517 Chartres St (between Franklin Ave and Spain St). 945.2339; fax 949.7321

72 FEELINGS

★★★$$ Gays and lesbians have been flocking to this atmospheric eatery for years, especially for Sunday brunch and weekend dinners. The eccentric structure, which merges a historic commercial building with slave quarters from the 18th-century D'Aunoy plantation, offers an airy dining room and a brick courtyard luxuriant with banana plants and elephant ears. Top choices from the menu include beef tournedos au poivre and medallions of veal D'Aunoy (with herb lemon butter and topped with sliced mushrooms and sauce hollandaise). The tangy crab cakes and barbecued shrimp are also stellar, but be sure to save room for the killer peanut butter pie. ♦ International/Creole ♦ M-Th, Sa dinner; F lunch and dinner; Su brunch and dinner. Reservations recommended. 2600 Chartres St (at Franklin Ave). 945.2222

Restaurants/Clubs: Red | Hotels: Purple | Shops: Orange | Outdoors/Parks: Green | Sights/Culture: Blue

ADDITIONAL HIGHLIGHTS

If you're ready to venture beyond Bourbon Street, New Orleans has its share of outlying—and outlandish—attractions well off the typical tourist map. **La Provence** and **Mosca's** are two celebrated restaurants worth a country drive, and even a quick trip to the suburbs is rendered palatable by a stop at **Andrea's, Crozier's,** or **La Riviera.** Outdoorsy types can wander the wetlands and forest of the **Louisiana Nature Center.** For indoor games, gamblers can try their luck at the **Treasure Chest Casino** in Kenner. And if you miss Carnival, you can always catch the spirit year-round at **Blaine Kern's Mardi Gras World** across the river in **Algiers.**

Wilder yet, for a look at New Orleans's unsung netherworld, offbeat roadsters can follow a lowdown, funky driving tour that leads all the way from an eccentric **Eighth Ward** shrine that honors St. Roch, patron of miraculous cures, right to **The End of the World,** where the concrete stops and the marsh begins.

The Ninth Ward is one of those unspoiled historic areas that will never surrender to gentrification, mainly because the gentry have always taken their business elsewhere.

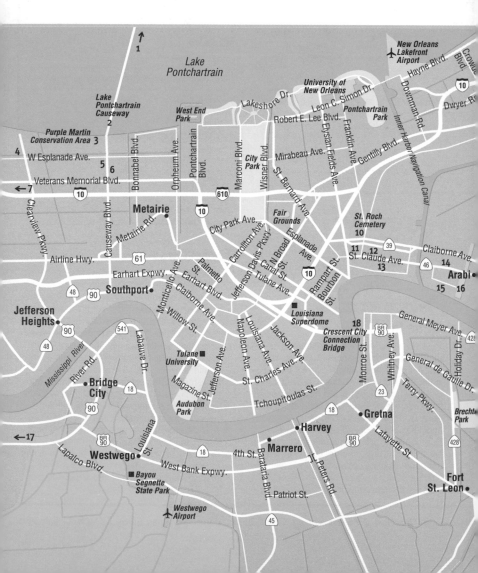

Unlike the uptown **Garden District,** an aging beauty struggling against hard times, Downtown's "Lower Nine" started with hard times and leveled out. Today the inner-city region that sprawls from **Faubourg Marigny** to the **St. Bernard Parish line** is still a crowded jumble of cheap shotgun houses, Creole cottages, and postwar bungalows. Many are shabby from decades of neglect; others are meticulously fitted out with carports, aluminum awnings, and chainlink fences.

Here, **St. Claude Avenue** flows past the deliciously downscale **Restaurant Mandich** and the one-in-a-million **Saturn Bar.** After the St. Bernard Parish line, St. Claude becomes **St. Bernard Highway**—the main drag through suburban **Chalmette** and points beyond. Along the way, you'll pass the **Jackson Barracks** (one of the country's oldest military bases) and the **Chalmette Battlefield and National Cemetery,** the historic site of the colorful Battle of New Orleans. Down the road in eastern St. Bernard Parish, far past the new housing developments and petrochemical refineries, the landscape returns to a more pastoral scene. Fishing villages and prime riverside grazing fields are reminders that there is a rich culture here that predates the oil boom, even the industrial revolution, and it continues to **The End of the World** (watch for the sign, so you don't fall off).

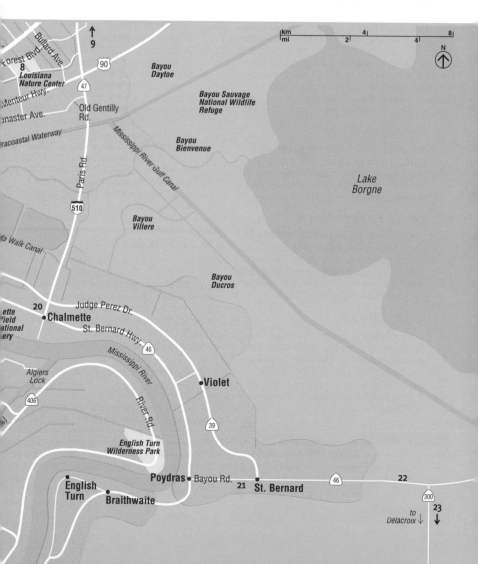

MANDEVILLE

When you reach the north shore from the Lake Ponchartrain Causeway, follow the well-marked exits to Mandeville. This 19th-century resort community was founded by Bernard Xavier de Marigny de Mandeville, the eccentric Creole who also laid out the New Orleans neighborhood of Faubourg Marigny. The historic summer retreats that line Mandeville's **Lakeshore Drive** offer a splendid introduction to Louisiana architecture. Many were built as speculative models of vacation homes and several date from the 1830s through the 1860s, which makes Mandeville's lakefront a prime attraction for students of mid-19th-century architecture. The early Louisiana cottages are characterized by high ceilings, deep roofs, tall shuttered windows, and ample porches for cool shelter from the steamy climate. The later Victorian shotgun houses, boxcar-shaped structures with rooms opening onto one another in a straight line, are so called because (theoretically) a bullet fired at the front door would exit through the back door. Most lakefront buildings are raised and sturdily constructed to withstand the frequent hurricanes and high water. For a do-it-yourself walking tour, be sure to stroll past the architectural beauties listed below. (All are private residences and closed to the public.) Picnicking is prohibited along Mandeville's oak-shaded lakefront, but if you follow Lakeshore Drive back toward the causeway, you will find a small waterside park with tables and other public facilities.

1 THE MAGNOLIAS

This raised cottage, built in the mid-1850s by Marigny for his then ex-wife, gets its name from the magnificent magnolia trees that shade the grounds. ♦ 1635 Lakeshore Dr (between Jackson Ave and Foy St)

1 LITTLE FLOWER VILLA

Constructed in the early 1800s, this symmetrically Classical and deliberately plain tropical-style house is set on low piers with a wraparound porch that's shaded by an overhanging roof. ♦ 1721 Lakeshore Dr (between Foy and Lamarque Sts)

1 FLAGSTAFF

Antoine James de Marigny and his wife, née Sophronie Claiborne (daughter of Louisiana governor William C.C. Claiborne), occupied this cottage from 1870 to 1890. It is listed on the National Register of Historic Places. ♦ 1815 Lakeshore Dr (between Lamarque St and Marigny Ave)

> Because the native bald cypress that grows in Louisiana's swamps is highly resistant to decay, it has been used for centuries to build houses, boats, and furniture. Known as "the wood eternal," it was one of the first American trees to be exported to Europe.

1 CHATEAU MARIGNY

This is one of Mandeville's oldest houses, built in 1838 by Juan Penas and Jean Pujol y Ripolle. The raised cottage has a central fireplace, a wide upper balcony, and two exterior staircases (one leading to the balcony, the other to the attic). ♦ 121 Marigny Ave (between Lakeshore Dr and Claiborne St)

1 DANIELSON HOUSE

Plain trim and the absence of gingerbread characterize this country cousin of the New Orleans shotgun house; it was built in 1900 by F. Edward Vix. ♦ 127 Marigny Ave (between Lakeshore Dr and Claiborne St)

1 LA PROVENCE

★★★★$$$ The name of this French restaurant is most appropriate, both for its idyllic country setting three miles east of Mandeville and for the origins of chef/owner Chris Kerageorgiou. Born in Port Saint Louis in Provence, he began as a baker and worked to fulfill his dream of opening a restaurant in America. Obviously, his dream is now a successful reality: This place celebrated its 25th anniversary in 1997. It is a charmer, with open fireplaces, warm wood paneling, and the ambience of a country estate. Among the appetizers, quail gumbo and eggplant custard are house specialties. Bouillabaisse, marinated rack of lamb, and tournedos in bordelaise sauce are some of the tempting entrées. It's very difficult to keep your eyes off the roving dessert cart. ♦ French ♦ W-Sa dinner; Su lunch and dinner. Reservations recommended; jacket recommended. Hwy 190, Lacombe. 626.7662 &

LAKE PONTCHARTRAIN

If this really were a lake, it would be among the nation's largest, at 610 square miles. But because it joins the **Mississippi River** and has a high salt content, it's actually an inland estuary, the largest in the US. That daunting name (say *Pont*-cher-train) comes courtesy of French nobleman Jerome Phelypeaux, Count Pontchartrain, who served as minister of marine under Louisiana's namesake, Louis XIV.

2 LAKE PONTCHARTRAIN CAUSEWAY

At 24 miles, the world's longest over-water bridge is a straight shot from suburban Metairie in Jefferson Parish to the town of Mandeville in St. Tammany Parish. The ride is smooth, thanks to a full-time maintenance crew, and the view is brilliant. For a long stretch, beyond sight of either shore, drivers experience the remarkable sensation of crossing the sea on a futuristic freeway. Sailboats and working tugs drift alongside, as pelicans and sea gulls swoop overhead. Plan to return near sundown so you can watch the great orange ball dip into the water as the distant New Orleans skyline gleams in the late-afternoon light. The twin one-way spans are composed of concrete supported by two- and three-pile bents. About 80 feet separate the 28-foot-wide, two-lane roadways, which are close to the water, with unobtrusive railings on each side. The first bridge, completed in 1956, has 56-foot spans, and the second, completed in 1969, has 84-foot spans. Motorist call boxes are located every half-mile in either direction. Causeway police, who arrive quickly to offer assistance, are also quick to offer tickets to anyone who exceeds posted speed limits, especially when the road is wet.

3 PURPLE MARTIN OBSERVATION AREA

Some of the commuters on the Lake Pontchar-train Causeway travel from the Arctic Circle to deepest Argentina. During peak season (late June and July), as many as 200,000 purple martins use the bridge as a roost stop on their migrations. An enthusiastic crowd gathers at the observation area just before sunset to watch the birds fly in from all directions, then wheel around the sky for several minutes before amassing under the bridge in a spectac-ular gang swoop. The largest of the swallows, martins are around eight inches long with distinctive triangular wings. Purple martins are named for the violet-headed males; females are gray with white bellies. Local bird-watcher Carlyle Rogillio discovered the roost in 1983 while doing work for **Audubon Zoo's Wild Bird Rehabilitation Center**. He noticed that all of the martins leaving the research area flew in the same direction and, after many observa-tions, spotted them flocking toward the lake, where they then disappeared. A sunset hike through tall weeds revealed their secret. For years he told no one of his discovery, but finally went public after deciding that mobs of bird-watchers would probably help protect the flocks. Today, naturalists travel miles to witness the phenomenon. Fencing guards the roost from fast moving traffic. To reach the concrete observation deck, park in the lot by the Causeway Commission office (located beside the tollbooths for the northbound span), then hotfoot it across both lanes to the stairs that lead beneath the southbound span. ◆ Causeway Blvd and Lake Pontchar-train Cswy

---

JEFFERSON PARISH
4 LA RIVIERA

★★★$$$ Oil paintings of the Italian Riviera add a little romance to the two spacious dining rooms at Valentino Rovere's restaurant, a local favorite since the 1970s. Chef Goffredo Fraccaro, salty co-star (with **La Provence's** Chris Keragiorgiou) of the syndicated TV show "Cooking with Chris and Goffredo," invites guests to visit his kitchen, where he makes his own pasta and spices dishes with herbs from his own garden. Don't miss the ravioli stuffed with lump crabmeat and topped with white cream sauce and parmesan. Known for his wide variety of veal dishes, Fraccaro also turns out fine cannelloni, eggplant parmigiana, and garlicky broiled chicken. ◆ Italian ◆ M, Sa dinner; Tu-F lunch and dinner. Reservations recommended. 4506 Shores St (between W Esplanade Ave and Belle Dr), Metairie. 888.6238 &

5 THE FRENCH TABLE

★★★$$$ An etched-glass door opens into chef Robert Krol's small and elegant restau-rant that gleams with dark wood paneling and polished brass trim. Hearty meat and poultry dishes include celebrated *coq au vin* and steak au poivre. For a lighter choice, try poached pompano drizzled with hollandaise or veal sweetbreads sautéed in lemon butter. ◆ French ◆ M-Fri lunch, M-Sa dinner. Reserva-tions recommended; jacket recommended. 3216 W Esplanade Ave (between Causeway Blvd and Hullen St), Metairie. 833.8108 &

6 ANDREA'S

★★★$$$ A native of Capri, chef Andrea Apuzzo now makes his home on the island of New Orleans, where he says, "I only buy fish so fresh it swims to my door." Try the homemade angel hair pasta, tossed with salmon, flamed in vodka, and topped with a light cream sauce and a sprinkling of caviar. Fragrant cioppino *Mediterraneo* is stocked with mussels, clams, scallops, shrimp, lump

---

crabmeat, and squid. Apuzzo's long menu of Northern Italian fare ranges from hot and cold antipasti to roasted duckling with raspberry sauce. The formal dining rooms are pale peach and lit by crystal chandeliers, a swank setting for the sumptuous Sunday Champagne brunch. ♦ Italian/Continental ♦ M-F lunch and dinner; Sa dinner; Su brunch and dinner. Reservations recommended. 3100 19th St (at Ridgelake Dr), Metairie. 834.8583 &

7 TREASURE CHEST CASINO

This floating casino is berthed on Lake Pontchartrain in suburban Kenner, a seven-minute drive from **New Orleans International Airport**. The glitzy, Las Vegas-style emporium, set on a replica of an old-fashioned riverboat that cruises the lake (in good weather) or operates dockside, is open around the clock. Gamblers can try their luck on three floors of slot machines, craps, blackjack, roulette, video poker, and other games. The casino also has live entertainment, cocktail lounges, and buffet dining. ♦ Daily 24 hours. Free admission and valet parking. 5050 Williams Blvd (north of 44th St), Kenner. 433.8000; www.treasurechest.com &

EASTERN NEW ORLEANS

8 LOUISIANA NATURE CENTER

One of the few natural preserves located in an urban community, LNC sprawls through an 86-acre bottomland hardwood forest near the **Bayou Sauvage National Wildlife Refuge**—20,000 acres of protected wetlands in eastern New Orleans. Three different trails loop through the woods, and a teaching greenhouse is filled with plants, drawings, and live butterflies. Ecology and biology exhibits in the **Interpretive Center** lead visitors to the second-floor **Discovery Loft,** where rocks, skeletons, fossils, and shells invite hands-on examination (only the resident fish and reptiles are untouchable). Back downstairs, an unobtrusive window overlooks squirrels, rabbits, birds, butterflies, and other native varmints who come to feed in the adjoining **Wildlife Garden**. The **Planetarium** presents star shows

> An estimated 400,000 alligators live in the swamps and marshes of Louisiana's coastal zone, where they feed on nutria, muskrats, garfish, turtles, and waterfowl.

and laser concerts on weekends. ♦ Admission. Tu-Su. Planetarium laser shows F-Sa 9PM, 10:30PM, and midnight. Joe W. Brown Memorial Park, 11000 Lake Forest Blvd (between Wright and Read Blvds). 246.5672, fax 242.1889; www.auduboninstitute.com &

9 JAZZLAND

This 140-acre family theme park includes a smattering of thrill rides, such as the spine-jarring wooden rollercoaster Mega-Zeph, with its 110-foot-high drop and the 360-degree Voodoo Volcano, along with water slides and milder thrill rides and midway games for the kiddies. They must have cut down every tree within miles when they planned this overwhelmingly concrete park—on a hot New Orleans summer day, about the only place that's bearable is the cool interior of the Festival Hall theater, where a terrific musical, *Jazz, Jazz, Jazz* and icy air conditioning refresh the body and soul. Shade is minimal, so stick to the water flumes when the temperatures climb. Makes you wonder why this place isn't open in the winter. Fee ♦ Open daily Memorial Day through Labor Day, weekends only April, May, Sept., and Oct. 12301 Lake Forrest Blvd. About 20 minutes outside of downtown, at the intersection of I-10 and I-510. Take exit 246A to Lake Forest Blvd East. 253.8100

EIGHTH WARD

10 ST. ROCH CEMETERY

It's hard to overemphasize the danger of wandering alone through the cities of the dead, where the mazes of crumbling tombs provide plenty of places for bad guys to hide. But do jump at the chance to join a group tour of a cemetery—particularly this one, which is modeled on *Campo Santo dei Tedeschi* (Holy Field of the Germans) near St. Peter's in Rome. It was founded by a German priest, Father Thevis, who was assistant pastor at nearby **Holy Trinity Church** during the yellow fever epidemic of 1868. Thevis prayed for assistance from St. Roch (who was canonized for his work with plague victims during the Middle Ages) and promised in return to build a monument with his own hands. Now the walls and altar of the **Gothic Chapel of St. Roch** are crammed with crutches, braces, glass eyes, and plaster casts of body parts left behind by those who have been cured after pilgrimages to this favored shrine. Hundreds more are in permanent storage, as the tiny building has been filled to capacity many times over the years. The chapel is located just inside the front gates of the cemetery. ♦ Daily. 1725 St. Roch Ave (between N Derbigny and N Roman Sts). 945.5961 &

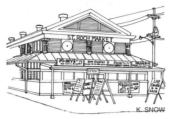

K. SNOW

11 St. Roch Seafood Market

★$ Fresh and boiled seafood, as well as very good plate lunches and sandwiches, are offered at this quaint old landmark (pictured above). Don't expect table service, or even air conditioning, but there's grungy atmosphere to spare and the prices are downright cheap. Best bets are gumbo, stewed chicken, and anything fried. Even if you don't stop for a meal, the historic fish market is a choice photo opportunity. ♦ Seafood ♦ M-Sa lunch and dinner. 2381 St. Claude Ave (at St. Roch Ave). 943.5778 &

Ninth Ward

12 Saturn Bar

This avant-funk masterpiece has probably not seen a dust cloth since the doors opened in 1947. The decor is an eclectic mix of neon chandeliers, tinsel, vinyl easy chairs, plaster madonnas, and straggly game trophies (a fighting cock and raccoon in fierce poses). Not to mention the moth-eaten life-size mummy suspended from the ceiling. That ceiling is a local treasure, frescoed in 1961 by native folk artist Mike Frolich. A riotous pattern of stars and planets swirls above his murals on the walls below. Frolich's canvases also crowd the back room and balcony. The collection includes Benny's *Victorious Chicken* and *How the West Was Won* (a three-dimensional collage of red dice, a full-house card hand, and a cow skull). This legendary watering hole is home to a hard-drinking crowd that doesn't warm to slumming sightseers, so dress down and don't gush. It's also no place for serious feminists, as the house T-shirts say . . . never mind, it would just upset you. Still, this is one hell of an experience if you can stand it. ♦ Daily from 2PM. 3067 St. Claude Ave (at Clouet St). 949.7532 &

13 Restaurant Mandich

★★$$ Although this neighborhood restaurant is a little bit fancier than most, it's still a no-nonsense place where you expect to see an old-fashioned ward boss holding court at the next table. Don't expect hoity-toity service, but the food can compete with some of the French Quarter's stars. Fried oysters are rendered even more heart unhealthy with a generous sousing of garlicky bordelaise sauce. Other highlights are the steaks and the trout Mandich topped with lump crabmeat. The bread pudding is a must. ♦ Seafood/Creole/Italian ♦ Tu-Th lunch; F lunch and dinner; Sa dinner. 3200 St. Claude Ave (at Louisa St). 947.9553 &

14 Fats Domino's House

Please don't disturb this local hero, but if you would like to sneak a peek at his house, you can see it from St. Claude Avenue. Look right behind **Puglia's Supermarket** (at the corner of Caffin Avenue) for the huge 1950s ranch-style job with the bright pink and yellow trim. You might even catch a glimpse of a pink Cadillac with gold-plated bumpers. Shine on! (But don't trespass—it's not open to the public.) ♦ 5525 Marais St (between Caffin Ave and Flood St)

15 Doullut Steamboat Houses

Two of the most exciting local specimens of the exuberant style known as Victorian Steamboat Gothic are located right on the river levee, where they were built by steamboat captain Milton Paul Doullut in 1905. Dual garlands of hand-carved cypress beads are draped from the rafters like strings of pearls, and elliptical stained-glass windows catch the light. The lower walls of white-glazed brick are surrounded by 27 tapered columns, and the broad galleries surrounding the second floors are reminiscent of riverboat decks. A glassed-in pilot house makes for a whimsical topknot on each roof. The facing houses, both private residences, are listed on the National Register of Historic Places. The Doullut Steamboat Houses as well as the private homes are closed to the public. ♦ 400 Egania St (just south of Douglas St)

16 Jackson Barracks

Continue just a few more blocks down St. Claude Avenue, where this military base borders the St. Bernard Parish line. Headquarters for the Louisiana National Guard since 1921, the facility was constructed during the administration of President Andrew Jackson (1829-1837) to house federal troops and defend the city. Robert E. Lee and Ulysses S. Grant were both stationed here in 1845. It also served as a US Army base during World War II. The base is closed to the public. ♦ St. Claude Ave (between Angela and Delery Sts). 271.6262

Restaurants/Clubs: Red | **Hotels: Purple** | **Shops: Orange** | **Outdoors/Parks: Green** | **Sights/Culture: Blue**

Within Jackson Barracks:

JACKSON BARRACKS MUSEUM COMPLEX

A crack collection of uniforms, weapons, flags, and other military relics dating from the Revolutionary War to Desert Storm is showcased at this small but fascinating museum. Walkways crisscross the grounds, leading to a variety of armored and amphibious vehicles, field artillery, and aircraft, including a Phantom jet that saw action in both Vietnam and the Persian Gulf. One of the newer acquisitions, parked on a bed of sand, is a Russian armored vehicle that was abandoned by Iraqi soldiers during the Gulf War. Many of the interior displays are housed in the powder magazine (built in 1837 and listed on the National Register of Historic Places), which has been used as a museum since 1974. ♦ Free. M-F and by appointment for groups. 6400 St. Claude Ave. 278.8242 &

WEST BANK

17 MOSCA'S

★★★$$$ Don't be deterred by the look of this nondescript roadhouse on the edge of a swamp. It doesn't have much curb appeal, the dining rooms are loud and frowsy, and the service is extremely casual. But it's packed with New Orleanians who didn't drive 15 miles for decor or amenities. Each of the old-fashioned Creole Italian dishes (no madcap pasta combos here) is big enough to serve at least two, and it's traditional for groups to order an assortment of appetizers and entrées

Animals you could encounter during a trek through one of Louisiana's swamps include white-tailed deer, bobcats, cougars, black bears, squirrels, rabbits, nutria, otters, raccoons, opossums, bald eagles, American woodcocks, catfish, sac-a-lait (crappie), bass, buffalo fish, gaspergou (also known as drum fish), alligator gars, crabs, crawfish, frogs, turtles, and American alligators.

Though many people use the terms interchangeably, a swamp is quite different from a marsh. A swamp is something like a waterlogged forest, while a marsh is a sea of grass, a wet lowland dominated by grasses.

to share. Be sure to get a pan of the famous oysters Mosca, sizzled under a thick blanket of seasoned bread crumbs. Add a whole baked chicken, crisp and spicy, and a plate of garlicky spaghetti bordelaise to make a feast for four. Even with reservations, you may have to cool your heels at the bar, and then the food (always prepared to order) will take a while to arrive—but it's definitely worth both waits. ♦ Creole/Italian ♦ Tu-Sa dinner. Reservations strongly recommended. No credit cards accepted. 4137 Hwy 90 (west of Avondale Garden Rd). 436.9942

18 BLAINE KERN'S MARDI GRAS WORLD

If you miss Mardi Gras, you can still catch some of its flavor with a visit to this huge float-building studio, where Kern and his staff create most of the entries in New Orleans's Carnival parades. The huge warehouses, called dens, are filled with giant props, including the Bacchus parade's elaborate Bacchusaurus float, the towering King and Queen Kong, and a 20-foot-high Michael Jackson head. Blaine Kern Artists, Inc. also creates floats for Macy's Thanksgiving Day parade and the Bastille Day parade in Cannes, France. Pick up Carnival souvenirs at the gift shop. When you're ready to leave, be sure to walk up on the levee behind the parking lot for one of the best views of the New Orleans skyline, with the river in the forefront. A shuttle van meets every crossing of the Canal Street ferry (on the Algiers side) from 9:30AM to 4:15PM. ♦ Admission. Daily. 233 Newton St (just west of Brooklyn Ave). 362.8211; www.mardigrasworld.com &

ST. BERNARD PARISH

19 CHALMETTE BATTLEFIELD AND NATIONAL CEMETERY

The famous Battle of New Orleans, in which General Andrew Jackson led a ragtag army of hastily assembled local civilians and Tennessee sharpshooters against a much larger force of trained British soldiers, was fought at this site on 8 January 1815. Perhaps it was the last-minute assistance from pirate Jean Lafitte and his Baratarians, or the all-night vigil by the Ursuline nuns, but when the smoke cleared, the Redcoats had been defeated and the city had been spared. It was an important moral victory, of course, but the Treaty of Ghent had actually been signed two weeks earlier. Annual reenactments of the historic battle are peopled by an international cast of musketeers and history buffs who each year come to take part in this colorful pageant. On the eve of the event, lantern tours simulate the nighttime atmosphere of the battlefield, as small groups are led by park rangers through the American and British camps. They pass by British headquarters as General Sir Edward Packenham and his officers plan their attack, then cross an American sentry line to watch Andrew Jackson holding a council of war with his staff. Back in the city, there's an annual Mass said on 8 January at the **National Shrine of Our Lady of Prompt Succor,** also known as **Ursuline Chapel.** The Ursulines promised God that if the Americans won, they would hold a Mass every year in thanks for the city's deliverance from the British. They have kept their promise without fail since 1815. The battlefield and cemetery complex is a division of the **Jean Lafitte National Historical Park and Preserve.** A well-marked driving tour skirts the ramparts, but it would be a shame to miss a walk on the oak-shaded grounds, the view from the levee, and the historic markers that line the rows of the cemetery. The visitors' center also features hands-on displays and a half-hour film about the battle. ◆ Free. Daily. 8606 W St. Bernard Hwy (at Chalmette Ave), Chalmette. 281.0510; www.nts.gov 占

20 ROCKY AND CARLO'S

★★$ There's a mighty temptation to award this joint four stars, as it does indeed qualify as an extraordinary experience, but **Commander's Palace** it ain't. This parish shrine of Creole Sicilian cuisine draws foodies and people watchers from all over the region. They come for sloppy po-boys, baked macaroni and cheese, excellent fried seafood, and fork-tender stuffed beef lavished with red gravy. If you're feeling politically correct, you can point to the vat and ask for a serving of the Italian salad, but don't be surprised if the septuagenarian waitress snarls at you in an accent that is pure Palermo, "Ya mean a wop salad?" Just say yes. Service is kind of iffy; most people belly up to the steam table and carry their own trays. The television over the bar is loud, the patrons are even louder, and this place couldn't be more downscale unless the roof blew off. But it's a local institution that must be seen to be believed—and the wop salad is great. ◆ Italian/Seafood ◆ Daily breakfast, lunch, and dinner. 613 W St. Bernard Hwy (between Lloyds and Trio Sts), Chalmette. 279.8323 占

21 ISLEÑO CENTER

Back on the road, resign yourself to a few hideous miles before the industry dies down. About a mile east of the town of Poydras, watch for a tiny museum set in a cottage on deep, oak-shaded grounds. A unit of the **Jean Lafitte National Historical Park and Preserve,** the museum is a tribute to the hardy people whose descendants still maintain a strong

hold in St. Bernard Parish. *Isleño* means islander—in this case, those who immigrated to the area from Spain's Canary Islands. Beginning in 1778, hundreds of Isleños were brought to Louisiana and stationed in strategic locations to protect the colony for the Spanish government. It took at least a year to sail over on wooden galleons; widows and the sick were abandoned at stops along the way. When they finally arrived, these mountain people were forced to eke out a living from the swampy land by hunting, trapping, and fishing. The rangers, members of the Isleño community, are excellent guides to the small collection of maps, portraits, models, craft items, household artifacts, and trappers' supplies. ◆ Free. W-Su. 1357 Bayou Rd. 682.0862 占

22 SAN PEDRO PESCADOR CATHOLIC CHURCH

Named for St. Peter the Fisherman, this simple church serves about 400 families from the tiny fishing communities that crowd the St. Bernard coast. To withstand frequent storms, the building perches on stilts high above the ground, and in honor of the local livelihood, the roof is shaped like the inverted bow of a boat and the altar is decorated with handmade nets and other nautical artifacts. Each year the parish comes alive for the two Sundays preceding the official opening of white shrimp season (always the third Monday in August). If you happen to be in town, don't miss the colorful Blessing of the Fleet, when a parade of gaily decorated fishing boats chugs by to receive blessings from the pastoral team that stands on shore. Meanwhile, stop by to admire the handiwork of the parishioners. Sister Diane Hooley, OP, resident pastoral administrator, says that visitors are always welcome to view the interior and the door on the left side is unlocked every day from 8AM to 5PM. ◆ Rte 46. 676.3719

23 THE END OF THE WORLD

Just beyond **San Pedro Pescador Church,** veer south onto Route 300 at the flashing light. This low-lying road is bordered on one side by huge fishing boats moored in the bayou. On the other, the fishermen's houses tower overhead on stilts. You are now on historic Delacroix Island heading straight for the end of the world. You won't need the sign to know when you've arrived, because there's nothing left but water and nothing left to do but turn back. ◆ Rte 300, Delacroix

---

Restaurants/Clubs: Red | Hotels: Purple | Shops: Orange | Outdoors/Parks: Green | Sights/Culture: Blue

Swamps to the left of you, swamps to the right—it's not easy to choose the best road trip from New Orleans. Here are suggestions that explore five of the dominant forces that shaped this rowdy culture: political shenanigans, plantations, Cajuns, pirates, and untamed nature. Drive on.

CAPITAL INTRIGUE IN BATON ROUGE

Back in the 17th century, the warring Bayou Goula and Houma tribes marked their grounds with a bloodstained cypress pole, an impressive landmark that inspired French explorers to christen the site "le Baton Rouge." From the earliest origins of "Red Stick," Louisiana's capital has enjoyed a colorful and contentious history, and the smooth 90-minute drive (west on **Interstate 10** from New Orleans) makes for an easy day trip to investigate this city sculpted by the **Mississippi River** and the infamous governor, Huey Long.

The LSU
Rural Life
Museum

Baton Rouge is in the heart of Louisiana's plantation country, surrounded by more than 30 stately homes. But one little-known local attraction presents a vivid picture of Southern living as it once was for the other 97 percent of the population. The **LSU Rural Life Museum** (I-10 and Essen La, 225/765.2437), an outdoor exhibit spread over five acres and incorporating more than 15 buildings, tells the real story of early times in Dixie. An authentic plantation complex (minus the big house) includes a commissary (the first general store), an overseer's house, kitchen, slave cabins, sick house, school-house, blacksmith shop, sugar house, gristmill, and 25 acres of formal and semiformal gardens. The folk architecture collection features a Gothic Revival church furnished with artifacts from several different faiths and walls brightened by exuberant decorations. Just across the road, a simulated graveyard contains authentic markers gathered from throughout Louisiana. Rustic paths lead from an 1840 pioneer's cabin to an 1870 dog-trot house (two separate cabins connected by a breezeway), and from an Acadian cottage to a common shotgun house. A huge barn displays hundreds of everyday rural items, prehistoric Indian artifacts, and an impressive fleet of antique vehicles. The museum is open daily and charges admission.

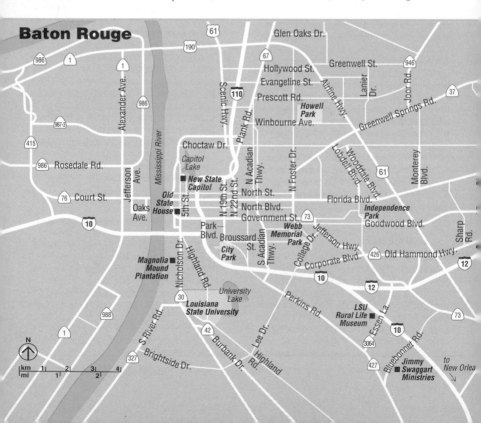

Baton Rouge

'o get there, take Interstate 10 to Exit 160; the entrance is just south of the highway. Once on the property, the museum is 1.5 miles down a curving, paved road.

he attractions lining the Baton Rouge waterfront are also worth a visit. To get there from Interstate 10, ake **I-110** to the **Convention Street** exit and follow the signs to the river. Your first stop could be the *USS Kidd*, a World War II Fletcher Class Destroyer estored to its VJ Day configuration. The 369-foot ship adjoins a nautical center (305 S River Rd, between Government St and North Blvd, 225/342.1942) with model ships and a P-40 Flying Tiger aircraft; the enter is open daily and charges admission. The neighboring **Louisiana Arts and Science Center/ Riverside Museum** (100 S River Rd, at North Blvd, 225/344.5272; www.lacsmuseum.com) is a restored train station with changing fine arts exhibits, hands-on children's science and art galleries, an Egyptian tomb, a restored five-car train, and more. It's open Tuesday through Sunday, and there's no admission charge on the first Sunday of each month.

But the main attraction of Baton Rouge is politics. The city was named the capital of Louisiana in 1846, and the riverside **Old State House** (100 North Blvd, at S River Rd) was completed in 1850. Unfortunately, the architecture of "the little sham castle" was not to everyone's taste. In fact, when a fire almost destroyed the turreted extravaganza during the Civil War, Mark Twain commented that "dynamite should finish the work a charitable fire began." But, thanks to persevering preservationists, the structure was spared to provide a suitably flamboyant setting for an in-house museum, **Louisiana's Center of Political and Governmental History** (225/342.0500). The museum is open daily and charges admission. www.sec.state.la.us

The 34-story **New State Capitol** (State Capitol Dr, between Fifth St and Riverside Mall, 225/342.7317) offers free self-guided tours and is open daily. The "new" capitol was built in 1932 during the reign of the legendary "Kingfish," Governor Huey Long. Designed by **Weiss, Dreyfous, and Sieferth,** America's tallest state capitol building was completed a little more than a year at the rock-bottom Depression price of $5 million. Construction of the Beaux Arts skyscraper required more than 2,500 railroad cars of material, including 50 loads of marble gathered from Vermont to Vesuvius." Each of the front steps has the name of a state engraved on it, as well as the date of its admission to the US; views from the 27th-floor observatory are spectacular. The House and Senate chambers still ring with double dealing and political maneuvering and you can see the elec-

tronic voting machines, among the first in the nation, where "the legislators pushed the buttons, but Huey pulled the switch." You can even run your fingers over the bullet holes that pit the marble columns outside the office where the big man was gunned down. Be sure to visit the formal gardens and **Old Arsenal Museum** (225/342.0401) on the capitol grounds; it's open daily and charges a separate admission.

Other area attractions include "Huey's University," **Louisiana State University** (Nicholson Dr, between Highland Rd and W Chimes St, 225/388.3202), and **Magnolia Mound Plantation** (2161 Nicholson Dr, between Johnson and Garner Sts), 225/343.4955; admission; open Tuesday through Sunday). www. magnoliamound.org

Fans of latter-day intrigue may want to visit **Jimmy Swaggart Ministries,** the headquarters of one of Baton Rouge's most famous (or infamous?) contemporary citizens. Jimmy is alive and kicking, and a representative from his **Family Worship Center** (8919 World Ministry Blvd, just east of Bluebonnet Rd, 225/768.8300) says that "Brother Swaggart preaches here nearly every Sunday."

You'll probably want to eat at some point, but be prepared—Baton Rouge is an island of lousy restaurants in Louisiana's sea of great cuisine. Two of the safer bets are right off the freeway, which should tell you something. A good choice for burgers and ribs, **J. Ribs** (2324 S Acadian Thwy, between I-10 and Hundred Oaks Ave, 225/383.7427), is a sports bar with a collection of **LSU** memorabilia; it's open daily for lunch and dinner. Exotic pizzas and crusty bread are baked in wood-fired ovens at **Louisiana Pizza Kitchen** (I-10 and Essen La, 225/763.9100), which also has a reasonable wine list and great salads; it's open daily for lunch and dinner. A popular student hangout on the edge of the LSU campus, **The Chimes** (3357 Highland Rd, at E Chimes St, 225/383.1754), serves breakfast, lunch (good sandwiches), and dinner daily, and showcases live music in an adjoining theater at night.

RIVER ROAD PLANTATIONS

The petrochemical plants assaulting the landscape are the strongest reminder that the great plantations of Louisiana have indeed gone with the wind. But to appreciate the beauty that still exists along this scenic drive, you must turn a blind eye to some hard facts. Just concentrate on the moody moss-draped oaks, the ancient whitewashed tombs of the country cemeteries, the wealth of historic houses (both large and small), and the mighty curves of the **Mississippi**. Concentrate on your driving, too, especially from 3 to 4:30PM, when day shifts end and plant workers race

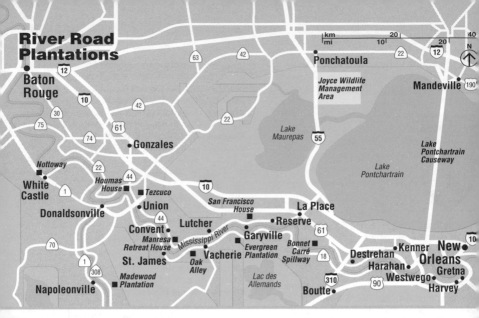

River Road Plantations

Baton Rouge · Ponchatoula · Mandeville · Gonzales · White Castle · Nottoway · Houmas House · Tezcuco · Donaldsonville · Union · Convent · Lutcher · San Francisco House · La Place · Reserve · Garyville · Manresa Retreat House · Vacherie · Evergreen Plantation · Bonnet Carré Spillway · Destrehan · Kenner · New Orleans · St. James · Oak Alley · Harahan · Westwego · Gretna · Napoleonville · Madewood Plantation · Lac des Allemands · Boutte · Harvey

Joyce Wildlife Management Area · Lake Maurepas · Lake Pontchartrain · Lake Pontchartrain Causeway

for home. As you leave the city far behind, industrial development thins out and the atmosphere thickens.

This is an easy day trip if you tour only one or two estates (and for some people the view from the roadside is more than enough), but plan an overnight stay if you want to trudge through every interior. Unless otherwise noted, all the plantations covered in this tour are open daily and charge an admission fee. Only **Madewood** and **Nottoway** offer luxurious bed-and-breakfast accommodations in the original bedrooms of the main house; others lodge guests in restored cottages or apartments on the grounds. Read on for details.

For the purest vistas—even though you'll miss a few mansions—take **Interstate 10** west from New Orleans and start at **La Place,** exiting the freeway and following the "River Road Plantations" signs until you see the levee. Turn right, after which the river should be on the driver's side. Here's where it gets kind of complicated. What is known locally as **"The River Road"** is actually twin two-lane blacktops that trace both sides of the Mississippi from New Orleans to Baton Rouge.

It's a very old trade route and the name on the street signs will change as you pass from town to town, but just keep hugging that levee. Also, most plantation manors have no street address other than River Road, so the addresses listed below locate the plantations between towns.

First up is **San Francisco House** (River Rd, between Reserve and Garyville, 535.2341), a colorful specimen of the rather raucous architectural style known as Steamboat Gothic. Built in 1856 by Edmond Bozonier Marmillion, it was dubbed by his son, Valsin *Sans Frusquin,* (French slang for "no money squirreled away") because of the financial drain it created for the family. No expense was spared on the famous ceiling frescoes, wrap-around galleries, and fussy exterior ornamentation.

Back on the road, steel yourself for about 15 miles of romantic (not!) oak-shaded oil refineries before you reach **Manresa Retreat House** (River Rd, between Lutcher and Convent), which is closed to the public but is one of the most impressive sights on this spectacular drive. Originally known as **Jefferson College,**

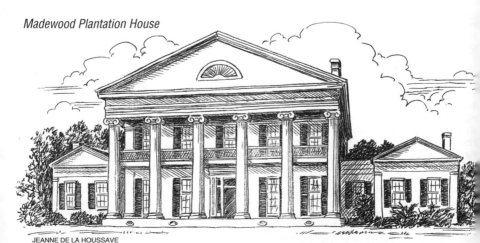

Madewood Plantation House

JEANNE DE LA HOUSSAVE

Tezcuco

KEELY EDWARDS

It was once the Jesuit-run center of education for the sons of wealthy Louisiana planters. The school was chartered by the state legislature in 1831 and was built entirely by subscription on the 65-acre riverfront tract. Still operated by the Jesuit order, today the facility hosts private religious retreats for men.

Continue another 12 miles to **Tezcuco** (River Rd, between Union and Burnside, 225/562.3929; fax 225/562.3923), aptly named from the Aztec word for "place of quiet rest." This splendid example of Louisiana cottage architecture was built between 1850 and 1855 by planter Benjamin Tureaud. The raised structure of cypress and plantation-made brick is furnished with museum-quality regional antiques and art. Of particular interest is the **River Road African-American Museum and Gallery,** a vibrantly mounted collection housed in one of the plantation outbuildings. Among the items displayed here are tools used by workers on area plantations, photographs of jazz musicians, soldiers, and slaves, purchase and emancipation documents for slaves, furnishings, and African musical instruments. Twenty bed-and-breakfast accommodations are available in restored cabins on the grounds and in an apartment in the attic of the main house. An on-site restaurant serves lunch daily.

A short two-mile hop leads to gorgeous **Houmas House** (River Rd, Burnside, 888/323.8314; www.houmashouse.com). Built in 1840 by Colonel John Smith Preston of South Carolina, it is perhaps the one stop on this drive which most closely matches the public's notion of a Southern plantation. The imposing, white-columned Greek Revival mansion originally commanded a 10,000-acre estate. It is flanked by two hexagonal *garçonnières,* the "bachelor quarters" which traditionally housed the young men of the household. A mile north, **The Cabin Restaurant** (Rte 44 and Rte 22, 225/473.3007) is a popular stop for tour buses, but the food (steaks, seafood,

Creole/Cajun fare) is good anyway. Lunch is served daily; dinner is served Tuesday through Saturday.

Backtrack just beyond **Tezcuco** and cross the river on the **Sunshine Bridge,** named in honor of former governor Jimmy Davis's hit tune, "You Are My Sunshine." Follow Route 1 beyond the town of **White Castle** to its namesake, **Nottoway,** the famous "white castle" on the Mississippi (Rte 1, between White Castle and Plaquemine, 225/545.2730; fax 225/545.8632; nottoway@worldnet.att.net). At a staggering 53,000 square feet, this is the largest remaining plantation house in the South. It was built in 1859 by John Hampden Randolph, a wealthy sugar planter, and was saved from destruction during the Civil War by a Northern gunboat officer who had once stayed there as a guest of the family. An exuberant blend of Greek Revival and Italianate architectural styles, **Nottoway** boasted many innovative features, such as hot and cold running water, a gas lighting system, and coal-burning fireplaces. Today, the interior retains the original hand-painted Dresden doorknobs, elaborate plaster frieze work, and marble fireplaces. A lovely sun-washed restaurant located on the grounds serves lunch and dinner daily.

Overnight visitors are treated to Sherry, a tour of the mansion, and a wake-up tray of sweet potato biscuits and coffee followed by a full breakfast in the first-floor dining room. Guests are also welcome to dive into the beautiful swimming pool, which is surrounded by a high brick wall that once enclosed the estate's rose garden. There are thirteen rooms, including the soft pink **Cornelia's Bedroom** on the third floor, with enormous windows overlooking the Mississippi; the majestic **Master Suite** and the **Randolph Suite,** both

Louis, the unhappy vampire Brad Pitt played in the movie *Interview with the Vampire,* lived at Oak Alley plantation. The actor himself, though, stayed at Madewood plantation during the filming.

Houmas House

KEELY EDWARDS

featured in the daily house tours; and a modernized first-floor **Bridal Suite** with a parlor, wet bar, private walled wading pool, and Jacuzzi.

Only one other area plantation quarters overnight guests in the original bedrooms of the main house. Located on **Bayou Lafourche, Madewood** (4250 Hwy 308, southeast of Napoleonville, 369.7151; fax 369.9848; www.madewood.com) is generally acknowledged as the most perfect Greek Revival manor in Louisiana (illustrated page 162). The accommodations have garnered rave reviews from **Vogue, Travel & Leisure, National Geographic Traveler,** and **Country Inns,** among other publications. Visitors sleep on feather pillows on oversize canopied beds in rooms graced by antiques and fresh flowers. There are five rooms in the main house and three suites elsewhere on the grounds (the more private cottage and cabin are great for families or honeymooners). Guests are treated to wine and cheese, candlelight dinner in the dining room, and continental breakfast. To get there from **Nottoway,** backtrack to the Sunshine Bridge and follow the "Bayou Plantation" signs to Route 70, Spur 70, and Route 308.

From **Madewood,** return to the foot of the Sunshine Bridge, then turn right onto the River Road to trace the west bank of the Mississippi back to New Orleans. Once again, the levee should always be on the driver's side. About 12 miles downriver is **Oak Alley** (3645 Hwy 18, between Vacherie and St. James, 800/44ALLEY; fax 225/265.7035; www.oakvalleyplantation.com), which has changed owners and fortunes many times since the spectacular tree-lined avenue was first planted in the 1700s. Now considered one of the most beautiful Southern mansions and toured by nearly 200,000 visitors annually, it began as a rustic cabin at the end of a double row of saplings. A French settler planted the 28 live oaks in 2 rows of 14 each, 80 feet apart, to form the quarter-mile avenue leading from the river to the house. The house was not built until 1839, when the property was acquired by planter Jacques Telesphore Roman. The architecture is a graceful amalgam of many

styles, dominated by the 28 Classical columns, each eight feet in circumference and made of solid bricks (which were baked in pie-shaped molds so they could be mortared together in a circle). An early masterpiece of passive solar design, the 16-inch walls were shaded most of the day by 13-foot verandas, while tall windows and doors provided plenty of cross ventilation. Legend has it that Roman's wife, Celina, named the plantation **Bon Sejour** (French for "pleasant sojourn"), but river travelers awed by the majestic trees dubbed it **Oak Alley,** and the name stuck. Anne Rice fans will recognize it as Louis and Lestat's home in the film *Interview with the Vampire.* A charming country-style restaurant located in one of the outbuildings serves breakfast and lunch daily, and overnight guests can choose from five informally restored cottages on the grounds.

Continue three miles downriver from Oak Alley to **Laura: A Creole Plantation** (2247 Hwy 18, Vacherie, 225/265.7690; www.lauraplantation. com). Built between 1805 and 1870, the complex of 12 National Register buildings, including two manors, plus slave quarters and Creole cottages, has gained nationwide attention for its rare focus on plantation life from the slaves' perspective. In fact, it was on these grounds in the 1870s that the West African folk tales of *Compère Lapin,* better known as Br'er Rabbit, were first recorded in America. One-hour guided tours dramatically detail day-to-day life of Creole women, slaves, and children over a period of 250 years. The meticulously researched accounts are based on 5,000 pages of historic French documents and former owner Laura Locoul's *Memories of My Old Plantation Home.*

From here, it's an easy shot back to New Orleans. You'll pass other private estates along the way, and those "Private: No Admittance" signs may be a sight for sore feet. (Note that nearby **Evergreen Plantation** is open only to groups with **New Orleans Tours**. For information call 504/592.0560.) Cross the **Huey P. Long Bridge** to **Airline Highway** or I-10, which will take you right into the city.

CAJUN COUNTRY

National fads come and go—the Cajun craze among them—but the independent bayou people will keep on with their *bon temps* whether the rest of the world is watching or not. The area settled in the mid-1700s by "Acadiens" (the Cajun forefathers who fled British persecution in what is now Nova Scotia) sprawls through several South Louisiana parishes. The local color cranks up about a three-hour drive west of New Orleans, a bit much for a day trip. But if you can spare a weekend or more, you'll go home with plenty of stories and exotic souvenirs. The following tour, though far from comprehensive, is a fun and efficient dip into the regional culture.

The first stop is for food, of course, and there's no better source than **Acadiana Catfish Shak**, **$ known for its award-winning chicken, sausage and seafood gumbos, this down-home Lafayette restaurant attracts tourists and locals alike. You can get catfish every imaginable way—try it stuffed Florentine style. The Rib-Eye Acadiana, a 10-ounce steak topped with crawfish étouffée, is equally enticing.
♦ 5818 Johnston St.(between Ambassador Parkway and Doc Duhon) in Lafayette, (337) 988-2200

Next priority: checking in to overnight accommodations. **Lafayette** is the largest city around and a good central location for people who prefer bright lights and a little nightlife; call the tourist commission (800/346.1958; www.lafayettetravel.com) for a list of area hotels and historic bed-and-breakfast inns. To bed down in lavish Southern style, **Chretien Point Plantation** (665 Chretien Point Rd, Sunset, 800/880.7050; fax 318/662.5876; www. virtualcities.com) lodges guests in five of the original bedrooms of a restored 1831 French Louisiana country manor with a famous stairway that was reproduced for Tara in the film *Gone With the Wind*. Seven guest rooms are available at the quaint **Old Castillo Bed and Breakfast** in St. Martinville (220 Evangeline Blvd, between Cemetery and S Main Sts, 318/394.4010), 800/621.3017; www.virtualcities.com, which is on the National Register of Historic Places. For homey atmosphere, the tiny New Iberia on oak-shaded

Chretien Point Plantation

KEELY EDWARDS

Bayou Teche is one of the state's prettiest towns. Call the tourist commission (318/365.1540; www.iberiaparish.com) or just pull up at their roadside Acadian cabin (2704 Hwy 14) when you hit town. Ask about bed-and-breakfast accommodations offered by several private homes or lodging in one of the local chain motels.

Once that's settled, hit the road again to cash in on a spate of nearby adventures. One of the best deals around is a whirlwind whoosh through the wetlands. **Airboat Tours Inc.** (318/229.4457; http://members.aol.com/baprioux/airboat.htm) departs **Marshfield Boat Landing** near **Loreauville** for one-hour spins through the shallow-water swamps, bayous, and coves of **Lake Fausse Pointe**. The boats are small and fast for a cooling cruise that skitters past 200-year-old cypress trees, then across brilliant floating fields of blooming lotus. Owner Lon Prioux is a knowledgeable and entertaining guide (ask him about his son, Lacy John, the state duck-calling champ for five years). Prioux stops often for close-up views of pelicans, herons, egrets—even alligators. All tours are by appointment only, and customized tours (sunset is popular) are available by request.

Vermilionville (1600 Surrey St, between Hwy 90 and Pinehook Rd, Lafayette, 318/233.4077, 800/992.2968; www.vermilionville.org) is sort of a Cajun version of Historic Williamsburg, a living folk museum that features blacksmithing, spinning, boat building, doll making, and other regional activities. It's open daily and charges admission. An old-fashioned ferry shuttles visitors across a bayou to **Fausse Pointe,** an 18th-century farm settlement where interpreters carry on daily chores and celebrate changing seasons and holidays in traditional fashion. Chefs at the cooking school demonstrate the secrets behind a successful

roux, fricassee, étouffée, or corn *maque chou* for an introduction to the intricate local cuisine. On weekends, strolling fiddlers, storytellers, and other entertainers guarantee that the atmosphere never gets too educational. Don't miss this fascinating complex—you might even see a real wedding at **Vermilionville**'s popular **La Chapelle**.

On Lafayette's southwestern outskirts, the more sedate **Acadian Village** (200 Greenleaf Dr, just north of New Hope Rd, 318/981.2364, 800/962.9133; www.acadianvillage.org) is another monument to the dominant local culture. Period houses, restored to their 18th-century appearance and furnished with native antiques, are set in 10 acres of gardens and woodland with replicas of a general store and chapel. A log building modeled on the frontier missions of the Mississippi River region houses artifacts of Native Americans and early missionaries. Stop here for a tranquil stroll through the past; the village is open daily and charges admission.

Avery Island, surrounded by water and marshland, is actually the tip of a subterranean mountain of salt, thousands of feet deep. Near New Iberia, the island is also the home of bright red Tabasco sauce, first produced here in the post-Civil War era by Edmund McIlhenny. Free tours of the quaint **McIlhenny Company Tabasco Factory** (318/365.8173; www.tabasco.com) are offered Monday through Saturday; the tours follow the tiny capsicum peppers from planting to packaging, with labels in Japanese, Swedish, Spanish, Italian, French, Chinese, Dutch, and English for customers in more than 100 countries. The founder's son, E.L. McIlhenny, was a noted naturalist and explorer who cultivated the island's other attraction, 200-acre **Jungle Gardens** (318/369.6243). He helped to save the snowy egret from extinction in the late 19th century, and now some 20,000 water birds nest here from early February into July on specially built, pierlike structures in his pond nicknamed "Bird City"; the gardens are open daily and charge admission.

Located on the neighboring salt dome known as **Jefferson Island, Rip Van Winkle Gardens** (5505 Rip Van Winkle Rd, 318/365.3332; www.ripvanwinkle.com) offers a gorgeous ramble over 20 landscaped acres fronting **Lake Peigneur** near New Iberia. Spring is the best time to visit, when more than 50,000 tulips, hyacinths, and daffodils are imported from Holland to complement the colorful explosion of Oriental azaleas. The grounds are graced by an aviary, rose garden, lily pool, Japanese teahouse, and a fine stand of ancient oaks. The estate was formerly the home of actor Joseph Jefferson—best known for his role as Rip Van Winkle—who purchased the site in 1865 to build his winter retreat. Today, the majestic Georgian estate (embellished with generous lashings of Moorish and Victorian steamboat gingerbread) houses an ever-changing exhibition of traditional arts and crafts. Both gardens and house are open daily and charge admission.

Charming **St. Martinville** is a town with an especially colorful past. One of the principal settlements of the Acadian refugees, this thriving Cajun community was subjected to a bizarre wave of immigration in the 18th century. Aristocrats fleeing the French Revolution established "Le Petit Paris," complete with opulent balls and opera productions, in this former trapper's camp. A small collection of handicrafts and plantation wedding costumes is on display at **Le Petit Paris Museum** (103 S Main St, at Evangeline Blvd, 318/394.7334); the museum is open every day and charges admission. Just across the town square, **St. Martin de Tours Church** (133 S Main St, between Port St and Evangeline Blvd) is the oldest continually occupied Catholic church building in Louisiana. Poet Henry Wadsworth Longfellow immortalized St. Martinville in his epic *Evangeline*, the sad tale of the beautiful Acadian refugee who waited for her lover, Gabriel, beneath the now-famous Evangeline Oak (Evangeline Blvd, between Cemetery and S Main Sts). Behind the church you'll find the grave of Emmeline Labiche, whose life inspired the legend. The cast of the film *Evangeline*, shot here in1927, donated the statue (which is actually a chiseled likeness of leading lady Dolores Del Rio). Just north of town, the **Longfellow-Evangeline State Commemorative Area** (1200 Hwy 31, between Burdin St and Teresa Dr, 318/394.3754; www.crt.state.la.us) on Bayou Teche is a gorgeous park, deep green and moody, with an **Acadian Handicraft Shop** and a splendid Caribbean-style **Acadian Plantation House**. The park's attractions can be visited daily; some charge admission.

MULATE'S

When you're ready for a little nightlife, head on over to **Mulate's** (325 Mills St, southwest of Rees St, Breaux Bridge, 318/332.4648, 800/42-CAJUN), where the sign promises *"bon temps et bon manger"* (good times and good eating), and this venerable landmark delivers. You know you're in Cajun country when you see alligator hides on the ceiling, bronzed dancing shoes on the walls, and four brands of hot sauce on every table. Try the boiled crawfish, fried crawfish, crawfish étouffée—or some of each. After all, **Breaux Bridge** tags itself "The Crawfish Capital of the World." The restaurant serves lunch and dinner daily and its old cypress floors stood up to more than five generations of two-steppers. There's still live Cajun music every night, as well as at noon on Saturday and Sunday.

For one of the best shows going, join the international crowd Saturday evening in **Eunice** at the **Liberty Theater** (300 S Second St, at Park Ave, 337/457-7389 or phone the **Eunice Chamber of Commerce** at 337/457.2565). This renovated 1918 vaudeville hall is the Acadian answer to the Grand Old Opry *(en français, naturellement)*, and the *"Rendez Vous des Cajuns"* is broadcast live to seven surrounding parishes every Saturday from 6PM to 8PM. Even French scholars may find it difficult to follow the raconteurs and singers who perform in the southwestern Louisiana dialect, but the lively music is accessible to everyone. The front rows of seats are cleared away so two-steppers can swing right by the stage, where the slanted dance floor is sprinkled with cornmeal for better traction. Ticket cost is negligible, but plan to line up early for first-come, first-seated admission.

BARATARIA, LAND OF JEAN LAFITTE

Some called him a scoundrel and a smuggler; others admired the so-called gentleman privateer. Historians argue about his birthdate (1780 or 1782), birthplace (France or West Indies), marriage (or marriages), and even the time and place of his death. But everyone agrees that Jean Lafitte helped save the city from the British in the historic Battle of New Orleans. He is remembered as the man who committed "a thousand villainies and a single heroism," but also as the namesake for Louisiana's first national park. No doubt about it, Creoles love a good rogue.

Lafitte and his men patrolled the intricate maze of watery highways that connected **Grand Isle, Cat Island,** and **Galveston,** but they were known as "the

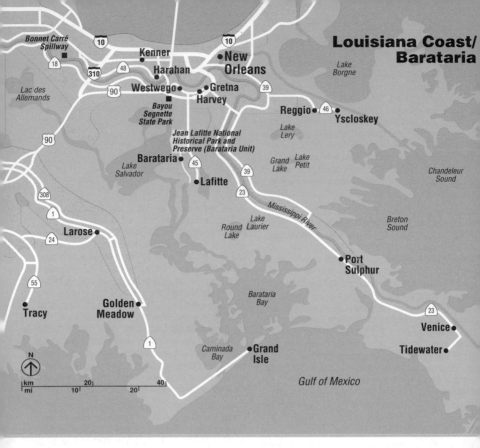

Baratarians" for their home base in the swampland about 30 miles south of New Orleans. An estimated one hundred ships and one thousand men created a pirate empire in Barataria, where many of the proud descendants still live. This modern-day fishing community is far from touristy, but there are a couple of attractions that should be of particular interest to sporting folk. Several local companies offer swamp tours aboard motorized pontoon boats that are enjoyable, even for the skittish. **Louisiana Swamp Tours** (467.8020; swamp@accesscom.net) and **Crown Point Swamp Tours** (689.4186; www.bigeasy.com) are two that operate trips daily and offer door-to-door transportation from downtown New Orleans Hotels. Anglers also can contact **Ripp's Inland Charters** (689.2665) and make an appointment to cruise fresh or salt waters in a 21-foot boat powered by a 200-horsepower engine. Package rates include rod, reel, bait, fish cleaning services, and ice. Overnight accommodations are also available.

Of course, you must eat. For great seafood and fried chicken, natives swear by **Boutte's** (Lafitte, 689.3889), which serves lunch daily, and dinner Tuesday through Sunday. Sit upstairs to watch the sun set over **Bayou Barataria**.

The **Barataria Unit of Jean Lafitte National Historical Park and Preserve** (Rte 45, 589.2330, www.nps.gov/jela) offers a museum and visitor's center (open daily; free) with exhibitions on hunting, fishing, trapping, and early life in the coastal wetlands. There are nine miles of carefully laid-out trails that explore three ecosystems: bottomland hardwoods,

tupelo gum/bald cypress swamp, and freshwater marsh. Along the way, you may spot alligators, frogs, turtles, nutria, and hundreds of different birds. Elevated boardwalks make the trekking easy, and ranger-guided walks are also offered daily at 2PM on the **Bayou Coquille Trail**. To reach the park from New Orleans, cross the **Mississippi River** bridge to the **West Bank Expressway** and turn left at **Barataria Boulevard (Route 45)**. Continue seven miles to the well-marked entrance.

You can rent canoes just outside the park at **Jean Lafitte** (Rte 45 and Rte 3134, 689.3271), which is licensed to deliver them into the park. Canoes are sometimes available at the neighboring **Bayou Barn** (689.2663), but renters must carry them into the park themselves. From March through mid-December, **Bayou Barn** also draws a fun crowd for its Sunday afternoon fais-do-dos, which feature jambalaya, gumbo, and two-stepping to lively Cajun bands in a covered pavilion on **Bayou des Familles**.

To spend more time in this fascinating area—or for country accommodations just 30 minutes from downtown New Orleans—contact **Victoria Inn and Gardens** (Lafitte, 689.4757, 800/689.4797; fax 504/689.3399; www.victoriainn.com). Constructed in 1978 on the site of an old plantation, two traditional West Indies houses are set on a large lake surrounded by six acres of gardens and woodland. Each of the 14 rooms is individually furnished with antiques, ceiling fans, and cable television. The complimentary full breakfast often features fresh local seafood, and tea is served daily.

A DRIVE ON THE WILD SIDE

For a close-up view of some indigenous creatures, and others that are far from their natural homes, here's a day trip that will take you from darkest swamps to deepest Africa. Bring the kids and the camera.

The **Joyce Wildlife Management Area**, on **Highway 51** near **Ponchatoula** (about 45 miles from New Orleans), maintains a **Swamp Walk**—a 1,000-foot boardwalk that leads deep into **Manchac Swamp** for bird watching, photography, general nature studies, and sports access. This well-maintained facility is free and open to the public, but rather obscure, so you can usually count on being one of the only humans on the grounds. It's great for outdoorsy types who won't get the heebie-jeebies from a solo wander through the murky environment, but no place for those who prefer guided tours and nature under glass. There are no guardrails, so children require close attention at all times. A ranger drives over to open the gate daily at sunrise and lock up at sundown, but that's about it for amenities. The **Tangipahoa Parish Tourist Commission** in **Hammond**, located right off I-55's Exit 28 (542.7520; www.tangi-cvb.org), will provide a detailed map and directions to the Swamp Walk, as well as a free flyer that lists the animals and birds common to the area. Numbers beside the plant listings correspond to markings along the trail for easy identification.

While you're at the tourism office, ask for directions to nearby **Kliebert's Turtle and Alligator Farm** (1264 W Yellow Water Rd, between Hoffman Rd and I-55, 800/854.9164). This quirky and charming family-run attraction, a short drive from the **Swamp Walk,** offers a close-up look at thousands of the two

most popular regional critters. Primarily a commercial operation to supply the booming restaurant trade with these unlikely entreés, the farm is open to visitors from March through November (there's an admission charge, but only for guided tours). Summer is the prime time to view fierce mother alligators guarding their nests as egrets and herons swoop overhead. Again, this is a simple place that won't appeal to the Disney World crowd, but the campy gift shop will bring back memories of the snake farms and other roadside attractions that used to be found on Southern highways. It's also the place to stock up on fresh alligator and turtle meat if you're of a mind to bring some home.

GLOBAL WILDLIFE CENTER

Hundreds of endangered and threatened exotic animals, and birds from all over the world, roam the 900 acres of the **Global Wildlife Center** (Rte 40, between Folsom and Rte 445, 796.3585, www.globalwildlife.com), about 20 miles from Hammond. The center is open daily February through December, Friday through Sunday in January; there's an admission charge, but only for tours. One of only three such wildlife education/research centers in the US, this nonprofit facility provides safe breeding grounds for a wide range of hoof stock: antelopes, bison, camels, gazelles, giraffes, llamas, zebras, and many other species (including a kangaroo or two). Maintaining the philosophy that animals, not humans, should run free, "interns" take visitors through the fields in covered wagons pulled by tractors. The drivers stop often for close-up views, and many of the animals have learned to approach the wagons for treats. The giraffes are especially sociable. In addition to the livestock, hills, trees, a lake, and 12 ponds create a breathtaking view of the Louisiana countryside.

From Folsom, an alternate route back to New Orleans will take you through **St. Tammany Parish** and the natural mineral springs and ozone-rich air that have made this region a popular health resort for centuries. From the wildlife center, take **Routes 40** and **445** to **Robert,** then follow the signs to **Interstate 12,** which leads east to the **Lake Pontchartrain Causeway** at **Mandeville.** Here, settle back for a cool 24-mile drive across the world's longest over-water bridge. If you happen to be here in late June or July and reach the south shore at sundown, park by the causeway office (next to the northbound approach lanes) and join the crowd that gathers each night to watch the spectacular air show, as an enormous flock of purple martins careens overhead before swooping *en masse* to their nests under the causeway. You'll find everyone (cameras and binoculars in hand) on the concrete observation pad, located just under the southbound lanes.

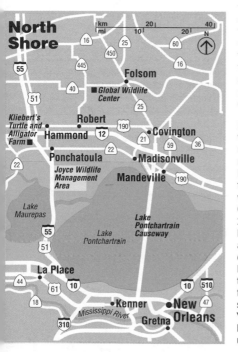

HISTORY

AD

1400 The indigenous population of the southeastern US is around 15,000. The major Native American tribes living in this region include the Caddo, Tunica, Atakapa, Chitimacha, Muskogean, and Natchez.

1492 Christopher Columbus sets sail, landing on the island of Hispaniola and beginning the race for territory in the New World.

1519 Alonso de Piñeda explores the southeastern US but leaves no settlements.

1530 Alvar Nuñez Cabeza de Vaca explores southern Louisiana for Spain.

1534 Jacques Cartier explores the St. Lawrence River for France.

1539 Fernando de Soto lands in Florida and begins the consolidation of Spanish control over the southeastern US.

1541 Members of de Soto's party reach the **Mississippi River**.

1608 The first permanent French colony is established in Quebec.

1668 French interest in the southeast US grows: The French see the Mississippi Valley as a natural barrier against British and Spanish expansion west.

1682 Robert Cavalier, Sieur de La Salle, leaves a French settlement in Canada and explores the Mississippi to the Gulf of Mexico. Claiming the vast territory for France, he names it **Louisiana** after King Louis XIV.

1699 The first French settlement in Louisiana is built by Pierre Le Moyne, Sieur d'Iberville, at Biloxi Bay.

1712 Wary of British territorial ambitions, the French build up the Louisiana territory. A commercial monopoly for all trade on the Mississippi is granted to Antoine Crozat, a French fur trader. The slave population is 20.

1714 Louis Juchereau de St. Denis establishes Natchitoches, the first permanent European settlement in Louisiana.

1717 The Louisiana concession is given to the Compagnie d'Occident (Company of the West). Planning begins for a new port city for the Mississippi.

1718 New Orleans is founded by Jean-Baptiste Le Moyne, Sieur de Bienville, and it is named for the French Regent, Philippe, Duc d'Orléans. Mosquito-infested swamps are cleared and plans are laid out for a town consisting of 66 squares forming a parallelogram. Prosperity comes slowly to the French outpost on the Mississippi (with its periodic outbreaks of yellow fever), but Gallic culture grows deep roots, planted by early settlers eager to imitate the manners of the court.

1721 The total population of New Orleans is about 470 Europeans and nearly 300 slaves.

1722 The capital of the Louisiana territories moves from Biloxi to New Orleans.

1724 The Code Noir (Black Code) is enacted as the basis for a system of laws regulating slavery.

1732 The Louisiana concession returns to the French crown. Growth remains slow; the main economic staples of tobacco and indigo are unprofitable.

1755 Two thousand French settlers in Acadia (later called Nova Scotia) are expelled by the British. Finding their way to Louisiana, they settle in the **Bayou Teche** and become known as Cajuns. People born in Louisiana of European ancestry become known as Creoles.

1762 France cedes the unprofitable Louisiana territory to Spain.

1769 The Spanish, under General Don Alejandro O'Reilly y McDowell, take control of New Orleans.

1789 New Orleans becomes a refuge for French royalists fleeing the French Revolution.

1800 Louisiana is returned to Napoléon's France in a secret treaty.

1803 US President Thomas Jefferson authorizes James Monroe to purchase New Orleans and western Florida from France. Napoléon, eager to avoid having to defend New Orleans against the British, offers to sell the entire territory for $15 million, or about four cents an acre. Changing hands for the fourth time, New Orleans becomes US territory. The population of New Orleans at this time is 8,000 (4,000 whites, and 4,000 blacks, about 2,700 of whom are enslaved).

1805 New Orleans is incorporated as a municipality. **Faubourg Ste. Marie** is added on the uptown side of the **French Quarter**. It becomes the American section and the city's commercial center.

1810 A population explosion: New Orleans now has 25,000 residents.

1812 Louisiana is admitted to the Union as the 18th state. An age of prosperity begins. The first steamboat, the *New Orleans,* arrives, ushering in the age of the steamboat and its impact on tourism and gambling.

1815 The Battle of New Orleans: threatened by the British during the War of

1812 New Orleans is successfully defended by Andrew Jackson.

1840 New Orleans is now the fourth largest city in the US, with a population of 102,000, and the second busiest US port after New York. Cotton and sugar fuel the economy. Opera houses, gambling dens, cafes, and bordellos coexist happily.

1841 Refugees of the Irish famine settle near **Adele Street,** soon to be called the Irish Channel.

1857 The first parading carnival group, the Mystick Krewe of Comus, make its debut.

1861 Civil War: Louisiana joins the Confederacy.

1862 New Orleans falls to Union forces.

1865 Political, economic, and social turmoil rip apart the city during Reconstruction.

1868 A new state constitution grants suffrage to blacks for the first time. Louisiana is readmitted into the Union.

1871 Mardi Gras celebrations grow increasingly lavish.

1872 Amnesty is granted to Confederate officers and the municipal government returns to local control. Rex Krewe debuts.

1879 Construction of jetties forces the Mississippi to cut a deeper channel. At the new depth of 30 feet, oceangoing vessels can now sail upriver. Population of New Orleans: 290,000.

1884 The Cotton Centennial Exposition is held in **Audubon Park.**

1890 Ragtime, a syncopated music played by marching bands, emerges and grows in popularity. Buddy Bolden's band improvises musical embellishments on set music.

1898 A new state constitution effectively disenfranchises blacks through literacy tests in a state with the highest rate of illiteracy in the US.

1901 Oil is discovered in Louisiana. In the next twenty years, a refinery industry emerges on the Mississippi between **Baton Rouge** and New Orleans.

1906 Yellow fever is finally eradicated. Port traffic declines with the rise of the eastern US ports and does not recover until after World War II.

1909 Zulu, the city's oldest black parading *krewe,* is founded. It satirizes white society, mocking the pretensions of Carnival "royalty."

1910 In **Storyville,** New Orleans's bordello

New Orleans has a long link with literary tradition. The roster of writers who have lived and worked here reads like a "Who's Who" of American letters: Ernest Hemingway, Gertrude Stein, Truman Capote, John Dos Passos, Walt Whitman.

district, black musicians, steeped in the blues tradition, develop and expand improvisational techniques and stretch the boundaries of ragtime into a style called "jass," probably local slang for sexual intercourse.

1917 The US Navy orders the closing of Storyville. Many of New Orleans's best musicians move north in search of work. "King" Oliver, the preeminent New Orleans trumpeter, heads for Chicago.

1922 Oliver becomes so popular that he sends for other New Orleans jazz musicians to join him in Chicago. The most brilliant of his disciples, Louis Daniel Armstrong, heads north. The jazz revolution begins.

1928 Running as a populist against the power of New Orleans, Huey Long is elected governor and launches a program of welfare and education reforms. Long's "Share Our Wealth" platform later influences the passage of the Social Security Act. Meanwhile, through his political machine he rules Louisiana as a virtual dictator.

1935 Huey Long is assassinated.

1938 Tennessee Williams arrives in New Orleans. The city and its characters become a backdrop for such works as *A Streetcar Named Desire* and *The Glass Menagerie*.

1948 The Long dynasty continues in a more benign fashion. Earl Long, Huey's brother, is elected governor for the second of three terms. Huey's son Russell begins his career as a powerful US Senator.

1954 The New Orleans city charter is revised, greatly enhancing the powers of the office of the mayor. A period of growth and development begins.

1961 NASA builds the Michoud Assembly Facility in New Orleans to assemble the Saturn booster rockets used in the Apollo flights to the moon.

1962 Development fever runs amok. A plan to construct a French Quarter Expressway is defeated by a grassroots campaign to preserve the historic district.

1963 The construction of port facilities along the **Mississippi Gulf** outlet diverts most wharf traffic away from the center of New Orleans. The old wharf area becomes the target of developers of commercial, residential, and tourism facilities.

1964 Federal Court intervention forces the collapse of efforts to resist school integration.

1969 The first New Orleans Jazz and Heritage Festival is held in **Congo Square**. It lasts five days and attracts more musicians than spectators.

1971 Louis Armstrong dies in Queens, New York.

1978 Ernest Morial is elected as the first African-American mayor of New Orleans.

1980 New Orleans strengthens its position as a leading international port. Over 5,000 oceangoing vessels dock annually and more than 40 countries maintain consular offices.

1984 The **Julia, Erato,** and **Poydras Wharves** become the sites of the 1984 World Exposition. Overshadowed by the Los Angeles Olympics in the same year and suffering from cost overruns, the expo nearly bankrupts the city.

1991 Legislation is passed to integrate the Mardi Gras *krewes*. The response is decidedly mixed. Some *krewes* threaten to disband or boycott the 1993 Carnival, rather than integrate. Among the old-line *krewes* which no longer have public parades—though they still sponsor exclusive masked balls—are Comus, Momus, and Proteus.

1991 Riverfront development explodes. Residential and commercial properties, including restaurants, parks, and tourist attractions, are built.

1993 The census counts nearly 500,000 residents in **Orleans Parish**.

1994 Democratic State Senator Marc Morial, following in his father's footsteps, is elected mayor of New Orleans.

1996 Mary Landrieu, daughter of former New Orleans Mayor Moon Landrieu, is the first woman in Louisiana to be elected to the US Senate.

1997 New Orleans hosts the 31st annual **Super Bowl** in the **Superdome** for the eighth time—more than any other city.

1998 **NFL** officials choose New Orleans as the site of the upcoming 36th annual **Super Bowl** games in the year 2002.

1999 Al Hirt, trumpeter extraordinaire and lifelong resident, dies in his Bourbon Street home 27 April, 1999. The virtuoso jazz musician played at John F. Kenedy's inauguration and serenaded Pope Paul II during the pontiff's visit to New Orleans. He won a Grammy award in 1964 for his signature song, *Java*.

2000 The **National D-Day Museum,** the only one of its kind in the world, opened to the public. The museum is located in New Orleans because Higgins Industries, the manufacturer of the landing craft that delivered US troops onto the beaches at D-Day, was based in New Orleans.

CREDITS

Writer and Researcher
for the Ninth Edition
Beth D'Addono

Writers and Researchers
for Gay New Orleans
David Appell
Paul Balido
Michel LaCroix

Writers and Researchers
for Previous Editions
Constance Snow
Kenneth Snow

Editorial Director
Edwin Tan

Jacket Design
Chin-Yee Lai

Design Director
Leah Carlson-Stanisic

Design Supervisor
Iva Hacker-Delany

Designers
Nicola Ferguson
Patricia Keelin

Map Designer
Patricia Keelin

Associate Director of Production
Dianne Pinkowitz

INDEX

RESTAURANTS

Only restaurants with star ratings are listed below. All restaurants are listed alphabetically in the main (preceding) index. Always call in advance to ensure a restaurant has not closed, changed its hours, or booked its tables for a private party. The restaurant price ratings are based on the average cost of an entrée for one person, excluding tax and tip.

★★★★	An Extraordinary Experience
★★★	Excellent
★★	Very Good
★	Good
$$$$	Big Bucks ($25 and up)
$$$	Expensive ($15–$25)
$$	Reasonable ($10–$15)
$	The Price Is Right (less than $10)

HOTELS

The hotels listed below are grouped according to their price ratings; they are also listed in the main index. The hotel price ratings reflect the base price of a standard room for two people for one night during the peak season.

$$$$	Big Bucks ($180 and up)
$$$	Expensive ($120–$180)
$$	Reasonable ($80–$120)
$	The Price Is Right (less than $80)

FEATURES

BESTS

MAPS